THE BUSINESS OF SYSTEMS INTEGRATION

The Business of Systems Integration

Edited by

ANDREA PRENCIPE, ANDREW DAVIES, AND
MIKE HOBDAY

UNIVERSITY PRESS

OXFORD
UNIVERSITY PRESS

Great Clarendon Street, Oxford OX2 6DP

Oxford University Press is a department of the University of Oxford.
It furthers the University's objective of excellence in research, scholarship,
and education by publishing worldwide in

Oxford New York

Auckland Bangkok Buenos Aires Cape Town Chennai
Dar es Salaam Delhi Hong Kong Istanbul Karachi Kolkata
Kuala Lumpur Madrid Melbourne Mexico City Mumbai Nairobi
São Paulo Shanghai Taipei Tokyo Toronto

Oxford is a registered trade mark of Oxford University Press
in the UK and in certain other countries

Published in the United States
by Oxford University Press Inc., New York

© Oxford University Press

The moral rights of the author have been asserted
Database right Oxford University Press (maker)

First published 2003

British Library Cataloguing in Publication Data

Data available

Library of Congress Cataloging in Publication Data
The business of systems integration/edited by Andrea Prencipe, Andrew Davies, and Mike Hobday.
p. cm
Includes bibliographical references and index.
1. Business enterprises—Computer networks—Management.   2. Information
technology—Management.   3. Management information systems. I. Prencipe, Andrea.
II. Davies, Andrew, 1960- III. Hobday, Michael.
HD30.2B878   2003   658'.05—dc22   2003065257

ISBN 0–19–926322–1

1 3 5 7 9 10 8 6 4 2

Typeset by Newgen Imaging Systems (P) Ltd., Chennai, India
Printed in Great Britain
on acid-free paper by
T. J. International Ltd., Padstow, Cornwall

This book is dedicated to the memory of Keith Pavitt, who died suddenly and unexpectedly on 20 December 2002. Keith was the main source of inspiration of this work and encouraged us to organize this interdisciplinary collection of papers on systems integration. He profoundly believed in the value of research on systems integration in the social sciences and both pushed and led our thinking on this issue. He himself contributed with a paper. During the preparation of the manuscript, we were, as usual, deeply influenced by his sharp thinking, historical understanding, and rigorous comments. This is a very small tribute to his great intellectual legacy.

Andrea Prencipe
Andrew Davies
Mike Hobday

Contents

Preface

Airplanes, automobiles, an electric power system, the process of producing a microprocessor, a hospital, all are complex systems, in the sense that each has a number of different components or elements, and for effective performance all these have to fit together, and work together. Making things work together well is what the authors of this book call the business of systems integration. The book is largely concerned with complex product systems and how these are designed, produced, integrated, and provided.

Although many contemporary product systems have properties many of us consider annoying, for instance personal computers, or the check-in process at airports, by and large the systems that we have work tolerably well. How does this minor miracle happen?

Partly it is the result of Adam Smith's invisible market hand working decently well. Producers of gasoline have powerful incentives to have their gas work with the engines in contemporary automobiles. Tire manufacturers design their wares so that they will fit on the wheels of contemporary cars. In many cases market mechanisms tend to create standards so that things that need to fit together do so, to the mutual benefit of the firms that produce the different things that need to fit, as well as of their customers.

Partly it is the result of Alfred Chandler's visible hand. Companies often themselves produce the key components that must fit together in their systems product or service they are selling. Indeed Chandler's historical discussion of the rise of the large and modern corporation is to a considerable extent a story of how companies selling systems products vertically integrated so that they could control the design and production of the components as well as the system as a whole.

Partly the mechanisms that generate effective systems involve the mixture of market mechanisms, and internal coordination. Often firms in an industry have formed industry associations for the express purpose of establishing standards. Sometimes government agencies have been involved in this process. Companies designing and selling large, complex systems traditionally have outsourced a number of their components, at the same time that they have produced certain key ones in house.

It is clear that the business of systems integration is both about engineering design, and about organization and management. A company cannot design both the overall system and the details of all of its components if it intends to contract for or generally use the market for the procurement of many of its components. If companies designing and producing components are very strong, a systems assembler is more or less forced to rely on them for much of component design, and in effect build the system design around the available components.

A central theme of many of the chapters of this book is that in recent years the technological aspects of systems have become more complex, and so have the organizational and managerial aspects of firms developing and integrating them, labeled in this book systems integrator firms. The requirements for components to work together effectively in a system have become more demanding. One might expect, therefore, that the systems integrator firm would be taking more of the component design job in house. But while there are exceptions, this has not happened. Rather, in many systems product fields, the systems integrator firm has been relying on contract and the market more, and on internal systems design and production less.

This is a fascinating development. It is a principal motivation for the book, and the authors of the book provide a considerable amount of light on what has been going on.

The purpose of a preface is not to summarize a book, but to wet the readers' appetite. The readers of this book will find it fascinating.

August 6, 2003
Richard R. Nelson
Columbia University

Acknowledgements

We are grateful to the Economic and Social Research Council's (ESRC) Complex Product System (CoPS) Innovation Centre at the Universities of Sussex and Brighton, which funded several chapters and themes of research within this book. We also thank the Engineering and Physical Sciences Research Council (EPSRC) for funding a major CoPS project on systems integration, focusing on the management of integrated system and service solutions, without which this book would not have been possible.

We would like to thank Susan Lees for her professional editing and proofreading of the manuscript and David Musson, who first acknowledged the value of publishing a book on systems integration.

Andrea Prencipe
Andrew Davies
Mike Hobday

Notes on Contributors

Michael H. Best is a Research Associate at the Center for Industrial Competitiveness, University of Massachusetts Lowell and an associate member of the Centre for International Business and Management, Judge Institute, Cambridge University, and was visiting at the Saïd Business School, Oxford University, during the academic year 2002–2003. Recent publications include *The New Competitive Advantage: The Renewal of American Industry* (Oxford University Press, 2001); *Transition in Malaysian Electronics* (a monograph co-authored with Rajah Rasiah, United Nations Industrial Development Organization, 2002); and *The Capabilities Perspective: Advancing Industrial Competitiveness in Northern Ireland* (Northern Ireland Economic Council, 2001).

Henry Chesbrough is the Executive Director of the Center for Strategic Management at the Haas Business School at the University of California, Berkeley. He is the author of *Open Innovation*, published in 2003 by the Harvard Business School Press. He holds a BA from Yale, an MBA from Stanford, and a PhD from Berkeley. He was previously a professor at Harvard Business School. Before joining academia, he worked as a senior executive at Quantum Corporation in the disk drive industry. His academic research has been published in *Research Policy, Industrial and Corporate Change, Business History Review*, and the *Journal of Evolutionary Economics*. He has also published managerial articles in the *Harvard Business Review, California Management Review*, and *Sloan Management Review*.

Andrew Davies is a Senior Fellow at SPRU—(Science and Technology Policy Research), University of Sussex and a senior researcher in the CoPS Innovation Centre at SPRU. His qualifications include a DPhil in political economy, an MA (with distinction) in the social implications of technical change, and a BA (1st Hons) in geography (economic) at the University of Sussex. Andrew has worked in SPRU focusing on (*a*) telecoms policy (1987–91) and (*b*) the management of innovation in CoPS (1994–2001). He has also worked as a Visiting Fellow at the Rotterdam School of Management (1998), a telecoms consultant (1994), and a Postdoctoral Fellow at the University of Amsterdam (1991–4). He has written extensively on telecommunications policy, large technical systems, firm strategy, innovation management, and organizational capabilities, including *Telecommunications and Politics* (1994) and articles in journals such as *Industrial and Corporate Change* and *Research Policy*. His research includes consultancy for the European Commission, OECD, governments and private companies. He was recently awarded a Teaching Excellence Scholarship by Sweden's STINT foundation to teach courses on CoPS in several leading Swedish Universities.

Giovanni Dosi is a Professor of Economics at the Sant'Anna School of Advanced Studies, Pisa. He is Continental Europe Editor of *Industrial and Corporate Change*. Professor Dosi is author and editor of various works in the areas of economics of innovation, industrial economics, evolution theory of economic change, and organizational studies, including *Technical Change and Industrial Transformation—The Theory and an Application to the Semiconductor Industry* (London, Macmillan, 1984; American edition: New York, St Martin Press, 1984); (with C. Freeman, R. Nelson, G. Silverberg, and L. Soete) *Technical Change and Economic Theory* (London, Frances Pinter and New York, Columbia University Press, 1988); 'Sources, Procedures and Microeconomic Effects of Innovation', in *Journal of Economic Literature*, 1988; *The Nature and Dynamics of Organizational Capabilities* (with R. Nelson and S. Winter) (eds.) (Oxford/New York, Oxford University Press, 2000); *Innovation, Organization and Economic Dynamics: Selected Essays* (Cheltenham, Edward Elgar, 2000).

Takahiro (Taka) Fujimoto is a Professor at Tokyo University's School of Economics, Faculty Fellow of Research Institute of Economy, Trade, and Industry, and Senior Research Associate at Harvard Business School. He specializes in technology and operations management. Fujimoto graduated from Tokyo University and joined Mitsubishi Research Institute in 1979. He received a doctoral degree from Harvard Business School in 1989. Fujimoto's main publications in English include: *Product Development Performance: Strategy, Organization, and Management in the World Auto Industry* (1991) with Kim B. Clark, and *The Evolution of a Manufacturing System at Toyota* (1999).

Eugene Gholz is an Assistant Professor at the Patterson School of Diplomacy and International Commerce at the University of Kentucky. He takes the lead role in the international commerce part of the curriculum, which trains master's students for government, non-profit, and private sector jobs that emphasize international skills. He teaches courses in globalization, economic statecraft, and defense statecraft. His research concerns how the government decides what weapons to buy, how and when to stimulate innovation, how to manage high-tech business–government relations, and US foreign military policy. He taught previously at George Mason University, and he was a national security fellow at Harvard University's Olin Institute of Strategic Studies. He received his PhD from the MIT Department of Political Science.

Michael Hobday is Director of the Complex Product Systems (CoPS) Innovation Centre at SPRU—Science and Technology Policy Research, University of Sussex. Michael Hobday has worked in SPRU since 1984 focusing on (*a*) innovation management in CoPS and (*b*) East and South Asian innovation studies. He has practical industrial experience in the semiconductor industry, in production, planning, and marketing management (Texas Instruments Ltd., UK, 1969–78). His qualifications include a DPhil (in telecommunications policy), an MA in economics, and a BA (1st Hons) in economics. Professor Hobday's work on CoPS has examined how innovation in high technology and high value capital goods contributes to competitiveness in the United Kingdom and other countries. His book 'Innovation in East Asia' (1995) was the first comprehensive analysis of East Asian firm innovation strategies, including detailed case studies of companies from Korea, Taiwan, Singapore, and Hong Kong. His international work includes extensive consultancy for governments, private companies, and international agencies, involving studies of the world semiconductor, telecommunications, and electronics industries. He has produced more than 100 publications, including three books, numerous articles on technology management, and major consultancy reports on industrial innovation, competitiveness, and project evaluation.

Stephen Johnson is an Associate Professor in the Space Studies Department of the University of North Dakota, teaching history and economics of space endeavours. He is the author of *The United States Air Force and the Culture of Innovation, 1945–1965*, published in 2002 by the US Air Force, and *The Secret of Apollo: Systems Management in American and European Space Programs*, published in 2002. He is also the editor of *Quest: The History of Spaceflight Quarterly*. His current research involves the development of cognitive psychology and artificial intelligence, space industry economics, and the history of space science and technology. Prior to joining the University of North Dakota, he worked in the aerospace industry for 15 years, managing computer simulation laboratories, designing space probes, and developing engineering processes. He received his doctorate in 1997 in the history of science and technology from the University of Minnesota, where he was also the Associate Director of the Babbage Institute for the History of Computing.

Luigi Marengo is Professor of Economics at the University of Teramo in Italy. He received his PhD at SPRU, University of Sussex in 1991, and worked as Research Fellow and then Associate Professor at the University of Trento in Italy, before moving to Teramo in 2001. He has also served as research fellow at the International Institute for Applied Systems Analysis (IIASA) in Austria and as invited professor at the University Louis Pasteur in Strasbourg, France. His main research interests concern organizational economics, models of bounded rationality and learning, decision theory, experimental economics, and game theory.

Maureen McKelvey is Professor in Economics of Innovation at Chalmers University of Technology, Sweden. Her academic degrees include a BA (1987) with a double major in political science and economics from Rice University (Houston, TX), an MA (1989) in science and technology policy from the Research Policy Institute, Lund University, a PhD (1994) in technology and social change from Linköping University, and a habilitation degree (1996) in technology and social change from Linköping University. In 1996, the International Joseph A. Schumpeter Society awarded her the prize for best scientific work for her Oxford book *Evolutionary Innovations: The*

Business of Biotechnology. She has been active in building up a research group with strong international linkages, as well as future undergraduate education. Her research interests focus on innovation processes.

Massimo Paoli is Professor of Innovation Management at the University of Perugia (Italy) and at S. Anna School of Advanced Studies, Pisa (Italy). His qualifications include a BA in economics (University of Pisa, 1981) and a DPhil (innovation management at S. Anna School of Advanced Studies, 1984). Before joining academia, Massimo Paoli worked in semiconductor and software European leader firms (1983–7). His research effort has been focused on links between technological and organizational innovation, and in particular about the relations between the nature of knowledge and dynamics of change in multi-technology systems. He has produced forty publications, including four books and numerous articles on the strategic management of innovation.

Keith Pavitt was Professor of Science and Technology Policy at Sussex University. He studied engineering, industrial management, and economics at Cambridge (UK) and Harvard (USA), and then worked at the Organization for Economic Cooperation and Development (OECD) in Paris. During his 30 years at SPRU, he has published widely on the management of technology, and science and technology policy. His central research interests were the nature, sources, and measurement of technology, and the reasons why countries, companies, and sectors differ in their rates and directions of technical change. He has published widely in economics and management journals, as well as those concerned with science and technology policy. Professor Pavitt advise numerous national and international bodies on policies for technical change. He has been a Visiting Lecturer at Princeton University, Visiting Professor at the Universities of Aalborg, Lumière-Lyon 2, Nice, Padua, Paris-Dauphine, Reading and Strasbourg (Louis Pasteur); and Visiting Scholar at Stanford University. He was a main editor of Research Policy.

Andrea Prencipe is a Research Fellow at SPRU—Science and Technology Policy Research, University of Sussex, and Associate Professor of Economics and Management of Innovation at the University G. d'Annunzio, Pescara, Italy. His qualifications include a DPhil in technology and corporate strategy (SPRU), an MA in innovation management (Scuola Superiore S. Anna, Pisa, Italy), an MSc (with distinction) in technology innovation management (SPRU), and a BA (1st Hons) in economics and business (University G. d'Annunzio). Dr Prencipe was awarded the Roy Rothwell Prize for the best SPRU Masters dissertation of the year in 1994–5. He has worked for the Italian National Research Council and in several European Union-funded projects. In collaboration with Ernst & Young, he has provided advice to the European Patent Office on the economic value of patents. His research interests include technology and corporate strategy, resource-based theory of the firm, modularity, and organizational memory. He has published in journals such as *Administrative Science Quarterly, Industrial and Corporate Change, Journal of Management Studies, Journal of Management and Governance*, and *Research Policy*.

Mari Sako is P&O Professor of Management Studies (International Business) at the Saïd Business School, University of Oxford. After reading philosophy, politics and economics at the University of Oxford, she studied for her MSc in economics at LSE, MA in economics at the Johns Hopkins University, USA, and PhD in economics at the University of London. During 1987–97, she was a Lecturer (and subsequently a Reader) in Industrial Relations at the London School of Economics. Professor Sako has published numerous books and articles on comparative business systems and human resources. She is a principal researcher of the International Motor Vehicle Program (IMVP), which funded the research reported in this book. She is also a member of the editorial boards of *Global Networks, Journal of International Business Studies*, and *Political Quarterly*.

Harvey M. Sapolsky is Professor of Public Policy and Organization in the Department of Political Science and Director of the MIT Security Studies Program. Dr Sapolsky completed a BA at Boston University and earned an MPA and PhD at Harvard University. He has worked in a number of public policy areas, notably health, science, and defence and specializes in effects of institutional structures and bureaucratic politics on policy outcomes. In the defence field he has served as a consultant to the Commission on Government Procurement, The Office of the Secretary of Defense, the Naval War College, the Office of Naval Research, the RAND Corporation, Draper Laboratory, and Johns Hopkins Applied Physics Laboratory, and has lectured at all of the service academies. He is currently focusing his research on three topics; interservice and civil/military relations, the impact of casualties on US use of force, and the future structure of defence industries. Professor Sapolsky's most recent defence-related book is entitled *Science and the Navy*, and is a study of military support of academic research. As a service to the wider defence community, Professor Sapolsky has organized an interorganizational curriculum development group called the Consortium on Military Innovation Studies.

W. Edward Steinmueller is Professor of Information and Communication Technology Policy at SPRU—Science and Technology Policy Research, University of Sussex. He received his PhD at and was formerly employed by Stanford University. His areas of research include the economics of the information and information technology industries, the economics of science and technology policy, and the relationships among social, organizational, and technological factors in the production and adoption of new technologies. He is internationally known for his work on the integrated circuit, computer, telecommunication, and software industries. He is currently engaged in studies of the relationships between information, networks and knowledge and their influence on scientific progress and technological innovation.

Akira Takeishi is Associate Professor at the Institute of Innovation Research, Hitotsubashi University. He received his PhD in management from the Sloan School of Management, Massachusetts Institute of Technology in 1998. His current research interests include management of the inter-firm division of labour for innovation, architecture of business systems, and innovations in mobile communication and computing. His work has appeared in the *Strategic Management Journal* and *Organization Science*. Recently, he has jointly edited a book with Takahiro Fujimoto and Yaichi Aoshima, *Business Architecture: Strategic Design of Products, Organizations, and Processes*, published by Yuhikaku (in Japanese).

Fredrik Tell is a Lecturer in the Department of Management and Economics at Linköping University (Sweden). He has been a visiting research fellow and lecturer at Stanford University, University of Sussex, and the London School of Economics. His research and publications lie within the broad areas of organization studies, business history, and evolutionary economics. On the organizational level, his research focuses primarily on the management of knowledge, particularly within project-based organizations. He also studies the evolution of organizational capabilities in the history of electrical manufacturing, while the dynamics of technological standards in network technologies, such as electrical power systems, is another locus of his research. Fredrik Tell is an associate research fellow of the CoPS Innovation Centre at SPRU—Science and Technology Policy Research, University of Sussex.

List of Figures

List of Tables

1

Introduction

MICHAEL HOBDAY, ANDREA PRENCIPE, AND ANDREW DAVIES

SPRU, University of Sussex, Brighton

1.1 Systems Integration: An Emerging Model of Industrial Organization

In the past decade or so, a new kind of systems integration has become a key factor in the operations, strategy, and competitive advantage of major corporations in a wide variety of sectors (e.g. computing, automotive, telecommunications, military systems, and aerospace). In the past, systems integration was confined to a technical, operations task—part of the wider area of systems engineering. Today, systems integration is a strategic task, which pervades business management not only at the engineering level but also in senior management decision-making. This book shows how and why this new version of systems integration has evolved into an emerging model of industrial organization whereby firms and groups of firms join together different types of knowledge, skill, and activity, as well as hardware, software, and human resources to produce new products for the marketplace.

At a technical level, systems integration has 'two faces' similar to the two faces of R&D highlighted by Cohen and Levinthal (1989). The first face refers to the internal activities of firms as they integrate the inputs needed to produce new products. The second face, which has assumed much greater importance in recent years, refers to the external activities of firms as they integrate components, skills, and knowledge from other firms, including suppliers, users, and partners, in order to deliver ever more complex products and systems. Both 'faces' of systems integration now go well beyond the engineering level, having become central to the business strategies and competitive advantages of many of the world's leading corporations including General Electric, Dell, Ford, IBM, Hewlett-Packard, Cable & Wireless, Siemens, Nokia, Rolls-Royce, and Boeing.

The business of systems integration has fundamental implications for the capabilities of firms. In many cases, firms have made a transition from being vertically integrated (doing nearly everything in-house) to being the integrator of somebody else's activities. These changes, while building on trends of the past, have accelerated in recent years, posing new challenges not only

1

to prime contractors and major systems integrators, but also their network of suppliers and partners in production and innovation.

The drivers of business systems integration are many. They include the increasing complexity of products and systems, the rapid pace of technological change, and the increasing breadth of knowledge required to manufacture and deliver both consumer and capital goods. Also, using 'modular' design strategies, firms operating in a large number of industrial sectors have begun to make extensive use of outsourcing to lower tier suppliers in order to move downstream to provide more lucrative services and solutions for their customers. Underlying this trend are continuing changes in the competitive environment, including the liberalization and deregulation of markets, globalization, and increasingly sophisticated service-intensive customer demands.

1.2 Objectives and Approach

To date, there has been no published research, which provides the theoretical, analytical, and empirical underpinnings needed to understand and explain the new systems integration. This edited collection therefore presents contrasting interdisciplinary perspectives on the evolution of systems integration. The aim of the book is to systematically explore the 'reinvention' of systems integration from various business, historical, and innovation perspectives, based on contributions from leading international scholars. The book delves deeply into the nature, dimensions, and dynamics of new forms of systems integration, deploying analytical techniques from a wide variety of disciplines, including the theory of the firm, the history of technology, industrial organization, regional analysis, strategic management, and innovation studies. The purpose is to develop deep and novel insights into the nature of systems integration based on recent empirical evidence from the United States, Europe, and Japan, which shows how systems integration has evolved to become a core industrial activity. The book also points to likely future trends as systems integration continues to unfold in the future.

The book is organized into three main parts. Part I traces the history of systems integration, from its military origins, and contrasts several early industrial examples. Part II presents emerging theoretical perspectives on systems integration in an effort to contextualize, understand, and explain the fundamental sources and directions of systems integration as an economic and business activity. Part III deals with how systems integration is shaping the competitive strategies and advantage of modern corporations, offering industrial and firm-level evidence on corporate strategies, capability building, and other key industrial processes. Each part uses empirical evidence to highlight the specific characteristics of systems integration across various industrial domains, stressing its importance for complex capital goods, such as aircraft, IT systems, engineering constructs, and telecommunications equipment, sometimes called 'complex product systems' (Hobday 1998).

The remainder of this introduction highlights the main contributions of each chapter, identifies the key debates in the field and shows how the chapters relate to each other. We also point to unresolved issues and gaps in our knowledge base in order to identify important research topics for the future.

Part I: The History of Systems Integration

Part I presents four chapters which analyse the history of systems integration. In Chapter Two, Sapolsky charts the military and cold war origins of systems integration in the United States, the first country to develop and institutionalize formal systems integration processes. The US Government required more than financial investment, effective strategy, and determination to wage the cold war. It also needed to invent the institutions that could sustain and coordinate the long-term enlistment of technology and industry for military purposes. The Second World War, with its near total societal mobilization, produced most of the weapons technologies needed to wage the cold war, but not the organizational systems required for the development, deployment, and renewal of these technologies over the prolonged half-peace/ half-war that characterized the cold war. The existing military structures that could command coordination, when most in society were ready to accept military discipline and priorities, proved to be inadequate for managing the 'less than total' mobilization that followed. Sapolsky describes the creation and institutionalization of a variety of special organizations and skills that allowed the military to manage effectively the design and development of complex weapons systems during the cold war. Prime among them were the systems analysis and integration skills required for building and operating complex weapons, including new project-based organizational structures.

In Chapter Three, Johnson picks up this theme of building and deploying reliable systems, emphasizing the enormous technical and social challenges facing systems producers. The difficulties confronting builders of reliable, complex, high technology systems are manifold, but most revolve around the communication of heterogeneous forms of information and knowledge between design engineers. This problem, in turn, is compounded by the difficulty of assuring foolproof manufacturing and integration of many thousands of components. Johnson shows that most technical failures ultimately result from human error or miscommunication and, furthermore, that the solutions to these problems, including systems integration, are likewise *social* in nature. Using a combination of engineering and historical analysis, Johnson highlights not only the social basis of failure, but also the social origins of dependability and reliability.

Chapter Four goes on to examine how different degrees of complexity, relating to organization, technology, and markets, shape the 'capability needs' of various forms of systems integration (and integrator organizations) during different stages of the life cycle of complex technology networks. Tell uses electrical power systems manufacture as an example, distinguishing three 'epochs' in the product life cycle of their evolution, each of which had different implications for systems integration among the supplier firms involved. During the first epoch, inventors and engineers at newly established electrical utilities could perform systems integration on their own. In the second epoch, due to the division of labour between departments and the integration of partitioned knowledge through elaborate managerial hierarchies, systems integration was characterized by the 'visible hand' of large industrial enterprises such as electrical manufacturers and utilities. The third epoch, which began in the mid-1970s ushered in new strategies and structures as waves of deregulation and privatization of public utilities spread across the world. As Tell shows, during this contemporary epoch, electrical manufacturers engaged in systems integration were forced to become 'loosely coupled' federations of businesses and projects assembled to complete certain tasks. This contemporary trend in deregulation, downsizing, and privatization may well have impacted other infrastructural sectors (e.g. telecommunications, air traffic management, railways, gas supplies, and air travel) which have all been subject to similar trends.

In Chapter Five, Pavitt develops a broad historical interpretation of the growing role of individual firms specializing in systems integration. Pointing to the powerful underlying logic of systems integration as a form of industrial specialization, Pavitt argues that there are both imperatives for and barriers against the take up of systems integration, which encourage and constrain the growth of firms specializing in the area. Firms specializing in systems integration are the result of two common characteristics of technical change that have shaped historical forms of industrial organization. First is the continuous increase in specialization in both the production of artefacts and knowledge. Second are periodic waves of major innovations. For example, major innovations in the second half of the nineteenth century led to the emergence in the twentieth century of R&D laboratories, integrated within large manufacturing firms, as the main agents of technical change. However, recent increases in knowledge specialization and product complexity, coupled with advances in IT, have increased the opportunities for 'disintegration', both within product development activities themselves and between product development and manufacturing. Firms specializing in systems design and integration have therefore grown to challenge large-scale manufacturing firms. However, Pavitt argues that there are limits to a complete division of labour, because arm's-length relationships often remain an inefficient means for exchanging and integrating fast-changing fields of knowledge. He also points out that, contrary to popular argument, these specialist firms are not 'post-industrial' or 'service' firms but concentrate on the knowledge-intensive elements of industrial activity, rather than on manufacturing itself.

Part II: Theoretical and Conceptual Perspectives on Systems Integration

Having delved into the origin and history of systems integration, Part II asks a series of basic theoretical questions: 'How can we best conceptualize the activities of systems integrators?'; 'In what ways does systems integration relate to and, in some cases, confer competitive advantage at the firm and regional levels?', 'How does the nature of technological progress in complex systems industries shape the choice of institutions and governance structures needed for establishing industry-wide standards?' Underlying these questions are fundamental issues concerning the cognitive basis of systems integration and the functioning of systems integration within the economic system.

To explore the economics of systems integration, Chapter Six makes a first attempt to place the idea of systems integration within the context of evolutionary economics, arguing that systems integrators (as firms) and systems integration (as an activity which goes on within and across firms) perform a central function as the 'visible hand' of much modern industrial activity, especially in complex products and systems. Dosi et al. reveal new facets of the relationship between systems integration and the co-evolution of knowledge accumulation and organizational boundaries, describing puzzling divergences between 'what firms do' and what 'firms know'. They show that in many complex industrial activities, firms need to 'know more' than what is seemingly required by current production tasks. In addition, and contrary to recent interpretations of modularity (e.g. Langlois 2001), this chapter argues that increasing 'modularization' across components and accompanying specialization among firms does not lead to a vanishing of the visible hand of management, but rather to an increasing requirement for integrative knowledge. In consequence, systems integrators will continue to be crucial repositories of such knowledge across many industrial landscapes. Because product complexity is here to stay (and likely to grow), so is the knowledge required to master interfaces and compatibilities across different components, especially in circumstances where product/system properties are not driven by innovation in any single crucial component. In these cases, coordinating the learning trajectories of different component suppliers might well lead to an expansion of the knowledge bases which systems integrators need to embody in the future. According to this interpretation, systems integrators represent the ever present visible hand of purposeful 'Chandlerian' organizations painstakingly and imperfectly trying to master the diverse learning trajectories of 'Smithian' suppliers.

Building on the Dosi et al. framework, in Chapter Seven, Prencipe explores the nature of systems integration from a strategic management perspective, showing how systems integration relates to competitive advantage. Prencipe identifies two distinct categories of systems integration in multi-technology, multi-component products, namely 'synchronic' and 'diachronic'. Synchronic systems integration refers to the static (intra-generation) technological capabilities required to set the product concept design, decompose it, coordinate the network of suppliers, and then recompose the product within a given technological family. By contrast, diachronic systems integration refers to the dynamic (inter-generation) technological capabilities required to envisage and then move progressively towards different and alternative paths of product architectures across new product families. The evolutionary dynamics of new products derive from the interaction of a variety of technological fields, so that the most important strategic problem facing systems integrator companies is how to establish dominion over these diverse technological fields which cross organizational boundaries.

Chapter Eight explores theoretical interpretations of the role of standardization processes in influencing, shaping, and supporting division of labour in the development of complex products and systems, particularly those involving software, integrated circuits, and telecommunications. Steinmueller identifies and discusses three fundamental aspects of systems integration, namely coordination, negotiationanol memory. While the discussion on coordination concentrates on the assessment of the feasibility of interorganizational division of labour, the discussion on negotiation highlights that technical compatibility standards provide incentive-compatible means for solving transaction issues between systems integrators and external suppliers. Steinmueller argues that systems integration creates a distributed memory of specialized competencies with their own trajectories, amongst organizations involved in the networked development of complex products.

In Chapter Nine, Paoli turns to the cognitive underpinnings of systems integration, arguing that strategic control over the technological and commercial evolution of complex multi-technology platforms (i.e. families of products) requires full control of the processes of systems integration. Paoli defines the key elements of the cognitive nature of systems integration and provides an epistemological reflection on both the personal and social knowledge involved in successful systems integration. It is argued that the meta-process of systems integration is above all the integration of knowledge. Using new concepts of personal and social knowledge, the chapter proposes that firms must retain and dominate, in-house, a whole host of generative contexts of knowledge in order to control systems integration. Contexts are conceptualized here as the 'bricks' that generate the knowledge that supports the firm's capability for systems integration.

In Chapter Ten, Chesbrough proposes a cyclical model of technical advance based on the dynamics of product modularity and systems integration in the hard disk drive industry. He argues that although our understanding of the interaction between technological change and organizational structure has made many advances, our prevailing conceptions of these interactions remain fundamentally static in nature. A more dynamic conceptualization of the relationship is needed in order to capture the dynamics of systems integration in disk drives and other high-technology industries. Chesbrough's research shows that organizational 'traps' may emerge in companies which are not properly aligned with their technologies and that, in these cases, adaptation to technological change is difficult. Path-dependent behaviours can intensify these traps. These dynamics of systems integration qualify earlier interpretations of organizational structure and technological change, providing a rich agenda for further empirical research.

Part III: Competitive Advantage and Systems Integration

Part III presents empirical research on systems integration, identifying key industrial trends and showing precisely how systems integration is emerging as a new model of industrial organization, and why this model requires particular forms of corporate capability and new capability building strategies. The six chapters in Part III examine and, in some cases, compare the processes of systems integration in cars, hard disk drives, defence, building and construction, healthcare, biotechnology, telecommunications, railways, flight simulation, engineering infrastructure, and corporate IT networks.

Chapter Eleven goes beyond the level of the firm to show how systems integration relates to the dynamics of regional clusters and regional innovation patterns. Best proposes a new model of technology management and regional innovation based on the principle of systems integration. The principle of systems integration is manifested in the organizational capability of firms, individually and networked, collectively fostering rapid technological change. The effect is a network or cluster of entrepreneurial firms in which design is decentralized within the enterprise and diffused amongst networked enterprises. Individual entrepreneurs and high-technology firms draw upon dense regional pools of knowledge and skill, implying that the technology pool exists above and beyond the contributions of any individual firm. The regional model is ideally suited to product-led competitive strategies and technological innovation, especially in high-technology complex products and systems. The combination of entrepreneurial firms and inter-firm networks is shown to foster a range of dynamic cluster processes that, in turn, underlie the growth of Silicon Valley and the unexpected resurgence of Boston's Route 128.

As Chapter Twelve shows, one of the significant worldwide responses to the need for systems integration has occurred in the car industry where suppliers have turned to the strategy of 'modularity' to cope with technical change, operational efficiency demands, and new market requirements.

Sako uses the car industry as an empirical setting for clarification of the concept of modularity in product architecture. Three arenas of modularity are identified: design, production, and use. Each present alternative business criteria for making boundary choices in cars. The chapter illustrates the strategic drivers pushing product architectures towards modularity, including marketing needs, operational efficiency, financial pressures, and technological change. Sako argues that different combinations of these drivers force car companies to choose different modular boundaries, and different decision paths towards outsourcing modules. The chapter considers the implications of these different paths for industry dynamics and, in particular, the power balance between customers and suppliers, as well as supply chain management.

Chapter Thirteen further explores this theme by examining the way modularization in the car industry has impacted on interlinked, multiple hierarchies of product, production, and supplier systems. Takeishi and Fujimoto show that modularization in the world car industry has involved architectural changes in each of the product, production, and supplier systems in the industry across Japan, Europe, and the United States emphasizing different purposes and dimensions. To understand these multifaceted processes, the chapter proposes a conceptual framework which interprets development and production activities as multiple, interconnected hierarchies of products, processes, and inter-firm boundaries. Using this framework, the chapter draws on case studies and questionnaire survey data to examine the ongoing processes of modularization in the industry. Takeishi and Fujimoto argue that tensions exist among the three hierarchies, which are likely to lead to further changes in product, production, and supplier-system architectures in the future.

Systems integration capability is not only essential for the production of complex products and systems as shown by Sapolsky (Chapter Two) and Johnson (Chapter Three) but also central to the use of such systems within their wider infrastructural settings. In Chapter Fourteen, Gholz shows, through a case study of the US defence industry, that a number of different kinds of organizations lay claim to specific types of skill and expertise and share the overall task of systems integration. These include major 'prime contractors' that build weapons systems, for-profit and non-profit technical advisors, government laboratories, organizations that manage weapons acquisition, and the military users of the weapons themselves. As Gholz points out, these groups often mean different things by the term 'systems integration', which confuses debates over defence investment and poses a major problem for national defence policymaking. For prime contractors that manufacture weapons, systems integration involves the ability to control supplier networks to produce efficiently. Acquisition planners that award development and production contracts need systems integration expertise in

order to set technical requirements and evaluate bids from prime contractors. Military planners and doctrine writers need technical advice about
systems integration to make tradeoffs in understanding the capabilities and
limitations of various weapons platforms. This chapter helps clarify the
meaning of systems integration by describing the supply and demand
structure for various types of systems integration capability and considers
the various techniques for measuring the quality of systems integration
capabilities.

In Chapter Fifteen, McKelvey deepens the argument discussed in Chapter
Fourteen and proposes to broaden the concept of systems integration by
analysing the demand side of it. McKelvey analyses the systems integration
phenomenon in pharmaceutical and open software industries taking an
innovation systems perspective. She argues that the boundaries of the
innovation system shift over time and so does the role of systems integrator
firms. From a dynamics point of view, systems integration can take place
through various coordination arrangements. The activities of actors involved
in a network can be carried out through the activities of a systems integrator
firm or through more distributed coordination mechanisms, such as market
transactions, which provide price signals to influence many distributed
individuals, or more loosely coordinated networks, such as communities of
developers or informal relationships. When the boundaries of a system shift,
then the types and relative importance of these different ways of coordinating arrangements may also shift.

While McKelvey assesses systems integration by linking analysis of supplier and demand, in Chapter Sixteen Davies looks specifically at how
supplier organizations are adopting 'integrated solutions' strategies to meet
user needs and thereby gain competitive advantage in the marketplace. As
Davies shows, some of the world's leading companies are changing the
strategic focus to compete by selling whole solutions, rather than individual
products or service lines. As a result, a new type of supplier firm is emerging,
namely 'the integrated solutions provider', which has created a new business
model centred on integrated solutions to meet the wide ranging requirements
of large business or government customers. To provide truly integrated
solutions, complex system suppliers are taking new positions in the industry
value chain and developing novel combinations of capabilities. This does not
mean, as some authors suggest (e.g. Wise and Baumgartner 1999) that firms
are uniformly marching 'downstream' from manufacturing to services.
Instead, suppliers are moving from both downstream and upstream positions to try and capture the higher value territory situated *between* manufacturing and services. To achieve this, firms are combining products and
systems with services in order to specify, deliver, finance, maintain, support,
and operate a system throughout its life cycle. This chapter provides
evidence on the strategies of five major solutions suppliers across different

sectors: railways, mobile communications systems, corporate networks, flight simulators, and the built environment.

1.3 Future Research Priorities

The sixteen chapters presented here provide a wealth of new insights and information on the business of systems integration, dealing with its origins, history, and conceptualization, as well as highlighting key industrial trends, new corporate strategies, and important debates in the field. Above all, the research indicates that systems integration has moved beyond the technical field in which it has traditionally been embedded (within the discipline of systems engineering) to the strategic business domain. The business of systems integration is vital to the strategy of many of today's modern corporations. It is also profoundly important to the unfolding regional and national economies in which it plays a crucial role as a new principle of industrial organization.

While many important aspects are dealt with in the book, there remain gaps in the field and several important unresolved problems, which require further investigation. At the theoretical level, there is on the one hand a pressing need to try to integrate the existing strands of theory and develop one or more coherent models of systems integration. On the other hand, it is also important to look more widely at the implications of systems integration for evolutionary economics, strategic management, and innovation studies. While the chapters here demonstrate the importance of systems integration, as yet, the implications of systems integration as a core industrial activity have not yet been accepted widely in any of the disciplines mentioned, partly because of the early stage of research. Perhaps, systems integration is best situated within evolutionary economics, as suggested here. However, it may also have deep implications for modern resource-based theories of the firm as this field grapples with the internal dynamics of firm behaviour.

It is also true to say that the 'strategic management' of systems integration is only touched upon in this book. However, if major firms, especially those producing complex products and systems, are increasingly the integrators of other firms' activities, then systems integration should be at the core of modern debates over strategic management, rather than at the periphery as it is at the present time. How do firms exploit systems integration successfully for competitive advantage? What future confronts firms which fail to build up the capabilities required for integrating systems and services to provide solutions for their buyers? How are business and government purchasers dealing with the challenge of outsourcing activities previously undertaken in-house? While these questions are all analysed in this book, there is a need to extend current work to industrial and service sectors not covered in order to test the propositions outlined in this volume, and to compare the importance of systems integration with other key drivers of industrial competitiveness.

One key area of weakness is that current research barely scratches the surface of systems integration from the user perspective. As business and government users (e.g. airports, telecommunications service suppliers, energy suppliers, air traffic controllers, and military organizations) increasingly outsource the design and production of systems, they need to ensure that they retain sufficient systems integration capabilities in-house in order to outsource effectively. This is a major challenge facing the private sector and governments as they form 'public private partnerships' to build and install the economic and social infrastructure of the future. This issue often involves complex financial deal structuring in areas of uncertainty (e.g. over transportation costs, traffic flows, and system development costs) over very long periods of time. This, in turn, requires a deep understanding of the system being installed, the financial risks involved and the changing nature of the services to be supplied on the part of the user/operator.

The business users of complex products and systems (e.g. rail travel companies, telecommunication providers, and internet service suppliers) often have to resolve conflicting priorities and pressures. In some cases, users may even have to establish a formal systems integration function or body where it does not already exist (e.g. in the case of European air traffic control where no formal systems integration function yet operates). In these cases, the political dimension of systems integration comes into sharp focus. Future research could help show how, for example, in European air traffic management, the processes of conflict and compromise (e.g. over the environment versus capacity growth) can be worked through in order to reconcile the different objectives of the various institutions involved.

More generally, the evolution of some systems integration roles (and their primary objectives) cannot be a forgone conclusion but will depend crucially on which agent or agents gain control over the integrator role. This outcome might well favour one trajectory (e.g. growth) over another (e.g. protecting the environment). In many cases, systems integration cannot be 'neutral' with respect to the system's evolution, or the interests of wider society, but has a political dimension, driven by the interests of a dominant organization or group. Scholars of political economy may well find this question of interest in areas such as military systems, rail, air, and road transport, and large infrastructural projects such as dams, nuclear power stations, and airports, which often pose controversial choices in areas such as the environment, energy, growth, innovation, and sustainability.

From the supplier side, this book clearly shows the emergence of systems integration and the accompanying process of outsourcing (other 'side of the coin' of systems integration) as key factors in organizing the production of products and services. However, there is a need to further test systems integration as a model of industrial organization. In fact, we need to understand whether and how far lessons learnt from one sector can be transferred to other sectors of the economy. In order to achieve this, more in-depth empirical research in other industries is needed to enable cross-sector comparisons. In addition, more focused analytical work is needed to properly define the domain of systems integration and the terminology used by the various scholars and business practitioners concerned. In bringing together current thinking and evidence at this stage, this book represents an early milestone in the development of the new business of systems integration.

References

COHEN, W. and LEVINTHAL, D. A. (1989). 'Innovation and Learning: The Two Faces of R&D', *The Economic Journal*, 99: 569–96.

HOBDAY, M. (1998). 'Product Complexity, Innovation and Industrial Organisation', *Research Policy*, 26/6: 689–710.

LANGLOIS, R. N. (2001). 'The Vanishing Hand: The Modular Revolution in American Business', invited paper for DRUID's Nelson—Winter Conference, June.

WISE, R. and BAUMGARTNER, P. (1999). 'Go Downstream: The New Profit Imperative in Manufacturing', *Harvard Business Review*, September–October: 133–41.

PART I

The History of Systems Integration

2

Inventing Systems Integration

HARVEY M. SAPOLSKY

Massachusetts Institute of Technology, Cambridge, MA, USA

2.1 Introduction

The United States's world position changed dramatically during the twentieth century from that of being a large industrial power absorbed by its own vastness and rapid internal growth to that of being the world's dominant economic and military power, although unaware yet of the limits of its global writ. This new status not necessarily fully understood or even sought by its citizens, required significant changes in the scale and role of government in American society. Most important among these for US global dominance has been the role its armed services came to play in the development of technology. In turn, the American military has been and continues to be transformed by technology.

The United States was a late entrant in both of the World Wars that marked the first half of the twentieth century. Nevertheless, its unmatched ability to generate and project great military power in a relatively short time proved decisive in these conflicts, which were fought primarily far from American shores. Its army was built on a militia base called to national service for the war and filled out by conscription (Flynn 1993). The equipment needed to arm, train, and transport large expeditionary forces was produced rapidly via a mobilization effort that surpassed the output of all other participants (Harrison 2000: 103).[1] The feat was a largely industrial one, with government allocating private industry the resources to produce vast quantities of weapons from pre-selected designs, often borrowed from allies (Holley 1983). Although there was a parallel mobilization of scientists and engineers that had more than an occasional spectacular success—the atomic bomb, for example—the wars were won on the assembly lines producing divisions, aircraft, and ships.

A series of confrontations with the Soviet Union over the future of a war-devastated Europe and Asia led to the reconstruction, in the early 1950s, of American military power which had been mostly demobilized after the Second World War. The resulting conflict evolved into a long-term ideological struggle that required a continuous if less than full-scale societal mobilization and a military strategy that would offset the large manpower advantage the Soviet Union and its allies had over the United States. Having used nuclear weapons to hasten the end of the Second World War, it was natural for the United States to adopt a technology-focused strategy that would substitute weapon development investments for mass production and the maintenance of a large army.

Most of the weapons needed to fight the cold war—jet aircraft, heli-copters, high endurance submarines, cruise and ballistic missiles, and nuclear weapons—would be found in the inventory of Second World War weapon experiments or plans. But major changes in organization and administrative practices were required for the effective development and employment of these weapons in the cold war. At American insistence, the cold war became a contest in demonstrating prowess in creating advanced technology weapons, a contest that eventually forced the bankruptcy of the Soviet Union. America avoided the same fate because it was more efficient than the Soviet Union in combining complex technologies into weapon systems and integrating advanced weapons systems into its fielded forces (Sapolsky, Gholz, and Kaufman 1999).

This Chapter describes the innovative organizational structures and administrative processes that facilitated the development and deployment of advanced weapon systems by the American military. Prime among them are system analysis and integration skills required for building and operating complex weapons (Johnson, Chapter Three, this volume; Gholz, Chapter Fourteen, this volume).

2.2   The Quest for Coordination

The Second World War gave the United States all the worries of a global power. Political leaders were concerned about the nation's ability to manage distant conflicts. The armed services were anxious to seize emerging national missions as their own. And technologists could envision potential security threats that would justify support for their most ambitious projects. Even before the war was in its final phases several of the governmental agencies managing the war effort had developed plans for the nation's long-term security needs (Friedberg 2000). Much attention was focused on the expansion of peacetime forces or activities to match new responsibilities. Victory would require an ever-vigilant global presence for US forces.

But the failures of the war were also recognized. It was usually difficult, at times impossible, to gain cooperation among the various branches of the military. In the European theatre, the Navy and the Army Air Forces argued over control of long-range aircraft important in the fight against the U-boats. In the Pacific theatre, three separate commands were established to accommodate the conflicting plans and ambitions of the services. Priorities for allocating scarce resources such as manpower and shipping were never fully reconciled. The governmental authority for assigning production priorities was in near constant flux (Gropman 1996). The national strategy for fighting the war, which gave primacy to the European Theatre over the Pacific, although clearly stated, was often contradicted by implementing agencies (Greenfield 1982). Recommendations for postwar reorganization of the defence agencies offered on the promise of solving these coordination problems gained widespread sympathetic attention.

The argument for significant reorganization was that the United States needed to create a coherent structure for managing its expanding global security responsibilities (Caraley 1965; Kinnard 1980). The mechanisms to develop and integrate broad-based intelligence, political analysis, and military assessments that many thought were required to support the formulation of international security policies were inadequate, if not entirely absent. More important, given the decentralized nature of American government, inter-agency coordination on important matters was achievable only through cumbersome layers of committees, most of which lacked staff and continuity. Short of commanding presidential attention, it was impossible to set enforceable priorities across agencies on national security matters or any other topic.

The main legislative expression of the reforms was the National Security Act of 1947, which created a number of entities including the National Security Council (NSC), the Central Intelligence Agency (CIA), and the Department of Defense (DOD) (Hoffman 1999). The members of the NSC are the President, the Vice President, the Secretary of State, and the Secretary of Defense with the Director of Central Intelligence and the Chairman of the Joint Chiefs of Staff as their advisors. The Director of Central Intelligence heads the CIA and coordinates the activities of other intelligence agencies. DOD brought together the Army, Navy, and the newly independent Air Force to coordinate the acquisition of weapons and the training of forces through these military departments and the use of fielded forces through unified theatre and functional commands. Formally, the President considers national security policy options in a NSC-managed process and issues directives for DOD, the CIA, and other agencies to implement his decisions. It was a plan to centralize control over defence matters to avoid the policy conflicts and confusion that many said characterized the war effort. The hope was that there could be a systematic approach to policymaking that would lead to an integrated and effective strategy to deal with the troubles that seemed certain to lie ahead.

The challenges of the early cold war years, however, brought more bureaucratic conflict, not less. The easily achieved consensus on the strategy to contain Soviet expansion did not reduce the competitive urges of the armed services and other agencies to gain the choicest defence missions. Each real or imagined threat—the war in Korea, conflict over Germany's future, the Sputnik crisis, the bomber and missile scares—generated proposals to counter the Soviets and perhaps a bureaucratic rival as well.

Budgets were up, but so were the fears of agencies worried about the ambitions of bureaucratic rivals to absorb them entirely. Attempts to achieve government coordination with additional reorganizations continued but were largely unsuccessful.

The intense competition for missions may well have been beneficial. The US armed services were certainly less wedded to old military technologies and doctrines and more willing to adopt new ones than was the Soviet military. And divided as they often were over policies, the services also were less able to resist civilian interventions and the innovative idea than is their reputation (Owens 2000). Only when the bureaucratic stakes diminished as the cold war aged and the Soviet threat waned did the centralizing preferences of defence reformers seem to gain hold (Sapolsky, Gholz, and Kaufman 1999).

2.3 Building Project Organizations

Effective coordination was achieved earlier at an entirely different organizational level and for an entirely different organizational purpose. The rigid functional structure of the technical branches of the military proved inadequate for the development of aircraft and missiles needed for the cold war. So did the technical capabilities and management responsiveness of the military's own network of weapon research laboratories and arsenals. By taking one halting step after another the military learned to think about weapons as systems and to find the organizational arrangements that would facilitate the development of the most complex types. Now institutionalized, it is this way of conceiving weapons that has moved up the organizational hierarchy and that has potential for revolutionizing warfare (MacGregor 1997).

Militaries generally separate weapon procurement and supply activities from the management of combat forces. In the US military, these procurement and support activities acquired an independence that brooked little challenge to their authority. Their ties to powerful congressional committees ensured that their jurisdictional interests were protected from interference by line officers responsible for combat operations. The technical branches of the Army were organized by function (e.g. quartermaster, ordnance, signals, engineers, medical, etc.) and controlled their own depots, arsenals, and field units. In the Navy, there was from the early 1840s a sharp division between what was called the shore establishment (the technical bureaus managing shipbuilding, ordnance, and engineering activities) and the fleet.

Proposals to give a strong hierarchy to the services and to integrate their support and operating activities were slow to be adopted. The Army began to build a general staff at the turn of the twentieth century. Gradually the technical branches came under the control of the Army's Chief of Staff, but it was not until the Second World War that the technical branches themselves were linked together under a coordinating command, the Army Service Forces. There was not a unified commander for all naval forces until the Second World War, when the posts of Commander in Chief US Fleet and Chief of Naval Operations (CNO) were combined into the latter, but even then the material bureau chiefs—all naval officers—were left outside of the CNO's control—reporting, as they had for a hundred years, directly to the Secretary of the Navy. The addition of aircraft to the military's armaments meant only that eventually separate procurement and supply activities were created for aviation, a separate material unit for the Army Air Corps, and a separate bureau in the Navy. When the Air Force was made independent of the Army in 1947, it took the appropriate slice of support facilities and units with it.

Weapon procurement projects were generally managed functionally as well, with project offices assigned as subunits in type commands that were in turn parts of component divisions of functionally defined technical branches or bureaus. Airframes were acquired independently of engines and guns and bombs. Mismatches and disappointments were common as coordinated developments were rarely organized and were difficult to sustain, but it was only with the intense quest to acquire advanced weapons in the early cold war years that the problems became acute. For Americans at least, the Second World War was a weapon production race while the cold war was a weapon development race, where technological performance mattered more than numbers (Jones 1990: 315).

The effort to develop turbojet aircraft, a field in which Britain and Germany substantially led the United States in the Second World War, demonstrated the need for changes. Advances in aerodynamics had undermined the utility of reciprocating engines and forced adoption of a more systemic approach to aircraft design. Intent on gaining the advantage in jets, the US Air Force discovered that it had to coordinate its work in human physiology, aircrew training, weapon design, avionics, combat tactics, and several other fields in order to achieve the full benefits of the rapid progress it made in turbojet technology (Young 1997).

However, it was the rush to develop a competing technology, like ballistic missiles, that precipitated substantial restructuring of weapon acquisition processes and organizations. Ballistic missiles were a disruptive technology in more than just the sense that Clayton Christensen (1997) identified in his important book, *The Innovator's Dilemma*, where new technology destroys the market for existing technology. German advances in rocket technology had showed the potential for attacking from great distances and without the concern about defences. Perfected and carrying nuclear warheads, such weapons would force the retirement of fleets of strategic bombers. But they were also the weapons that prevented a direct clash between Soviet and American forces during the cold war. The potential consequences of the use of nuclear weapons were too great to risk direct engagement. And it was the development of such weapons that altered the aircraft industry, transforming it into the aerospace industry.

But because it represented work in a new technology, the development of ballistic missiles did not fit easily into the existing weapon acquisition structure. Almost from the first proposal to initiate a ballistic missile development programme, there was intense competition both within and among the services to gain approval to establish a project. The stakes seemed high. There was pressure to limit the number of projects. The costs were significant and the pool of available experts limited. A central role in the nation's security strategy seemed assured for the service or services that deployed ballistic missiles. The risk of exclusion in either the development effort or the deployment could be the loss of budget share because the projects were likely to pull resources away from other defence activities (Sapolsky 1972; Neufeld 1990: 88).

For the Air Force, ballistic missiles were an Air Force mission because they were an extension of pre-existing cruise missile projects, pilotless aircraft, only a lot bigger, longer-ranged, and faster. For the Army, they were artillery shells with a much bigger punch and obviously, the development province of its Ordnance branch that had experience with rockets. The Navy, which had both a Bureau of Ordnance and a Bureau of Aeronautics, found it had an internal rivalry as well as external quest. Multiple projects were started and the struggle to win official sanction was a public event and bitterly fought—the epitome of American bureaucratic politics at its best or worst, depending on one's policy perspective.[2]

The Air Force projects were managed by the Air Force Research and Development Command (AFRDC), but in a separate division situated nearly a continent away from its parent organization and given special contracting authority that allowed it to by-pass most standard procurement and reporting procedures (Neufeld 1992: 4–5). Top level advisory and oversight boards were established to help, guide, and protect what became known as the AFRDC's Ballistic Missile Division, even though it was in essence an independent special project command that managed the entire development, procurement, and basing of ballistic missiles. For ballistic missiles the functional organization gave way to a system manager structure.

The Navy, the other service that gained authorization to develop long-range ballistic missiles, created approximately the same management structure but by a different route. With both the Bureau of Ordnance and the Bureau of Aeronautics vying for the management task within the Navy, the decision was made to create an independent office with the status of a bureau that would be responsible for the development and deployment of the submarine-launched Fleet Ballistic Missile, what became the Polaris missile system. The Navy's Special Projects Office (later the Strategic Systems Projects Office) managed the entire Polaris system which included the development of specialized submarine navigation equipment, missile guidance and launch subsystems, the missiles themselves, crew training facilities, special communication facilities, and support bases. Like the Air Force, the Navy had established a systems management organization dedicated to the task of creating a nuclear deterrent for the United States (Sapolsky, Gholz, and Kaufman 1999).

Having two separately managed ballistic missile programmes likely accelerated technical progress. The Navy, unhappy with the prospect of utilizing volatile liquid fuels for missiles aboard ships, invested heavily in the development of solid fuels for rocket motors, a technology that the Air Force had initially supported. Success in developing safer fuel motors not only led to the deployment of the Polaris missile on submarines, but also to the Air Force's decision to abandon its liquid fuelled Atlas missiles for the more flexible and quicker reacting Minuteman missile system. Independent judgements by the programmes had similar beneficial effects on warhead design, command and control technology, and missile maintenance procedures. It also allowed for special focus on system unique needs such as defences, and crew training and support.

2.4 The Contract State

The creation of independent project organizations to manage the development of complex systems was only a partial solution to the system coordination problem. Project organizations dealt with uncooperative agencies largely by avoiding them. They could appeal to higher authority for support, but more often they duplicated needed facilities or help outside the government. There already had been a shift towards a reliance on contractors for weapon development. The use of project management offices—increasingly popular after the success of the ballistic missile programmes—accelerated it. Why risk being overruled in appeals to higher authorities when the cooperation that one sought could be achieved through the award of a contract?

The US military traditionally relied on government owned and managed arsenals and shipyards for development of its weapons. Although their work pace was slow, these facilities nurtured military technologies between wars when the government purchases of military equipment were too little to hold the interest of many commercial suppliers. When wars broke out demand for this equipment would increase sharply and contractors would be hired to fill it. When the wars ended, orders dried up and the contractors turned again to commercial business while the arsenals soldiered on experimenting with new designs for weapons, but building few of them. Such was the general pattern until the Second World War.

Aviation was a major exception. Although the federal government did establish a civilian agency—the National Advisory Committee for Aeronautics—to conduct aviation research and the Navy did maintain its own aircraft factory—an aviation arsenal, so to speak—that designed and built aircraft, the military let the private sector take the lead in the development of aviation. The romance of flight mixed with a belief on the part of some investors that the aeroplane would be the next car, the next mass consumer product, kept fledgling aircraft manufactures funded even when there were few aeroplanes being purchased. In fact, the services exploited the enthusiasm for aviation by not always fully reimbursing the manufacturers when they won military aircraft design and production contracts (Holley 1964).

After the Second World War, the armed services came to rely more and more on contractors for weapons. Many of the contractors drafted for the Second World War wanted to stay on with defence work. The cold war promised continuing large defence budgets, enough at least to make armaments an attractive business in which to invest. The military viewed contractors as being more responsive to their direction and more competent technically than arsenals and military laboratories. Contractors were usually eager to work on the advanced technologies that the military sought to master. They also could pay their scientists and engineers higher compensation than civil service schedules allowed. And contractors were willing to lobby for projects while the arsenals and shipyards tended to believe that their futures were assured.

One administrative challenge was to find contracting mechanisms that would appropriately compensate contractors for the risks involved with defence work. This was a politically sensitive issue because wartime pressures to increase arms production rapidly with the award of lucrative non-competitive contracts had led to postwar charges of lax government oversight and contractor profiteering. The cold war's emphasis on the development of advanced military technologies meant that there were relatively few qualified contractors to do the work and that much work would be unpredictable in terms of outcomes, schedule, and costs. Although fixed price, competitive contracting where the risks of failure (not meeting the performance, schedule, or budget goals) fall entirely on the contractors is the standard for most government procurement, it was obviously inadequate for developing and buying the cold war's weapons. Instead, the practice became to limit competitions to select firms and to negotiate cost plus fixed fee contracts with winners, just skirting scandal and giving the firms little incentive to control costs. Projects were plagued by technical faults, delays, and overruns, largely because their goals were so ambitious, but also because it was so difficult to instil discipline and accountability into the process (McNaugher 1989).

Discipline and accountability were problems in weapon projects due to the dependencies that increased reliance on contractors created. The shift away from arsenals and government laboratories meant that the government's own experts were less involved in design and project management decisions. Moreover, for many of the technologies being explored, contractor or university based scientists and engineers were the most knowledgeable experts available rather than civil servants or military officers. Once a firm acquired deep expertise in some specialty, it was expensive and disruptive of carefully constructed production and deployment schedules to replace them, and it was often awarded follow-on contracts.

The policy was to shift detailed management responsibility for weapon development onto an often very willing prime contractor or weapon system manager. The prime contractor would identify and coordinate the mix of technologies and subsystems required to develop and produce complex weapon systems for the government via a network of subcontractors. The formal choice of what and to which firms to subcontract would be the government's, but obviously the prime contractor would have great influence over such decisions because of the systems knowledge it had and its necessarily special relationship with the project offices. The government needed help in defining the internal and external parameters of complex weapon systems and a way to coordinate the diverse talents and technologies required to develop them. It found such help in prime contractors able to attract skilled scientists and engineers. And it found the required coordination through the cooperation that subcontracting dollars could elicit.

As Don K. Price pointed out, the Contract State blended the public and the private in American society. The government took over the role of the private sector entrepreneur by absorbing through cost plus contracts the risks of developing new technology. Defence was the major justification for the federal government's substantial R&D investments during the cold war. In turn, the contractors became the managers of important public programmes, the design, and acquisition of weapons (Price 1954). The contractors' financial viability was dependent upon the continuing goodwill of their government customers—the only permitted buyers of exotic weapon systems costing a billion dollars. And the government was dependent upon capabilities and honest judgements of its contractors. Given that the armed services were the government buyers, the contractors maintained goodwill by serving military priorities. This meant contracts were won and maintained largely by emphasizing weapon system performance over costs (Gholz 2001). Given the limited technical training of most officers, the government customers had to search for reassurance when making judgements on the basis of advice received from the prime contractors and other contractors, or risk disaster.

2.5   The Non-profit Solution

The prime task that the prime contractors performed was systems integration. Weapons were being conceived as complex systems that required the design and simultaneous development of component subsystems such as the platforms, sensors, weapons, and propulsion that were both compatible with each other and optimized for overall systems performance (Johnson, Chapter Three, this volume; Gholz, Chapter Fourteen, this volume). Tradeoffs had to be made among the component subsystem to meet standards and achieve desired system characteristics. Systems reliability, ease of maintenance, and crew needs also had to be considered. The prime helped qualify and monitor subcontractors and provide necessary documentation for the system. Military officers serving as project monitors usually rotated to other assignments, but the primes assured continuity, staying on because the systems could not operate without them. For fielded systems they often managed the provision of spare parts and periodic overhauls and upgrades. Thus, the integration was across disciplines and time.

Two concerns worried senior officials. One was the ability of contractors to be sufficiently knowledgeable about the full range of relevant technologies. The obvious candidates for prime status were the large manufacturers, especially the aircraft builders. For familiar weapons like aircraft where systems thinking evolved through experience, the risk was low that the job was too much for a Boeing or a Lockheed. There were several firms with sufficient background in managing major projects to provide the government with the opportunity to complete the systems integration task. But for newer systems such as ballistic missile, early warning, and nuclear-powered submarines there were no firms with broad enough experience to give comfort about their ability to handle the work.

The other worry was that the firms given the integration task for new and evolving systems could abuse their position. The primes would have an intimate knowledge of the systems and government preferences. It could reserve for itself the most lucrative and commanding technologies. Or it could take information obtained from subcontractors to enter their businesses at opportune times, including competing with them on other projects. Proprietary information could be jeopardized. The involvement of one giant firm might discourage another from offering its services. Little firms might fear bigger ones. And because manufacturing promised the greatest returns through the provision of spare parts as well as the purchase of original equipment, the judgement of manufacturing primes about design tradeoffs and systems assignments had to be taken with some scepticism.

Air Force programmes demonstrated these problems most clearly. The Air Force had pioneered the weapon systems manager concept and was inclined to utilize the same programme format for its major new efforts in ballistic missiles, early warning systems, and satellites. Although still preoccupied with the acquisition of its bomber fleet, the Air Force had responsibility for developing land-based intercontinental ballistic missiles. The civilian officials and scientists who advocated the acceleration of ballistic missile projects in the face of reports in the early 1950s of Soviet progress in long-range missiles had doubts about the capabilities of the Air Force's usual primes and standard procedures to do the job even if a crash programme were initiated to ensure an American lead. When such a programme did in fact gain quick approval, they reiterated their advice about the need for rethinking project management arrangements. The Air Force responded by selecting an engineering consulting firm, the Ramo–Wooldridge Corporation, to be the deputy to General Bernard A. Schriever, the officer in charge of the ballistic missile development effort, and gave it responsibility for the programme's systems engineering and technical direction. Thus Ramo–Wooldridge was made part of the Air Force's command structure and held line control over the other contractors working on the ballistic missile projects. It was to be the systems integrator for Air Force ballistic missiles (Neufeld 1990: 102–5, 111).

Several of the contractors objected to Ramo–Wooldridge's favoured position. Even though the Air Force had barred Ramo–Wooldridge from competing for hardware contracts, they thought it was rewarded too much and had too much inside information. Their concerns grew when the firm merged with Thompson Productions, an automotive parts manufacturer, forming Thompson–Ramo–Wooldridge, now TRW. Under congressional pressure, the Air Force required TRW to spin-off its ballistic missile engineering integration business, conveniently housed as a subsidiary called Space Technology Laboratories (STL), into a non-profit organization chartered to do Air Force work. Soon STL was renamed the Aerospace Corporation (Neufeld 1990: 210–12).

The Air Force in another major programme—the effort to create an early warning system of radars across Northern Canada and Alaska—had addressed similar issues with a similar solution. Known as the DEW Line (for Distant Early Warning) the radars were intended to detect and track Soviet bombers on a mission to attack the United States with nuclear weapons. The concept and design for such a system evolved from studies produced by various scientific advisory committees and Lincoln Laboratory, a radar research facility managed by the Massachusetts Institute of Technology (MIT) (Needell 2000: 199–258). When a deployment decision was made, the Air Force assumed that MIT would be the systems integrator, coordinating the advanced development and site engineering of various radar, computer, and communications components required for this large network. MIT was reluctant to become so involved with the detailed engineering of the project and the direct supervision of firms like IBM, General Electric, and AT&T that were likely to be the component contractors. In turn, none of these companies were comfortable with one of the others as the systems integrator, given the advanced technologies involved. The Air Force then helped MIT spin-off sections of Lincoln Laboratory into a separate non-profit organization called MITRE, to do the required systems engineering and technical direction work for the DEW Line. MITRE would go on to do systems integration and design consulting for the Air Force on a number of other command and control programmes (Trainor 1966; Wats 1970; Office of Technology Assessment 1995; Defense Science Board 1997).

The Aerospace Corporation and MITRE are what are called Federally Funded Research and Development Centers (FFRDCs), non-profit organizations dedicated to serving federal agency interests related to technology and usually given long-term contracts for their services. Some are policy focused like RAND and the Center for Naval Analyses; others are basic research and applied engineering oriented. Lincoln Laboratory, mentioned above, is in that category. Aerospace and MITRE are the only FFRDCs dedicated in providing systems engineering assistance. Most are chartered to work for a single agency, although RAND actually manages four FFRDCs, one for the Air Force, one for the Army, one for the Office of the Secretary of Defense, and one for the Department of Health and Human Services. The biggest are the systems engineering FFRDCs that worked for the Air Force (Neufeld 1997).

At least into the 1960s, systems integration was more of a government developed and furnished skill in the Navy than it was in the Air Force. The Navy had more of an in-house industrial base and engineering tradition than did the Air Force. When nuclear power arose as a propulsion option for submarines, the Navy built its own engineering staff to manage the development effort. The desire was to build the true submersible, a submarine that did not need to come to the surface to recharge batteries. The officer in charge of the programme, Admiral Hyman G. Rickover, feared the political consequences of reactor accidents for the Navy's ability to deploy nuclear submarines and took tight control of all aspects of the programme to avoid them. He recruited able assistants for the Nuclear Power Division in the Bureau of Ships (now the Naval Reactors Directorate in the Naval Sea Systems Command), his Navy billet, and insisted that all commanding officers assigned to the submarines be qualified in nuclear reactor operation. He was tyrannical in his relations with the contractors and shipbuilders involved in the programme, demanding rigid conformity to his directions and total dedication to the task of building a nuclear fleet, and became a hero to the Congress in large part because of it (Duncan 1990). Admiral Rickover, however, had a dual appointment in the Atomic Energy Commission (AEC; now the Department of Energy), the civilian-managed agency responsible for the development and manufacturing of nuclear weapons as well as the promotion of peaceful applications of nuclear energy. Through the AEC he had access to the AEC's network of very capable national laboratories, including two dedicated to his needs in the design and development of naval reactors, the Bettis Atomic Power Laboratory in Pennsylvania operated by Westinghouse, and the Knolls Atomic Power Laboratory in New York State operated by General Electric (Hewlett and Duncan 1974).

As effective as it was, Admiral Rickover's office in either the Navy or the AEC did not control all aspects of the nuclear submarine system. Other parts of the Navy shore establishment held jurisdiction for the hull design, weapons, and sensors. The development of the nuclear submarine as an effective weapon system was evolutionary. The first nuclear-powered submarine was the Nautilus, commissioned in 1954. The first submarine utilizing the efficient teardrop hull was the Albacore, a 1953 diesel-powered submarine, but it was not until the Skipjack was commissioned in 1959 that the design was incorporated into the nuclear-powered fleet. The Polaris missile first went to sea in 1960. And the Mark-48 torpedo, an effective anti-submarine weapon, did not reach service until the mid-1970s (Cote 2003).

The Special Project Office (SPO), the organization that developed the Polaris ballistic missile, had a larger writ. It was created to develop a ballistic missile capability for the Navy. Initially, that capability was expected to be a version of the Army's liquid Jupiter missile. At the time the Army had the approved development programme and the Navy did not. Because it was teamed with the Army's Jupiter project, SPO chose Chrysler, the Jupiter prime contractor, as its own to marry the missile to a naval platform, a submarine or a surface vessel. But once the Navy gained permission to develop a new solid fuelled ballistic independent of the Army, SPO decided against hiring a prime and chose instead to do much of the systems design and integration inside its own organization. Like Naval Reactors, it brought into the project a number of capable engineers to supervise the contractors that would be selected to develop subsystems, which in the case of the Polaris included the missile, the submarine, the missile guidance and fire-control systems, the launcher, the submarine navigation system, and required bases and communication systems. Only the reactors for the submarines and the warheads for the missiles lay beyond SPO's management scope.

The SPO's immediate task was to define and assure the compatibility of the systems interfaces, the boundary requirements for each subsystem. Captain (later Vice Admiral) Levering Smith, the project's technical director, oversaw the process. Smith, like Rickover, earned a reputation for being in control of the details and for his devotion to the mission, acquiring a vital new capability for the Navy. But unlike Rickover, Smith was not willing to rely entirely on programme civil servants and naval officers, as capable as he thought they were, for the programme's systems integration and monitoring needs. Instead, he brought in two contractors to advise and assist, one a non-profit and the other a commercial entity. The Applied Physics Laboratory at Johns Hopkins University, a FFRDC, helped by conducting system tradeoff studies, proposing component boundary lines, and analysing system test results. The Vitro Corporation documented and monitored system interfaces. Lockheed, as the contractor responsible for the keystone systems component, the missile, was called upon to perform additional staff services such as report preparation and public relations, but neither it nor the Applied Physics Laboratory and Vitro could be fairly described as weapon systems manager or the programme's systems integrator. Instead Smith managed a team that included them and the SPO staff to do these jobs (Sapolsky 1972: 82).

The big technological steps the American military took during the cold war required the coordination of many disciplines and organizations. Although some defence contractors had experience in managing complex aircraft projects for the government, the belief was that the financial opportunities the new technologies appeared to offer would be too tempting to place them in charge again. The government itself could take control, but many worried that there would soon be recruitment and retention problems. Government careers, except for the military, lack status in American society. There were some very able military officers available to run the projects, but would there be enough of them to sustain the effort required?[3] The answer to this problem lay in the creation of a new set of institutions, non-profit organizations dedicated to government service, but able to pay salaries competitive with industry to attract talent. These organizations overlapped in function with industry, but were restricted in terms of the kinds of contracts they could accept from government. MITRE, the Aerospace Corporation, Lincoln, the Applied Physics Laboratory, and the AEC's national laboratories taken together were a social invention that helped the United States win the cold war. To varying degrees the armed services had to rely on specially created non-profit systems design and integration organizations to build the strategic deterrent, warning, reconnaissance, and command and control systems that kept America ahead and that exhausted the Soviet Union in its attempt to match them.

2.6   Thinking Systemically About Policy and War

Systems thinking appeared first on the operational side of the military, but was slower to spread there than on the weapons development side. Pioneering work in operations research techniques was applied on several fronts during the Second World War. In the Battle of the Atlantic, American, British, and Canadian scientists calculated the preferred convoy routing, and ship and aircraft search patterns to thwart the highly destructive attacks by German U-Boats on Allied shipping (Tidman 1984: 17–94). Earlier, British scientists had demonstrated the military effectiveness of operations research in their effort to improve the intercept rates of fighters in the Battle of Britain, the Royal Air Force's defence of Britain against German air attacks. These were interdisciplinary efforts that applied scientific methods to military problems in order to improve the efficiency of operations and the design of equipment (Tidman 1984: 12–16).[4]

Although American practitioners of the art found employment in nearly every corner of the military after the war, operations research had less impact on warfare than its Second World War contribution seemed to promise. Generals and admirals resisted intrusions into their domain by scientists with little or no combat experience. To many of them, success in war was certain to remain as the product of sound professional training and judgement in the face of the great confusion and horror of the battlefield (Rau 2000). Moreover, the reliable quantitative information needed to analyse military problems was hard to obtain due to the difficulty in conducting realistic experiments short of war.

The military's resistance grew stronger when scientists broadened their inquiry to include policy issues as they did almost immediately on questions related to nuclear weapons. Senior officers were worried that the pacifist/ arms control inclinations of the scientists would influence the public and interfere with plans for rapidly expanding nuclear forces (Needell 2000: 241–5).[5] Much to their annoyance, the systems analytic framework that scientists developed both in and outside of government to consider nuclear weapons issues did gain legitimacy and was later used by civilian officials, most especially Secretary of Defense Robert McNamara who served in the 1960s, to limit military requests for nuclear and non-nuclear weapons. Secretary McNamara countered the military claim to professional expertise with a claim of expertise in systems analysis, the quantitative oriented approach to defence policy problems that scientists favoured (Kantor 1979; Rosen 1984).

Although political and professional judgements still dominated policy-making, the rational scientific approach that systems analysis seemed to offer found widespread appeal in official discussions of policy where politics and personal agendas cannot easily be expressed. At a disadvantage in these policy discussions, the military built up their own systems analysis capabilities and support organizations. RAND, The Center for Naval Analyses, and other FFRDCs that served a single armed service were often the generators of studies that promoted service programmes in the face of challenges by the Secretary's staff or the other services. Analysis, easily shaped to reach desired outcomes because of its dependence on the policy assumptions and measures selected became another weapon in the bureaucratic wars over programmes and budget (Esell 1968; Lucas and Dawson 1974; Lehman 1988; Donohue et al. 1993; Vistica 1997).

Secretary McNamara retained the initiative by exploiting the natural competitiveness of the services. He would pit one against another, selectively offering opportunities or imposing penalties, to avoid having them form a united front against his policies. The policies McNamara favoured were greater centralization of support functions, joint weapon developments, limits on nuclear forces, and coordinated operations (Hitch 1967; Johnson 2000). During his tenure he reduced significantly the government's ability to design and build its own equipment by closing arsenals and shipyards (Assistant Secretary of the Navy for Manpower, Reserve Affairs and Logistics 1978). Contractors were asked to bid on the entire acquisition of a weapon, the so-called Total Package Procurement initiative first used with less than stellar results in the purchase of the C-5A transport (McNaugher 1989: 176). And the services were forced to buy the same aircraft irrespective of which one of them had developed it (Art 1968; Hallion 1994). An unpopular war, America's long struggle in Vietnam eventually forced McNamara, its senior manager, out of office. Many of his specific reforms did not survive very long—the Navy, for example, cancelled its participation in the joint acquisition with the Air Force of the F-111 aircraft within hours of his departure—but his underlining criticism that the services focused too narrowly on their interests and neglected common ones clearly did survive (McNaugher 1989: 176). Nearly every military failing since then, from disappointment in weapon acquisition to combat disaster in the field, has been blamed on service parochialism and lack of integration among the armed services (Hoffman 1999). McNamara's endorsed proposals that there should be more jointness in both procurement and military operations became gospel, with the Congress, long the protector of service interests, enshrining them into law in the Goldwater–Nichols Act in 1986, which amended The National Security Act of 1947, and which increased the authority of the military's joint organizations. Even the F-111 idea of joint service development of aircraft is back in the form of the tri-service Joint Strike Fighter, the F-35 (Brinkley 2000). The services too have embraced jointness in the belief that greater coordination among them did not necessarily mean greater integration. They have used the increased importance of the Joint Staff and the joint commands in the US military structure, mandates of Goldwater–Nichols, to gain agreement among themselves about the sharing of missions. They rarely break ranks publicly when resources are at issue. Joint projects are increasingly common, but without much impact on the share of the budget or the assignment of missions among the services.[6] The promise of real integration, however, lies just ahead, we are told. Advances in communications and computers lead many to believe that a revolution in military practice is about to take place. There are visions of networked battlefields where surveying sensors identify targets and pass the information on to dispersed weapons platforms, which engage as needed while remaining aware of the location and status of friendly forces. Queued from space or unmanned aircraft, the weapons are precise. The connections are seamless between platforms, services, and commands. In these visions wars are fought by a military that utilizes 'systems of systems' (Owens 2000). The American military, according to its own documents, is working to transform itself into precisely such a force (Flournoy 2001).

2.7 Discovering the Limits

The American military in the cold war forced the pace of technology in a number of large complex weapon projects. Spurred on by its own internally competitive structure, it learned and helped others to learn systems integration skills, the art of conceiving, designing, and managing the development and deployment of large systems involving multiple disciplines and many participating organizations. The skills became central to the work of several aerospace firms, some government agencies, and a few specially created non-profit organizations dedicated to public service. Their efficiency in creating complex weapon systems eroded the Soviet Union's confidence in its ability to compete and surely contributed to the peaceful end of the cold war.

The systems integration skills were narrowly focused on weapons. They did help increase America's military power relative to others. But the thought that a similar level of integration can be achieved in policymaking or that war fighting can be made into a manageable systems problem seems illusionary. Reorganizations have centralized authority within the American Department of Defense without offering a comparable increase in the ability to process relevant information, make effective decisions, or gain full compliance in their implementation. Moreover, too much of importance to America's security lies beyond the scope of the Department of Defense or the influence of weapons.

The danger is to expect too much from those practising the art of systems integration.[7] The success achieved in building weapon systems for the cold war has led to much hubris about the efficacy of systems thinking and the ability of the military to manage very complex operations. At least some of today's generals and admirals could benefit from a bit of the scepticism their predecessors showed when dealing with the claims of the operations researchers and other scientists after the Second World War. Technology has changed much about the way wars are fought, but it has not yet lifted the fog of war.

To the engineering mind, however, the need is to keep trying to apply a systems approach to all problems, civil or military. As Simon Ramo of Ramo–Wooldridge and systems integration fame expressed it, 'The system is there. It exists, designed or not, analyzed or not' (1969: 106). For Ramo, the systems approach/systems integration was the cure for chaos. Most organizations want very much to order their environments and thus cannot resist the call of the engineers. The result, however, is always another partial system, perhaps a step better, but inevitably only the reason for the next try for more order, and not the cure for chaos.

Notes

1. See Figure 5.1 Fitted logistic curves of war production: five cases.
2. The list of studies of missile programmes with this focus is long. A place to start is with Armacost (1969).
3. Apparently, the Air Force still struggles with this issue. See Simon (2002).
4. A claim for the first business application of systems engineering/systems design is made in Aris (2000).

5. For a British parallel, see Mary Jo Nye's comments on P. M. S. Blackett, the British geophysicist, who was an Operations Research leader (Nye 2002).
6. Cindy Williams (2001) explores a defence budget where the shares move due to competition for missions, but the total stays fixed.
7. The promise of great contributions of the systems approach in solving social problems, also disappointed, came earlier. See Webb (1969), Sayles and Chandler (1971), and especially Jardini (2000).

References

ARIS, J. (2000). 'Inventing Systems Engineering', *IEEE Annals of the History of Computing*, July–September: 4–15.
ARMACOST, M. H. (1969). *The Politics of Weapons Innovation: The Thor–Jupiter Controversy*. New York: Columbia University Press.
ART, R. J. (1968). *The TFX Decision: McNamara and the Military*. Boston, MA: Little, Brown.
ASSISTANT SECRETARY OF THE NAVY FOR MANPOWER, RESERVE AFFAIRS, AND LOGISTICS (1978). *Naval Ship Procurement Process Study, Final Report*. Washington, DC: Department of the Navy.
BRINKLEY, C. M. (2000). 'Jones Not Committed to Future Jump Jet', *Marine Corps Times*, 25 December: 12.
CARALEY, D. (1965). *The Politics of Military Unification*. New York: Columbia University Press.
CHRISTENSEN, C. (1997). *The Innovator's Dilemma: When New Technologies Cause Great Firms to Fail*. Boston, MA: Harvard Business School Press.
COTE, Jr., O. (2003). *The Third Battle of the Atlantic*. Newport, RI: The Naval War. College Press.
DEFENSE SCIENCE BOARD (1997). *Report on Federally Funded Research and Development Centers (FFRDC) and University Affiliated Research Centers (UARC) Independent Advisory Task Force*. Washington, DC: Office of the Under Secretary of Defense for Acquisition and Technology.
DONOHUE, G., LORELL, M., SMITH, G., and WALKER, W. (1993). 'DOD Centralization: An Old Solution for a New Era?', RAND Issue Paper. Santa Monica, CA: RAND Corporation.
DUNCAN, F. (1990). *Rickover and the Nuclear Navy: The Discipline of Technology*. Annapolis, MD: The US Naval Institute Press.
ESELL, E. (1968). 'The Death of the Arsenal System?', paper presented at the Annual meeting of the Organization of American Historians, Dallas, Texas, 18 April.
FLOURNOY, M. A. (ed.) (2001). *QDR 2001 Strategy-driven Choices for America's Security*. Washington, DC: National Defense University Press.
FLYNN, G. Q. (1993). *The Draft, 1940–1973*. Manhattan, KS: University of Kansas Press.
FRIEDBERG, A. L. (2000). *In the Shadow of the Garrison State: America's Anti-statism and its Cold War Strategy*. Princeton, NJ: Princeton University Press.

GHOLZ, E. (2001). 'The Curtiss-Wright Corporation and Cold War-era Defense Procurement: A Challenge to Military–Industrial Complex Theory', *Journal of Cold War Studies*, 2/1: 35–76.

GREENFIELD, K. R. (1982). *American Strategy in World War II: A Reconsideration.* Malabar, FL: Robert E. Krieger Publishing Company.

GROPMAN, A. L. (1996). *Mobilizing US Industry in World War II* (McNair Paper 50). Washington, DC: National Defense University Press.

HALLION, R. P. (1994). 'A Troubling Past: Air Force Fighter Acquisition since 1945', *Airpower Journal*, Winter: 30–40.

HARRISON, M. (2000). 'Wartime Mobilization: A German Comparison', in J. Barber and M. Harrison (eds.), *The Soviet Defence–Industry Complex from Stalin to Khrushchev.* London: Macmillan Press, 99–117.

HEWLETT, R. G. and DUNCAN, F. (1974). *Nuclear Navy 1946–1962.* Chicago, IL: University of Chicago Press.

HITCH, C. J. (1967). *Decision-making for Defense.* Berkeley, CA: University of California Press.

HOFFMAN, F. (1999). 'Goldwater–Nichols after a Decade', in W. Murray (ed.), *The Emerging Strategic Environment.* Westport, CT: Praeger, 156–82.

HOLLEY, I. B., Jr. (1964). *Buying Aircraft: Matériel Procurement for the Army Air Forces.* (United States Army in World War II, Special Studies). Washington, DC: Department of the Army.

——(1983). *Ideas and Weapons.* Washington, DC: Office of Air Force History.

JARDINI, D. R. (2000). 'Out of the Blue Yonder: The Transfer of Systems Thinking From the Pentagon to the Great Society', in A. C. Hughes and T. P. Hughes (eds.), *Systems, Experts, and Computers: The Systems Approach in Management and Engineering, World War II and After.* Cambridge, MA: MIT Press, 311–58.

JOHNSON, S. P. (2000). 'From Concurrency to Phased Planning: An Episode in the History of Systems Management', in A. C. Hughes and T. P. Hughes (eds.), *Systems, Experts, and Computers: The Systems Approach in Management and Engineering, World War II and After.* Cambridge, MA: MIT Press, 93–112.

JONES, W. D., Jr. (1990). *Arming the Eagle: A History of US Weapons Acquisition Since 1775.* Fort Belvoir, VA: Defense Systems Management College Press.

KANTOR, A. (1979). *Defense Politics: A Budgetary Perspective.* Chicago, IL: University of Chicago Press.

KINNARD, D. (1980). *The Secretary of Defense.* Lexington, KY: University of Kentucky Press.

LEHMAN, J. (1988). *Command of the Sea: Building the 600 Ship Navy.* New York: Scribner.

LUCAS, W. A. and DAWSON, R. H. (1974). *The Organizational Politics of Defense* (Occasional Paper No. 2, International Studies Association). Pittsburgh, PA: Center for International Studies, University of Pittsburgh.

MACGREGOR, D. A. (1997). *Breaking the Phalanx: A New Design for Land Power in the 20th Century.* Westport, CT: Praeger.

MCNAUGHER, T. L. (1989). *New Weapons Old Politics: America's Procurement Muddle.* Washington, DC: The Brookings Institution.

NEEDELL, A. A. (2000). *Science, Cold War and the American State: Lloyd V. Berkner and the Balance of Professional Ideals.* Amsterdam: Harwood Academic Publishers.

NEUFELD, J. (1990). *Ballistic Missiles in the United States Air Force 1945–1960.* Washington, DC: GPO.

NEUFELD, J. (ed.) (1992). *Reflections on Research and Development in the United States Air Force*. Washington, DC: Center for Air Force History.

—— (1997). 'Ace in the Hole: The Air Force Ballistic Missile Program', in J. Neufeld, G. M. Watson, Jr., and D. Chenoweth (eds.), *Technology and the Air Force: A Retrospective Assessment*. Washington, DC: Air Force History and Museum Program, United States Air Force, 111–23.

NYE, M. J. (2002). 'The Most Versatile Physicist of His Generation', *Science*, 296: 49–50.

OFFICE OF TECHNOLOGY ASSESSMENT, US CONGRESS (1995). *A History of the Department of Defense Federally Funded Research and Development Centers* (OTA-BP-ISS-157). Washington, DC: US Government Printing Office.

OWENS, W. (2000). *Lifting the Fog of War*. New York: Farrar, Straus and Giroux.

PRICE, D. K. (1954). *Science and Government*. New York: New York University Press.

RAMO, S. (1969). *The Cure for Chaos: Fresh Solutions to Social Problems Through the Systems Approach*. New York, NY: David McKay Company.

RAU, E. P. (2000). 'The Adoption of Operations Research in the United States During World War II', in A. C. Hughes and T. P. Hughes (eds.), *Systems, Experts, and Computers: The Systems Approach in Management and Engineering, World War II and After*. Cambridge, MA: MIT Press, 82–4.

ROSEN, S. P. (1984). 'Systems Analysis and the Quest for Rational Defense', *Public Interest*, Summer: 3–17.

SAPOLSKY, H. M. (1972). *The Polaris System Development: Programmatic and Bureaucratic Success in Government*. Cambridge, MA: Harvard University Press.

——, GHOLZ, E., and KAUFMAN, A. (1999). 'Security Lessons from the Cold War', *Foreign Affairs*, 78/4: 77–89.

SAYLES, L. R. and CHANDLER, M. K. (1971). *Managing Large Systems: Organizations for the Future*. New York: Harper & Row.

SIMON, S. (2002). 'US Air Force Mulls Engineer Institute', *Defense News*, 17–23 June: 56.

TIDMAN, K. R. (1984). *The Operations Evaluation Group: A History of Naval Operations Analysis*. Annapolis, MD: US Naval Institute Press.

TRAINOR, J. L. (1966). 'Government Use of Nonprofit Corporations', *Harvard Business Review*, May–June: 38–52.

VISTICA, G. L. (1997). *Fall From Glory: The Men Who Sank the US Navy*. New York: Touchstone.

WATS, N. (1970). *Problems in the Management of Federal Contract Research Centers* (MTP-119). MITRE Corporation.

WEBB, J. E. (1969). *Space Age Management: The Large Scale Approach*. New York: McGraw-Hill.

WILLIAMS, C. (ed.) (2001). *Holding the Line: US Defense Alternatives for the Early 21st Century*. Cambridge, MA: MIT Press.

YOUNG, J. O. (1997). 'Riding England's Coattails: The Army Air Forces and the Turbojet Revolution', in J. Neufeld, G. M. Watson, Jr., and D. Chenoweth (eds.), *Technology and the Air Force: A Retrospective Assessment*. Washington, DC: Air Force History and Museum Program, United States Air Force, 28–9.

3

Systems Integration and the Social Solution of Technical Problems in Complex Systems

STEPHEN B. JOHNSON

Space Studies Department, University of North Dakota, USA

With the advent of large-scale, complex systems in the middle of the twentieth century, the problem of systems integration has preoccupied many engineers, particularly in the aerospace and computing industries. We can define a complex system as a set of humans and technologies united to perform a specific function, which are collectively incomprehensible (in total) to any single person. Examples are legion, but include nuclear power plants, modern jet aircraft and ballistic missiles, computerized command and control systems, etc. In the United States, military officers, academic researchers, and industrial leaders created systems engineering primarily on ballistic missile and air defence programmes of the 1950s (Johnson 2002a; Sapolsky, Chapter Two, this volume). From these programmes the methods spread into other industries and countries, and have been codified into procedures of the US military[1] and that of its allies[2] (Gholz, Chapter Fourteen, this volume). Through these regulations they have become the standard for those industries that develop technologies for the military and for many other industries as well. These disciplines have therefore been a significant element in the economic development of developed and developing countries.

Only since the 1980s, with research into the economics of innovation, the politics and sociology of complex systems, and the history of technology, has systems integration come to the attention of social scientists. Social scientists who are now investigating systems integration use the tools and methods in which they were trained. However, they are less likely to utilize insights and debates of engineering researchers and designers. Also, it is unlikely that social scientists can form a true picture of systems integration without understanding the technical and social problems that engineers face. If firms gain competitive advantage from systems integration, economists and organizational theorists must understand the technical and social issues of system integration. To do this, we must turn our attention to systems engineering, which is the disciplinary home of systems integration.

Systems engineering has been a hot topic among engineers for nearly half a century, as engineering practitioners and researchers have debated whether it is 'really' engineering, or whether it is 'mere management'. Understanding this debate requires us to step back in time to the foundation of systems engineering in the 1950s and 1960s. During these decades, engineers faced for the first time the complex problems of deep and heterogeneous technologies, and along with military officers, managers, and scientists, created systems management to deal with the many problems they encountered. These problems became obvious due to many technological failures, which required the creation of new sociotechnical methods to deal with their causes. For both engineers and social scientists, understanding the social nature of systems engineering is essential.

It is the purpose of this chapter to define and dissect systems integration from an engineering viewpoint, to describe how it historically evolved, to understand the role of failure in this evolution, and finally to use these technical and humanistic approaches to suggest new methods to improve systems integration in the future. To do so, I divide the chapter into four sections that analyse these four issues, respectively.

3.1 Systems Engineering and Systems Integration

Systems integration is an element of 'systems engineering', which historically developed during the 1940s to 1960s as a means to coordinate and control the development of complex aerospace and computing systems. Systems engineering addresses the processes and issues involved with: early analyses and trade studies of possible future systems (systems analysis); development of requirements and specifications for a particular concept; progressive design and development of the hardware, software, and operations concepts; integration of the components built by the various engineering and other organizations involved; testing and verification of these components separately and as they are progressively integrated into prototypes; and finally, deployment of the design into manufacturing and operations.[3]

When systems engineers refer to systems integration, they typically refer only to integration of components, along with the testing and verification of these components and of the system. Thus, systems integration is only one element of a much larger process of the creation and development of a complex system. For example, the United Kingdom's Defence Evaluation and Research Agency (1997) refers to systems integration in its manual of systems engineering practices.

Integration and verification process. In the integration and verification process, tested subsystems/components are delivered from the system development process or component development process at the level below, assembled (possibly with supplier support) and tested as configured subsystems items, ready for delivery to the higher level system development process or system acquisition process. The integration and verification process is the final process in the system development process. (para 6.5.1)

In its standard for engineering management, the US Department of Defense (DOD) defines systems integration similarly.

System element integration and verification. The system elements shall be progressively integrated (bottom-up) into items that provide an end-use function. At each level, the resulting design requirements, physical configuration and physical interfaces shall be verified to ensure that the functional requirements are satisfied. The correlation amongst interfunctionally related elements shall be established and controlled. The techniques and procedural data for development, production, test/verification, deployment/installation, operation, support, training, and disposal shall be determined, documented and implemented, as applicable. To provide a satisfactory solution set, each configuration item shall be evaluated to verify that it meets performance, functional and design requirements as well as user needs/requirements.[4]

In both definitions, and in the regulations and procedures that follow, systems integration requires not simply that components be put together, but also that the components, when assembled, are tested to ensure they perform as advertised. Systems integration is thus the penultimate test of the technology to determine if it will function as originally envisioned. The final test comes when the system goes into operation with its final user.

As critical as systems integration is to the success of the system, it is only one element of the technological life cycle. Programme managers and engineers believe that success in the development of any complex technology requires 'womb to tomb' planning and control—for them the critical issue is not systems integration, but systems engineering. If a programme is not well planned and coordinated from the start, they believe it is a virtual certainty that failures will ensue upon integration. I too will refer primarily to systems engineering and systems engineers, as opposed to the final stage of systems integration.

Systems engineers have long recognized the links between their discipline and the management of technology. Systems engineering acts as the process and disciplinary link between engineers that design and test technologies, and managers that oversee the process and distribute funds. In the 1950s, the new discipline of 'project management' came into being as the managerial analogue to systems engineering, and from that time onwards, project managers and systems engineers have worked together and fought with each other to create complex new technologies (Johnson 1997).

For some 50 years, systems engineering has been a topic of intense debate among engineers. Much of the debate has revolved around the failure to transform systems engineering into a mathematical discipline on the model of the physical sciences. This failure has left systems engineering largely without a disciplinary home in academia. Academic engineers that rely heavily on mathematical methods criticize it on these grounds, believing that any 'real' discipline must be so grounded. They dismiss it as mere management or bureaucracy. Design engineers, who frequently use systems engineering methods, often criticize systems engineering as 'something that any good engineer does'. Their criticism is not that systems engineering lacks mathematics, but rather that since they occasionally use systems engineering methods themselves, systems engineering has no unique attributes in comparison to other engineering disciplines such as electrical or mechanical engineering.[5]

Because the nature of their job involves the coordination and direction of other engineers and organizations, systems engineers have always had to deal in some measure with social issues. It is perhaps enlightening to note that few if any managers or business theorists have had trouble understanding the function, utility, or theories of systems engineering. While most systems engineers have conceived of these social interactions in terms of technology management, a few unconventional engineers recognize that social issues have a more subtle and important role than most acknowledge.

The social environment places a number of fundamental obligations on those undertaking systems engineering, some in the form of legal requirements, some in the form of social norms. These obligations can have a profound impact on the opportunities available and on the acceptability of solutions. They present constraints, for example, health and safety legislation, standards of behaviour, Montreal Protocol, employment regulations, international trading agreements/restrictions. They may also present opportunities, for example, environmentally friendly products, systems meeting social trends, politically expedient international collaboration.

These overriding social influences most immediately impact on the enterprise and project environments in which systems engineering sits. However, it is still common for social influences to be evident explicitly and, more challengingly, implicitly in the activities and decisions associated with systems engineering, for example in energy conservation, product aesthetics, disposal criteria, system safety.

According to the Defence Evaluation and Research Agency (DERA) document referred to previously: 'Systems engineering practices are thus subject to the effect of the social environment. Its impact can be fundamental and decisive and the systems engineer needs to be familiar with its existence and influences.'[6]

This statement is atypical in its explicit recognition of social factors that have important influences on technology design. Here, the social environment is conceived as an external influence that may enhance or inhibit the job of the systems engineer, or may influence the requirements and goals of the system. While this statement goes further than most, it shares with common engineering opinion complete silence about the possible social interactions of the engineers and managers themselves in the process of engineering design. This is due to the prosaic fact that engineers are neither by inclination nor by training disposed to see their own work as inherently social. Nor are they inclined, even if they realize that communication and coordination are important, to think through the technical implications of the social nature of their work.

A substantial number of engineers perform tasks clearly identified in industry and the government as systems engineering. The function of systems engineering clearly exists, even according to those engineers that are sceptical of its disciplinary status. Systems engineers coordinate, and to some extent control, the overall technical direction of the project. The processes, methods, and tools by which this occurs has drawn some attention in engineering circles, leading to books (1957), standards (1969), and eventually (1990) to its own professional organization, the International Council on Systems Engineering (INCOSE).[7] To better understand the processes of systems engineering, as espoused in these various publications and organizations, we must return to the 1940s and 1950s, to the problems facing systems engineering's founders.

3.2   The Tribulations of the Early Systems Engineers

During the Second World War, scientists and engineers developed a plethora of new technologies, many of them critical to military success. On the Allied side, radar and the atomic fission bomb were the most prominent new developments. It is often said that radar won the war, while the atomic bomb ended it. Other less obvious technologies were also very important, such as operations research to organize bombing and anti-submarine operations, the proximity fuse for anti-aircraft shells and naval torpedoes, and proto-computers for cryptological analysis and anti-aircraft guns. The Germans deployed the first ballistic missiles, jet engines, and submarine snorkels. By the end of the war, scientists and engineers had garnered tremendous prestige, and the US military was determined to continue rapid development of new technologies as a means to ensure the security of the nation.

For aviation engineers of the 1940s, many of these technologies were novel. Aviation design up to the late 1930s primarily involved designing efficient aerodynamic structures and hydraulic pilot controls. Normally engineers would develop a new airframe design, which the Army Air Corps or the Navy would accept for manufacturing. The military mounted radios and weapons (bombs or machine guns generally) into each aircraft. Aircraft designers therefore did not concern themselves with electronics or weaponry (Holley 1964). This changed during the Second World War, as weapons and electronics became structurally integrated into aircraft. Aviation firms had to learn new skills, particularly those related to electronics and jet engines, since these had to be designed into the aircraft right from the start (van der Muelen 1995: 11–29). This was even more pronounced for missiles, which had the added complication of requiring automatic controls without pilots or ground intervention. Aircraft and missiles were becoming too complex for the mechanically oriented aircraft designers of the 1930s. Teams of engineers and scientists from many disciplines now had to contribute to the design of 'weapons systems'. Coordination among these different experts became an issue of importance, which was most pronounced for ballistic missiles (Johnson 2002a: 6–7, 46–54).

Nuclear weapons and the means to deliver them dominated military thinking for most of the cold war. Heavy bombers such as the B-29, B-36, and eventually the jet-propelled B-52 were the delivery mechanisms of choice from 1945 to 1953. However, in 1953, the first successful test of the thermonuclear fusion bomb changed that dominance. Although the military had been intrigued by the ballistic missile ever since the deployment of the Nazi V-2 in 1944, ballistic missiles could not carry effective fission warheads due to their large mass and relatively small explosion. Put another way, ballistic missiles would hit too far away from their targets for fission warheads to destroy the target. Fusion weapons changed this, as their explosion was so huge compared with its mass that even a miss by a few miles would still obliterate the target. This made ballistic missiles, which were impossible to destroy when in flight, the delivery mechanism of choice (Neufeld 1990).

Ballistic missiles posed a number of difficult challenges to engineers of the late 1940s and 1950s. They included many new technologies with which most aviation engineers had little expertise, including most prominently rocket engines, radio communications, automatic guidance and control, and high-speed aerodynamics. Rocket engines, for example, required novel expertise in fluid dynamics, and also needed ultra-clean manufacturing facilities because a single bit of dirt could clog a fuel valve and lead to a catastrophic explosion. The combination of these technologies posed entirely new problems, such as the interaction between the near-random vibration of rocket engines and their detrimental effect on sensitive electronics by breaking wires, solders, and casings. Another example was the interaction of electronic signals, which would interfere with each other unless protected from each other's electromagnetic radiation. Ballistic missiles flew all the way into and through the vacuum of space, which was an environment completely alien to earth-bound engineers. The lack of air meant that new means had to be devised to carry heat away from hot electronic components since many terrestrial thermal designs used air convection to distribute heat energy (Johnson 2002a: 4–7).

Finally, complexity caught up with 1950s missile designers. The sheer number and variety of components, which in the 1930s numbered in the hundreds or low thousands for aircraft, multiplied in the 1950s to the tens of thousands, with a variety of types that matched the diversity of disciplines. A frequent problem of the 1950s was a mismatch between the paper design and the manufactured vehicles. Engineers thought that a certain missile was flying with a certain set of components interconnected as documented on paper. Unfortunately, that missile often flew with different components than what appeared on the design drawings due to modifications made somewhere in the design or manufacturing. Since each missile flew only once, missile tests required an entire assembly line, which had to be kept up to date with the many changes being made as engineers struggled to build this radically new device. The missile's 'configuration' thus became a critical concern (Johnson 2002*a*: 10–11, 89–102).

Equally significant were the 'interfaces' between components. With each additional component and device added to the missile came a new connection between that device and the rest of the missile. The proliferation of components and component types greatly amplified the problem of ensuring that each component mated properly with its neighbours, and also that their collective performance matched engineers' expectations. Analysing and making consistent these many interfaces became a critical task (Johnson 2002*b*: 13–14).

Engineers reacted to these issues with a number of strategies. To deal with the new environment of space and the problem of rocket engine vibrations, engineers developed new environmental tests. For the vacuum environment outside of the atmosphere, thermal vacuum chambers were created, which mimicked the heating and cooling effects of solar radiation and shade without the mitigating effects of air. Vibration problems could be uncovered through the creation and use of random vibration, or 'shake' tables. When tested with these new devices, engineers could detect thermal problems and poorly connected electrical components, since poor thermal and mechanical designs appeared through overheating or overcooling, and electrical connections broke (Johnson 2002*b*: 9–12).

Testing also provided a means to detect unexpected interactions among components and subsystems. Each time engineers connected a new component, they ran 'functional tests' that ensured proper electrical and mechanical connectivity. System tests replicated the events and environments that the vehicle would undergo during its mission as much as possible without actually flying the vehicle. These frequently uncovered problems in timing and sequencing of events such as stage separation, as well as unexpected interactions between thermal, electrical, propulsion, and mechanical subsystems (Johnson 2002*a*: 95; 2002*b*: 86, 127–9).

While testing could find many problems, system testing and retroactive redesign was an expensive proposition. It would be much better to prevent the problems in the first place. Problem prevention required that engineers create a better design, that factory workers improve manufacturing quality, and that communication between all involved become more effective right at the start. Many, if not most design problems ultimately arose from one of two situations: when engineers or organizations miscommunicated information required to connect components; or when the information needed to detect possible design flaws simply did not flow from those who had the information to those who needed it. Put another way, most engineering problems were not due to lack of knowledge about phenomena or artefacts, but rather that engineers did not grasp the system-wide implications of making local design decisions.

Better coordination was called for. The method that became most prevalent was the 'design freeze' followed by rigorous 'change control'. By 'freezing' the design, the engineer in charge, often called the chief engineer or the systems engineer, would stop any other engineer from making design changes in that portion of the system that was 'frozen'. Since designs changed continually in the early design phases and slowly stabilized as engineers worked out the various problems, this could be done only with those portions of the design that had reached sufficient maturity. Once frozen, engineers could make changes only if the systems engineer approved the proposed change. If a change was proposed, the systems engineer communicated the change to all potentially affected parties in what became known as a 'change board'. This allowed all parties to determine any ramifications of that change on their own designs, and could then submit their resulting changes to the systems engineer. The systems engineer typically allowed only those changes absolutely necessary. Changes that improved performance past the minimum requirements were frequently disallowed (Johnson 2002*a*: 94–7; 2002*b*: 90–2).

Manufacturing quality control required different methods. Many of the difficulties with missiles (and later, computers) arose from the processes of connecting components together. Factory workers knew very well how to crimp a connector or solder a wire. The problem was to do so every time for thousands of connectors and wires. Repetitive tasks such as these were problematic simply because workers' attention wandered. Since a single bad connection could cause loss of the vehicle, some means to guarantee proper work was required. One solution was to have quality control inspectors double-check, and then to sign off on each and every connection or solder. Each component had to be verified for proper function, and then rigorously tracked to ensure that only those components found their way into the missile (Johnson 2002*a*: 131, 135; 2002*b*: 125–7).

A similar system of component tracking tied to engineering change control formed the solution to mismatches between the paper design and the manufactured vehicle. This system, known as configuration control, became the primary method to ensure one-to-one match between engineering conception and manufacturing reality. The system traced each and every design element to a specific manufactured component, and vice versa. Change control boards regulated engineering changes. Once approved, the change control board released the new design paperwork, and required that the assembly and manufacturing processes and components also change to match. When a vehicle was ready to fly, inspectors then crosschecked the actual hardware components versus the current design drawings (Johnson 2002*a*: 96–8).

By the early 1960s, managers gained control of these processes. Realizing that the chief systems engineer exerted control over other engineers through the change control board, project managers inserted themselves into the process, and required that engineers not only gave technical information about changes, but also cost and schedule. If they did not, the project manager vetoed the change. Cost and schedule data provided a proxy for the technical data that the project manager might or might not understand. By monitoring predicted costs and schedules, which were updated regularly, managers converted configuration control into configuration management, a critical tool of what became known as 'systems management' (Johnson 2002*a*: 100–2).

Systems management required formal documentation. Engineers had to develop their specifications in far greater detail than they had done previously, so as to match specific specifications to specific design attributes. By the early 1960s, The Aerospace Corporation had developed this into a formal set of procedures known as System Requirements Analysis (Johnson 2002*a*: 97–8). Once developed, engineers had to prove that their designs met the performance detailed in the specifications. They did this by verifying each specification through inspection, testing, or analysis. In addition, the specifications, designs, and tests came under review through formal design reviews, from the Preliminary Design Review that ensured validity of specifications, to the Critical Design Review that crosschecked the design, to the Flight Readiness Review that ensured the vehicle components and configuration matched the design requirements and specifications. At each of these reviews, outside experts assessed performance of the design and testing teams (Johnson 2002*b*: 127, 142, 148–9). Interfaces received special attention through the creation of Interface Control Documents that documented all relevant information about component and subsystem boundaries to ensure compatibility (Johnson 2002*b*: 128–9).

Common to all of these new processes was their social nature. Engineers did not find many technological fixes to quality control and design complexity problems. Instead, they relied on social processes of communication and control. In retrospect, this is not surprising, since the fundamental issues were communication between engineers, and psychological characteristics of human inattention in manufacturing. While it is possible in some cases to replace humans with machines in manufacturing, that is far less likely for engineering design, which is an essentially creative process. Machines cannot ultimately resolve communication issues between human beings, although they can act as intermediaries. Systems engineering, which encompasses all of these processes, is a fundamentally social enterprise, having to do with enhancing social processes of communication and control to create new artefacts and new human–machine systems.

3.3 The Role of Failure

Failure has a critical role in technology development (Petroski 1982). We usually think of failure in technological terms. However, a deeper analysis of the concept reveals that it is a social construct. Failure is defined by the expectation of the builders and users. If a system does not perform the functions that the builder or the user intends, then it has failed (Campbell et al. 1992: 3). Implicit in the definition is that for a system to function properly, user intentions as well as designer intentions must be communicated to all involved in the design. This goes far to explain why systems engineering is ultimately about information coordination and communication.

Engineers often create new technologies by extracting increased performance out of their technological bag of tricks. This is by its nature an exploration of the unknown, combining existing methods, techniques, and ideas in a new, unexpected manner. Insights often occur through an unstructured interplay of old and new. This implies that designers require some measure of freedom from rigid rules (Gorman and Carlson 1990).

In contrast to creativity, which requires unstructured thinking and tinkering, the fear of failure fosters bureaucratic processes. This is particularly true of complex technologies in which humans find it difficult to ascertain the danger or risks (Perrow 1984; Weick 1987). The failure of the space shuttle Challenger in January 1986 was such a case. Ultimately, the failure was due to operating the vehicle at temperatures lower than the solid rocket booster O-rings could safely function. This fact was unclear at the time, even to the engineers at Thiokol who understood the boosters best and the NASA engineers and managers who operated the shuttle (Vaughan 1996). Engineers and managers tried to manage the risk of the shuttle through extensive processes to check against possible faults. In the case of Challenger, the processes uncovered anomalies, but the complexities of the data, which reflected the complexities of the system, made interpretation difficult and ultimately flawed.

Systems engineering developed in the 1950s and 1960s partly to foster communication required for creativity, but equally to ensure that the new systems functioned properly. Ballistic missile, air defence, and space systems required new technologies that travelled into new environments (high altitudes and the vacuum of space), individually and collectively requiring much higher performance than prior technologies (high-speed computing, high-accuracy guidance, much stronger structures), and attempting to harness extremely powerful and dangerous forces (nuclear warheads, cryogenic propellants). Some engineers began to realize that they did not understand the ramifications of all of these collective novelties.

Engineers at first did not grasp that these complex new systems required new social processes. It would have been quite surprising if they had, considering that their training was primarily in technologies and physical and mathematical theories to the near-exclusion of social and cognitive issues. Failure was a major spur to action, as old methods did not suffice, and engineers tried new ones on an *ad hoc* basis to deal with the problems as they occurred. The initial development of ballistic missiles and real-time computing systems required visionary and creative processes, which fostered small teams and groups that came into and went out of existence as needed. These teams largely ignored military and industrial regulations and adopted creative processes largely borrowed from academia. Experts from various disciplines came together in committees to share knowledge and resolve problems. They also shared decision-making power, since no single group or individual had the expertise required. This led to interesting (and some-times illegal!) organizational developments, such as the use of the Ramo–Wooldridge Corporation to double-check Air Force contractors, or the Massachusetts Institute of Technology's (MIT) Lincoln Laboratory, which informally coordinated the air defence development programme *in lieu* of military direction. Similarly, the California Institute of Technology's Jet Propulsion Laboratory developed ballistic missile programmes for Army Ordnance.[8]

Informality began to disappear when testing began, because the tests showed that these early systems did not work very well. Reliability of the early ballistic missile systems hovered in the 40 to 60 per cent range, and the prototype air defence computing systems functioned for only a few hours at a time before failing (Johnson 2002*a*: 92–3, 135–6). This did not surprise many programme managers, as they realized that testing would uncover many problems. By far the vast majority of failures transcended specific artefacts and disciplines. In general, the biggest issues had to do with the interactions among components and the consistency of manufacturing, and hence the interactions among the people designing and manufacturing components and the inability of humans to work with absolute consistency. These issues required social solutions. Along the various social responses discussed previously, such as configuration control, parts tracking, and environmental and systems testing, aerospace managers and engineers cre-ated a plethora of other social processes and organizations to improve communication and control of technical development. The most obvious changes were the creation of organizations whose job was to explicitly coordinate other engineering tasks. Examples include the Air Force's crea-tion of non-profit corporations such as Aerospace and MITRE to act as the Air Force's systems engineers and institutional memory (Johnson 2002*a*: 174–97) and JPL's creation of its systems department in late 1959 (Johnson 2002*b*: 94). In late 1963, George Mueller reorganized NASA's Office of Manned Space Flight, creating systems engineering, programme control, test, and reliability and quality assurance departments at NASA Headquarters and field centres (Johnson 2002*b*: 134). The European Space Agency began importing American managerial and engineering methods from the 1960s, culminating in the creation of its own systems engineering department in 1979 (Johnson 2002*b*: 206–7).

Not all engineers were happy about being second-guessed. Some contractors complained that the Air Force's new systems engineers at Ramo–Wooldridge simply searched for 'errors, mistakes, and failures' (Johnson 2002a: 88). To ensure that engineers and project managers could not interfere with cross-checking, some organizations separated failure reporting from the normal chain of command. The Air Force's separation of technical monitoring from contractors by placing these functions in Aerospace and MITRE achieved this end. So too did JPL's separation of quality assurance functions from the project manager's authority in 1962 after a series of embarrassing failures of its Ranger spacecraft (Johnson 2002b: 103).

Project managers might be hostile to external oversight, but they were often eager to investigate their own workers and contractors. At NASA's Marshall Space Flight Center, director Wernher von Braun used a system of 'Monday Notes' to acquire data from managers two levels below him that his direct underlings could not edit (Tompkins 1993: 62–6). He also got to know many of his workers personally, so as to be able to assess the credibility of their reports. As von Braun put it,

This [MSFC] is like being in the earthquake prediction business. You put out your sensors. You want them to be sensitive enough, but you don't want to get drowned in noise. We have enough sensors, even in industry. There are a lot of inputs about trouble. Some are too sensitive; they overreact. Someone else might underestimate. You want to know the name of the guy. Is he one of the perennial panic-makers? Some guys always cry for help. You need balance in the system—to react to the critical things. Exposure teaches you how to react. Some create problems and then proudly announce they have solved them. Others make a lot of noise just to get the mule's attention. (Tompkins 1993: 58)

Others used different means to 'penetrate' organizations in the search for problems. When JPL realized the seriousness of Hughes Aircraft Company's problems with the Surveyor programme, JPL managers assigned hundreds of engineers to investigate (Johnson 2002b: 104–5). Marshall Space Flight Center frequently did the same. In 1967 they had over 700 engineers assigned to remote sites to collect information (Tompkins 1993: 68–70). NASA established Resident Manager's Offices at each of their major contractors to maintain surveillance on the contractors. Less successfully, NASA Administrator James Webb used contractors to monitor NASA's field centres on the Apollo programme (Johnson 2002b: 124–5).

Major problems triggered major organizational responses. At the first signs of trouble, managers could order a 'Tiger Team' for an intense short-term review. Perhaps the first of these was the team that Atlas Technical Director, Colonel Charles Terhune sent to gather information at Convair in San Diego in the early phases of that programme. After two gruelling weeks, Terhune revealed forty shortcomings with the president of Convair and Atlas manager. This got Convair's attention. Terhune later sent a similar team to investigate the Martin Company's Titan programme (Johnson 2002a: 108–9). When Apollo Program Director, Brigadier General

Samuel Phillips encountered problems with North America's second stage programme, he assembled a NASA Tiger Team to the troubled plant to 'terrorize the contractor'. The result became the infamous 'Phillips Report' later uncovered in Congressional investigations of the Apollo 204 fire (Grey 1992; Johnson 2002*b*: 143–5).

The most traumatic social responses to failure were Congressional investigations. Six consecutive failures of the Ranger programme led to a Congressional investigation of JPL, in the aftermath of which JPL had to give up much of its organizational independence from NASA Headquarters, despite its status as a division of California Institute of Technology (Koppes 1982: 156–77; Johnson 2002*b*: 99–104). Congressional investigations also followed testing problems and cost overruns on Surveyor, the Atlas and Titan failures in the early 1960s, and human flight disasters. All of these led to significant tightening of bureaucratic procedures and to increased centralization of management, as well as technical fixes to reduce risks (Lambright 1995: 142–88; Johnson 2002*b*: 104–6, 146–9).

Engineers and technical managers often disdained external investigations because of the reviewers' perceived technical amateurism. Project personnel believed that at best the investigators simply got in the way of getting to the business of fixing technical problems, and at worst completely misunderstood the issues. While there was some truth to these beliefs, investigators' emphasis on organization was not misplaced. Since the fundamental causes of technical failures were frequently social, attention to organization was vital. In fact, the organizational and process changes that resulted from investigations were largely beneficial to the technical outcomes of these projects, to the extent that they called attention to and ameliorated communication dysfunctions.[9]

Systems management was a mature process by the 1970s. Technical failures of space and missile systems had receded to a rate around 5 and 10 per cent, in comparison with 40 to 60 per cent failure rates typical of the 1950s and early 1960s. This did not end debate about systems management, or about the utility of systems engineering. Much of the debate had to do with the costs involved. Critics complained that systems management was an over-bureaucratic process that consumed far more paper and resources than necessary. These critics pointed to other technologies that had been developed with much less cumbersome methods.[10]

Some argued for a 'Skunk Works' approach, which relied on a relatively small team with much greater initiative and authority than typical of systems management (Rich and Janos 1994). Others admired Japanese management techniques that made highly reliable automobiles and electronic systems at relatively low costs. They promoted Total Quality Management or 'Theory Z' team approaches.[11] By the late 1980s and early 1990s, these critics and reformers were making headway in aerospace circles, as many aerospace companies and government organizations tried out these techniques.

The most public showcase for trying out new methods was NASA's 'Faster, Better, Cheaper' (FBC) initiative, strongly promoted by Administrator Dan Goldin. Goldin, who had been an executive at Thompson–Ramo–Wooldridge (TRW), had significant experience developing robotic spacecraft that used smaller teams than NASA's manned programmes. Upon taking the helm at NASA, Goldin found that his main problem was the tremendous cost of the human flight programme, combined with Congressional reluctance to give NASA any more money. With the space shuttle's costs unlikely to decrease and the space station's costs uncontrollable for both political and technical reasons, NASA had to save money elsewhere. The primary target was space science (McCurdy 2001: 48–52).

Joining NASA's critics, Goldin encouraged robotic spacecraft programmes to take more risks. Instead of running a small number of large expensive projects, he promoted a larger number of small programmes. Failure of any one of these small programmes would not be such a disaster, as many others would be ongoing. The idea of (FBC) had actually come from the DOD, and NASA already had some smaller satellite programmes. Goldin used these as the basis for the Discovery programme, which trolled industry and academia for new programme ideas in which the spacecraft cost less than US$150 million in 1992 dollars. Ongoing studies such as a proposed Pluto flyby came under significant pressure to reduce costs (McCurdy 2001: 52–9).[12]

The initiative spurred new cost reduction ideas such as using airbags to land on Mars, and cancelled programmes that significantly overran budgets. Each programme manager took risks of various kinds. However, these frequently came at the cost of procedural crosschecks. Systems engineering and integration took much of the brunt of these measures. Some risks paid off, while others did not. The FBC programme appeared in good shape in 1998, with several remarkable successes, such as Lunar Prospector, Mars Pathfinder, Near Earth Asteroid Rendezvous, and Mars Global Surveyor. However, 1999 featured the loss of the Wide Field Infrared Explorer, Mars Climate Orbiter, Mars Polar Lander, and the Deep Space 2 micro-probes. The many failures showed that too many projects had cut too many corners (McCurdy 2001: 6–7, 57–9).

While detailed comparative analysis of these projects has yet to be done, most analysts and informed observers believe that NASA's cost-cutting efforts went too far. Project managers eliminated too many of the procedural checks and tests required to ensure high reliability, and failure rates increased beyond the point of acceptability. The pendulum is now swinging back towards decreasing risks, and reimplementing some of the lessons learned in the early days of the space programme. While it is possible to succeed on some programmes some of the time without the social controls of systems management, it is impossible to maintain consistently high rates of success.

This is not surprising, since the reforms implemented between 1955 and 1965 were put in place to ensure reliability.

The history of FBC reifies processes described nearly two decades ago by engineer Henry Petroski. Petroski observed in his studies of mechanical and electrical engineering that each successful design brings up a societal and engineering question. Could we have created this bridge or cathedral more efficiently? Thus, the next iteration of the design frequently cuts back on some aspect of the design, by making trusses lighter, by reducing safety margins, and so on. If the new design succeeds, the process repeats itself, until at some point the cutbacks go too far and failure ensues (Petroski 1982). Dan Goldin posed the same question to NASA. Could NASA cut back on processes put in place to ensure reliability, and still successfully reach the stars? The FBC initiative showed the possibilities and the limits of reducing procedural checks. NASA has once again shown that failure is an essential part of engineering learning.

3.4   Towards a Social Theory of Systems Engineering

The histories of the early systems engineers and of their descendants at NASA show that failure is the mother of social invention, at least in engineering. To build large-scale complex systems, the critical problems have to do with the limitations of humans' ability to perform simple but repetitive tasks, and to communicate between individuals and groups. As the problems are primarily social, so too are the solutions. This comes as good news to social scientists, who are naturally inclined to seek social issues and explanations. However, social issues are inextricably bound together with technical issues, of which many social scientists are as unfamiliar as engineers are with social theory. Neither social scientists nor systems engineers are likely to generate optimal solutions, since neither fully grasp the fundamental, sociotechnical issues. How might reconceptualizing systems engineering in social terms modify the practice of systems engineering? In this section, I will speculate as to some possible new avenues to bring this knowledge to bear.

With complex systems, one of the primary problems is knowledge-sharing across disciplines. We can conceive of this problem statistically, by saying that an expert in one field has a much lower rate of correct knowledge about other knowledge domains, for example, a 70 per cent rate of correctness as opposed to a higher rate within his or her own discipline. Dealing with cross-disciplinary issues still requires reviews by experts, but with few if anyone expert in two or more disciplines, more rigorous and formal means are likely to be needed, as indeed we see in the creation of Interface Control Documents and the use of design reviews. By conceiving of this systems engineering problem in terms of information flow, and of error rates within these flows, systems engineers could revise their knowledge-sharing and knowledge-validation processes to reduce the error rates of the entire system.

The history of systems engineering shows that many complex systems problems relate to communication between organizations and engineers. Two kinds of communication problems predominate: miscommunication, and the lack of communication. In the first case, the persons involved each speak somewhat differently about similar issues, due to disciplinary, personality, and cultural differences. These differences lead to misinterpretation of attempted communication. In the second case, different individuals have correct (or nearly correct) knowledge of their individual domains, but information sharing is restricted by organizational or other issues, such that relevant information does not flow to others that need it.

The end result is the same in both cases, a mismatch between expected and actual performance of the system. This occurs because the artefacts, whether hardware, software, or procedures, will embed the knowledge of their creators. If that knowledge is flawed or incomplete, then the artefacts will mirror those knowledge inadequacies. When separate artefacts are integrated together, communication inadequacies often become obvious, as the logic and knowledge embedded in them interact directly, independent of previous human interpretation of what they should be doing. Technical artefacts are information repositories, in ways far more precise than natural language communication or engineering drawings.

At the beginning of the design process there are few means to detect miscommunications, and thus many of them go unnoticed. What exists is a vision of what the end products will be, but there are as yet no end products. The only way to detect miscommunications early on is for engineers to exchange information about their conceptualizations. Engineers have implemented means to formalize and exchange conceptualizations through specifications written in natural language or formal languages such as mathematics, computer languages, symbolic logic, and through design drawings. Detection of flaws rests upon the ability to communicate this information between engineers, and then analyse them together.

If we combine the ideas of information flows and error rates with the recognition that artefacts embed that knowledge, some fundamental principles emerge. Perhaps the most important is the 'principle of redundancy', which applies both to artefacts and to communications. Engineers typically develop redundant hardware or software components so that if one fails, others can continue their function. However, this is not the only use of the principle.[13]

One common use of redundancy is to determine whether an error in the system exists. Many systems have active internal monitoring for errors, and automatic detection and correction of those errors. In these systems, known under various names, such as redundancy management, integrated diagnostics, vehicle health management, or fault protection, one of the fundamental issues is determining whether a sensor reading is correct, or whether the sensor itself is malfunctioning.[14] The only way to determine whether a sensor is malfunctioning is by use of redundant information.

One common technique is 'voting'. In this method, typically at least three identical sensors measure the same thing, or three computers calculate the same data item. Since the chance of more than one of these sensors failing at the same time is very small (unless there is some problem common to all of them, known as a 'common mode failure'), if one of the sensors deviates from the other two, it is outvoted by them. The system uses the middle-valued sensor of the three. In the case where only two sensors measure the same information, it becomes more difficult to determine which of them is faulty if the two diverge. In this case, the faulty sensor typically behaves in ways known by other means to be erroneous. For example, if a temperature sensor measures 100° at one moment, and then a few microseconds later reads zero, engineers know through laws of physics that the temperature cannot change that fast. This sensor is quickly identified as faulty. In all situations, the only way to crosscheck a potentially faulty reading is by comparing that with other information that is at least equally legitimate.[15]

Another typical design issue for complex systems is the engineering concern for 'clean interfaces'. This refers to the desire to have the connections between components be as simple as possible. Many engineers believe it is a good practice because simplification of interfaces reduces the chances for error. This is generally true, but the reasons for it are not usually elaborated.

The reason that 'clean interfaces' are a good practice is social. Simple connections between artefacts lead to simple communications between organizations, for the reason that different organizations design the artefacts. Artefact interfaces are also organizational interfaces. Simplifying connections between components also simplifies communications between organizations, thus reducing the chances for error. Seen in social instead of technical terms, the reason for simplified interfaces becomes obvious. The same also holds for 'object oriented programming' and other software engineering methods, which aim to do the same thing. Systems engineers could leverage this knowledge to create better 'architectures' for their systems, once they use information complexity as a primary design criterion.

If conceived in social instead of technical terms, systems engineering could be significantly improved. Analysis of systems integration in terms of information, communication, and error rates of individuals and between individuals could lead to changes in engineering practice.

3.5 Conclusion

Systems integration is an important element of designing any complex technology. It involves social and technical elements that interlock in myriad ways in the design and validation process. A critical element of systems integration is the desire to uncover interactions among humans and technologies in the system, particularly those that do not match the designers' expectations. Difficulties of this kind led to the creation of new testing techniques in systems integration, and also to the social processes that we now know as systems engineering and systems management. The complex problems that engineers face in the creation of large-scale technologies are fundamentally due to human capabilities, or lack thereof. Humans are not very good at performing repetitive processes for long periods of time, and despite their social nature, frequently miscommunicate with each other. Both problems require primarily social solutions, often using the principle of redundancy. In both cases, humans must find means to crosscheck designs and manufactured items using information that is at least as dependable as the process or product being checked.

It is useful to conceive of engineering complex systems as a problem of accurately and completely communicating vast quantities of heterogeneous information. The early phases of design require the communication of a vision for how the system should operate at the highest level, and then communicating the many visions of the lower level components among those that must ultimately integrate them together. When the visions become artefacts, any communication problems or just simple errors made in the design become obvious once those artefacts are connected to each other. All of the information that the designers used, either implicitly or explicitly, in the creation of the artefact become elements of that artefact. Unlike humans, who might not recognize the implications of lack of information or wrong information, the artefacts interact with each other the moment they are connected and operated together. This is why systems integration is the ultimate point at which social misunderstandings become manifest.

An understanding of the social nature of the systems integration problem and of systems integration solutions will be beneficial not only for social scientists trying to understand technical and organizational issues, but also for engineers who actually develop complex systems. With better understanding, social scientists can help foster better organizations and communications, and engineers can use these new and better processes to build more dependable technologies.

Notes

1. Department of Defense, MIL-STD-499A, Engineering Management, paragraph 3.3. www.incose.org/stc/mil499A.htm. Accessed 7 June 2002.
2. Defence Evaluation and Research Agency, DERA Systems Engineering Practices Reference Model.

3. According to the International Council on Systems Engineering, 'Systems Engineering is an interdisciplinary approach and means to enable the realization of successful systems. It focuses on defining customer needs and required functionality early in the development cycle, documenting requirements, then proceeding with design synthesis and system validation while considering the complete problem: Operations, Performance, Test, Manufacturing, Cost and Schedule, Training and Support, Disposal. Systems Engineering integrates all the disciplines and specialty groups into a team effort forming a structured development process that proceeds from concept to production to operation. Systems Engineering considers both the business and the technical needs of all customers with the goal of providing a quality product that meets the user needs.' International Council on Systems Engineering, 'What is Systems Engineering' webpage. www.incose.org/whatis.html. Accessed 7 June 2002.

4. Department of Defense, Air Force Systems Command, MIL-STD-499B, Engineering Management, draft, 5/15/91, paragraph 4.5.3.2. Standard 499B has morphed into an industry-wide standard known as Electronics Industry Alliance 632, Standard: Processes for Engineering a System. See the INCOSE website, and Rainey (2003), Chapter 2.

5. I paraphrase here from a meeting by the author with a group of engineers from the National Aeronautics and Space Administration (NASA) Marshall Space Flight Center in the early 1990s. The leading propulsion engineer at the meeting dismissed systems engineering on these grounds. I, and many other systems engineers, encounter this sentiment frequently. It is important to note that 'systems theory' has developed in parallel with, but somewhat separately from most working systems engineers. Theorists working in this tradition have certainly noted the difficulties of complex technologies. However, for the most part, these theories have remained separate from the prosaic tasks of practicing engineers, and from the development of standards for the practice of systems engineers. For this reason, I will not address it further. Systems theory developed initially from several sources. These include biological roots in the works of Ross Ashby and Ludwig von Bertalanffy, and cybernetics as developed by Norbert Wiener and Heinz von Foerster. An interesting elaboration of these ideas for complex systems can be found in Beer (1979).

6. DERA Systems Engineering Practices Reference Model, section 3.2.1.

7. The first books solely on systems engineering were Goode and Machol (1957), and Hall (1962). The first standard was DOD MIL-STD-499, published in 1969. The Air Force's Systems Management Standard, AFSC 375–5, came out in the early 1960s. It contained the germs of MIL-STD-499. INCOSE's founding date refers to the informal founding, as opposed to incorporation, which apparently came in 1992. I gleaned from the document 'Introduction to NCOSE (The National Council on Systems Engineering)' dated 2/92, no author. I believe this came from NCOSE itself in 1992. This paper contains a brief history of the organization at that time.

8. For JPL and its relationship to Army Ordnance, see Koppes (1982). On Ramo–Wooldridge, see Johnson (2002*a*) chapters 3, 5; and Dyer (1998). On Lincoln Laboratory, see Johnson (2002*a*, chapter 4); and Redmond and Smith (2000).

9. It is also worth noting that investigations are a treasure-trove for later research into what was really going on in these organizations.

10. I would argue that systems management is likely to be cost-effective when you calculate the amount spent on additional bureaucracy and compare that with the cost of rebuilding and relaunching failed systems. The additional processes generally cost far less than the replacement cost of rebuilding and relaunching most space vehicles (Johnson 2002*b*: 221–5).

11. There are hundreds of books on Total Quality Management, I note here only some representative works—Ishikawa (1985); Williams (1994); Lewis (1985).

12. On the Pluto programme, these included such ideas as moving from nuclear to solar sources and batteries. Given the incredibly small amount of solar energy available in the outer solar system, these ideas bordered on the ridiculous. This information comes from the author's experience with this programme, 1993–6.

13. Engineers have used redundancy for decades, if not centuries. I am here elevating it to a principle of more fundamental importance than normally attributed to it.

14. Redundancy management is a term used in NASA's human flight programme. Integrated diagnostics is a typical Department of Defense designation. Vehicle health management (or integrated VHM) is a NASA-wide term used by researchers, and by launch vehicle designers. Fault protection is the term used by NASA Jet Propulsion Laboratory for their deep space probes. The multiplicity of terms is itself an indication of the fragmentation of the field, as there is no standard term or set of methods. The source for this information is the author's experience in the field from 1990 to 1996.

15. A good introduction to some of these practices is Siewiorek and Swarz (1982).

References

BEER, S. (1979). *The Heart of Enterprise*. New York: John Wiley & Sons.

CAMPBELL, G., JOHNSON, S., PUENING, R. L., and OBLESKI, M. (1992). *System Health Management Design Methodology*. Martin Marietta Space Launch Systems Company, Purchase Order #F435025, 14 July.

DEFENCE EVALUATION and RESEARCH AGENCY (1997). DERA Systems Engineering Practices Reference Model DERA/LS(SEC-FH)/PROJ/018/G01, 13 May. Farnborough, Hampshire: DERA, paragraph 6.5.1.

DYER, D. (1998). *TRW: Pioneering Technology and Innovation since 1900*. Boston, MA: Harvard Business School Press.

GOODE, H. H. and MACHOL, R. E. (1957). *Systems Engineering*. New York: McGraw-Hill.

GORMAN, M. E. and CARLSON, W. B. (1990). 'Interpreting Invention as a Cognitive Process: The Case of Alexander Graham Bell, Thomas Edison, and the Telephone', *Science, Technology & Human Values*, 15/2: 131–64.

GREY, M. (1992). *Angle of Attack: Harrison Storms and the Race to the Moon*. New York: Penguin.

HALL, A. D. (1962). *A Methodology for Systems Engineering*. Princeton, NJ: D. Van Nostrand.

HOLLEY, I. B., Jr. (1964). In S. Conn (ed.), *Buying Aircraft: Matériel Procurement for the Army Air Forces. United States Army in World War II* Vol. 7. Washington, DC: Office of the Chief of Military History, Department of the Army.

ISHIKAWA, K. (1985). *What is Total Quality Control? The Japanese Way* (trans. David J. Lu). Englewood Cliffs, NJ: PTR Prentice Hall.

JOHNSON, S. B. (1997). 'Three Approaches to Big Technology: Operations Research, Systems Engineering, and Project Management', *Technology and Culture*, 38/4: 891–919.

—— (2002*a*). *The US Air Force and the Culture of Innovation, 1945–1965*. Washington, DC: Air Force History and Museums Program.

—— (2002*b*). *The Secret of Apollo: Systems Management in American and European Space Programs*. Baltimore, MD: Johns Hopkins University Press.

KOPPES, C. (1982). *JPL and the American Space Program: A History of the Jet Propulsion Laboratory*. New Haven, CT: Yale University Press.

LAMBRIGHT, W. H. (1995). *Powering Apollo: James E. Webb of NASA*. Baltimore, MD: Johns Hopkins University Press.

LEWIS, J., Jr. (1985). *Excellent Organizations: How to Develop and Manage Them Using Theory Z*. New York: J. L. Wilkerson Publishing Company.

McCURDY, H. E. (2001). *Faster, Better, Cheaper: Low-cost Innovation in the US Space Program*. Baltimore, MD: Johns Hopkins University Press.

NEUFELD, J. (1990). *Ballistic Missiles in the United States Air Force 1945–1960*. Washington, DC: Office of Air Force History.

PERROW, C. (1984). *Normal Accidents*. New York: Basic Books.

PETROSKI, H. (1982). *To Engineer is Human: The Role of Failure in Successful Design*. New York: St. Martin's Press.

RAINEY, L. B. (ed.) (2003). *Space Systems Modeling and Simulation: Roles and Applications Throughout The System Life Cycle*. Reston, VA: American Institute of Aeronautics and Astronautics.

REDMOND, K. C. and SMITH, T. M. (2000). *From Whirlwind to MITRE: The R&D Story of the SAGE Air Defense Computer*. Cambridge, MA: MIT Press.

RICH, B. and JANOS, L. (1994). *Skunk Works: A Personal Memoir of My Years at Lockheed*. New York: Back Bay Books.

SIEWIOREK, D. P. and SWARZ, R. S. (1982). *The Theory and Practice of Reliable System Design*. Bedford, MA: Digital Equipment Corporation.

TOMPKINS, P. K. (1993). *Organizational Communication Imperatives: Lessons of the Space Program*. Los Angeles, CA: Roxbury.

van der MUELEN, J. (1995). *Building the B-29*. Washington, DC: Smithsonian Institution Press.

VAUGHAN, D. (1996). *The Challenger Launch Decision: Risky Technology, Culture, and Deviance at NASA*. Chicago, IL: University of Chicago Press.

WEICK, K. E. (1987). 'Organizational Culture as a Source of High Reliability', *California Management Review*, 29/2: 112–27.

WILLIAMS, R. L. (1994). *Essentials of Total Quality Management*. New York: AMACOM.

4

Integrating Electrical Power Systems
From Individual to Organizational Capabilities

FREDRIK TELL

Department of Management and Economics, Linköping University, Sweden

4.1 Introduction

This chapter discusses the role of systems integration in a large technical system—the electrical power system. It examines how innovation activities have been organized along the system's historical trajectory. In other words: how does the innovation context change as a large technical system matures? One prominent feature of large technical systems is its systemic character, with components connected in a network (Hughes 1983; Davies 1996). This chapter focuses on both the evolution of the system as a whole, and also on specific inventions that made 'component connections' possible in the system. Innovation in systems technologies requires an understanding of specific component technologies, the functioning of the system as a whole, as well as the various components in the system design that need to be connected. These are the crucial aspects of systems integration that are investigated in the historical overview of innovation in electrical power systems given below.

The chapter suggests that large technical systems follow a general pattern of historical development. The evolution towards increasingly complex systems is accompanied by a shift from (*a*) an emphasis on individual human creativity, ingenuity, entrepreneurship, and vision in an initial system building phase to (*b*) more collective and organized patterns of corporate-led innovation in components, subsystems, architectures, and their integration in maturing systems (cf. Davies 1997). The chapter attempts to specify some critical issues in the management of innovative activities in large system technologies, in particular focusing on the cognitive abilities of man and organizations in understanding, as well as providing solutions to complex technical and social problems. This analysis points to issues related to the integration of systems, not only as they already exist, but also in the process when they are envisaged and invented.

The empirical context of the chapter is the evolution of the electric power system and the emergence of the electrical equipment manufacturing industry.[1] Electrical power systems consist of subsystems for generation,

56

transmission, and distribution/utilization of electrical energy. In this chapter, transmission and distribution systems will be given particular emphasis. A central idea in the modern electrical power system is that energy generation can be located at one central point at quite some distance from where this energy is to be used. Transmission and distribution systems thus serve an important connecting function in the electrical power network. As this design of the electrical power system emerged in the late nineteenth century, there was a concomitant rise of industrial enterprises delivering the equipment for these systems.

A number of inventors/entrepreneurs were active at the inception of the electrical manufacturing industry (Passer 1953, Tell, 2004 forthcoming). As noted by Hughes (1983, 1989) some of these were particularly adept at 'system building', for example, Thomas Alva Edison, Werner von Siemens, and George Westinghouse. The peculiarities and complexities of electrical power systems required an ability to understand the functioning and use of the system as a whole and not only particular subcomponents. The remarkable progress made in the early development of the electrical power system was, however, achieved under fairly simple institutional and organizational conditions. In the case of Edison, a single man, with the help of a small group of assistants, was able to develop and integrate the components of an electrical power system. Despite having been very influential in the formation and management of Edison General Electric, Edison played no part in the management and developmental activities of the company after the merger with Thomson-Houston in 1892 (David 1992). Under the presidency of Charles A. Coffin from Thomson-Houston, General Electric put a great deal of effort into restructuring the company to utilize Thomson-Houston's advances in technology and sales combined with the production capabilities of Edison General Electric. In conjunction with the banker Henry Villard, Coffin designed the company as a single centralized structure, and by 1900, engineering had become a separate department (Chandler 1977: 428). Thus, by the turn of the century, General Electric (GE) was a company characterized by the managerial hierarchies of a modern industrial enterprise. In 1890, an electrochemical R&D laboratory was created, after repeated proposals from the company's chief consulting engineer, Charles Proteus Steinmetz (Wise 1985: 75–7). In the context of the industrial enterprise the role of inventive activities changed, and the manufacturing aspects of new inventions had to be considered. Moreover, patents and the defence of patents within existing technologies had 'to shape the entire innovative process, rather than be tacked on as an afterthought' (Wise 1985: 139).

In what way did the increased complexity of the underlying technology interact with the organization of innovative activities and systems integration? Hounshell (1989: 122–3) argues: 'the degree to which a laboratory can focus its research on an emergent technology often correlates with the success of that laboratory in contributing to that technology'. Hence, one can suspect that early attempts and the development of a less refined technology may benefit from an organization that allows for separation and focused learning (cf. Levinthal and March 1993). There is also an issue regarding to what extent the maturation of power system technology affected the organization of systems integration.

This chapter focuses on the firms and inventors/entrepreneurs that played a crucial part in forming the industry. This delimitation restricts our analysis to the electrical manufacturers, disregarding the large emerging utilities that were established for the operation of the electrical systems. As noted by Hughes (1983), innovation in systems integration and control also took place in the early utilities, such as, for instance, Chicago Edison Electric, headed by Samuel Insull. Although such utilities did take some part in systems development, innovative efforts were undoubtedly concentrated on the manufacturers of electrical equipment. The men involved in forming the systems design and the subcomponents of the system were also building industrial enterprises with organizational capabilities. The chapter primarily concentrates on systems integration internal to the firm, with less emphasis on the function of systems integration as a means for integrating resources and knowledge external to the firm (cf. Brusoni, Prencipe, and Pavitt 2001). Instead, the main thrust of this chapter is that as complexity increased in electrical power systems, single individuals were no longer able to comprehend or work with all aspects of the system. In order to deal with technological depth and breadth of these systems, distinctly organizational capabilities had to be developed (cf. Prencipe 2000; Wang and von Tunzelmann 2000). Larger groups of engineers with an increasing degree of specialization invented subsystems and components, with ramifications for the design of the entire electrical power system. How are we to understand such specialization in conjunction with the apparent need for systems integration in a large technical system?

The chapter is organized accordingly. The next section describes the early efforts of Thomas Alva Edison in inventing a general direct current (DC) system design for incandescent lighting. The third section of the chapter shows how this system was refined and amended by George Westinghouse, who not only used the new alternating current (AC) technology, but also organized innovation activities differently. The fourth section of the chapter discusses the role of emerging formal R&D organization in the electrical manufacturing industry. The fifth section looks at one example of systems renewal, namely the introduction of high voltage direct current (HVDC) transmission. In the sixth section, a discussion and some conclusions are offered.

4.2   Systems Integration in the Invention of the Incandescent Lighting System

The electrical system for incandescent lighting marks the entry of electrical power system design; specifically, electrical energy generated centrally to be distributed for illumination of larger areas. The system was the brainchild of American inventor Thomas Alva Edison. As such, it has been hailed as an outstanding example of the invention of a complex system and its necessary subsidiary equipment, achieved by one man almost singlehandedly. Edison was, as Hughes (1983: 18) puts it, a 'holistic conceptualiser'; well equipped to develop a system for generation and utilization of electrical energy that required the understanding of systemic interrelationships. Edison's interest and strength lie in inventing and developing whole systems and not only component parts of larger systems (Byatt 1979: 15). One can view Edison as the innovator of power distribution systems; he managed to develop a system for incandescent lighting in only 4 years (between his initial idea in 1878 and the inauguration of the Pearl Street Power Station in New York City in 1882).

Edison described the conceptualization of the new invention with which he was working as the 'subdivision of light' (Friedel, Israel, and Finn 1986: 23). Returning from a trip with Professor George Baker of the University of Pennsylvania, to recover from a period of tiredness, in late August 1878, Edison commenced work upon incandescent lighting within 2 weeks. What was the impetus? Recommended by Baker, Edison visited the factory of Wallace & Sons (in Ansonia, CT) in September 1878. The dynamo developed by the inventor William Wallace fed eight electric lights at one time; and this was the system Edison wanted to emulate on a grander scale. He wanted to devise a distributed lighting system reaching into every house. The existing gas-system provided an obvious model for any electric lighting system (Friedel, Israel, and Finn 1986: 64). The subdivision of light, that is, the development of small illuminating units of electric lights in a system analogous to the illuminating units of gas distribution, had been discussed previously, but was deemed impossible (Jehl 1937: 197). However, this did not prevent Edison from probing forward in this direction.

According to Edison's assistant Francis Jehl (1937: 215), Edison aimed at developing an electric system that not only imitated the gas system in its simplicity, but which would also meet the requirements posed by commercial, technological, and natural conditions. There were many aspects of the system that needed attention, if it was to become a viable alternative to gas. Characteristically, Edison approached the task sequentially, but without ever letting go of the vision of the system in its entirety. Jehl (1937: 217) comments: 'the secret [of rapid success] lay in his early vision, far in advance of realization'. The first focus was to provide a unit for incandescent lighting. In order to provide incandescent lighting, Edison foresaw how a spiral-formed filament could be heated to incandescence (albeit many inventors previously had worked on the idea of incandescence). He set out to write a document that outlined the design of such an incandescent lighting system, and deemed the major problem to be how to prevent the filament from reaching its melting point. Therefore, in this document he described forty-four different regulating devices for temperature regulation (Friedel, Israel, and Finn 1986: 9–13). He was sufficiently confident that his new design would rapidly solve all the problems that had eluded previous inventors. He boasted in the *New York Sun*, 16 September 1878:

With the process I have just discovered I can produce a thousand—aye, ten thousand [lights]—from one machine. Indeed, the number may be said to be infinite. When brilliancy and cheapness of the lights are made known to the public—which will be in a few weeks, or just as soon as I can thoroughly perfect the process— illumination by carbonated hydrogen gas will be eliminated. (Friedel, Israel, and Finn 1986: 13)

He then went on to describe how he could light all of lower Manhattan with a 500 hp engine, through a system of underground wires that would bring electricity into buildings. Several newspapers reported the story and Edison's representative and friend Grosvenor P. Lowrey requested a business meeting with Edison and various financiers on how to capitalize on the invention. Everything was based on the single document produced by Edison in his investigations into incandescent lighting! On 15 October 1878, the Edison Electric Light Company was incorporated. Edison got help from Lowrey who assembled a dozen men to come up with the capital stock of $300,000 (Passer 1953: 84–5). At this stage, one could say, Edison formally turned from an inventor into an innovator. Although his earlier inventions already had commercial purposes, he was now able to commercialize new inventions himself through this company. The J. Pierpoint Morgan banking group supported the company and its activities.

However, the incandescent lighting system would not be a system if it only consisted of incandescent light bulbs. The struggles of Edison and his team of associates between 1878 and 1880 provide an illuminating tale of how the realization of a system as a whole first required identification of 'reverse salients' (Hughes 1989: 79). Progress towards the final objective of an electrical system for illumination required identification of various components and then designing these components (if they did not exist), bearing in mind how the components of the system were to be integrated. Starting out with the problem of incandescent light, Edison identified the filament as a critical problem. A number of materials were tested: for example, platinum, iridium, platinum–iridium, carbon, chromium, aluminium, silicon, tungsten, molybdenum, palladium, and boron. But there were few visible and positive results. Without solving the question of what material should be used or what shape the filament should be, he jumped to working on other parts of the system. Apart from the filament question, there were a number of issues involved in completing the system, for example, (*a*) regulation and control; (*b*) parallel wiring; (*c*) a new dynamo; (*d*) a meter; and (*e*) a motor. Not only had new things to be invented or refined, but Edison and his team also had to understand how to integrate the new apparatus into a functioning system.

Friedel, Israel, and Finn (1986: 31) contest that Edison was working at the whole system at this time. Rather, focusing on the filament's self-regulation of heat as the key to successful light 'other aspects were simply not seen as important'. It thus seems that Edison did not hold a very sophisticated view of the system requirements at the time (1878), and that this allowed for decomposition and analysis of a crucial subcomponent. Matters were thus studied sequentially. Edison's associate Jehl provides a somewhat rosier and idolized picture:

Edison's fertile brain conceived the new system and the conditions under which it should be operated, and put that system into a tangible form step by step. First, he required a lamp that would fulfil the conditions of the system. Then, he had to have an efficient generator, an electric meter for registering the current, a mode of regulating the system, sockets, switches, fuse wires, underground conductors, and all the other equipment. It was a Herculean job for one man. (Jehl 1937: 243)

Towards the end of 1878, all work on filaments had ceased in favour of the new design of the generator for the system (Friedel, Israel, and Finn 1986: 43, 69). Series connection, or winding, of the system was not viable since it did not allow for the extinguishing of one lamp at a time. Therefore, a parallel winding system had to be devised. It was also recognized that the Wallace generator (dynamo) design was insufficient for a large system of incandescent lamps and in April 1879, the engineers at Menlo Park came up with a new and improved design, called Jeanette, with low internal resistance (Jehl 1937: 301). During the same year an electric meter was devised. Finally, a new motor design was invented with its armature arranged in parallel with the magnet instead of transversely, and with the magnet formed of one single casting. Responding to these problems alleviated the return to the filament issue and Edison suggesting that carbon was the best filament found so far. However, it could not easily be formed into a spiral, but a horseshoe-shaped filament made from carbonized cardboard became the working prototype (Friedel, Israel, and Finn 1986: 105). After further experimentation, the first incandescent lamps from Edison had filaments made of bamboo. On New Year's Eve 1889, the first functioning system was demonstrated in Menlo Park (Jehl 1937: 421). However, attention shifted away from the Menlo Park laboratory, when commercial manufacturing began (Hounshell 1989: 126).

Production of Edison's lamp was carried out at the Menlo Park laboratory in Newark until the end of 1880. Then Edison and some of his associates formed the Edison Lamp Company. This partnership reached an agreement with the Edison Electric Light Company in Spring 1881. At first, production continued in Menlo Park but in 1882, it was moved to Harrison where the supply of labour was superior. About the same time, Edison also became a partner in a newly established firm, Bergmann and Company, formed to supply components and accessories to the Edison system. For the manufacturing of dynamos, Edison established the Edison Machine Works in

1881. Further, to manufacture underground conductors, Edison founded the Electrical Tube Company the same year. Following the success of this development, one can view Edison as the innovator of power distribution systems, in particular after the inauguration of the Pearl Street Power Station in New York City in 1882. For the installation of the Pearl Street Station system, the Edison Illuminating Company of New York was founded. Edison also needed funding for the heavy investments in R&D required for inventing a complete system for incandescent lighting. More stock was issued and Passer (1953: 88) estimates the cost of putting the incandescent lighting system into a commercial stage to be nearly half a million dollars.

The Edison system was a DC electrical distribution system adapted for limited areas. When demand for larger scale distribution appeared, both in respect of load and area, there were some problems not easily solvable within the technology, since no DC transformer existed to raise voltages for increased efficiency in long-distance transmission. This was to cause a fierce 'battle of the systems' between two competing technologies. We will focus here on the development work of the competing technology—the AC system.

4.3   Systems Integration in Electrical Power Transmission—'Westinghouse Style'

The next generation of electrical power systems was based on AC technology. This technology allowed for transmission over larger distances. By refining the function of the system, the inventors of the AC system were able to perfect the idea of central generation combined with possibilities of long-distance transmission, which lie at the core of the electrical power system. The driving force in this development was George Westinghouse, who saw the large-scale implications of the AC system. His was a different strategy for innovation and systems integration than Edison's. Not being an inventor of many subsystems in the AC system, Westinghouse rather provided a general idea of the systems design. He then acquired necessary patents and let engineers and hired consultants work on the specific problems and solutions.

The major invention that made the AC system such an attractive alternative was the invention of the static transformer. This was a device that could 'step up' voltages from generation to high-voltage transmission, and then 'step down' voltages again for power consumption. This invention opened up the possibility for connecting systems of high-voltage transmission with low-voltage distribution networks. George Westinghouse founded his first company in 1867, at the age of 21, to market a railway device he had invented. This company was dissolved the year after but, in 1869, when he invented the air brake, the Westinghouse Air Brake Company was founded. During the next decade, he spent much time in Great Britain marketing these brakes. There, he found out about switching and signalling devices, and decided to enter that business. In 1881, he acquired one company in Pennsylvania and another in Massachusetts, which he combined to form the Union Switch and Signal Company. He also found out how to utilize natural gas and in 1883, formed the Philadelphia Company for the distribution of gas to factories and residences in the Pittsburgh area (Leupp 1919). In these operations, the company developed capabilities in long-distance systems for conveying gas. Ingeniously, Westinghouse saw the potential analogy with electrical power distribution. In the gas system, the high pressure used for long-distance transmission had to be reduced for consumer utilization. By connecting wider pipes in areas of distribution, pressure was reduced. The transformer exerted the same function in the electrical power system (Passer 1953: 131).

Already in 1883 Westinghouse had commenced studying the DC system that was Edison's forte, and hiring people to work with it, 'but not until he had his vision of the possibilities of the alternating current [AC] was his interest thoroughly aroused' (Prout 1921: 91). Westinghouse realized how the use of AC technology could provide an economical system for electricity distribution by the 'stepping up' and 'stepping down' of voltages. George Westinghouse pursued the development of an AC-based system for electricity distribution, despite the fact that he was not yet knowledgeable in the field of electrical engineering (Passer 1953: 132). The development work, however, was so promising that the electrical department of the Union Switch and Signal Company was formed as a separate company, the Westinghouse Electric Company, on 9 January 1886 with a capital stock of $1 million (Passer 1953: 136).

As pointed out by Usselman (1992), Westinghouse differed quite dramatically from Edison in his approach to innovation. Whereas Edison invented for public showcases, Westinghouse was more interested in industrial applications and the interest of industrialists. Moreover, he organized innovation and production concomitantly, in a manner that would be quite the norm in electrical equipment manufacturing for years to come (cf. Chandler 1977; Wise 1985). A pertinent example of this strategy is the development of the transformer-based AC transmission system. The founding father of the transformer's application for power systems was Frenchman Lucien Gaulard, who, together with his British associate John Gibbs introduced a system for transformation of AC voltages in 1882. In 1885, Westinghouse read in an English engineering periodical about their AC system for electrical transmission using the system of transformers (Hughes 1983: 95).

The main advantage with this solution was that when transmission voltages increased, losses in transmission decreased, allowing for much more cost-efficient long-distance energy distribution (Philipson and Willis 1999: 55–6). Gaulard and Gibbs had designed a system connecting the transformers in series. George Westinghouse understood that using the transformers in parallel would be a much better idea, facilitating the transformation from low to high voltages and vice versa (Passer 1953: 135–6). William Stanley, when working for Westinghouse, came up with a parallel solution (Prout 1921: 110–11). Elihu Thomson in the United States also developed a parallel design concomitantly (Carlson 1991: 251–3). Another important suggestion from Westinghouse was that this system facilitated the introduction of larger and more centralized power generation stations, allowing for the transmission of large amounts of electrical energy to low-voltage users or distribution networks. The use of transformers initiated research on how to solve problems involved with AC power transmission. In 1886, the newly established Westinghouse Electric Company (Westinghouse) installed the first commercial single-phase AC system for lighting in Buffalo (Passer 1953: 277).

As with Edison's DC system, there were a number of problems to deal with and Westinghouse, as well as other firms, came up with ingenious solutions to most of them. There were several new components used and integrated into the systems by the Westinghouse Electric Company, which was to make the AC technology a superior contender for the epitaph 'the universal system'. David and Bunn (1990: 135) single out: (*a*) the induction motor, (*b*) the AC meter, and (*c*) the rotary converter.

The invention of the polyphase induction motor for alternating currents was invented at approximately the same time (1888) by Nikola Tesla in the United States, Galileo Ferraris in Italy, and Michael Osipowitch von Dolivo-Dobrowolsky in Germany. Westinghouse was able to acquire the patent rights of Tesla's induction motor, which seems to have been the most developed one at that time, in July 1888 (Passer 1953: 277–9). By this move, Westinghouse had the opportunity to try out the workings of the motor in an AC lighting circuit. The results were a little discouraging, as the Westinghouse engineers found that the Tesla motor could not be used in the AC systems then in commercial use. It was necessary to develop a complete power system, including generators and transformers as well as the motor.

Hence, it was only through continuous development work that a universal AC system would become a reality. It seemed that DC technology still had a great advantage in that the system's metering capabilities were compatible with both lighting and motors. DC motors were also very suitable for traction purposes since the speed could be easily adjusted, which was not the case for the induction, polyphase motor invented by Tesla. Still in 1888, however, Oliver B. Shallenberger, who was working for Westinghouse, came up with a meter for AC (Prout 1921: 128–9; Passer 1953: 138–9).

American inventor Charles S. Bradley invented the rotary converter. The converter was a device designed for conversion of electrical power not only between AC and DC, but also between different technologies (e.g., single-phase and polyphase AC) within each technology (Prout 1921: 99–100; Byatt 1979: 108; Hughes 1983: 121; David and Bunn 1990: 137). It was essentially a motor-generator set mounted together. When integrated in a

system, the combined effect of these component innovations was impressive. Within a few years, AC technology superseded DC, in what has become
known as the 'battle of the systems (or currents)'.[2]

All this means that within a period of, say, five years the source of direct current for
large plants in particular, had shifted from direct-current generation at low voltage to
alternating-current at comparatively high voltage, with transmission at high voltage
and with conversion, by means of the rotary converter, to any desired direct-current
voltage at any desired place. Surely this was revolutionary. (Prout 1921: 133)

Not only did it mean that the AC technology for power systems became
universally acknowledged, but also another consequence of the displacement
in systems technology was a drift from a model of innovation and integration
of the power system by one single 'holistic conceptualiser' (i.e. Edison) to a
mode where innovation and integration were made by a community of
inventors, to an increasing extent, assigned to larger companies. Whereas,
Edison had developed his electrical DC distribution system primarily
in-house, the increasing complexity and 'collectiveness' of the AC system
required new innovation strategies. The preferred way of Westinghouse to
deal with this problem was to purchase patents and short-term consulting
services from independent consultants (Wise 1985: 69). Westinghouse was
much more focused towards specific pratical problems than Edison was
(Usselman 1992: 275). Instead of cherishing the possibility of being given
credit for an invention, Westinghouse more pragmatically went about
acquiring whatever was necessary (even designs developed outside his own
laboratory) and implemented it, or let a hired consultant such as William
Stanley, for example, implement it. In doing so, the emphasis lay on
refinement within technical and economical constraints—a move towards
what Vincenti (1990: 7) describes in engineering as normal design, where 'the
engineer engaged in such a design knows from the outset how the device in
question works, what its customary features are, and that, if properly
designed along such lines, it has a good likelihood of accomplishing the
desired task'. This was the direction in which much invention and systems
integration in the electrical power system would proceed, away from the
radical design of Edison's Menlo Park experience (cf. Hughes 1989).

4.4 The Corporate R&D Lab: System Integration in the Modern Industrial Enterprise

As the electrical industry developed, and R&D became institutionalized, the
'corporate' inventors grew in number. In electrical engineering, we find
Charles P. Steinmetz (USA), Willis Whitney (USA), William Coolidge (USA),
Irwing Langmuir (USA), Friedrich von Hefner-Alterneck (Germany),
Michael Dolivo-Dobrowolski (Germany), Uno Lamm (Sweden), among
others. These engineers worked more or less within the confines of an

organized hierarchy. Most often, they also belonged to a formal R&D organization and worked within a community of professional scientists. As discussed by Chandler (1977, 1990), the modern industrial enterprise was characterized by a formal hierarchy and division of labour into multi-functional units and the rise of professional management. What effects did this have on innovative activities in developing and integrating electrical systems?

Industrial leader, GE can serve as a case in point. GE's organized central research laboratory came about at the beginning of the twentieth century and conducted basic research in the service of commercial interest (Wise 1985). The reason for GE to set up industrial research was the threat from European innovations regarding the incandescent lamp, which might make the Edison-based light bulb obsolete at the turn of the century. However, Edison had scolded the old European professors and basic scientific research and instead focused on applied research with short-term payoff. Since this was a policy that had been continued and amplified by his successors, neglecting pure science and advanced development work, this neglect was in danger of taking its toll (Reich 1985: 53; Wise 1985: 69).

The idea of developing capacity in R&D for GE was primarily defensive. Especially in the lighting business, patent suits were pending continuously. Among other things, the firm was threatened by the independent inventor, Peter Cooper-Hewitt's work on mercury-arc lamps, which was financed by Westinghouse on the premise of exclusive patent rights (Reich 1985: 64). A research laboratory could provide an option to negotiate with other patent holders, for example, a 'stalling' negotiating strategy could be used, giving the laboratory time to 'invent around' too expensive patents (Hughes 1983: 166).

The GE research laboratory idea granted approval from the board on the premise that a proper manager could be found. Under the direction of Willis Whitney, a faculty member of the Massachusetts Institute of Technology (MIT) with a PhD in Chemistry from Leipzig University, the laboratory not only took on basic research, but also minor assignments stemming from the operations at the works. The laboratory began operating in late 1890, and had success in defending GE's lamp filament patents. The first years in action, this defence consumed all the time and effort of the new department, and became instructive for the department's way of working.

In electrical power system technology, GE hired inventor Charles Bradley and gained access to his patents and knowledge. This resulted in the development of an efficient rotary converter in the mid-1890s (Reich 1985: 60). However, Coffin decided that the most important long-term strategy for the laboratory had to be diversification. Instead of trying to crowd out Westinghouse and other competitors, the laboratory should be used to develop new product lines that could increase profits for the company (Wise 1985: 115). A centralized research laboratory could facilitate both new product development as well as helping the manufacturing plants in increasing efficiency. One such process innovation was the hot swaging method for metal filaments invented by William Coolidge in 1909. The laboratory made findings leading to products for consumer use in the first decade of the twentieth century. Research by the manager of the laboratory, Willis Whitney, on heating units that could be used in consumer products such as stoves and percolators was important for this diversification (Wise 1985: 170–1).

William Coolidge (also with a PhD from Leipzig University, in Physics) took over as director when Whitney left, suffering from a physical and mental breakdown in 1907–8 (Reich 1985: 79). As Whitney came back, GE was able to extend and exploit a knowledge base in electricity furthering the development of new products, leading to diversification in areas, such as, for example, chemical materials, X-ray technology, and nuclear energy. Electrical systems were also complex products where many components could be refined and innovations multiply, creating new business opportunities in electrical generation and transmission systems in themselves. A third trend was also that the American companies observed the use of electricity and developed products for consumer markets. In 1912, Irving Langmuir at the laboratory made discoveries that enabled GE to pursue wireless telegraphy. By the end of 1913, the only rival left in this business was AT&T. The laboratory had made a leap from defence to diversification (Wise 1985: 177)!

The consequence was that GE diversified into 'lighter' electrical engineering before the war. Reich (1985: 91) elaborates on the diversification: 'Although its defence of GE's market position in electric lighting may have been the Research Laboratory's most profitable service, the lab did not reach its full potential until research results began to open up entirely new commercial opportunities.' With such new opportunities, there followed an increased breadth of products, and consequently further specialization. A number of new technologies as well as markets (e.g. consumer markets) meant that the scope for systems integration within the large industrial enterprises that came to dominate the industry throughout the twentieth century increased dramatically.

4.5 Systems Integration and Renewal in a Maturing System

The continuing development of electrical power systems further illustrates the move from individual to corporate innovativeness and systems integration. As the world was left after the battle of the systems with one universal system for power transmission, that is, the AC system, few observers thought that DC technology would ever revive for this usage (e.g. see Prout 1921; David 1992). However, the development of HVDC transmission technology shed some light on how new system designs can emerge in a

mature large systems technology (Tell 2000). It also highlights the importance of connecting technologies that serve in integrating subsystems or even
competing systems.[3] Finally, the HVDC story illustrates the orchestration of
resources necessary, and provides questions about which type of industrial
firm will undertake efforts to try to alter an established design.

One important aspect of high voltage power transmission is the ability to
transmit energy over long distances. As power generation plants were located
farther away from the place of utilization, for example, in the case of
hydroelectric power, utilities demanded more efficient transmission systems.
By increasing voltages in the power systems, higher transmission efficiencies
could be obtained. The AC power system went to high voltage alternating
current (HVAC) and experiments were conducted using ultra-high voltages
(UHV). Facing these requirements, it turned out that high voltage DC
transmission could be an alternative to the AC transmission systems. This
caused a 'second battle of the systems' (Fridlund and Maier 1996: 4). At the
centre of this development was one technological device that had already
played an important role in the first battle of the systems—the converter
(e.g., see David and Bunn 1990). However, it was given a new name—the
rectifier. What was the difference?

In 1901, Peter Cooper Hewitt, trying to convert the quartz lamp (that
operated by DC) to AC, found that in this operation there was a change into
DC through the mercury-arc, and that, henceforth, it could be used for
AC/DC conversion generally. Hewitt's research was supported financially by
Westinghouse. The invention had far greater implications than just being
able to use the quartz lamp on AC (Siemens 1977: 116–17; Fridlund 1995:
43). What Cooper Hewitt, concomitantly with Ezekiel Weintraub at the GE
research laboratories, had discovered was the mercury-arc rectifier—a static
AC/DC converter.

A patent litigation battle took place, lasting 10 years and ending with a
final victory for Cooper Hewitt. At that time, however, the financially
stronger GE licensed the technology, and in 1921 acquired Cooper Hewitt's
firm (Wise 1985: 100). In 1922, Irwing Langmuir at the GE Laboratory in
Schenectady started working with Albert W. Hull on electrical discharges and
ionization (Cobine 1961: xvii). During the 1920s, Langmuir and his associates continued the research on arc discharges, and found ways in which it
could be controlled by means of a grid in a gas-filled tube. They called this
grid-controlled arc tube a 'Thyratron' (Anschütz 1985: 23). Hull had become
interested in high-voltage transmission and the stability problems of long
distance AC transmission. The alternative of developing a DC transmission
line was discussed. Together with two other GE associates, C. W. Stone and
D. C. Prince, Hull erected a small DC testing transmission line between
Schenectady and Mecanicville (Suits and Lafferty 1970: 223). In 1935, GE
carried out experiments with high voltage DC transmission (Maier 1993: 128;
Fridlund 1999: 158). Despite its potential for high voltage DC power

transmission, no commercial DC transmission line was developed and sold. At Westinghouse, Joseph Slepian developed the competing 'Ignitron'. As for the Thyratron, the Ignitron found its primary use in converting AC into DC in steel manufacturing mills. In Europe, the vacuum-based Thyratron, and its subsequent designs came to be used in traction, electrochemical processes, and rolling mills (Anschütz 1985: 27, 32–5).

Hence, the first mercury-arc rectifiers found their applications at lower voltages and/or currents (Robinson 1992: 3).[4] In order to facilitate high voltage DC applications in power transmission, one needed a rectifier for both high voltage and high currents. Features in a rectifier design that were conducive for higher voltages were usually unfavourable for higher currents, and vice versa. Moreover, the device needed to be able to rectify in both directions, that is, from AC to DC (rectifier) and from DC to AC (a so-called 'inverter'), if it was to be used in high voltage DC transmission. It was this solution that electrical engineers in the research departments at the American, British, German, Swedish, and Swiss manufacturers all worked on.

The most ambitious programme for the development of transmission occurred between 1941–5 in Germany. This was the Elbe–Berlin transmission line, in which first AEG, and later, Siemens and Felten & Guillaume participated. It was decided that an effort should be made in developing a system for HVDC transmission. The argument put forward was military: for DC transmission underground cables could be used instead of overhead transmission lines, decreasing the risk of exposure to the allied air force attacks (Fridlund and Maier 1996: 8). There was also a need for the Germans to exploit the hydroelectric power resources of Scandinavia. The main German manufacturers allocated their joint resources in order to quickly come up with a solution (von Wieher and Goetzeler 1983: 99). The progress of work was impressive, and in only 4 years, the Germans were able to develop and complete testing of the HVDC system between Elbe and Berlin. However, this was also the time in history when the Third Reich was overpowered by the Allied Forces, and most technical equipment in Berlin was to be dismantled by the Red Army (Adamson and Hingorani 1960: xvi; Siemens 1977: 280–2).

As the Swedish firm ASEA was quite late in adopting mercury-arc rectifying technology in the 1920s, they hired Bela Schäfer as a technical consultant. Using the Hungarian Engineer Schäfer had been able to install the first Mercury-Arc rectifier with a steel tank in 1911 the specifications delivered by Schäfer, ASEA manufactured a rectifier that suffered from severe technical problems. Research led by Uno Lamm resulted in an idiosyncratic design in 1929. Lamm collected a group of engineers and in 1932 ASEA built a laboratory for rectifiers. Within a few years, ASEA was able to successfully compete internationally with its own design of mercury-arc rectifiers for low currents (Fridlund 1995: 44–6).

Development work and experimentation began with rectifiers for high currents/high voltages, so-called ion-valves. Since these designs had to be empirically tested to a large extent during the development work, this was an extremely costly operation that needed large amounts of electricity. In 1934, ASEA was able to present results that made its ion-valve a competitor on the global scene. However, delay caused by leakage and poor materials postponed any further progress (Fridlund 1995: 52). A new sealing method helped Lamm and his associates to succeed in maintaining the vacuum in the rectifier. The company presented its first commercial rectifier using this new sealing method in 1940 (Fridlund 1999: 159). In 1943, ASEA and the Swedish State Power Board (Vattenfall) signed a contract agreeing on the establishment of a test plant for HVDC transmission.

In 1947, there were discussions in the Swedish parliament about the possibilities of connecting the island Gotland to the national grid. Vattenfall and ASEA carried out an investigation, and reached the conclusion that it was not possible to use AC, since that would give rise to very large losses (ca. 30 per cent) of effect in the cables. They considered the use of a HVDC transmission, the most economically and technically viable alternative. The decision on such an alternative was made in 1950. However, there were still great uncertainties, at the time the contract between ASEA and Vattenfall was signed (Fridlund 1999: 183). The completion of the Gotland link was preceded by further joint development efforts by ASEA and Vattenfall. This particularly concerned the ion-valves to be used in the transmission. There were no mathematical operations yet applicable to the design and physical principles of the ion-valves (Robinson 1992: 5; Fridlund 1999: 164, 180–1). This made development work both an arduous and, indeed, a very empirical venture, where full-scale experiments were necessary. A new ion-valve laboratory was put into operation in 1951, designed for the final development and testing of rectifiers. The transmission link was formally commissioned in 1956, after a couple of years in test operation. Outside the Nordic countries, the first HVDC scheme was put into operation between Great Britain and France in 1961, and English Electric took up licensing of the Swedish technology.

The HVDC transmission system based on mercury-arc rectifier technology had several advantages when it finally saw daylight. The first was related to the distance and location of a power transmission system, and reactive power. Because of reactive effects, AC was inappropriate when it applied to underground and underwater transmissions. For overhead power transmission over very long distances, requiring very high voltages, the stability of AC systems became problematic, usually solved by installing a system of shunt-reactors for compensation. DC systems did not have these inductance and capacitance effects, and therefore did not need shunt devices (Arrilaga 1998: 258–259). A DC system 'leaked' less energy than a comparable AC transmission line (Blalock 1998: 318). A cost-saving aspect of

HVDC schemes was the earth return capability, and less cable or wire was required (Arrilaga 1998: 261); HVDC was also highly controllable, which gave additional benefits. In a high-voltage AC transmission system it was extremely hard to change the direction of the electricity transmitted, as stability was affected. In a DC system the direction could be changed within hundreds of a second. This implied that the energy source of least cost, or energy available, could be utilized.[5] In regional grids, thus, a more cost-efficient use of electrical power was possible. The control aspect also contributed to the use of HVDC schemes as so-called 'back-to-back' stations, connecting asynchronous AC systems or AC systems operating at different frequencies (Arillaga 1998: 93–4).

The main disadvantage of HVDC was the high cost for substations and the relatively complicated technology involved, requiring more maintenance. In particular, HVDC required rectifiers, which increased the cost compared with a comparable AC system (Le Du 1996: 125). A number of HVDC transmission links has been installed throughout the world, although HVDC has not replaced AC as the dominating technology for transmission of electrical energy (compare Hauge 1987).

This story does not only illuminate interesting dynamics in the competition between technologies, but also serves the purpose of showing how quite radical and systemic innovation continued to thrive also in a completely different institutional setting. The inventors/entrepreneurs were no longer single inventors/entrepreneurs, but innovation of and conceptualization of new systems took place within professional R&D laboratories, by more or less scientifically trained engineers, often in cooperation with utilities. Within the framework of the existing system, developed by incumbent firms, a new and competing system was thus developed for power transmission. The HVDC story illustrates how important the development of interconnecting devices is for such a radical change to take place. This type of equipment *per se* serves an integrating function in the overall system. In order to develop the rectifier, firm capabilities needed to be developed for the integration of commercial and technological opportunities.

4.6 Discussion and Conclusions

Historian David Hounshell (1995) has pointed out that much research still remains to be done in the intersection between the history of large industrial enterprises (as promoted, for example, by Alfred Chandler 1977; 1990) and the history of large technological systems (in the tradition of Thomas Hughes 1979, 1983). This chapter contributes by cross-fertilizing insights from the history of electrical power systems with the history of the large electrical manufacturing firms. As the electrical power system evolved over time, new forms of organization of the electrical manufacturers have emerged. Some determinants of new organizational patterns can be found in the requirements involved in the management of the systems integration process. From an initial situation where a single inventor/entrepreneur could integrate most aspects of the system, a number of shifts have taken place towards organizational capabilities for the design and integration of increasingly complex systems.

Whether in the rapid development by Edison of the incandescent lighting system or the long and tedious process towards the HVDC system, the various examples of innovative efforts in power systems technology demonstrate a number of issues involved in systems integration of complex systems technologies. Admittedly, this chapter has focused on very early stages of inception and innovation of such systems, neglecting the important aspects of organizing for implementation and manufacturing. Nevertheless, there are some salient features in the narratives provided. Going back to the initial question concerning the relationship between the complexity of a technology and the organization of development work, one has to agree with Hounshell's (1989) emphasis on focusing of activities. The innovator needs an ability to focus on the system as a whole, by demarcating the organization of innovation from other entrepreneurial activities, such as financing, marketing, and manufacturing. Separating innovation activities in a research laboratory, for example, provides opportunities for testing the systemic links in a somewhat self-contained way. Crucial links between system components may be explored and tested. In particular, in the early stages, where the vision of the system to be formed is to be conceptualized, such isolation of activities seems particularly important. As the system evolves, this may not be the most important aspect of focus and separation. In order to integrate a complex system, the examples discussed here also show the importance of identifying particularly crucial subsystems or components, which retard further development (cf. Hughes 1983). Whether these were filaments, transformers, rotary converters, or rectifiers, they all deserved long and special attention in order to attain a workable solution that was viable for the system as a whole. In several instances, these particular innovations had a 'connecting' character, with ramifications for the entire system.

In this light the innovating R&D organization faces a familiar dilemma. On the one hand, separation of activities is conducive for 'deep' learning and solving critical reverse salients. On the other hand, separation of activities promotes barriers to integration. How much can attributes, components, and activities pertaining to a complex technological system be separated? An interesting case in point is the strategy of George Westinghouse when developing the alternating current transmission system. Westinghouse seemed to have been able to rely on a high degree of separation, making use of patents, components, and people devoted to other causes. Although there may be several reasons for this, one aspect that can be highlighted is the collective process of innovation. In intensive periods of search, a technological community may emerge looking for solutions to a common problem.

This common perception of the problem and possible system solutions at hand may open up linkages between designs and activities that were developed in separation. It then becomes important, as also shown in the case of HVDC, to not only have an inward focus of system development, but to develop an 'absorptive capacity' (Cohen and Levinthal 1990), through interaction with external actors and by the testing of solutions developed elsewhere. As discussed by Brusoni, Prencipe, and Pavitt (2001) and Prencipe (2003, Chapter Seven, this volume), such outward focus may cause multi-technology firms to develop knowledge in excess of what is strictly related to what they currently make. It is then not possible to discern the boundaries of the individual firm solely from knowledge relating to production, but a definition of firm boundaries needs to take into account specialized knowledge developed for the maintenance of system integration capabilities of increasingly complex systems.

The complexity of an evolving large technical system is like a two-edged sword. First, as the system matures, its complexity decreases in the sense that more parts and their interactions are properly understood. Second, however, the system also becomes more complex in the sense that new applications are found and the user of the system becomes more involved in its design. The first point can be illustrated by the diversification of electrical systems to encapsulate not only generation, distribution, and lighting, but with the development during the twentieth century of electrical appliances and electronics. The development of an electrical consumer society has implications for the scope and range of systems integration. How many parts belong to the system and to what extent are they integrated? The capacity for systems integration will then be one important parameter for judging decisions on, for example, make/buy, acquisitions, divestitures, and the general core competence of the corporation.

The second point is illuminated by the development of HVDC, both in Sweden and Germany, where the interaction with an industrial (state-owned) customer played a crucial part. The electrical utilities developed high engineering skills in-house, and became an integral part in developing power systems further. Recent trends of deregulation of utilities as electricity suppliers and telecommunication providers suggest, however, that this trend may be reversing (Davies et al. 2001). Such a perspective on complexity and systems integration thus emphasizes the role of public policy. For instance, will future procurement of the large technical system be made by a knowledgeable customer willing to cooperate in innovative systems integration activities, or will this be a case of arm's-length contracting? If electrical manufacturers and other providers of large technical systems are to continue to dominate future innovation through systems integration, this may imply that they may have to take into account aspects previously considered as being on the fringe of the scope of the system, such as financing, maintenance, and operation. Current changes in regulation may put such services at the core of future systems integration capabilities of the manufacturers of large technical systems (Davies 2003, Chapter Sixteen, this volume). Whether this implies new forms of organizing large industrial enterprises active in this sector of the economy remains to be seen, and should be the object of further inquiry.

Acknowledgements

A previous draft of this chapter was presented at a seminar at the Business History Unit of the London School of Economics. The author would like to thank the Unit's Director, Terry Gourvish and the seminar participants for stimulating comments and discussions. The chapter also benefited greatly from the insightful comments and suggestions of book editor Andy Davies. Remaining errors are solely attributable to the author. Financial support from Jan Wallander's and Tom Hedelius' Foundation for Social Science Research and The Bank of Sweden Tercentenary Foundation is gratefully acknowledged.

Notes

1. In this chapter this industry will be denoted simply the electrical manufacturing industry.
2. For a historical account of this episode in electrical power technology, see, for example, David (1992), Fridlund (1999), Hughes (1983), Leupp (1919), and Prout (1921).
3. David and Bunn (1990) describe such technologies as 'gateway innovations'.
4. Examples would be low-voltage/low-current applications in industrial drives, and high-voltage/low-current applications in radar transmitters.
5. One argument for the cross-channel link was the displacement in time of electricity demand between France and Great Britain (see Fridlund 1999: 186).

References

ADAMSON, C. and HINGORANI, N. G. (1960). *High Voltage Direct Current Power Transmission*. London: Garraway Limited.

ANSCHÜTZ, H. (1985). *Gescichte der Stromrichtertechnik mit Quecksilberdampfgefäßen*. Berlin: VDE-Verlag.

ARRILAGA, J. (1998). *High Voltage Direct Current Transmission* (2nd edn.). London: The Institution of Electrical Engineers.

BLALOCK, T. J. (1998). *Transformers at Pittsfield: A History of the General Electric Plant at Pittsfield, Massachusetts*. Baltimore, MD: Gateway Press.

BRUSONI, S., PRENCIPE, A., and PAVITT, K. (2001). 'Knowledge Specialization, Organizational Coupling, and the Boundaries of the Firm: Why Do Firms Know More Than They Make?', *Administrative Science Quarterly*, 46: 597–621.

BYATT, I. C. R. (1979). *The British Electrical Industry 1875–1914: The Economic Returns to a New Technology*. Oxford: Clarendon.

CARLSON, W. B. (1991). *Elihu Thomson and the Rise of General Electric, 1870–1900*. Cambridge: Cambridge University Press.

CHANDLER, A. D. Jr. (1977). *The Visible Hand: The Managerial Revolution in American Business*. Cambridge, MA: Belknap Press of Harvard University.

——(1990). *Scale and Scope: The Dynamics of Industrial Capitalism*. Cambridge, MA: Belknap Press of Harvard University.

COBINE, J. D. (1961). 'Fundamental Phenomena in Electrical Discharges' (Introduction to Vol. 4), in C. G. Suits and H. E. Way (eds.), *The Collected Works of Irving Langmuir* (Vol. 4: *Electrical Discharge*). Oxford: Pergamon Press, 154–61.

COHEN, W. M. and LEVINTHAL, D. A. (1990). 'Absorptive Capacity: A New Perspective on Learning and Innovation', *Administrative Science Quarterly*, 35: 128–52.

DAVID, P. A. (1992). 'Heroes, Herds and Hysterisis in Technological History: Thomas Edison and "The Battle of the Systems" Reconsidered', *Industrial and Corporate Change*, 1/1: 129–80.

——and BUNN, J. A. (1990). 'Gateway Technologies and the Evolutionary Dynamics of Network Industries: Lessons from Electricity Supply History', in A. Heertje and M. Perlman (eds.), *Evolving Technology and Market Structure—Studies in Schumpeterian Economics*. Ann Arbor, MI: University of Michigan Press, 121–56.

DAVIES, A. (1996). 'Innovation in Large Technical Systems: The Case of Telecommunications', *Industrial and Corporate Change*, 5/4: 1143–80.

——(1997). 'The Life Cycle of a Complex Product System', *International Journal of Innovation Management*, 1/3: 229–56.

——, TANG, P., BRADY, T., HOBDAY, M., RUSH, H., and GANN, D. (2001). *Integrated Solutions: The New Economy between Manufacturing and Services*. Brighton: SPRU, University of Sussex.

FRIDLUND, M. (1995). 'Ett svenskt utvecklingspar i elkraft: ASEAs och Vattenfalls FoU samarbete, 1910–1980', Sandvika: Senter for Elektrisitetsstudier, Handelshøyskolen BI.

——(1999). 'Den gemensamma utvecklingen: Staten. Storföretaget och samarbetet kring den svenska elkrafttekniken', Doctoral Dissertation. Stockholm: Brutus Östlings Bokförlag, Symposion.

——and MAIER, H. (1996). 'The Second Battle of the Currents: A Comparative Study of Engineering Nationalism in German and Swedish Electric Power 1921–1961', *Working Paper 96/2*. Stockholm: Department of History of Science and Technology, Royal Institute of Technology.

FRIEDEL, R., ISRAEL, P., and FINN, B. S. (1986). *Edison's Electric Light: Biography of an Invention*. New Brunswick: Rutgers University Press.

HAUGE, O. (ed.) (1987). *Compendium of HVDC Schemes throughout the World*. Paris, France: CIGRÉ Working Group 04 of Study Committee 14 (DC Links).

HOUNSHELL, D. A. (1989). 'The Modernity of Menlo Park', in W. S. Pretzer (ed.), *Working at Inventing: Thomas A. Edison and the Menlo Park Experience*. Dearborn: Henry Ford Museum & Greenfield Village.

——(1995). 'Hughesian History of Technology and Chandlerian Business History: Parallels, Departures, and Critics', *History and Technology*, 12: 205–24.

HUGHES, T. P. (1979). 'The Electrification of America: The System Builders', *Technology and Culture*, 20: 124–61.

—— (1983). *Networks of Power: Electrification in Western Society 1880–1930*. Baltimore, MD: The Johns Hopkins University Press.

—— (1989). *American Genesis: A Century of Invention and Technological Enthusiasm, 1870–1970*. New York: Viking Penguin.

JEHL, F. (1937). *Menlo Park Reminiscences* (3 Vols.). Dearborn: Edison Institute.

LE DU, A. (1996). 'Histoire de L'Interconnexion France-Angleterre de 2,000 MW en Courant Continu', *Bulletin d'Histoire de l'Électricité, 27: 125–47*.

LEUPP, F. E. (1919). *George Westinghouse: His Life and Achievements*. London: John Murray.

LEVINTHAL, D. A. and MARCH, J. G. (1993). 'The Myopia of Learning', *Strategic Management Journal*, 14 (Winter Special Issue): 95–112.

MAIER, H. (1993). 'Erwing Marx (1893–1980)'. Ingenieurwissenschaftler in Braunschweig, und die Forschung und Entwicklung auf dem Gebiet der elektrischen Energieübertragung auf weite Entfernungen zwischen 1918 und 1950. Doctoral Dissertation. Stuttgart: Verlag für Geschichte der Naturwissenschaften und der Technik (GNT).

PASSER, H. C. (1953). *The Electrical Manufacturers 1875–1900: A Study in Competition, Entrepreneurship, Technical Change, and Economic Growth*. Cambridge, MA: Harvard University Press.

PHILIPSON, L. and WILLIS, H. L. (1999). *Understanding Electric Utilities and De-regulation*. New York, NY: Marcel Dekker.

PRENCIPE, A. (2000). 'Breadth and Depth of Technological Capabilities in CoPS: The Case of the Aircraft Engine Control System', *Research Policy*, 29: 895–911.

PROUT, H. G. (1921). *A Life of George Westinghouse*. New York: The American Society of Electrical Engineers.

REICH, L. S. (1985). *The Making of American Industrial Research: Science and Business at GE and Bell, 1876–1926*. Cambridge: Cambridge University Press.

ROBINSON, T. S. (1992). *Mercury-arc Valves for HVDC Transmission*. Stockholm Papers in History and Philosophy of Technology TRITA-HOT-9002. Stockholm, Sweden: Royal Institute of Technology.

SIEMENS, G. (1977). *History of the House of Siemens* (Vol. II). New York: Arno Press.

SUITS, C. G. and Lafferty, J. M. (1970). *Albert Wallace Hull 1880–1966*. National Academy of Sciences, Reprint from: Biographical Memoires, New York: Columbia University Press.

TELL, (2000), Organizational Capabilities–A study of Electrical Power Transmission Equipment Manufacturers, 1878–1990, Doctoral Dissertation, Linköping: Linköping University.

—— (2004) Organization Capabilities and Technological change, Cheltenham: Edward Elgar (forthcoming).

USSELMAN, S. W. (1992). 'From Novelty to Utility: George Westinghouse and the Business of Innovation during the Age of Edison', *Business History Review*, 66: 251–304.

VINCENTI, W. (1990). *What Engineers Know and How They Know It*. Baltimore, MD: The Johns Hopkins University Press.

VON WIEHER, S. and GOETZELER, H. (1983). *The Siemens Company—Its Historical Role in the Progress of Electrical Engineering 1847–1980*. Berlin: Siemens Aktiengesellschaft.

WANG, Q. and VON TUNZELMANN, N. (2000). 'Complexity and the Functions of the Firm: Breadth and Depth', *Research Policy*, 29: 805–18.

WISE, G. (1985). *Willis R. Whitney, General Electric, and the Origins of US Industrial Research*. New York: Columbia University Press

5

Specialization and Systems Integration
Where Manufacture and Services Still Meet[*]

KEITH PAVITT

SPRU: Science and Technology Policy Research,
University of Sussex, Brighton, UK

5.1 Introduction

In this chapter, I shall speculate about the future development of firms'
activities in systems integration.[1] I shall do this by exploring the long-term
changes in industrial organization that are likely to emerge as a consequence
of present trends in technical change. A certain humility is required in such
an exercise, given the many failed attempts over the past 20 years to foresee
the consequences of what is now called the information and communication
technology (ICT) revolution, the nature and implications of which have
often turned out differently from what had been expected earlier.

My main assumption is that two long-term and related trends have
underpinned the processes and organization of technical change since the
industrial revolution. The first—clearly identified by Adam Smith—is
the continuous increase in specialization in both the production of artefacts,
and in the production of knowledge on which they are based. The second is
the appearance of periodic waves of major innovations based on rapid
changes in specific technologies. It is in the context of these two trends that
the effects on industrial practice and on organization of the latest of the
periodic radical changes in technology (ICT) can best be judged.

These technical changes are of course embedded in wider processes
of economic, social, and political change, which they both help to create
and to which they respond. These processes include the search for profit
in a world of competition, increasing wages, changing tastes, urbaniza-
tion, the progressive destruction of distance, uneven development across
regions and countries, and changing methods of corporate governance and
regulation. But, as Rosenberg (1974) and others have demonstrated,

An earlier version was the basis of the Welcome Lecture ('What are advances in knowledge
doing to the large industrial firm in the new economy?'*) on 6 June 2002, at the DRUID Summer
Conference on *Industrial Dynamics of the New and Old Economy—who embraces whom?*

technical changes are not entirely 'socially constructed'. They have a cognitive logic of their own, so that R&D activities undertaken in recognition of a technical problem or social need do not automatically lead to its solution. He illustrated this point by comparing the historical developments until the twentieth century in mechanics and medicine. Strong social demands existed in both cases, but progress in the former was much greater than in the latter, because the problems were easier to understand and solve. Contemporary examples of the same phenomenon would include the very different rates of progress now being made in the storage of information and of energy. For these reasons, I shall concentrate here on the influences of changes in the state of technological knowledge, whilst being fully aware that the partial processes of organizational disintegration that I am describing are also strongly influenced by economic, social, and political factors (Loasby 1998).

I shall argue that the appropriate organizational processes for generating and exploiting advances in technological knowledge—in particular, markets or integration—have been heavily influenced by the nature of technical change itself. Briefly stated, initial trends towards disintegration in the early nineteenth century, were later reversed because subsequent technological changes favoured tight coordination between the increasing specialized functions of product development, production, and marketing. Now there are renewed pressures towards disintegration within the process of product development, and between product development and production. We shall examine their nature, causes, and extent, before drawing conclusions about the future role of systems integration.

5.2 Technology in Integration and Disintegration

To begin with, Adam Smith's pin factory is mainly a story about innovation in production processes. The conditions for the mechanization of repetitive manual operations emerged from the specialization of tasks within the factory. They also depended critically on access to water and (increasingly) steam-power, and on continuing and largely craft-based improvements in the quality of the metals, and the accuracy with which they could be cut and shaped (Bernal 1953). As anticipated by Smith, the design and building of these machines would increasingly often become 'the business of a peculiar trade' (Smith 1776: 8). This happened with the spread and the growing codification and standardization of specific mechanical operations (e.g. spinning and weaving in textiles). More generally, the provision of product components and parts became a specialized business as they became standardized and interchangeable. And the provision of mechanical inventions itself became a specialized trade, with the development of specialized intermediaries, namely, patent agents (Lamoureaux and Sokoloff 2002). So there developed a division of labour between the manufacturers, the machine builders, and the mechanical inventors.

However, a number of complementary radical innovations from the middle of the nineteenth century reversed these trends towards specialization. Both have been documented by Chandler (1977, 1990) and Mowery and Rosenberg (1989), amongst others. The first is the emergence of mass production through the exploitation of economies of scale and speed in production, and the reduced transport costs, both made possible by the availability of the new power sources (e.g. coal, electricity, oil) and better materials (e.g. iron and steel). Increasing size led to increasing functional specialization with the firm, and the need for coordinated planning between material purchase, production, and marketing.

Second, advances in specialized mechanical, chemical, and electrical knowledge opened major new opportunities for product innovation, not only in machinery and parts, but also in consumer goods, transportation, materials, and communications. The development of these new products required the integration of partly tacit knowledge across disciplines (e.g. purely mechanical products became electromechanical), and between the R&D and other functions within the firm. Under these circumstances, integration has been more efficient than markets (Mowery 1982).

As a consequence, the dominant sources of technical change in the twentieth century became large manufacturing firms with in-house R&D labs, combined with a myriad of small firms providing specialized capital goods. The mix of firms and technologies changed over the period reflecting the differential rates of growth of innovative opportunities generated by the different rates of growth of specialized knowledge. However, in the last 20 years, new forces have surfaced to begin to modify this pattern.

5.3 Modular Designs for Increasingly Complex and Multi-technology Products?

The first is that products are becoming increasingly complex, embodying both an increasing number of subsystems and components, and an increasing range of fields of specialized knowledge. Increasing product (or system) complexity is one consequence of increased specialization in knowledge production that has resulted in both better understanding of cause–effect relations, and better and cheaper methods of experimentation (Perkins 2000; Mahdi 2002). This has reduced the costs of technological search, and thereby enabled greater complexity in terms of the number of components, parts, or molecules that can be successfully embodied in a new product or service. Developments within ICT itself are accelerating this trend: digitalization opens options for more complex systems, and simulation techniques reduce the costs of experimentation (Pavitt and Steinmueller 2001).

Specialization in knowledge production has also increased the range of fields of knowledge that contribute to the design of each product. Compare what originally was the largely mechanical loom, with the many fields of specialized knowledge—electrical, aerodynamic, software, materials—that are now embodied in the contemporary design; or observe the contemporary automobile that must increasingly integrate plastic and other new materials, as well as electronic and software control systems (Granstrand, Patel, and Pavitt 1997).

Firms designing these increasingly complex products have found it difficult to master advances in all the fields embodied in them. Hence the growing importance of modular designs, where component interfaces are standardized, and interdependencies amongst components are decoupled. This enables the outsourcing of design and production of components and subsystems, within the constraints of overall product (or system) architecture (Ulrich 1995; Sanchez and Mahony 1996). However, as is pointed out elsewhere in this book, modularity does not reduce the function of systems integration to one of simply defining architecture, subcontracting the design and production of components, and then assembling them. In complex systems, it is also important to have the competence to deal with unpredicted interactions between components (e.g. resonance and vibrations in mechanical systems), and uneven rates of development in the technologies underlying different components and subsystems (e.g. electronic versus mechanical control systems). This competence comprizes a capacity to design and test systems with new architectures, as well as knowledge of the technological fields underlying the outsourced components and subsystems (Brusoni, Prencipe, and Pavitt 2001).

5.4   Technological Convergence and Vertical Disintegration in Production

In addition to this specialization and partial disintegration in product design, there are also signs of further progress in the partial disintegration between product design and production, following a further step-jump in technology. As we have seen, the rise of the large manufacturing company since the nineteenth century is closely associated with the economies of scale and speed made possible by a combination of major technical innovations in materials, machines, and energy sources, with the major organizational innovation that was the vertically integrated company (Chandler 1977). When the firm was manufacturing standard commodities with relatively simple production techniques, vertical disintegration and the emergence of a specialized machine-building sector happened relatively quickly (Rosenberg 1963). However, when advances in the technologies of machinery and transport, chemicals, and electrical and electronic products enabled the combination of economies of scale and scope (that is, new products), disintegration became less frequent.

As Mowery (1982) has shown for the USA, a growing proportion of industrial R&D in the twentieth century was integrated within large manufacturing firms. Until about ten years ago, business-funded R&D in all Organization for Economic Cooperation and Development (OECD) countries was almost exclusively performed within manufacturing firms. Mowery explained this lack of vertical disintegration by the difficulties of writing contracts for an activity whose output is uncertain and idiosyncratic. Today, this writer would place greater emphasis on the advantages of integration in coordinating product and process change, which requires the combination of specialized and often tacit knowledge across functional boundaries, and where accumulated experience matters (see also Kogut and Zander 1992).

In any event, the strongly recommended practice in innovation management has traditionally been close collaboration and feedback between product design and production operations, often involving personal contacts and exchanges to deal with tacit elements of both product design and its successful transfer to manufacture (Tidd, Bessant, and Pavitt 2001). There are many stories of product designs that turned out to be technically difficult (even impossible) to manufacture, and of the importance of largely informal processes that ensure effective feedback between the design of product and process (Iansiti and Clark 1994).

However, even in industries with heavy investments in product innovation, some vertical disintegration in manufacturing process innovation has been happening since the nineteenth century, stimulated at each stage by technological advances. Thus, Rosenberg (1963) has shown how specialized machine tool firms emerged in the nineteenth century, because advances in metal cutting and metal forming techniques led to technological convergence in operations that were common to a number of manufacturing processes (e.g. boring accurate circular holes in metal was common to the making of both small arms and sewing machines). Although the skills associated with such machining operations were often craft-based and tacit, their output could be codified and standardized. The size of the market for such common operations therefore often became large enough to sustain the growth of small specialized firms designing and making the machines to perform them. Large manufacturing customers could therefore buy machines incorporating the latest improvements fed back from many users, and therefore superior to what they could do by themselves. In contemporary terms, designing and making such machines in-house no longer gave large manufacturing firms a distinctive competitive advantage.

As Table 5.1 shows, similar processes involving technological convergence and vertical disintegration have been frequent since then. New opportunities for technological convergence have emerged from breakthroughs that have created potentially pervasive applications in production across product groups: material shaping and forming, properties of materials,

TABLE 5.1 *Examples of technological convergence and vertical disintegration*

Underlying technological breakthrough	Technological convergence	Vertical disintegration
Metal cutting and forming	Production operations	Machine tool makers
Chemistry and metallurgy	Materials analysis and testing	Contract research
Chemical engineering	Process control	Instrument makers
		Plant contractors
Computing	Design	CAD makers
	Repeat operations	Robot makers
New materials	Building prototypes	Rapid prototyping firms
ICT	Application software	KIBS
	Production systems	Contract manufacture

Abbreviation KIBS, Knowledge-intensive business services.

continuous chemical processes, storage and manipulation of information for controlling various business functions (manufacturing operations, design). They have led to the emergence of contract research firms specializing in materials analysis and testing (Mowery and Rosenberg 1989), and firms making measurement and control instruments used in continuous processes, systems of computer-aided design and manufacture originally developed in the transport sectors, robots in metal manufacture, and specialized applications software and rapid prototyping in a whole range of industries. In the heavy chemical industry, vertical disintegration in production has gone further. Specialized chemical engineering firms began designing and building complete large-scale continuous production facilities for a number of products, based on technological convergence emerging from improved understanding of chemical processes (Landau and Rosenberg 1992; Arora and Gambardella 1999).

Recently, we have begun to see signs of a further step in the disintegration of product design from subsequent manufacture. Unlike most of the cases in Table 5.1, the technological convergence is not between similar elements of manufacturing operations in different industries, but between the total manufacture of different product designs in the same industry. Sturgeon (2002) has documented the rise of contract manufacturing in electronics: namely, firms that take over electronic product designs from other firms, and do the detailed engineering and manufacture. He reports that contract manufacturing is also growing in other industries.[2] He stresses the importance of the development of

the modular production network, because distinct breaks in the value chain tend to form at points where information regarding product specifications can be highly formal... within functionally specialized value chain nodes activities tend to be highly integrated and based on tacit linkages. Between these nodes, however, linkages are achieved by the transfer of codified information.

In addition to Sturgeon (2002), a number of other scholars (such as Zuboff 1988; D'Adderio 2001; Balconi 2002) have analysed the nature and effects of advances in modularity and in ICT on the links between product design and manufacture. Their studies suggest that ICT increased technological convergence in two dimensions.

- First, it has radically reduced the costs of search to identify standard components and subsubsystems to undertake a specified function within a product architecture.
- Second, it has progressively increased the standardization of production through automation (see Sturgeon 2002), and through the widening adoption of standard software tools (e.g. integrated enterprise software systems like PDM and ERP; see D'Adderio 2002).

In addition, advances in ICT have reduced the costs of vertical disintegration to the product-designing firm.

- Simulation technology and modelling have increased the possibilities of 'learning before doing' (Pisano 1997), thereby reducing the risks of 'bugs' and technical difficulties in subsequent production (D'Adderio 2001).[3]
- ICT has also increased the ease with which digitized information about new products can be transferred from product designer to producer. This both reduces ambiguity, and provides a common basis for debates and agreements amongst the specialized groups involved in product development and production.
- ICT now enables product designers to monitor subsequent production instantaneously.

However, in spite of these advances, ICT has yet to achieve completely the conditions for a modular production system, as specified by Sturgeon. Linkages between product design and production are not like activating the <print> instruction on a PC, after writing a paper. They are not based entirely on codified information. Products are more difficult to formalize than language, and product designers are typically dealing with products considerably more complex and technically demanding than the car trailers and desks that Ulrich (1995) uses as exemplars for modularity.

As D'Adderio (2001) has shown, the process of digitizing a product's characteristics by its designers involves simplification; digitized models must subsequently be reactualized by the groups responsible for production. This therefore still requires personal contacts and the transfer of tacit knowledge. An equivalent division of labour in knowledge thus does not mirror the division of labour in production: product designers still have to know something about production, and producers about product design. Although vertically disintegrated, producers and designers are 'relational' and not 'arm's length', which is no different from the earlier disintegration between product designers and makers of specialized capital goods (Lundvall 1988; Lorenzoni and Lipparini 1999).

To sum up, the complete disintegration of product design and manufacture has not yet been achieved, but recent advances in modularity and ICT have apparently shifted the balance in its favour in some industries. Amongst other things, this is reflected in the growth in markets for technology (Arora, Fosfuri, and Gambardella 2001). In the next section, we explore how far and in what direction the two processes of disintegration—within product design itself, and between product design and manufacture—are likely to go in future.

5.5 How Far (and Where) Will Disintegration Go?

Limits to the Division of Labour: Systems Integrators Not Legoland

The economic pressures for greater modularity and disintegration in product design and related manufacture are considerable. For example, Carpenter, Lazonick, and O'Sullivan (2002) have recently shown how pressures for shareholder value have increased the outsourcing of manufacture in optical networks. Brusoni and Prencipe (2001) identify a variety of economic factors behind increases in outsourcing design and production in aircraft engines and chemical plant: spiralling development costs, pressure from developing countries, reduced defence budgets, shrinking profit margins and the advantages of specialization. And in a special report on car manufacturing, *The Economist* (2002) points to market saturation, product differentiation, and uncertainty of customer reactions as the factors behind the growing experimentation with modular components and subsystems, and with radically new product architectures.

But it is doubtful whether we are moving towards a complete, arm's-length division of labour, with product designers defining modular product architectures and functions in anticipation of customers' needs, subcontracting firms designing components and subsystems within the constraints of the overall product architecture, and manufacturing firms making the components and subsystems. The reasons are as follows.

First, in some industries, possibilities for vertical disintegration may be limited by a lack of technological convergence in the manufacturing of different products. Unlike the production of electronic products, certain critical manufacturing operations may be difficult to codify and automate. For example, Balconi (2002) insists on the difficulty of automating skill-intensive mechanical assembly (including welding), where components are often heavier and more varied in size and shape than those in electronics.

Second, product design will continue to design and manufacture components and subsystems that are part of their strategic core competencies, in that they are difficult to imitate and critical to their overall competitiveness. Thus, Prencipe (1997) has shown that aero-engine manufacturers, in spite of an increase in outsourcing of production, continue to design and manufacture central components and subsystems. Furthermore, product designer firms will themselves often prefer to undertake at least initial production, when new and untested techniques are involved. As Sturgeon (2002) himself points out, contract manufacturers tend to concentrate on routine production operations, where they specialize in a *base process* which is used to manufacture products in a wide range of end markets, or a *base component* which is used in a wide variety of end products, or *base service* for a wide variety of end-users. In such cases, product designers have no strategic advantage for continuing their own production.

Third, although there may be increasing specialization between firms in the provision of product designs, of their subsystems, and of their manufacture, this increasing specialization will not extend to the knowledge bases that underlie them. This is because, as we have seen, completely arm's-length markets are not efficient in dealing with the exchange and integration of specialized, partly tacit, and often fast-changing knowledge into increasingly complex product systems. These will continue to require, at the very least, 'relational' links between firms, characterized by overlapping skills and knowledge exchanges. They may also require 'loose coupling', characterized by occasional periods of organizational integration, particularly when new product architectures are developed. The development of products (systems) of great complexity with unpredictable interdependencies and uneven rates of change in the technologies underlying component performance, will require full integration (Brusoni, Prencipe, and Pavitt 2001).

Finally, even when firms design products purely on the basis of standard modularized components that are relatively easy to manufacture and assemble, they may deploy increasingly sophisticated technical skills (often based on ICT), for the logistics of the supply and the control of assembly of components, and for customer delivery and support (e.g. Dell's personal computers).

To sum up, the division of labour within product development, and between product development and manufacture will probably grow, but will be incomplete. For some products, associated manufacture will remain a strategic resource. Specialized firms will need to maintain and develop technological competencies beyond what they make themselves. In particular, firms specializing in product development and systems integration will need to maintain competencies in related manufacture, components, and subsystems, and in evolving applications of ICT in design, logistics, production, customer support, and coordination and control.

Will Manufacturing Continue to Migrate to Developing Countries?

How will the above trends affect the migration of manufacturing to developing countries? Over 45 years ago, Vernon (1966) was right in his prediction that the emergence in developing countries of local demand, coupled with lower labour costs, would attract an increasing share of world manufacturing production. Much more recently, Feenstra (1998) has written about the 'Integration of trade and disintegration of production in the global economy', showing that manufacturing firms are outsourcing an increasing share of their production to foreign locations. Vernon (1966) originally argued that relocations to developing countries would happen only in products in the 'third stage' of the product cycle, when product characteristics and production methods had stabilized, and the main skills were those of combining stable (and cheap) factors of production. Sturgeon (2002) argues that the emergence of contract manufacturing is associated with the revival of US manufacturing, and Best (2001) makes a similar point about US developments in systems integration.

However, a number of factors point to a growing share of certain developing countries in contract manufacture in the second stage of the product cycle. As Hobday (1995) has shown, firms in certain East Asian countries began their process of modernization by offering contract manufacturing services for mature products in the third stage of the product cycle, but then proved capable of offering manufacturing services—and even component design capabilities—for new products in the second stage. Advances in ICT have now facilitated the transfer of product information[4] to, and production monitoring in, distant countries (Ernst 2002*a,b*). They have also increased the importance of formal education in production operatives, compared with experience-based craft skills (Balconi 2002). Recent developments in ICT will therefore enable developing countries that have invested in education and IT infrastructure to build their success somewhat beyond what Leamer and Storper (2001) call 'routine intellectual labour'. They will be able to transform the 'higher order' activities of invention and innovation immediately into manufacturing production. These trends can already be detected in the transformation of multinational firms into what Ernst and Kim (2002) call 'global production networks'. The 'network flagships' at the core of these networks resemble closely what we call 'systems integrators'.

5.6   Conclusions and Speculations

We have tried to demonstrate that increasing specialization in the production of artefacts and knowledge, coupled with recent advances in the applications of ICT, are important factors contributing an increase in disintegration and specialization within product development activities, and between product development and manufacturing.

We may speculate that this trend reflects a major shift in the opportunities for major technical changes from the processing of materials into products, towards the processing of information into services. As a consequence, we argue that the locus of competition through innovation in leading companies could shift from discrete physical product and process innovations associated with manufacturing, to innovations in the design, development, integration, and marketing of increasingly complex products and systems.

As foreseen by Drucker (2001),[5] this could lead to an increased—but still incomplete—disintegration between systems integration firms and manufacturing firms. It could also reinforce the shift of manufacturing towards certain lower-wage countries. However, the high-skilled 'services' in which the high-wage countries specialize would not be 'immaterial' in the conventional sense. They would comprise high-tech machines (processing information rather than materials), mastery of the knowledge underlying manufacturing, and a capacity for designing, integrating, and supporting complex physical systems, including simulations and modelling products and processes, production and logistic operations, monitoring and control, and customer support: in other words, the skilled activities that manufacturing firms undertake, except manufacturing itself. The fact that most of these activities are defined as 'services' often confuses rather than clarifies.

In this sense, firms specializing in systems design and integration are *not* post-industrial. They are instead the prolongation of the industrial system into a period of growing specialization and complexity, and of growing capacities to store, transmit, and manipulate information. High-wage countries may indeed find themselves specializing increasingly on 'services', but not as an alternative to manufacturing activities but as the skill-intensive components within them. The Visible Hand of manufacturing will not become invisible (Langlois 2001), but continue to exploit economies of physical scale, speed, and scope. At the same time, the Visible Brain of systems integration could become the dominant form of business organization in the world's advanced countries.

Notes

1. For the purposes of this chapter, systems integration includes product (or system) design, together with the integration of components, subsystems, and related knowledge.
2. He lists apparel and footwear, toys, data processing, offshore oil drilling, home furnishings and lighting, semiconductor fabrication, food processing, automotive parts, brewing, enterprise networking, and pharmaceuticals. In addition, Prencipe (1997) has shown increases in the outsourcing of production of aircraft engine components.

3. See, also, 'Our global vision is that by 2005, every production factory will be planned, built, launched, and operated first using full simulation, before going to bricks and mortar. Every digital vehicle must pass the digital factory quality gate—meeting cost, quality, and timing targets—before approval will be given for the actual factory.'—Sue Unger, Chief Technology Officer, DaimlerChrysler AG (*Manufacturing Daily*, 28 August 2002).
4. Although S. Brusoni insists on the continuing importance of long-distance jet travel as an effective means of international (tacit) knowledge transfer. Personal communication.
5. See his contrasting visions of the futures of GM and Toyota (pp. 18–19).

References

ARORA, A. and GAMBARDELLA, A. (1999). 'Chemicals', in D. Mowery (ed.), *US Industry in 2000: Studies in Competitive Performance*. Washington: National Academy Press, 45–74.

——, FOSFURI, A., and GAMBARDELLA, A. (2001). *Markets for Technology: The Economics of Innovation and Corporate Strategy*. Cambridge, MA: MIT Press.

BALCONI, M. (2002). 'Tacitness, Codification of Technological Knowledge and the Organisation of Industry', *Research Policy*, 31: 357–79.

BERNAL, J. (1953). *Science and Industry in the Nineteenth Century*. London: Routledge and Kegan Paul.

BEST, M. (2001). *The New Competitive Advantage: The Renewal of American Industry*. Oxford: Oxford University Press.

BRUSONI, S. and PRENCIPE, A. (2001). 'Unpacking the Black Box of Modularity: Technologies, Products and Organisations', *Industrial and Corporate Change*, 10/1: 179–205.

—— —— and PAVITT, K. (2001). 'Knowledge Specialization and the Boundaries of the Firm: Why do Firms Know More than they Make?', *Administrative Science Quarterly*, 46: 597–621.

CARPENTER, M., LAZONICK, W., and O'SULLIVAN, M. (2002). 'Corporate Strategy and Innovative Capability in the "New Economy": The Optical Networking Industry'. Fontainebleu: INSEAD.

CHANDLER, A. (1977). *The Visible Hand*. Cambridge, MA: Belknap Press.

—— (1990). *Scale and Scope: The Dynamics of Industrial Capitalism*. Cambridge, MA: Belknap Press.

D'ADDERIO, L. (2001). 'Crafting the Virtual Prototype: How Firms Integrate Knowledge and Capabilities across Organisational Boundaries', *Research Policy*, 30/9: 1409–24.

—— (2002). *Bridging Formal Tools with Informal Practices: How Organisations Balance Flexibility and Control*. Edinburgh: Research Centre for Social Sciences (RCSS).

DRUCKER, P. (2001). 'The Next Society: A Survey of the Near Future', *Economist*, 3 November.

ECONOMIST (2002). 'Incredible Shrinking Plants'. 23 February.

ERNST, D. (2002*a*). 'Global Production Networks in East Asia's Electronics Industry and Upgrading Perspectives in Malaysia', *Working Papers, Economics Series, No. 44*. Hawaii: East-West Centre.

—— (2002*b*). 'Digital Information Systems and Global Flagship Networks: How Mobile is Knowledge in the Global Network Economy', *Working Papers, Economics Series, No. 48*. Hawaii: East-West Centre.

—— and KIM, L. (2002). 'Global Production Networks, Knowledge Diffusion, and Local Capability Formation', *Research Policy*, 31/8–9: 1417–29.

FEENSTRA, R. (1998). 'Integration of Trade and Disintegration of Production in the Global Economy', *The Journal of Economic Perspectives*, 12/4: 31–50.

GRANSTRAND, O., PATEL, P., and PAVITT, K. (1997). 'Multi-technology Corporations: Why They have "Distributed" rather than "Distinctive Core" Competencies', *California Management Review*, 39/4: 8–25.

HOBDAY, M. (1995). *Innovation in East Asia*. Aldershot: Edward Elgar.

IANSITI, M. and CLARK, K. (1994). 'Integration and Dynamic Capability: Evidence from Product Development in Automobiles and Mainframe Computers', *Industrial and Corporate Change*, 4: 557–605.

KOGUT, B. and ZANDER, I. (1992). 'Knowledge of the Firm, Combinative Capabilities and the Replication of Technology', *Organisation Science*, 3: 383–97.

LAMOREAUX, N. and SOKOLOFF, K. (2002). 'Intermediaries in the US Market for Technology, 1870–1920', *Working Paper 9017*. Cambridge, MA: NBER.

LANDAU, R. and ROSENBERG, N. (1992). 'Successful Commercialization in the Chemical Process Industries', in N. Rosenberg, R. Landau, and D. Mowery (eds.), *Technology and the Wealth of Nations*. Stanford: Stanford University Press, 73–119.

LANGLOIS, R. (2001). 'The Vanishing Hand: The Modular Revolution in American Business', *mimeo*. Storrs, CT: University of Connecticut. Richard.Langlois@ Uconn.edu

LEAMER, E. and STORPER, M. (2001). The Economic Geography of the Internet Age, *Working Paper 8450*. Cambridge, MA: NBER.

LORENZONI, G. and LIPPARINI, A. (1999). 'The Leveraging of Interfirm Relationships as a Distinctive Organizational Capability', *Strategic Management Journal*, 20: 317–38.

LOASBY, B. (1998). 'The Organisation of Capabilities', *Journal of Economic Behaviour and Organisation*, 35: 139–60.

LUNDVALL, B.-Å. (1988). 'Innovation as an Interactive Process: From User– Producer Interaction to the National System of Innovation', in G. Dosi, C. Freeman, R. Nelson, G. Silverberg, and L. Soete (eds.), *Technical Change and Economic Theory*. London: Pinter, 349–69.

MAHDI, S. (2002). 'Search Strategy on Product Innovation Process: Theory and Evidence from the Evolution of Agrochemical Lead Discovery Process', *SPRU Electronic Working Paper No. 79*. Brighton: SPRU, University of Sussex www.sussex.ac.uk/SPRU/publications/imprint/sewps/sewps79.pdf.

MANUFACTURING DAILY (2002). 28 August: 4. Provided from Mailing@manufacturingnews.com.

MOWERY, D. (1982). 'The Relationship between Contractual and Intrafirm Forms of Industrial Research in American Manufacturing, 1900–1940', *Explorations in Economic History*, 20/4: 351–74.

——and ROSENBERG, N. (1989). *Technology and the Pursuit of Economic Growth*. Cambridge: Cambridge University Press.

PAVITT, K. and STEINMUELLER, W. E. (2001). 'Technology in Corporate Strategy: Change, Continuity and the Information Revolution', in A. Pettigrew, H. Thomas, and R. Whittington (eds.), *Handbook of Strategy and Management*. London: Sage Publications, 344–72.

PERKINS, D. (2000). 'The Evolution of Adaptive Form', in J. Ziman (ed.), *Technological Innovation as an Evolutionary Process*. Cambridge: Cambridge University Press, 159–73.

PISANO, G. (1997). *The Development Factory*. Boston, MA: Harvard University Press.

PRENCIPE, A. (1997). 'Technological Competencies and Product's Evolutionary Dynamics: A Case Study from the Aero-engine Industry', *Research Policy*, 25: 1261–76.

ROSENBERG, N. (1963). 'Technological Change in the Machine Tool Industry, 1840–1910', *Journal of Economic History*, 23: 414–46.

——(1974). 'Science, Invention and Economic Growth', *Economic Journal*, 84: 333.

SANCHEZ, R. and MAHONEY, J. T. (1996). 'Modularity, Flexibility, and Knowledge Management in Product and Organization Design', *Strategic Management Journal*, 17: 63–76.

SMITH, A. (1776). *An Inquiry into the Nature and Courses of the Wealth of Nations* (Dent edn., 1910). London. W. Straham and T. Cadell.

STURGEON, T. (2002). 'Modular Production Networks: A New American Model of Industrial Organization', *Industrial and Corporate Change*, 11/3: 451–96.

TIDD, J., BESSANT, J., and PAVITT, K. (2001). *Managing Innovation: Integrating Technological, Market and Organizational Change* (2nd edn.). Chichester: Wiley.

ULRICH, K. (1995). 'The Role of Product Architecture in the Manufacturing Firm', *Research Policy*, 24: 419–40.

VERNON, R. (1966). 'International Investment and International Trade in the Product Cycle', *Quarterly Journal of Economics*, 80: 190–207.

ZUBOFF, S. (1988). *In the Age of the Smart Machine: The Future of Work and Power*. Oxford: Heinemann.

PART II

*Theoretical and Conceptual Perspectives on
Systems Integration*

6

The Economics of Systems Integration
Towards an Evolutionary Interpretation

Giovanni Dosi

S. Anna School for Advanced Studies, Pisa, Italy

Mike Hobday

SPRU, University of Sussex, Brighton, UK

Luigi Marengo

DSGSS, University of Teramo, Italy

Andrea Prencipe

SPRU, University of Sussex, Brighton, UK and Faculty of Economics,
University G. D'Annunzio, Pescara, Italy

6.1 Introduction

The aim of this chapter is to explore some theoretical aspects of the economics of systems integration (and disintegration) by placing the idea of systems integration within the context of evolutionary economics. We argue that systems integrators (as firms) and systems integration (as a key capability within and across firms) perform a central function as the 'visible hand' of much modern industrial activity, especially in complex product systems. The latter include a significant subset of capital goods such as mobile communication systems, military systems, corporate IT networks, high-speed trains, aircraft, intelligent buildings, air traffic control systems, and tailored software packages.

The chapter identifies important facets of the relationship between systems integration and the co-evolution of knowledge accumulation on one hand, and organizational boundaries on the other. Some recent interpretations of modularity (e.g Langlois 2001) are challenged. We show that the increasing modularity across components and its accompanying specialization among firms do not necessarily lead to the disappearance of the visible hand of management, but rather to a need for additional integrative knowledge on the part of the firm as 'integrator'. We also argue that systems integrators and systems integration as a capability represent the ever-present visible hand of the 'Chandlerian' organizations in their efforts to coordinate the diverse and complex learning trajectories of 'Smithian' suppliers.

Complex product systems (CoPS) are shown to differ from mass-produced goods in terms of product and production characteristics as well as patterns of innovation, competitive strategies, market characteristics, and managerial constraints (Hobday 1998). For example, design and implementation are usually carried out through major projects which often consist of temporary multi-firm alliances. Moreover, the multi-component and multi-technology nature of CoPS requires manufacturers to be active in multiple technological fields in order to design, develop, integrate, and manufacture products.

Research on CoPS has often emphasized the role of some key manufacturers as coordinators of their own internal activities as well as the activities of a network of actors (such as component suppliers, but sometimes also universities, regulatory bodies, etc.) involved in the industry. Indeed, across many CoPS industries, a particular class of leading producers are responsible for the overall coordination of production and innovation: in the definition originally proposed by Rothwell (1992), they act as systems integrator. In turn, such distinctive patterns of industrial organization hint at major interpretative questions with bearings well beyond the domain of CoPS themselves, and which touch upon the very core of the analysis of economic organizations, their boundaries, their relationships with each other, and their evolution.

In Section 6.2, we briefly outline some of the key issues which motivate our study. Section 6.3 presents an overview of evidence on the organization of design and production of CoPS. Finally, in Section 6.4 we attempt to interpret the evidence within an evolutionary theory of knowledge accumulation and organizations.

6.2   The Changing Boundaries Between Organizations and Markets: Some Background Issues

It would be futile to try to tackle here in any depth the determinants of those fuzzy and proximate boundaries, separating what is done inside relatively coherent organizational entities, versus what occurs through the intermediation of exchanges amongst independent actors. Here, it suffices to recall some different, albeit not mutually exclusive, lines of interpretation.

A first one, dating back to (parts of) Adam Smith's (1776) *Inquiry*, leading on to Stigler (1951, 1968) and to the refinements on 'complementarities' by Milgrom and Roberts (1990), focuses on the performances of particular tasks and on the advantages of specialization under certain indivisibilities and scale conditions. The famous pin-making example of Adam Smith is the archetype. Indeed, there is little doubt that 'virtuous circles' between expanding scales of production, division of labour, and increasing efficiency have been a powerful driver of secular productivity growth.

However, a distinct issue concerns the relationships between specialization across tasks versus specialization across firms. Historically, the former is a robust stylized fact; much less so the latter. Firms are typically multitask (and often multi-product) entities which internally govern the processes of division of labour and the coordination amongst separated tasks. What accounts then for such systematic discrepancies?

An answer is suggested by a second line of interpretation of the boundaries of the firm, based on the nature of transactions and the related transaction costs—inspired by Coase (1937) and developed by Williamson (1975, 1985). Here the unit of analysis is not 'technical' tasks but elementary transactions: hierarchical organizations are compared to market forms of coordination in terms of relative efficiencies in transaction governance. The scope for opportunistic behaviour, depending in turn on asset specificities and other characteristics of transactions, twists the balance one way or another and— the theory suggests—shapes the approximate boundaries between organization-based and market-based mechanisms of coordination.

Third, a different (but, to repeat, not necessarily alternative) interpretation focuses upon the division of knowledge—as distinct from the division of 'operational' tasks—across organizations and upon organization-specific learning processes. It is a perspective which finds its roots in seminal works of Herbert Simon and collaborators (Simon 1981, 1991; March and Simon 1993).[1] In a nutshell, such a perspective conjectures that proximate boundaries of corporate organizations are heavily shaped by the nature of the competences/capabilities organizations which they embody, and by their learning patterns. For more detailed recent discussions of these concepts, see Dosi, Nelson, and Winter (2000). Organizational knowledge, in turn, applies to diverse domains such as (*a*) allocative capabilities (e.g. deciding what to produce, how to price it, etc.); (*b*) transactional capabilities (deciding whether to make or buy, etc.); (*c*) administrative capabilities (concerning, for example, the designing of effective governance structures); (*d*) problem-solving capabilities (concerning, at large, the organization of design, planning, production, etc.); (*e*) search capabilities (covering technological search for new products and processes of production, new organizational arrangements, new strategic positioning, etc.) (Teece, Pisano, and Shuen 1994).

Note also the likely overlapping amongst the three preceding perspectives. For example, if organizational capabilities have mainly to do with the dynamics of transaction characteristics, the explanatory variables of the (changing) organizational boundaries mainly concern the features of the mechanisms for transaction governance (compare the discussions in Langlois (1992) and Foss (1993)). Conversely, if one were able to neatly decompose 'chunks' of knowledge and map them into organizational activities, one would also get a large overlap between 'knowledge-centred' views of firm boundaries. Indeed, many analyses focusing on product modularity hint at this interpretative perspective. In the management literature, modularity was first proposed as a product design strategy aimed at defining stable interfaces amongst components (modules) of a product. Together, it is suggested, each module may be improved (e.g. via changes in design, the introduction of new materials, etc.) within a predefined range of variation, with little or no impact on the design of the other modules (Ulrich 1995). A further step is the claim that modularity carries over from product design to the very characteristics of organizations. As, for example, Sanchez and Mahoney (1996) argue, if components' interfaces can be fully specified and standardized, they also determine relatively stable product and production architectures. Hence, the processes for improving single modules may also be decoupled and carried out by independent organizational entities. Firms, therefore, may well choose to either specialize in the design (and/or assembly) of final products or in specific modules, largely leaving the interfaces to market exchanges.

Somewhat similar considerations apply to the role of market transaction concerning the very 'chunks of knowledge' and, *in primis*, technological knowledge. Clearly, codification and (lack of) context-dependency influence the importance of market exchanges. In this respect, Cowan, David, and Foray (2000) and Arora, Fosfuri, and Gambardella (2001) suggest that, in fact, an increasing codification of technological knowledge fosters the growing importance of a 'market for technologies'. The robustness and extent of this tendency is the subject of lively debate. For another view, see Brusoni, Prencipe, and Pavitt (2001).

In any case, we have here some major interpretative questions, including:

(a) the relationships between division of labour (e.g. amongst operational tasks) and division of knowledge within and across corporate organizations;
(b) the ensuing determinants of the proximate boundaries between activities internalized within single organizations and those mediated by market relations;
(c) the very nature of interorganizational relations, hardly reducible to impersonal exchanges.

6.3 'Making' versus 'Knowing': Some Empirical Evidence on the Relevance of Systems Integration

There is growing empirical evidence that division of labour and division of knowledge, though connected, follow different and often apparently uncorrelated dynamics both within business organizations (Brusoni and

Prencipe 2001) and in the economy at large. In particular, the less than perfect overlap between knowledge and product boundaries of business firms has been corroborated by in-depth industry case studies based on both qualitative and quantitative evidence, as shown below.

Based on systematic observations on US patent statistics in several industrial sectors, Granstrand, Patel, and Pavitt (1997) argue that decisions related to products are distinct from those concerning their underlying capabilities (e.g. technological). Thus, for example, outsourcing the production of components does not necessarily entail outsourcing the sets of knowledge employed to specify, design, integrate, manufacture, test, and assemble them. They argue that 'firms should maintain capabilities in exploratory and applied research in order to have the capability to monitor and integrate external knowledge and production inputs' (p. 20).

Miller et al. (1995), in their study on the flight simulation industry, underline the role of leading firms that act as integrators of other firms' knowledge and activities. The knowledge bases of these systems integrators span many different knowledge domains and include:

- the scientific and technological fields underpinning the high variety of components and subsystems;
- organizational (for example, project management) and relational (e.g. marketing) capabilities required to manage and integrate the activities of multiple actors involved in the industry;
- knowledge about client requirements; and
- knowledge about rules and regulations for engine certification.

This in-depth study showed that the revolutionary changes (being technological or institutional in nature) that occurred in the industry heavily affected component suppliers, but not so much the final flight simulator producers (i.e. the systems integrators).

Prencipe (2004) argues that in the aircraft engine industry, although engine manufacturers make extensive use of collaborative agreements, they maintain a broad and deep range of in-house capabilities in order to understand and coordinate the technological workings of the network of suppliers involved in the industry. In particular, this industry is characterized by a set of driving forces whose combined effect 'enables' and 'pushes' engine makers to resort to suppliers to a greater extent than hitherto. The former forces include accumulated knowledge of the behaviour of the engine system, the knowledge codification process, and the increasing use of powerful computers, while major 'pushing' factors include spiralling development costs, pressures from developing countries, and advantages of specialization.

The modularization of the engine is just one (albeit an important one) of these driving forces. The impact of these forces has resulted in a greater division of labour between engine manufacturers and suppliers. In particular, due to accumulated knowledge about the behaviour of components as well as of the entire system, manufacturers are able to conceive engines in terms of modules and delegate the design and manufacture of larger engine parts to suppliers. As an industry expert put it: 'If I want to make a list of these 10,000 [engine] parts and I want to put a price against each of them, then the name of the supplier, you will find that between 60–80 per cent of the total value is outside the systems integrator.'

However, despite increasing outsourcing of components, as the study by Prencipe shows, engine makers maintain a broad range of in-house technological capabilities and the breadth of these capabilities is shown to increase over time. While there is a trend in the industry towards a greater division of labour between engine manufacturers and suppliers, there is no evidence of increasing 'technological focusing' and knowledge specialization of engine makers themselves.

The persistence of in-house multi-technology bases, despite the increasing use of outsourcing, points to untidy trends followed by division of labour and division of knowledge. Indeed, if product decomposability does not necessarily entail knowledge decomposability, then the knowledge boundaries and the product boundaries of the firm are likely to differ. Decisions to outsource components do not necessarily entail outsourcing technological knowledge. Component outsourcing and technology outsourcing, though connected, are distinct phenomena. Prencipe (2004) argues that the scope for technology outsourcing for engine manufacturers is limited by two interrelated factors, namely, (*a*) the technological and product requirements for the engine integration, and (*b*) the need to coordinate the network of actors involved in the industry.

Both factors foster the possession of profound knowledge in different technological fields. Engine manufacturers divide up engine development tasks across a number of external suppliers, but this task-partitioning capability (von Hippel 1990) hinges on their multi-technology bases. Moreover, the capabilities of engine manufacturers must span a wide spectrum of technologies in order to coordinate from a technological viewpoint the work of suppliers, airframers, airlines, and regulatory bodies. Coordination in this industry, therefore, is not achieved through arm's-length relationships, but needs to be actively pursued by all-round knowledgeable engine manufacturers. Engine manufacturers act in other words as the *systems integrators* of the industry. Their multi-technology bases constitute their systems integration capabilities.

Brusoni (2001) finds similar evidence in his study of the chemical engineering industry. By comparing the evolution of the pattern of division of labour between operators and contractors, notwithstanding increasing product modularity, he highlights the persistent need for explicit efforts of coordination by so-called operators, which play the role of the systems integrators of the industry. In his words:

Despite the increasing involvement of contractors in high-level design decisions, all the operators involved in this study have retained in-house capabilities related to critical components. In particular, they maintain both conceptual and detailed design capabilities related to the reactor, which is the key component of the plant. Changes in this specific piece of equipment are likely to bring about systemic changes. Operators also maintain research units focused on the theory and modelling of reactor behaviour. (Brusoni 2001: 181)

More specifically, it is worth noting that evidence shows that many CoPS products are characterized by two persistent trends, namely (*a*) incorporation of an increasing number of functionalities that increase the integration of the number of parts and components (multi-component) as well as services, and (*b*) incorporation of an increasing number of new and sometimes distant scientific and technological disciplines (multi-technology). These two trends impact heavily on the definition of the boundaries of the firm (particularly make-or-buy decisions), since CoPS suppliers must increasingly resort to external sources of components, equipment, and technologies. Firms are required to set up and manage a network of institutions that are involved in the industry. As a consequence, systems integration capabilities could become even more important in the future.

The incorporation of services (e.g. maintenance and finance) and the move towards the supply of 'bundled' systems rather than individual sub-systems (Tidd, Bessant, and Pavitt 1997) is a trend that deserves separate treatment. Research on CoPS (Davies 2003, Chapter 16, this volume; Prencipe 2004) has stressed that suppliers are moving downstream to provide bundled systems (integrated solutions or turnkey projects) to buyers. Bundled systems are composed of hardware and software components, often linked by proprietary interfaces, that tie customers into a product and service solution with a single point of purchase and after-sales support. Suppliers of such solutions generate an increasing proportion of revenues through service-enhanced activities (e.g. maintenance and technical support) rather than manufacturing (Chadran, Chua, and Kabonovsky 1997).

In some industries, the move towards downstream business activities and the ensuing development of service capabilities by systems integrators has become a 'strategic imperative'. So, for example, the rebirth of IBM is ascribed to its reinvention as 'solutions provider'. In the aircraft engine industry, shrinking margins, high development costs, and long payback periods to recoup the initial financial investment have prompted engine makers to explore new ways of pricing engines that would better stabilize their revenue stream. Leasing agreements, where manufacturers lease their engines rather than sell them, represents one option. Rolls-Royce in the 1970s had already introduced power-by-the-hour agreements for operators of corporate jets, according to which customer airlines pay a fixed rate that includes both capital and operating costs. This agreement provides an incentive to the manufacturer to improve engine reliability and reduce maintenance costs because it manages the entire engine life cycle: engine manufacturers provide an integrated system solution. Airlines might benefit too, since with improved engine reliability, they have less down time.

All the preceding examples suggest patterns of: (*a*) vertical disintegration in production, (*b*) (complementary) 'Smithian' specialization in particular components, and (*c*) persistent concentration of broad knowledge bases within a few 'systems integrators'.

Partial counter-examples to these patterns are equally revealing. Consider, for instance, the case of telecommunications, where a tendency toward vertical disintegration in production still applies. However the importance of broad-based knowledge carried by systems integrators might actually be diminishing, this does not imply a diminishing importance of systems integration, rather the latter appears to be pushed 'upward' and embodied into the producers of crucial components. To a significant extent, systems integration is increasingly incorporated into the underlying microelectronic components. For a detailed discussion on the relationships between electronics and systems integration, see Steinmueller (Chapter 8, this volume).

6.4   Empirical Patterns and Theoretical Interpretations

The above evidence supports the argument that system integration, in the presence of widespread component specialization, constitutes a fundamental coordination mechanism which hardly falls within the scope of the rudimentary representations of market exchanges familiar to a good deal of economic theory. Systems integration is performed by specific types of organizations—distinct in terms of technological and coordination capabilities. At the same time, the degrees of vertical integration of these firms vary according to the nature and dynamics of multiple competencies and subsystem technological trajectories.

How does one interpret this evidence? Teece et al. (1994) conjectured that the proximate boundaries of firms are shaped by: the interplay between technological opportunities; convergence/divergence of technological trajectories; degrees of cumulativeness of idiosyncratic technological learning; and asset specificities. The patterns displayed by CoPS broadly corroborate the general notion emphasized by Teece et al., and are consistent with the evolutionary literature, according to which the nature and dynamics of technological knowledge is a fundamental determinant of the vertical and horizontal boundaries of firms. However, the evidence from CoPS also vividly illustrates a further distinction between different types of knowledge which organizations embody.

A first type relates, roughly speaking, to the 'ability to do things' and the way doing *A* affects or not the ability to do *B* and/or the advantages and costs of governing market relations when selling and buying *A* or *B*. Clearly, this is also a domain where evolutionary, knowledge-centred analyses overlap significantly with both transaction cost interpretations of make versus buy behaviours and 'Smithian' interpretations based on specialization-driven increasing returns.

A second, somewhat distinct, type of knowledge regards 'how products are put together', that is, how multiple components, possibly manufactured by independent producers, are ultimately assembled into complex products (aeroplanes, steel plants, flight simulators, and submarines) which generally perform the task they are meant to, not withstanding the lack of either central planners or magic pre-existing modularity between components.

Finally, organizational knowledge concerns how to 'search for what is not already there', and possibly how to coordinate search efforts among independent agents. CoPS, we suggest, highlight dynamic patterns whereby knowledge accumulation in these three preceding domains are only loosely coupled. An important observable consequence entails diverging dynamics in the scope of what firms do compared with what (some) firms know. Brusoni, Prencipe, and Pavitt (2001) argue that distinct systems integrating organizations are a fundamental node in loosely coupled systems which emerge when complex products are characterized either by uneven (and relatively high) rates of change in the underlying technologies (even when component complementarities remain rather predictable), or, conversely, when interdependency patterns tend to change in unpredictable ways. In these circumstances, systems integration entails technological and organizational capabilities to integrate multiple changes in components and subsystems only partly designed or even forecasted by the integrators themselves. Together, systems integrators are crucial in the persistent, imperfect, efforts to match the untidy dynamics of division of operational labour, knowledge accumulation, and cross-corporate division of competencies.

Accepting all this, what kind of 'reduced form' formal representations can one offer of such organizational structure, if any? A basic building block regards the explicit account of organizations as repositories of problem-solving procedures. Marengo et al. (2000) develop a formalism aimed at capturing diverse and (usually suboptimal) routines of production and search embodied in different firms. Let us start by presenting the basic qualitative features of such modelling exercises, also discussed in Dosi, Hobday, and Marengo (2003).

In the view proposed here, the basic units of analysis for problem-solving behaviour (PSB) are, on the one hand, elementary physical acts (such as moving a drawing from one office to another) and elementary cognitive acts (such as a simple calculation) on the other. Problem-solving can then be defined as a combination of elementary acts within a procedure, leading eventually to a feasible outcome (e.g. an aircraft engine or chemical compound). Or, seen the other way round, given the possibly infinite set of procedures leading to a given outcome or product, it is possible to decompose these procedures into diverse series of elementary cognitive and physical acts of varying lengths, which may be executed according to various possible execution architectures (e.g. sequential, parallel, or hierarchical).

Problem-solving behaviour straightforwardly links with the notion of organizational competencies and capabilities. First, a firm displays the operational competencies associated with its actual problem-solving procedures—in line with the routines discussed by Nelson and Winter (1982) and Cohen et al. (1996). Second, the formal and informal organizational structure of the firm determines the way in which cognitive and physical acts are distributed, and the decomposition rules which govern what is and what is not admissible within a particular firm (providing a route into the analysis of incentive structures and processes). Third, the organization shapes the search heuristics for, as yet, unresolved problems, thereby governing creative processes within the firm.

This theoretical approach to PSB within the firm also closely corresponds to empirical accounts of firm behaviour from the economics of innovation (Freeman 1982; Dosi 1988; Pavitt 1999). Moreover, it has the benefit of being applicable both to the analysis of intra-firm structures and to the analysis of the boundaries between firms and the market. Indeed, such boundaries can be seen as particular patterns of decomposition of an overall problem-solving task. In other words, the boundary of the firm is shaped, in part, by the problem to be solved, often corresponding to the product to be created (e.g. a car or a piece of steel). Particular decomposition strategies may notionally range from the totally centralized and autarkic types (with no decomposition at all) to the equivalent of an ideal pure market, where one person acts on each task with market-like transactions linking each elementary act.

It is helpful to think of complex problem-solving activities as problems of design: the design of elaborate artefacts and the design of the processes and organizational structures required to produce them. In turn, these processes require the design of complex sequences of moves, rules, behaviours, and search heuristics involving one or many different actors to solve problems, create new 'representations' of problems themselves, and ultimately to achieve the technoeconomic goals at hand. Common to all these design activities is that they involve search in large combinatorial spaces of 'components' (as defined above in terms of elementary physical and cognitive acts) which have to be closely coordinated. To complicate matters still further, the functional relations among these elements are only partly understood and can only be locally explored through a process of trial and error learning, often also involving the application of expert, partly tacit knowledge.

For example, the design of a complex artefact, such as an aircraft or a flight simulator, requires the coordination of many different design elements, including engine type and power, wing size and shape, and other materials. The interaction between each of the subsystems and components is only partly understood, and each comprises many smaller components and subsystems (Miller et al. 1995; Prencipe 1997). The interactions between the elements of the system can only be partly expressed by general models and have to be tested through simulation, prototype building, and trial and error moves where learning and tacit knowledge play an important part. Producing an effective solution, such as a new aircraft, involves a long sequence of moves, each of which is chosen out of an enormous set of possibilities. In turn, the relationships between the moves in the sequence can only be partly known as a full understanding would (impossibly) require knowledge of all the endless possibilities. The likelihood of combinatorial explosion within the search space presents a computationally intractable task for bounded rational agents.

Business firms as well as collaborative ventures among them can be seen as complex, multi-dimensional bundles of routines, decision rules, procedures, and incentive schemes, whose interplay is often largely unknown both to the managers of the organization and to managers, designers, and engineers responsible for single projects. Of course, over time many repeated technical and business activities become routinized and codified, allowing for stable, formal structures and established codified routines as, for example, in the volume production activities of cars or commodity chemicals. In these circumstances, some sort of 'steady state' problem decomposition becomes institutionalized, also allowing the establishment of neat organizational structures, and, together, the exploitation of economies of scale and scope. The 'Fordist' and 'Chandlerian' archetypes of organization are classic examples. This is also the organizational arrangement which most forcefully highlights potential advantages (and also the inbuilt rigidities) of division of labour and specialization. However, even in this stable case there remain many nonroutine, complex activities within the firm, including new product design, R&D, new marketing programmes, etc. Even more so, under conditions of rapid market and technological change, all organizations are ultimately forced to shape their structures in order to respond to new market demands and to exploit new technical opportunities (see, for example, the related discussions by Coriat and by Fujimoto in Dosi, Nelson, and Winter (2000) on Japanese—'Toyotist'—organizational arrangements and routines).

During the multi-stage product design task, the basic elements to be coordinated are characterized by strong interdependencies, which create many local optima within the search space. For instance, adding a more powerful engine could lead to a reduction in the performance of an aircraft or prevent it from flying altogether if the other subsystems and components are not simultaneously adapted. Similarly, at the organizational level, the introduction of new routines, practices, or incentive schemes which have proven superiority in another context could also prove counterproductive, if other elements of the organization are not appropriately adapted to suit the new inputs (Dosi, Nelson, and Winter 2000).

A helpful, although rough, 'reduced form' metaphor of the complex task problem is presented in Kaufman's model of selection dynamics (1993) in the biological domain with heterogeneous interdependent traits. Kaufman considers a model of the selection mechanisms whereby the units of selection are complex entities made of several nonlinearly interacting components. Units of selection are combinations of N elementary components which can assume one of a finite number of states, and a fitness value is exogenously assigned to each combination, producing a fitness landscape on the space of combinations whose characteristics reflect the interdependencies among the constituent elements. His model shows that as the number of interdependent elements increases, the fitness landscape presents an exponentially increasing number of local optima. In the presence of strong interdependencies (as is often the case in many complex products), the system cannot be optimized by separately optimizing each element from which it is made. Indeed, in the case of strong interdependencies, it might well be the case that some, or even all, solutions obtained by tuning each component 'in the right direction' yield a worse performance than the current one.

In the presence of strong interdependencies, the problem cannot therefore be decomposed into separate subproblems which could be optimized separately from the others (Marengo 2000). As argued by Simon (1981), problem-solving by boundedly rational agents must necessarily proceed by decomposing a large, complex, and intractable problem into smaller subproblems which can be solved independently. Within the firm, this is equivalent to a division of problem-solving activities. Clearly, the extent and efficacy of the division of such problem-solving efforts is limited by the existence of interdependencies. If, in the process of subproblem decomposition, interdependent elements are separated, then solving each subproblem interdependently does not allow overall optimization. As Simon (1981) pointed out, a perfect decomposition—which isolates in separate subproblems all and only the elements which are interdependent with each other—can only be designed by someone who has perfect knowledge of the problem: boundedly rational agents will normally try at best to design 'near-decompositions'. The latter are decompositions which try to isolate the most relevant interdependencies (in terms of performance) into separate subproblems.

However, unlike the biological analogy above, the design space of a problem faced by an engineer or firm is not given exogenously but, rather, is constructed by the agents as a subjective representation of the problem itself, in turn shaping a good deal of the search strategy. If the division of problem-solving labour is limited by interdependencies, the perceived structure of the latter, in turn, depends on how the problem is framed by the problem-solvers. Sometimes with major innovations, problem-solvers are able to make major leaps forward by reframing the problem itself in novel ways: for striking illustrations of the paramount importance of different combinations among already known system elements, compare Levinthal (1998) on wireless communications and Sapolsky (1972) on the Polaris missile system.

For the purpose of this work, note, first, that specific decomposition schemes do not only mark the division of labour within individual firms but also the proximate boundaries between firms themselves. Second, in this framework, one may straightforwardly represent the distinction between competencies on 'how to do given things' and integrating and search capabilities. The former clearly include abilities in handling subproblems, holding decompositions constant. Conversely, the latter refer to both the ways solutions to subproblems are put together and to search patterns for new decompositions/recombinations of knowledge bases and physical components. Third, as conjectured in Simon (1981), near-decomposable systems have an evolutionary advantage over systems which do not have this feature, because near-decomposability increases the speed of adaptation, confines the consequences of errors and damaging events to subcomponent of the system, and guarantees the 'evolvability' of the system, that is, its capability to produce innovation without jeopardizing its overall viability and coherence. In particular, there are two types of near-decomposable architectures which are particularly relevant for our discussion, namely (*a*) an architecture of partially overlapping modules, and (*b*) an architecture of nested modules. In the former, modules are separated apart from some components they share. A system of nested modules is instead similar to Russian dolls in which there exists a small set of core components which belong to all modules, then another larger set which includes the former and is contained in all the others and so on. Figure 6.1 depicts the architecture of both systems.

A system made of partially overlapping modules is in fact very close to Simon's idea of near decomposability, and enjoys its properties of high adaptability and evolvability. With respect to search processes, in systems having this feature, components where modules overlap, obviously have a special role, since they are also the components for which search cannot be effectively decentralized. It is also easy to verify that those components which two subsystems have in common must be kept relatively stable, because changes imposed by one subsystem will jeopardize the search process in the other subsystem. Some form of control over these

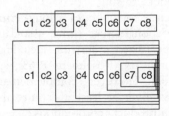

Fig. 6.1 Systems with partially overlapping and nested components

interfaces among subsystems is therefore fundamental in order to keep the system coherent.

A system of nested modules also has specific characteristics investigated at greater length in Marengo, Pasquali, and Valente (2002): they are characterized by very strong interdependencies but, nevertheless, the search space remains highly decomposable, provided that search proceeds sequentially from the 'core' components, which must be set first, to the more peripheral ones which can be adjusted sequentially.

Both partially overlapping and nested architectures have properties which are very similar to some of the stylized facts about systems integration presented in the previous section. Both architectures are based on the presence of some key components (and key agents) which are crucial for adaptation and evolvability and have to be kept relatively stable. According to this interpretation, systems integrators are those agents which possess critical knowledge about such major overlaps and interfaces.

6.5   Conclusions: Some Conjectures on the Co-evolution of Knowledge Accumulation and Organizational Boundaries

The long-term history of many contemporary industries and, closer to the concerns of this work, the dynamics of industries producing CoPS reveals puzzling divergences between what 'firms make' and what 'firms know' (Brusoni, Prencipe, and Pavitt 2001). Putting it another way, there are systematic divergences between firms' boundaries revealed by the scope of production activities, compared to the scope of knowledge bases which firms master.

These patterns are explained by an evolutionary approach to the role of knowledge specificities in both production and innovation in different industries (Freeman 1982; Pavitt 1984; Teece et al. 1994; Nelson and Mowery 1999; Piscitello 2000). Ultimately, the simple fact is that, in many activities, firms need to 'know more' than what is seemingly required by current production tasks. Such breadth of knowledge is often a necessary requirement for firms to produce complex outputs, and even more so to prepare for future generations of product. So, for example, General Motors reveals significant technological competencies in plastics and glass, even though it does not produce them.

Indeed, robust evidence corroborates a long-term tendency towards an increasing division of labour across firms, associated with the historical emergence of novel specialized industries, including the emergence of a distinct machine tool industry (Rosenberg 1963), and the pharmaceutical industry (Freeman 1982). However, complementary to such long-term trends, one can observe over at least a century the emergence of large multi-technology, multi-product corporations, characterized by varying degrees of vertical integration, but always embodying rich integrative capabilities among multiple components and multiple technological bases.

Is something radically new happening today? A few analysts have emphasized a growing division of labour across firms, corresponding to a spreading modularity between components which ultimately make up complex products (e.g. Langlois 2001; Sturgeon 2002). Certainly, such a process is at work in many industries. However, it is hardly a new phenomenon. At least since the nineteenth century, processes involving (a) 'technological convergence' in operations common to a number of manufacturing processes; (b) 'output codification'; and (c) the growth of markets large enough to sustain a number of small specialized firms (Pavitt 2002: 6) have frequently led to the birth of new specialized industries and to vertical disintegration. The evidence on CoPS is broadly in line with this pattern: specialization in the production of knowledge and task-specific increasing returns, and frequently a drive towards the separation of 'modules' of tasks between distinct firms.

However, a more controversial issue concerns whether 'modularity' supported by the codification of knowledge will be sufficient to make the *Chandlerian Visible Hand* of multi-technology, often big, corporations vanish (see Langlois 2001 for the idea of the 'vanishing hand'). Our conjecture, drawing on the evidence from CoPS, is somewhat different and suggests that, other things being equal, increasing 'modularization' across components and specialization across firms goes hand in hand with increasing requirements of integrative knowledge. As a result, systems integrators will continue to be crucial repositories of such knowledge. Clearly, the balance between what these types of firm 'know' and what they directly 'make' will continue to depend upon product- and technology-specific patterns of knowledge accumulation and their interfaces. Relatedly, while it is likely that such balances will move away from the profiles of heavy vertical integration displayed by classic 'Chandlerian' firms, it is equally unlikely that they will lead towards 'hollow corporations' performing just the role of 'brokers' or 'middlemen' bringing together demand and supply of different components.

Product complexity is here to stay (and possibly to grow), and so is the knowledge required to master interfaces and compatibilities across different components: this is indeed the first crucial task of systems integrators. A second, equally significant task is to bridge learning trajectories at the component level. This is particularly important in circumstances where system properties are not driven by innovation in any single crucial component (as in the case of high-speed computers, aircraft engines, and telecommunications). In these cases, coordinating the diverse learning trajectories followed by independent component suppliers might require the expansion of the knowledge bases which systems integrators need to embody (although not necessarily the number of intermediate inputs they directly manufacture).

In summary, our conjecture, based primarily on CoPS, has much broader implications. It implies that the tendencies toward vertical disintegration and 'Smithian' specialization (a secular feature of modern economies) do not correspond to any general trend towards symmetric in the patterns division of knowledge across firms. On the contrary, the more dispersed is the production of knowledge and the more complex are products, the higher also are the requirements of explicit integrative capabilities embodied in systems integrators. In many ways, these firms represent the enduring visible hand of purposeful organizations, which painstakingly and imperfectly try to master through time the expanding combinations of product components and knowledge, as well as the diverse learning trajectories of 'Smithian' suppliers.

Note

1. Nelson and Winter (1982), Freeman (1982), Chandler (1977, 1990), Richardson (1990), further developed in Winter (1987), Dosi and Marengo (1994), Patel and Pavitt (1997), Pavitt (1998), Teece (1996), Teece, Pisano and Shuen (1994); Teece et al. (1994), Dosi, Nelson and Winter (2000) amongst many others; and largely overlapping with 'core competences' theories of the firm (Prahlad and Hamel 1990).

References

ARORA, A., FOSFURI, A., and GAMBARDELLA, A. (2001). *Markets for Technologies*. Cambridge, MA: MIT Press.

BRUSONI, S. (2001). 'The Division of Labour and the Division of Knowledge: The Organisation of Engineering Design in the Chemical Industry', Unpublished PhD Thesis, Brighton: SPRU, University of Sussex.

—— and PRENCIPE, A. (2001). 'Unpacking the Black Box of Modularity: Technologies, Products, Organizations', *Industrial and Corporate Change*, 10: 179–205.

——, ——, and PAVITT, K. (2001). 'Knowledge Specialization and the Boundaries of the Firm: Why Firms Know More Than They Make', *Administrative Science Quarterly*, 46: 597–621.

CHANDLER, A. D. (1977). *The Visible Hand: The Managerial Revolution in American Business*. Cambridge, MA: Harvard University Press.

—— (1990). *Scale and Scope: The Dynamics of Industrial Capitalism*. Cambridge, MA: Harvard University Press.

CHADRAN, A., CHUA, G., and KABANOVSKY, A. (1997). 'Transforming Technical Support', *Public Network Europe*, 7/5: 31–3.

COASE, R. M. (1937). 'The Nature of the Firm', *Economica*, 4: 386–405.

COHEN, M. D., BURKHART, R., DOSI, G., EGIDI, M., MARENGO, L., WARGLIEN, M., WINTER, S., and CORIAT, B. (1996). 'Routines and Other Recurring Action

Patterns of Organizations: Contemporary Research Issues', *Industrial and Corporate Change*, 5: 653–98.

CORIAT, B. (2000). 'The "Abominable Ohno Production System". Competencies, Monitoring, and Routines in Japanese Production System', in G. Dosi, R. Nelson, and S. Winter (eds.), *The Nature and Dynamics of Organizational Capabilities*. Oxford: Oxford University Press, 213–43.

COWAN, R., DAVID, P., and FORAY, D. (2000). 'The Explicit Economics of Knowledge Codification and Tacitness', *Industrial and Corporate Change*, 9: 211–53.

DOSI, G. (1988). 'Sources, Procedures and Microeconomic Effects of Innovation', *Journal of Economic Literature*, 26: 1120–71.

——— and MARENGO, L. (1994). 'Towards a Theory of Organisational Competencies', in R. W. England (ed.), *Evolutionary Concepts in Contemporary Economics*. Ann Arbor, MI: Michigan University Press, 157–78.

———, HOBDAY, M., and MARENGO, L. (2003). 'Problem Solving Behaviours, Organizational Forms and the Complexity of Tasks', in Constance E. Helfat (ed.), *The Blackwell/Strategic Management Society Handbook of Organizational Capabilities: Emergence, Development and Change*. Oxford: Blackwell.

———, NELSON, R., and WINTER, S. (eds.) (2000). *The Nature and Dynamics of Organizational Capabilities*. Oxford: Oxford University Press.

FOSS, N. (1993). 'Theories of the Firm: Contractual and Competence Perspectives', *Journal of Evolutionary Economics*, 3: 127–44.

FREEMAN, C. (1982). *The Economics of Industrial Innovation* (2nd edn.). London: Frances Pinter.

FUJIMOTO, T. (2000). 'Evolution of Manufacturing Systems and Ex-post Dynamic Capabilities', in G. Dosi, R. Nelson, and S. Winter (eds.), *The Nature and Dynamics of Organizational Capabilities*. Oxford: Oxford University Press, 244–80.

GRANSTRAND, O., PATEL, P., and PAVITT, K. (1997). 'Multi-technology Corporations: Why They Have "Distributed" Rather than "Distinctive Core" Competencies', *California Management Review*, 39/4: 8–25.

HOBDAY, M. (1998). 'Product Complexity, Innovation and Industrial Organisation', *Research Policy*, 26: 689–710.

KAUFMAN, S. A. (1993). *The Origins of Order*. Oxford: Oxford University Press.

LANGLOIS, R. (1992). 'Transaction Costs Economics in Real Time', *Industrial and Corporate Change*, 2: 99–127.

LANGLOIS, R. N. (2001). 'The Vanishing Hand: The Modular Revolution in American Business', invited Paper for DRUID's Nelson–Winter Conference, June.

LEVINTHAL, D. (1998). 'The Slow Pace of Rapid Technological Change: Gradualism and Punctuation in Technological Change', *Industrial and Corporate Change*, 7: 217–47.

MARCH, J. G. and SIMON, H. A. (1993). *Organizations* (2nd edn.). New York: Wiley.

MARENGO, L. (2000). *Decentralisation and Market Mechanisms in Collective Problem-solving* (mimeo). Trento: Department of Economics.

———, DOSI, G., LEGRENZI, P., and PASQUALI, C. (2000). 'The Structure of Problem-solving Knowledge and the Structure of Organisations', *Industrial and Corporate Change*, 9: 757–88.

———, PASQUALI, C., and VALENTE, M. (2002). 'Decomposability and Modularity of Economic Interactions', in W. Callebaut and D. Rasskin-Gutman (eds.),

Modularity: Understanding the Development and Evolution of Complex Natural Systems. Cambridge, MA: MIT Press.

MILGROM, P. and ROBERTS, J. (1990). 'The Economics of Modern Manufacturing', *American Economic Review*, 80: 511–28.

MILLER, R., HOBDAY, M., LEROUX-DEMERS, T., and OLLEROS, X. (1995). 'Innovation in Complex Systems Industries: The Case of Flight Simulation', *Industrial and Corporate Change*, 4: 363–400.

NELSON, R. and MOWERY D. C. (eds.) (1999). *Sources of Industrial Leadership: Studies of Seven Industries.* New York: Cambridge University Press.

—— and WINTER, S. (1982). *An Evolutionary Theory of Economic Change.* Cambridge, MA: Harvard University Press.

PATEL, P. and PAVITT, K. (1997). 'The Technological Competencies of the World's Largest Firms: Complex and Path-dependent, but not much Variety', *Research Policy*, 26: 141–56.

PAVITT, K. (1984). 'Sectoral Patterns of Innovation: Toward a Taxonomy and a Theory', *Research Policy*, 13: 343–75.

—— (1998). 'Technologies, Products and Organization in the Innovating Firm: What Adam Smith tells us and Joseph Schumpeter Doesn't', *Industrial and Corporate Change*, 7: 433–52.

—— (1999). *Technology, Management and Systems of Innovation.* Cheltenham: Edward Elgar.

—— (2002). *Systems Integrators as 'Post-Industrial' Firms?* (mimeo). Brighton: SPRU, University of Sussex. (Presented at DRUID's New Economy Conference, June 2002, Aalborg, Denmark.)

PISCITELLO, L. (2000). 'Largest Firms' Patterns of Technological and Business Diversification. A Comparison between European, US and Japanese Firms', *Dynacom Working Paper Series*, Pisa: Sant'Anna School of Advanced Studies, LEM.

PRAHALAD, C. K. and HAMEL, G. (1990). 'The Core Competence of the Corporation', *Harvard Business Review*, 68: 79–91.

PRENCIPE, A. (1997). 'Technological Competencies and Product's Evolutionary Dynamics: A Case Study from the Aero-engine Industry', *Research Policy*, 25: 1261–76.

—— (2004). *Strategy, Systems, and Scope: Managing Systems Integration in Complex Products.* London: Sage (forthcoming).

RICHARDSON, J. B. H. (1990). *Information and Investment.* Oxford: Oxford University Press.

ROSENBERG, N. (1963). 'Technological Change in the Machine Tool Industry, 1840–1910', *Journal of Economic History*, 23: 414–43.

ROTHWELL, R. (1992). 'Successful Industrial Innovation: Critical Factors for the 1990s', *R&D Management*, 22: 221–39.

SANCHEZ, R. and MAHONEY, J. (1996). 'Modularity, Flexibility, and Knowledge Management in Product and Organisation Design', *Strategic Management Journal*, 17: 63–76.

SAPOLSKY, H. M. (1972). *The Polaris System Development: Bureaucratic and Programmatic Success in Government.* Cambridge, MA: Harvard University Press.

SIMON, H. A. (1981). *The Sciences of the Artificial.* Cambridge, MA: MIT Press.

—— (1991). 'Organizations and Markets', *Journal of Economic Perspectives*, 5: 25–44.

SMITH, A. (1776). *An Inquiry into the Nature and Causes of the Wealth of Nations* (Dent Edn., 1910). London: W. Straham and T. Cadell.

STIGLER, G. T. (1951). 'The Division of Labor is Limited by the Extent of the Market', *Journal of Political Economy*, 59: 185–93.

—— (1968). *The Organization of Industry*. Homewood, IC: Irwin.

STURGEON, T. J. (2002). 'Modular Production Networks: A New American Model of Industrial Organization', *Industrial and Corporate Change*, 11: 451–96.

TEECE, D. J. (1996). 'Firm Organization, Industrial Structure, and Technological Innovation', *Journal of Economic Behaviour and Organization*, 31: 193–224.

——, PISANO, G., and SHUEN, A. (1994). 'Dynamic Capabilities and Strategic Management', *CCC Working Paper #94–9*, Berkeley: University of California.

——, RUMELT, R., DOSI, G., and WINTER, S. G. (1994). 'Understanding Corporate Coherence: Theory and Evidence', *Journal of Economic Behaviour & Organization*, 23: 1–30.

TIDD, J., BESSANT, J., and PAVITT, K. (1997). *Managing Innovation: Integrating Technological, Market and Organisational Change*. Chichester: John Wiley & Sons.

ULRICH, K. T. (1995). 'The Role of Product Architecture in the Manufacturing Firm', *Research Policy*, 24: 419–40.

VON HIPPEL, E. (1990). 'Task Partitioning: An Innovation Process Variable', *Research Policy*, 19: 407–18.

WILLIAMSON, O. (1975). *Markets and Hierarchies: Analysis and Antitrust Implications*. New York: Free Press.

—— (1985). *The Economic Institutions of Capitalism*. New York: Free Press.

WINTER, S. G. (1987). 'Knowledge and Competence as Strategic Assets', in D. J. Teece (ed.), *The Competitive Challenge*. Cambridge, MA: Ballinger, 159–84.

7

Corporate Strategy and Systems Integration Capabilities
Managing Networks in Complex Systems Industries

ANDREA PRENCIPE

SPRU, University of Sussex, UK; Faculty of Economics,
University G. D'Annunzio, Italy

7.1 Introduction

A growing body of theoretical and empirical literature argues that the relevance of external sources of component and knowledge for a firm's competitive advantage has increased in the last two decades. This is due to two closely interrelated sets of factors: increasing complexity of products in terms of number of components composing them and the expanding set of component knowledge bases deriving from the increasing specialization of scientific and technological disciplines. Hence, managing external relationships (through the development and maintenance of an extensive flow of information across the boundaries of the firm) becomes critical for developing and sustaining a competitive advantage.

The concept of network has emerged as a form of organization of economic activity as opposed to markets and hierarchies (Powell 1990). Empirical studies emphasized the relevance of network forms of organization as patterns of economic organization in an increasing number of industrial sectors (Lorenzoni and Lipparini 1999; Kogut 2000). As argued by Richardson (1972: 895) 'Firms are not islands but are linked together in patterns of co-operation and affiliation. Planned co-ordination does not stop at the boundaries of the individual firm but can be effected through co-operation between firms'.

The importance of network relationships and the management thereof has also been emphasized in studies of complex product systems industries (Hobday 1998). Complex product systems (CoPS) are capital-, engineering- and IT-intensive, business-to-business products. They are multi-technology, multi-component products, often produced in multi-firm alliances, as a one-off or in small batches for specific customers. Examples include global business networks, aircraft engines, civil airliners, power stations, off-shore oil platforms, mobile telephone systems, and large civil engineering projects. The multi-technology, multi-component nature of CoPS poses significant implications for firms' strategies in terms of critical 'make or buy' decisions (Brusoni, Prencipe, and Pavitt 2001).

The multi-technology, multi-component nature provides a vantage point for researchers looking at network capabilities since firms producing CoPS do not and cannot develop in-house all the technologies relevant for product design and manufacturing and increasingly adopt outsourcing strategies. Despite the interest of numerous scholars in networks, however, relatively little has been said and researched on the strategic features of the firms that lead CoPS networks and the typology of the capabilities that such firms develop to integrate and coordinate the work of external sources such as suppliers, research centres, and universities. By identifying the capabilities required by systems integrator firms to manage networks relationships, the chapter sets out to analyse one of the major aspects of corporate strategy in multi-technology, multi-component settings.[1]

The resource-based view of the firm conceives firms as collections of resources of various nature (Penrose 1959). The coordination of such resources paves the way for the development of unique organizational capabilities that in turn constitute the basis of a firm's competitive advantage (Grant 1996*a*). Within this view, each firm has its own distinctive history and capabilities that place a boundary (small or large) around their freedom to manoeuvre. The more recent theoretical conceptualization of the firm as a knowledge-based entity argued that the most important resource is knowledge (Grant 1996*b*). Firms are understood as integrators of information and knowledge, whose source could be both internal and external to the firms.

The aim of this chapter is to analyse the network phenomenon with a capability perspective and to provide a framework within which to analyse a firm's network capabilities in CoPS industries. Following the theoretical contribution by Grant (1996*a,b*) who understood firms as integrators of in-house and external knowledge, this chapter deepens and extends the work of Lorenzoni and Baden-Fuller (1995), and Brusoni, Prencipe, and Pavitt (2001) to introduce the concept of *systems integrator firm* as the organization that sets up the network and leads it from an organizational and technological viewpoint. The research question this chapter attempts to address is, what are the capabilities that lead firms are required to develop to manage networks? In particular, the chapter focuses on *systems integration* as the distinctive capability of the lead firms. Systems integration is understood as the primary coordination mechanism that firms use to compete through the introduction of incremental and radical innovations.

The chapter argues that systems integration comprises a set of different technological and organizational skills, ranging from component assembly through the understanding and integration of the technological disciplines underlying a product to project management. The chapter identifies two analytical categories of systems integration, namely *synchronic* and *diachronic*. Synchronic systems integration refers to the capabilities required by firms to sustain competitive advantage in the short term. Synchronic systems integration enables firms to access external resources in order to reduce transaction costs, development risks, time-to-market, quality defect rates, and stocks. More specifically, synchronic systems integration refers to the capabilities required to set the product concept design, decompose it in modules, coordinate the network of suppliers, and then recompose the product within a given architecture. It is argued that from a static point of view, products can be seen as 'interlocking pieces' and the main task of firms is to dovetail the work of suppliers to meet customer requirements.

Diachronic systems integration refers to the capabilities that firms require to compete in the long term, enabling them to keep pace with technological developments, enhancing and expanding the firms' capabilities for innovation and flexibility, and knowledge creation (through combination). It therefore contributes to the creation of the basis of the firm's competitive advantage. In particular, diachronic systems integration refers to the capabilities to envisage and move progressively towards different and alternative paths of product architectures (that is, new product families) to meet evolving customer requirements. From a dynamic point of view, products are better conceptualized as a continuous flow of innovations deriving from different, distant and, often intertwined, technological paths. The evolutionary dynamics of products, therefore, derives from the joint interaction of a variety of technological fields, so that the most important strategic problem facing companies resides in the need to interpret user needs and coordinate change across technological fields and organizational boundaries to meet them.

The chapter relies on empirical evidence from a 4-year field study in the aircraft engine industry (Prencipe 2004). The aircraft engine industry is an example of a complex product systems industry as identified by Hobday (1998). Although the chapter is focused on empirical evidence from a study on a CoPS industry, the chapter also makes reference to case studies in multi-technology, multi-component industrial settings where systems integration capabilities are increasingly relevant to manage network relationships (e.g. Lorenzoni and Lipparini 1999; Takeishi 2002; Sako, Chapter Twelve, this volume).

The chapter is organized as follows. Section 7.2 reviews literature on firm networks. Section 7.3 introduces the concept of systems integration firms and highlights their primary capabilities. Section 7.4 concludes the chapter.

7.2   Literature Review

Strategic Networks as Forms of Organization

The strategic management literature has for long highlighted the importance of external sources of components and knowledge for a firm's competitive advantage. Empirical research in the 1960s demonstrated the vital importance of the role of external sources of scientific, technical, and market information for successful innovating firms and, therefore, of networks. As Freeman noted 'networking for innovation is an old phenomenon and networks of suppliers are as old as industrialized economies' (1991: 510–11). External sources of R&D were intensively used by firms who had their own internal R&D. Such external sources were an important ancillary and complementary source of scientific and technical information rather than a substitute for indigenous innovative activities (Freeman 1991).

Empirical studies have underlined both quantitative changes and qualitative changes in firm's networking activities (Mowery 1988). As regards quantitative changes, an extremely rapid growth of inter-firm innovative networks was observed in several industrial sectors, and particularly in high-tech ones, for example, materials, biotechnology, and information technology (Hagedoorn and Schakenraad 1992). As regards qualitative changes, network relationships have shifted from a one-way to two-way flow of information so that suppliers began to be considered as knowledge generators (e.g. Japanese firms). Also, information technology has profoundly changed firm functions (e.g. design: CAD; manufacturing: robotics; marketing: computer-based inventory) as well as enabling electronic networks of communications within and between firms.[2]

According to Powell (1990), know-how development, demand for speed, and trust-based relationships are three critical components for the emergence of networks. 'Economizing is obviously a relevant concern in many instances. . . . But it alone is not a particularly robust story, it is but one of among a number of theoretically possible motives for action. . . . The reduction of uncertainty, fast access to information, reliability, and responsiveness are among paramount concerns that motivate the participants in exchange networks' (Powell 1990: 323). Jarillo (1988) defined strategic networks

as long-term, purposeful agreements among distinct but related for-profit organizations that allow firms in them to gain or sustain competitive advantage vis-à-vis their competitors outside the network . . . . It is a mode of co-ordination that is not based strictly on the price mechanism, or on 'hierarchical fiat' (Williamson 1975: 101), but on co-ordination through adaptation. (Johanson and Mattson 1988: 32)

Here, we refer to productive network that is an organized group of institutions that interact to develop and/or manufacture a new product or new process. In particular, we refer to the definition proposed by Imai and Baba (1989) according to which, a network is an organization having a core firm with both strong and weak ties with constituent members, that is, other firms, research centres, universities, etc. The cooperative relationships among members include joint ventures, licensing agreements, subcontracting, and R&D collaboration, which are not mutually exclusive. Such network relations can be both formal and informal and both direct and indirect.

Systems Integrator Firms

Kogut (2000: 408) argued, 'Networks also provide capabilities to coordinate behavior among firms.'[3] This happens when a capable supplier base emerges or, in other words, when 'markets learn' (Stigler 1951).[4] Following Kogut (2000), we argue that network forms of organization led by lead firms equipped with the capabilities to manage external relationships (being direct or indirect ties) enable firms to exploit variety (typically offered by the market) and at the same time use authority to deal with and implement changes (a typical feature of hierarchies). Networks can combine the advantages of both traditional mechanisms of coordination and therefore can promote variety as well as coordination (Kogut 2000). 'Cooperation ... can also engender capabilities in the relationship itself, such that the parties develop principles of coordination that improve their joint performance ... in this sense, the network is itself knowledge, not in the sense of providing access to distributed information and capabilities, but in representing a form of coordination guided by enduring principles of organization' (Kogut 2000: 407).

It is important to understand therefore the strategic features of firms that lead the network. Following Brusoni, Prencipe, and Pavitt (2001), Miller et al. (1995), and Prencipe (1997, 2004), we propose the concept of systems integrator firms. From a strategic viewpoint, systems integrator firms configure the network in terms of number, type (direct and indirect), and intensity of relationships. They also define the specific contractual terms (formal, such as joint-ventures, alliances or informal) to be adopted in the relationships. Burt (1992), in fact, argued that configuration of the relationships has a strong impact on the networks' efficiency and effectiveness. The concept of systems integrator firms finds its origin in the concept of hub firms as proposed by Jarillo (1988) and that of strategic centres as proposed by Lorenzoni and Baden-Fuller (1995).

Jarillo (1988) argued 'essential to this concept of strategic networks is that of the "hub firm", which is the firm that, in fact, sets up the network, and takes a proactive attitude in the care of it' (1988: 32). According to Jarillo (1988), hub firms through conscious actions lower transaction costs, hence the emergence of strategic networks. In a similar vein, Gomes-Casseres contended, 'co-operation ... is never automatic. The structure of the partnership must provide incentives for performance. Without some sort of collective governance, a group [that is, a network] risks becoming no more than a haphazard collection of alliances' (1994: 66). Lorenzoni and Baden-Fuller (1995) put forward the concept of the strategic centres that create a shared vision among the members that constitute the network, develop brand power, select partners through, for instance vendor rating systems, develop capabilities of partners, and develop trust among the partners. Strategic centres develop relational capabilities to manage such external relationships.

Research on networks argued that network benefits include two types (Ahuja 2000). First, resource sharing that enables firms to combine knowledge, skills, and physical assets. Second, access to information spillovers in the sense that network relationships act as information conduits through which news about discoveries and failed approaches are exchanged. Grant (1996*b*) contended that firm networks based on relational contracts are efficient and effective means to access knowledge in three cases, (*a*) when knowledge is explicit; (*b*) when speed in acquiring knowledge is essential to achieve competitive advantage; and (*c*) when there is no perfect overlap between the knowledge domain and product domain of firms. This latter case is particularly relevant for the purpose of this chapter. The lack of perfect overlap between knowledge domain and product domain has become a typical feature of an increasing number of industrial sectors, where due to the multi-technology, multi-component nature of products, firms cannot maintain in-house all the relevant knowledge bases (Brusoni, Prencipe, and Pavitt 2001).

To secure both resource and informational benefits, a strategic decision for systems integrator firms is to configure the networks in terms of direct and indirect ties. While direct ties allow both resource sharing and access to information spillovers, indirect ties enable access only to information spillovers. Resource sharing involves the combination of partners' capabilities that in turn requires a close and continuous interaction between partners; hence, firms should develop a larger number of direct ties. Literature on new product development underlined the advantages of early and close involvement of suppliers in the development process (Rothwell 1992). Car makers acting as systems integrators take advantage and combine specialized resources held by suppliers and develop a competitive lead by shortening lead-time (using off-line assembled components) and cutting development costs (exploiting more efficient specialized suppliers) (Clark and Fujimoto 1991). Similarly, in science-driven environments such as pharmaceuticals, research performance was found to be positively associated with the ability to span the boundaries of the firm (Henderson and Cockburn 1994).

Access to new and relevant information sources constitutes the informational benefits of networks (Powell 1990; Kogut 2000). 'One of the key advantages of network arrangements is their ability to disseminate and interpret new information. Networks are based on complex communication channels' (Powell 1990: 325). Indirect ties provide access to the information held by the partner's partners (Gulati and Garguilo 1999). They increase a firm's catchment area in terms of relevant sources of information (information-screening) and in terms of access to new sources (information-gathering) (Ahuja 2000). According to Burt (1992), the most efficient and effective network is the one that (*a*) maximizes disconnections (or structural holes) and (*b*) selects partners with many other partners. In other words, a high-performing network must develop many indirect ties.[5] Partners have access to a large number of different information flows. In fact, networks rich in structural holes enable access to mutually unconnected partners and to many distinct information flows. Partners become sensing devices that enable the lead firm to exploit the variety of such distinct information flows.

7.3 Systems Integration as a Coordination Mechanism

What are the capabilities that lead firms are required to develop and maintain to sustain their competitive advantage through networking? We zero in on these issues using the aircraft engine industry as an illustrative example (Prencipe 2004). This industrial setting is particularly interesting for studies on coordinative capabilities for innovating activities. Indeed, the multi-technology, multi-component nature of the aircraft engine product poses significant strategic implications for the firms in terms of make–buy decisions, given that technologies and components are too many (and increasingly so) to be mastered within the boundaries of one single organization, let alone changes in the underlying product's technologies (Brusoni, Prencipe, and Pavitt 2001). Another feature also makes such a setting interesting. Although there is a trend towards increasing modularization of the product architecture and ensuing outsourcing of production and design activities, it has been highlighted that markets have not emerged as the principal coordinating mechanism of innovative activities (Brusoni and Prencipe 2001).

We propose that firms develop systems integration capabilities to lead networks and therefore exploit and explore network advantages. While prices are the main coordinating mechanisms in markets and vertical integration mainly prevails in hierarchies, we argue that coordination in networked arrangements takes place mainly through systems integration. The concept of systems integration proposed here is related to those of tapered integration and quasi-integration discussed by Porter (1980) as an intermediate type of coordination mechanisms in between markets and hierarchies. Porter (1980) argued that tapered integration in R&D 'reduces the risk of locked-in relationships to the extent of the degree of taper. It also gives the firm some access to outside R&D activities ... tapered integration also gives the firm many of the informational benefits of integration' (p. 320). Quasi-integration is somewhere in-between long-term contracts and full ownership (through minority equity investment, cooperative R&D, exclusive dealing agreements). Systems integration is also akin to the concept of architectural or integrative capabilities put forward by Henderson and Cockburn (1994) and defined as 'the ability to access new knowledge from outside the boundaries of the organization and the ability to integrate knowledge flexibly across disciplinary and therapeutic class boundaries within the organization' (p. 66).

Systems Integration Capabilities: Knowledge Integration and Component Assembly

Systems integration firm and systems integration capabilities have long been used in the aerospace and defence literature to refer to the prime contractors of large engineering projects and their capabilities (Sapolsky 1972; Sapolsky, Chapter Two, this volume). We rely on this literature to delve into the nature of systems integration. Based on a definition put forward by the UK Technology Foresight Defense and Aerospace Panel, we aim to untangle the different skills underlying systems integration at the technological level. Systems integration was defined as 'The ability to understand and model the overall requirements for a major system and the interaction and performance of its many interrelated parts in an unambiguous way, accommodating the various subsystems technologies; then to design the complete systems together with its manufacturing processes and production facilities' (Office of Science and Technology 1990).

Using this definition of systems integration and with the help of two experts of the aircraft engine industry, we identified five skills underlying systems integration. Table 7.1 reports the ranking by competitive importance of these skills based on interviews with twenty company engineers. The emphasis is on the understanding of the underlying bodies of knowledge and ensuing systems behaviour, rather than on the activities of design and assembly. In fact, systems integration as the ability to assemble component interfaces ranks the lowest, just below the ability to design most key components of the engine. Likewise, the ability to design most components (including key ones) is not considered a critical skill. The skills that rank

TABLE 7.1 *Systems integration: underlying skills*

Understanding of underlying technological disciplines and therefore ability to integrate them

Technological understanding of the entire system behaviour in terms of relevant parameters

Ability to design the entire system

Ability to design most key components of the system

Ability to assemble components interface

Source: Author's elaboration on interview data.

highest are those related to (*a*) the understanding of technological disciplines underlying the engine system and (*b*) the understanding of the engine system behaviour in terms of its relevant parameter. The ability to design the entire engine system receives an average ranking.

These results point to an interesting conclusion. Systems integration is primarily interpreted as the ability to understand and integrate the different scientific and technological disciplines underlying the aircraft engine. Similarly, understanding the engine behaviour is considered paramount for systems integration. Therefore, the integration of the engine product is primarily seen as the integration of technological knowledge rather than the mere assembly of components.

Based on this, it can be argued that integration of technological knowledge and assembly of components are two distinct skills. Research in multi-technology industrial settings highlighted that the product and its underlying technological knowledge may follow different yet related dynamics (Granstrand, Patel, and Pavitt 1997; Brusoni and Prencipe 2001). In networked arrangements, in fact, specialized suppliers design, develop, and manufacture components, which are then integrated by systems integrators. To effectively integrate externally developed and manufactured components, systems integrators develop and maintain systems integration capabilities to 'compose' what they have 'decomposed' (Prencipe 1997).

The distinction between division of labour and division of knowledge from a strategic viewpoint was highlighted by Prencipe (2000) in his study of the development of control systems for aircraft engines. He argued that the rate of change of components' underlying technologies heavily influenced interorganizational patterns of division of knowledge and labour. When control systems were based on hydromechanical technologies, components were relatively standardized and the technology was relatively stable (it quickly reached a performance ceiling) so that engine manufacturers delegated their design and development to external suppliers and a perfect overlap between knowledge and labour partitioning was in place. The advent of digital electronics radically changed the pattern of interorganizational division of labour. Although components based on the new technology became modularized, aircraft engine manufacturers started to develop and maintain capabilities in digital electronics because of the fast-moving nature of such technology.

The concept of systems integration capabilities proposed here, therefore, extends the seminal distinction put forward by Henderson and Clark (1990) between architectural and component knowledge. In fact, the coordination and integration of knowledge advances (in new scientific and technological disciplines) requires a fine and deep level of knowledge that goes well beyond the architectural level (Prencipe 2000).

Based on empirical studies on the packaging machine industry and the car industry, Takeishi (2002) and Lorenzoni and Lipparini (1999) respectively, reached similar conclusions in relation to systems integration capabilities. Takeishi (2002) distinguished between division of knowledge (knowledge-partitioning) and division of operational tasks (task-partitioning).[6] Drawing on an empirical study on carmakers' management of suppliers' involvement in product development in Japan, he showed that while the actual tasks of design and manufacturing could be outsourced, carmakers retain relevant knowledge to obtain better component design quality. His results illustrated that the effective pattern of knowledge-partitioning differed from the pattern of task-partitioning. The discriminator of the non-perfect overlapping between knowledge- and task-partitioning according to Takeishi was technological newness. In the case of the development of new components, the carmakers that performed better were those that developed and maintained both architectural and component knowledge, or, using our words, systems integration capabilities. In the case of the development of standard components, a perfect overlap between knowledge- and task-partitioning was in place.[7]

The longitudinal study of the Italian packaging machine industry by Lorenzoni and Lipparini (1999) is particularly telling in relation to the emergence of the systems integrator firms. The packaging industry has been characterized by a continuous trend of outsourcing of tasks of different nature (design, manufacturing, and assembly) to first- and second-tier suppliers. As Lorenzoni and Lipparini (1999: 328) underlined, the boundaries of the leading firms of such network organizations have shrunk over time due to the 'progressive disintegration of the manufacturing process'. The three case studies analysed by Lorenzoni and Lipparini, in fact, showed that all the lead firms under scrutiny increased their reliance on external suppliers. Notwithstanding this increasing reliance on external resources, Lorenzoni and Lipparini found that 'rather than using external ties as a substitute for capabilities which a firm has not yet developed, firms use collaborations to expand and improve their core competencies' (1999: 334). The complementarities of capabilities across firms pointed out that no strict division of knowledge amongst firms themselves occurred and that in network-like forms of industrial organization the role of lead firms that act as integrators of external specialized sources of components and knowledge for innovations, without being vertically integrated, is paramount.

To sum up, systems integrator firms outsource detailed design and manufacturing to specialized suppliers while developing and maintaining in-house systems integration capabilities to coordinate the work of suppliers. Their in-house knowledge bases stretch beyond their production activities: 'firms know more than they need for what they make' (Brusoni, Prencipe, and Pavitt 2001: 620). Systems integrators' knowledge bases are augmented through the direct and indirect networks relationships. Direct ties are means whereby systems integrators combine their resources with their partners and tap in to their technology bases. Indirect ties enable systems integrators to benefit from information spillovers of partners' partners. Systems integration capabilities are required for short-term competitive advantage where systems integrators orchestrate the network of suppliers to exploit an existing set of network relationships (within an existing product architecture). Systems integration capabilities are also required for long-term competitive advantage when systems integrators coordinate and integrate knowledge advances and innovative developments from outside sources and therefore explore new configurations of networks relationships to introduce innovative solutions to meet customer demand. Systems integrator firms therefore pursue both exploitation and exploration activities. This is discussed in the next section.

The Two Dimensions of Systems Integration: Synchronic versus Diachronic

The analytical framework proposed here revolves around two key dimensions of systems integration, namely *synchronic* and *diachronic*. *Synchronic* systems integration refers to the range of in-house capabilities of firms required to set the product concept design, decompose it, orchestrate the work of several companies, and then recompose the product within an existing architecture. Strictly speaking, this dimension relates to the firms' capabilities within a new product development programme. *Diachronic* systems integration refers to firm capabilities to introduce incremental (e.g. a new product family) and radical innovations at the architectural level to meet changing customer and regulatory requirements. In this respect, diachronic systems integration refers to the capabilities to coordinate changes across different technological fields and organizational boundaries. Although analytically distinct, the *synchronic* and *diachronic* dimensions of systems integration clearly overlap in practice. For ease of exposition, the following two sections discuss them separately.

The Synchronic Dimension.   The interpretation of systems integration as *synchronic* capability finds its historical antecedent in the study of the Polaris System Development carried out by Sapolsky (1972). The title of Chapter 5 of Sapolsky's book is *The Synchronization of Progress in Several Technologies.* Sapolsky argued that the primary objective of the Polaris project was the construction of a submarine system rather than advancement of its underlying technologies. In his words, 'The deployment of the Polaris submarines required the *synchronized development of a dozen different technologies....* To build a system that involved interdependent progress in a dozen technologies was, however, unprecedented' (p. 137, emphasis added). He then went on to explain

[T]he product of the development, the early deployment of the FBM [Fleet Ballistic Missile] submarine, was a greater and more uncertain achievement than the sum of its parts would lead one to believe. It was the synergistic effort or the tying together of progress in diverse technologies on a compressed schedule that was both the challenge and the breakthrough in the FBM Program and not the progress in any of its component elements. (p. 138)

Drawing on Sapolsky's work, *synchronic* systems integration refers to the technological capabilities required to coordinate the development of a new product within a predefined time period and financial budget. *Synchronic* systems integration also refers to the capabilities to exploit the potential of existing product architecture to develop new product versions to cater for different customer requirements. Within a product family, firms introduce incremental and radical technological innovations at the component level to adapt and improve the performance of the existing architecture.

From a technological viewpoint, *synchronic* systems integration relates to firms' capabilities to set the concept design, decompose it into subsystems and components, and delegate design and manufacturing tasks to suppliers. Within a new product development programme, the product decomposition process requires the definition of the interfaces between components and subsystems. This definition process is also called *systems engineering* (Fine and Whitney 1996). 'Systems engineering is a product realization process best exemplified in the aerospace industry, where its top-down process is called requirements flow-down. The process conceives the product as a series of levels, with lower levels defined in more detail or containing subsidiary components, subsystems, or single parts' (p. 11). Systems engineering is a capability *per se* since it involves the identification of design compromise among subsystems, analysis of subsystems, and supervision of system testing (Sapolsky 1972).[8] As found in the aircraft engine industry, after decomposing the product, engine manufacturers *synchronize* their work with that of suppliers and customers in order to assure the overall consistency of the system performance and to comply with the rules of the certification authorities. *Synchronic* systems integration should be seen as a two-way process. As explained by one of the company engineers interviewed 'Systems integration is a *top-down process* where engine makers model the engine, define the total systems requirements, and break it down into components. Systems integration is also a *bottom-up process* where engine makers must be able to recompose what they have decomposed. Engine makers must be competent in both legs'. Within a new engine development programme, engine manufacturers rely on state of the art component technologies and a defined engine architecture. As explained elsewhere, engine manufacturers make extensive use of technology acquisition and demonstrator programmes in order to acquire and prove new technologies to minimize risks, and cost and time overrun of development programmes (Prencipe 2003).

Within a product family, *synchronic* systems integration refers to the capabilities to refine, adapt, and optimize ('stretch') existing architectures through the development of 'derivative' engines in order to cater for different thrust requirements. The capability of manufacturers to 'stretch' architectures to develop 'derivative' product is a function of the degree of modularity of the architecture itself. Modularity enables manufacturers to use common cores to target different niche markets. It also allows manufacturers to considerably improve the performance of existing architectures through the introduction of incremental and radical technological innovations at the component level. The introduction of new technologies into existing product architectures comes under the name of 'retrofitting'.

From an organizational viewpoint, synchronic systems integration refers to the capabilities required to manage interorganizational communication processes, to promote a shared vision amongst partners, and create a network identity. Dyer and Nobeoka (2000) provided an interesting and detailed study on the network-level processes developed by Toyota to manage a production network. The aim of these processes is to create a network identity, 'creating an "identity" for a collective (e.g. firm, network) means that the individual members felt a shared sense of purpose with the collective' (p. 352), whereby interorganizational communication is improved and more importantly, tacit and explicit rules of coordination are established (Kogut and Zander 1996). These processes include a supplier association to promote mutual friendship and the exchange of technical information; Toyota's operations management consulting division for knowledge acquisition, storage, and diffusion within the network; voluntary small group learning teams; an inter-firm job-rotation programme. It should be noted that Toyota invested in these processes to develop such a network. This is consistent with Jarillo (1988) who argued that in a network form of organization, trust-building mechanisms should be in place to render such an organization efficient. Jarillo in particular, contended that the principal (that is, Toyota in this case) should take on some of the risk of the relationship, for instance a part of the cost of a specific asset.

The Diachronic Dimension.   Diachronic systems integration identifies a continuum of technological capabilities ranging from the introduction of incremental architectural innovations to the introduction of fundamentally new product architectures. In the case of the aircraft engine industry, an incremental architectural innovation is best exemplified by the introduction of a new engine family that meets unprecedented thrust requirements. For instance, the introduction of the Trent engine to meet the thrust requirements of the Boeing 777 represented a step change for the technological capabilities of Rolls-Royce. The Trent develops twice as much power as the previous RB211 engine.

Diachronic systems integration relates also to more fundamental changes. Drawing again from the aircraft engine industry study, the best example is probably the Rolls-Royce three-shaft engine configuration that in the early 1970s represented a major step change for the company's technological capabilities. Other examples of radically new engine configurations are under study by engine manufacturers, such as the geared-fan engine (probably the future architecture for Pratt & Whitney new engine families), the aft-fan and prop-fan engines, and the all-electric engine (under study by Rolls-Royce). In this respect, diachronic systems integration is better understood as a risk-bearing attitude to search and explore alternative paths of product configurations. The introduction of radically new configurations requires major coordination efforts between engine manufacturers, airframers, airlines, and certification authorities.

In this respect, diachronic systems integration refers to the capability to coordinate the development of new and emerging bodies of technological knowledge. These capabilities must be developed for the coordination of change across (*a*) different bodies of technological knowledge, since different bodies of technological knowledge relevant to production may be characterized by uneven rates of advance; and (*b*) different organizational boundaries, firms cannot master in-house all the relevant scientific and technological fields. The management of the relationships with and coordination of external sources of technologies, such as universities, research laboratories, and suppliers, becomes therefore a central task for multi-technology firms.[9]

7.4 Conclusions

The discussion carried out in this chapter has extended the research on network organizational forms focusing on the capabilities required by lead firms to lead and coordinate networks. Based on empirical evidence in the aircraft engine industry as an example of multi-technology, multi-component settings, this chapter has deepened and discussed the concept of systems integration as a coordination mechanism of economic activities in-between markets and hierarchies. Firms to compete successfully (should) develop and maintain systems integration capabilities in order to manage the integration of new components and new technological knowledge developed either in-house or externally. Change, and in particular technological change, can be identified, managed, and integrated via systems integration and does not necessarily require firms to be vertically integrated as extant literature on make-buy decisions argued. Specifically, the chapter introduced two analytical categories of systems integration, synchronic and diachronic. Synchronic systems integration refers to the capabilities required to compete in the short run and specifically to set the product concept design, decompose it in modules, coordinate the network of suppliers, and then recompose the product within a given product architecture. Therefore, synchronic systems integration refers to the exploitation of the potential of a given product architecture to meet customer demands. Diachronic systems integration refers to the capabilities required to compete in the long run and specifically to envisage and move progressively towards different and alternative paths of product architectures to meet evolving customer requirements through the coordination of change across technological fields and organizational boundaries. Diachronic systems integration relates to the search for and experimentation of new product architectures, and therefore, it refers to the exploration of different and alternative paths of product configurations.

March (1991) argued that firms specialize either in exploitative or explorative activities. The systems integration perspective taken in this chapter has deepened this argument to contend that systems integrator firms are required to pursue both types of activities simultaneously. Firms pursue exploitative activities to extract the most out of the technological trajectory underlying existing product architectures, also through the introduction of innovative technologies that can be added on. Within this, they entertain subcontracting relationships with suppliers to cut down on cost and improve quality to reduce time to market. Systems integrators also carry out explorative activities to envisage new paths of product architectures.

The chapter has also highlighted a number of issues that would require more research attention. The explorative dimension of systems integration points to a systems integration perspective on university–industry relationships focusing on the organization and management of such relationships. Also, the coordinating and incentive mechanisms put in place by firms and national (and supranational) governments to align research efforts constitute a key issue for future research.

The chapter also points to a reframing to understand the impact of modularity on organization forms and firms' capabilities. It is safe to say that modularity is a powerful design strategy as far as products are concerned. As regards applications of the principles of modularity to organizational design and knowledge management, then some heavy assumptions (or discounts) of the definition of modularity must be made. Whether product architecture shapes organization architecture and its underlying knowledge basis as argued by modularity advocates, is hard to say if we take into account that changes may occur and entail heavy reconfiguration of the product and more importantly the organization architecture and its knowledge basis.

Modularity, however, does have its bearing across different levels of analysis in some special cases. As argued by Brusoni, Prencipe, and Pavitt (2001) in their contingent explanation of the appropriate organizational arrangements to manage change, modularity is a pervasive design strategy in some particular industries, such as the computer industry. Modular networks of production are the appropriate organizational arrangements in situations where products are characterized by even rates of change among component technologies and predictable interdependencies at the product level. Such modular networks are coordinated via arm's-length market relationships as happens, for instance, in the personal computers (PCs) industry (Langlois and Robertson 1992; Baldwin and Clark 1997). A modular architecture, built around standardized interfaces, would enable a process of progressive specialization of R&D, production, and marketing activities in such a way that each component (e.g. disk drive, microprocessor, operating system, application software) would define the boundary of a firm whose relationships with the others would be mediated via decentralized market transactions.

Besides modular organizational forms, Brusoni, Prencipe, and Pavitt (2001) also discussed vertically integrated and network forms. These organizational forms are characterized by other distinct inter-firm coordination mechanisms, vertical integration and systems integration, respectively. Products characterized by both component technologies changing at uneven rates and by unpredictable interdependencies across components require large, integrated firms to maintain in-house both the knowledge and the activities involved in the design and production of their final products and component units: coordination is achieved via vertical integration. This situation fits the case of the telecommunication equipment industry (Davies 1997). Network organizations are appropriate structures when multi-technology products are characterized either by uneven rates of advance in underlying technologies and predictable product interdependencies (Chesbrough and Kusunoki 2001), or by even rates of advance in underlying technologies and unpredictable product interdependencies (Sako, Chapter Twelve, this volume). The coordination mechanism in the network organization is systems integration.

Acknowledgements

I would like to thank Mike Hobday and Fred Tell for comments on earlier drafts of this chapter. Normal disclaimers apply.

Notes

1. Davies (Chapter Sixteen, this volume) analysed both market positioning and financial issues of systems integrator firms.
2. Though Freeman noted 'networking of various kinds was a normal feature of the industrial and regional landscapes long before the advent of modern information technology' (1991: 510–11).
3. Kogut (2000) argued that the structure of the network may depend on the specific characteristics of the industry's underlying technologies or on specific institutional factors at work in a particular context (e.g. Italian industrial districts). Accordingly, science-driven industries lend themselves better to networking (between firms and research centres) as opposed to mass-production technologies.
4. The concept of capable supplier is also explored by Steinmueller (Chapter Eight, this volume).

5. 'Structural holes are gaps in information flows between alters linked to the same ego but not linked to each other' (Ahuja 2000: 431).
6. This resulted in the distinction proposed by Fine and Whitney (1996) between dependency for capacity and dependency for knowledge. In the case of dependency for capacity, the firm can make the item, but chooses to extend its capacity by means of a supplier. In the case of dependency for knowledge, the firm does not have the skill to make the item, and therefore it does not understand what it is buying or how to integrate it. Fine and Whitney emphasized that firms dependent for capacity but not for knowledge could live with outsourcing without substantial risks.
7. Liker et al. (1996) in their comparison of Japanese and US supplier involvement in car component design found that Japanese carmakers are less dependent on suppliers for product development knowledge than US ones. Their study revealed that US carmakers are not able to easily replicate a much higher percentage (63 versus 39.1%) of development effort than their Japanese counterparts.
8. Sapolsky (1972: 86) distinguished between systems engineering ('the identification of explicit tradeoffs between component values of a system'), general systems engineering ('the integration of alternative combination of system values into coherent system design proposals'), and technical direction ('choice among alternative system design proposals in terms of some objective or subjective preference function').
9. Besides coordination, systems integration can also be analysed in terms of negotiation and suppliers base memory (Steinmueller, Chapter Eight, this volume).

References

AHUJA, G. (2000). 'Collaboration Networks, Structural Holes, and Innovation: A Longitudinal Study', *Administrative Science Quarterly*, 45: 425–55.

BALDWIN, C. Y. and CLARK, K. B. (1997). 'Managing in an Age of Modularity', *Harvard Business Review*, September–October: 84–93.

BELL, M. and PAVITT, K. (1993). 'Technological Accumulation and Industrial Growth: Contrasts Between Developed and Developing Countries', *Industrial and Corporate Change*, 2/2: 157–209.

BRUSONI, S. and PRENCIPE, A. (2001). 'Unpacking the Black Box of Modularity: Technologies, Products, Organizations', *Industrial and Corporate Change*, 10: 179–205.

—— ——, and PAVITT, K. (2001). 'Knowledge Specialization, Organizational Coupling and the Boundaries of the Firm: Why Do Firms Know More Than They Make?', *Administrative Science Quarterly*, 46: 597–621.

BURT, R. S. (1992). *Structural Holes: The Social Structure of Competition*. Cambridge, MA: Harvard University Press.

CHESBROUGH, H. and KUSUNOKI, K. (2001). 'The Modularity Trap: Innovation, Technology Phase-shifts, and the Resulting Limits of Virtual Organizations', in I. Nonaka and D. Teece (eds.), *Managing Industrial Knowledge: Creation, Transfer and Utilization*. Thousand Oaks, CA: Sage Publications, 202–30.

CLARK, K. and FUJIMOTO, T. (1991). *Product Development Performance*. Boston, MA: Harvard Business School Press.

DAVIES, A. (1997). 'The Life Cycle of a Complex Product System', *International Journal of Innovation Management*, 1/3: 229–56.

DYER, J. H. and NOBEOKA, K. (2000). 'Creating and Managing a High-performance Knowledge-sharing Network: The Toyota Case', *Strategic Management Journal*, 21: 345–67.

FINE, C. and WHITNEY, D. E. (1996). 'Is the Make–Buy Decision Process a Core Competence?' (Unpublished manuscript). Boston, MA: MIT.

FREEMAN, C. (1991). 'Networks of Innovators: A Synthesis of Research Issues', *Research Policy*, 20/5: 499–514.

GOMES-CASSERES, B. (1994). 'Group versus Group: How Alliance Networks Compete', *Harvard Business Review*, 72: 62–74.

GRANSTRAND, O., PATEL, P., and PAVITT, K. (1997). 'Multitechnology Corporations: Why they have "Distributed" rather than "Distinctive Core" Capabilities', *California Management Review*, 39/4: 8–25.

GRANT, R. (1996a). 'Toward a Knowledge-based Theory of the Firm', *Strategic Management Journal*, 17: 109–22.

—— (1996b). 'Prospering in Dynamically–competitive Environments: Organizational Capability as Knowledge Integration', *Organization Science*, 7/4: 375–87.

GULATI, R. and GARGUILO, M. (1999). 'Where do Networks Come From?', *American Journal of Sociology*, 104: 1439–93.

HAGEDOORN, J. and SCHAKENRAAD, J. (1992). 'Leading Companies and Networks of Strategic Alliances in Information Technologies', *Research Policy*, 21: 163–90.

HENDERSON, R. M. and CLARK, K. B. (1990). 'Architectural Innovation: The Reconfiguration of Existing Product Technologies and the Failure of Established Firms', *Administrative Science Quarterly*, 35: 9–30.

—— and COCKBURN, I. (1994). 'Measuring Competences? Exploring Firm Effects in Pharmaceutical Research', *Strategic Management Journal*, 15: 63–84.

HOBDAY, M. (1998). 'Product Complexity, Innovation, and Industrial Organisation', *Research Policy*, 26: 689–710.

IMAI, K. and BABA, Y. (1989). 'Systemic Innovation and Cross-border Networks: Transcending Markets and Hierarchies to Create New Techno-economics System', paper presented at the OECD Conference on Science and Technology and Economic Growth, Paris, June.

JARILLO, J. C. (1988). 'On Strategic Networks', *Strategic Management Journal*, 9: 31–41.

JOHANSON, J. and MATTSON, L.-G. (1988). 'Internationalization in Industrial Systems—a Network Approach', in P. J. Buckley and P. N. Ghauri (eds.), *The Internationalization of the Firm: A Reader*. London: Academic Press, 303–21.

KOGUT, B. (2000). 'The Network as Knowledge: Generative Rules and the Emergence of Structure', *Strategic Management Journal*, 21: 405–25.

—— and ZANDER, U. (1996). 'What do Firm's Do? Coordination, Identity, and Learning', *Organization Science*, 7: 502–14.

LANGLOIS, R. N. and ROBERTSON, P. L. (1992). 'Networks and Innovation in a Modular System: Lessons from the Microcomputer and Stereo Component Industries', *Research Policy*, 21: 297–313.

LIKER, J. K., KAMATH, R. R., NAZLI WASTI, S., and NAGAMACHI, M. (1996). 'Supplier Involvement in Automotive Component Design: Are there Really Large US Japanese Differences?', *Research Policy*, 25: 59–89.

LORENZONI, G. and BADEN-FULLER, C. (1995). 'Creating a Strategic Center to Manage a Web of Partners', *California Management Review*, 37/3: 146–63.

—— and LIPPARINI, A. (1999). 'The Leveraging of Inter-firm Relationships as a Distinctive Organisational Capability: A Longitudinal Study', *Strategic Management Journal*, 20: 317–38.

MARCH, J. G. (1991). 'Exploration and Exploitation in Organisational Learning', *Organization Science*, 2/1: 71–87.

MILLER, R., HOBDAY, M., LEROUX-DEMERS, T., and OLLEROS, X. (1995). 'Innovation in Complex Product Systems Industries: The Case of Flight Simulation', *Industrial and Corporate Change*, 4/2: 363–400.

MOWERY, D. C. (ed.) (1988). *International Collaborative Ventures in US Manufacturing*. Cambridge, MA: Ballinger.

OFFICE OF SCIENCE AND TECHNOLOGY (1990). *Technology Foresight Progress through Partnership: Defence and Aerospace*. London: Office of Science and Technology.

PENROSE, E. (1959). *The Theory of the Growth of the Firm*. London: Basil Blackwell.

PORTER, M. E. (1980). *Competitive Strategy: Techniques for Analyzing Industries and Competitors*. New York: The Free Press.

POWELL, W. W. (1990). 'Neither Markets Nor Hierarchies: Networks Forms of Organizations', *Research in Organizational Behavior*. JAI Press, 12: 295–336.

PRENCIPE, A. (1997). 'Technological Capabilities and Product Evolutionary Dynamics: A Case Study from the Aero-engine Industry', *Research Policy*, 25: 1261–76.

—— (2000). 'Breadth and Depth of Technological Capabilities in Complex Product Systems: The Case of the Aircraft Engine Control System', *Research Policy*, 29: 895–911.

—— (2004). *Strategy, Systems, and Scope: Managing Systems Integration in Complex Products*. London: Sage (forthcoming).

RICHARDSON, G. (1972). 'The Organisation of Industry', *Economic Journal*, 82: 883–96.

ROTHWELL, R. (1992). 'Successful Industrial Innovation: Critical Factors for the 1990s', *R & D Management*, 22/3: 221–39.

SAPOLSKY, H. M. (1972). *The Polaris System Development: Bureaucratic and Programmatic Success in Government*. Cambridge, MA: Harvard University Press.

STIGLER, G. J. (1951). 'The Division of Labor is Limited by the Extent of the Market', *Journal of Political Economy*, 59: 185–93.

TAKEISHI, A. (2002). 'Knowledge Partitioning in the Inter-firm Division of Labor: The Case of Automotive Product Development', *Organization Science*, 13/3: 321–38.

TEECE, D. J. and PISANO, G. P. (1994). 'The Dynamic Capabilities of Firms: An Introduction', *Industrial and Corporate Change*, 3: 537–56.

WILLIAMSON, O. (1975). *Markets and Hierarchies: Analysis and Antitrust Implications*. New York: The Free Press.

8

The Role of Technical Standards in Coordinating the Division of Labour in Complex System Industries

W. Edward Steinmueller

SPRU—Science and Technology Policy Research, University of Sussex, Brighton, UK

8.1 Introduction

The idea of complex products and systems has featured in a number of recent studies (Miller et al. 1995; Rycroft and Cash 1999; Hobday, Rush, and Tidd 2000). A central aim of these studies has been to identify the specific managerial, technological, and organizational issues that arise when engineering-intensive design processes are required to create systemic products or other complex artefacts such as civil engineering projects or sophisticated producer goods. Some of these studies use a specific term of art, complex products and systems (CoPS), to refer to a subset of these design-intensive activities that involve relatively small production 'runs' of unique design.

The organizational arrangements necessary for the creation of CoPS are a focus of recent research. It is recognized, for example, that the division of labour involved in CoPS often involves multiple technologies and competences that must be effectively integrated (Prencipe, Chapter Seven this volume). This division of labour often spans organizational boundaries and, in the words of one recent study, will 'depend heavily on continuously adaptive organizational networks that know how to do more than any individual can understand in detail' (Rycroft and Cash 1999: 3), wording that mirrors, at an organizational level, Polanyi's (1962: 87–95) discussion of the tacit components of personal knowledge. Issues of how knowledge is accumulated, modified, and applied in these organizational networks have become central features of the research agenda for understanding innovation.

This chapter exists because of Andrea Prencipe's energy and enthusiasm for organizing research on systems integration, a vitally important area which demonstrates the value and vitality of interdisciplinary research.

Correspondingly, for authors in this literature (e.g. Prencipe and Paoli 1999; Davies and Brady 2000; Hobday, Rush, and Tidd 2000), the arrangements for design and production of a given artefact are a more telling indication of whether it should be regarded as a CoPS than a physical examination of the number of components incorporated in the artefact. In effect, the issue is not the definition of the physical complexity of the product. Instead, it is the difficulty of 'integrating' the components of the system, which, in turn, is shaped by what knowledge is required for integration and how this knowledge is acquired, retained, and applied to the integration process.

This chapter considers one type of knowledge underlying the systems integration process, the problem of creating technical interface standards, particularly in areas of technology where digital electronics are involved. Technical interface standards are the collection of explicit rules that permit components and subsystems to be assembled in larger systems and hence are also called technical compatibility standards (Greenstein and David 1990). This usage of the term 'standards' is distinct from, but often related to, two other uses of the word 'standards'. 'Reference standards' are the explicit rules that are used to characterize the physical properties of raw materials or artefacts and often play a background or foundational role in defining the building blocks for compatibility standards (e.g. the definition of a unit of electrical resistance, the ohm, involves reference standards). 'Quality standards' are explicit rules that further elaborate and combine reference standards to address health, safety, or other desired attributes of the materials and artefacts used in industrial processes or the resulting manufactured outputs. Although reference and quality standards accompany the processes of defining and using compatibility standards that are discussed in this chapter, their specific role is not examined.

Technical compatibility standards are determined through various public and private processes of consultation and 'published' by standards organizations (referred to as *de jure* standards), through processes of market leadership (de facto standards), and through processes of design and problem-solving within organizations, or between organizations that lead to 'privately held' technical compatibility standards. This last class of standards has not previously been analysed within the standardization literature and will be referred to in this chapter as 'local standards'. The standardization literature (e.g. Farrell and Saloner 1988; Greenstein and David 1990; Hawkins, Mansell, and Skea 1995), has, to date, included considerations of the technical deliberation processes necessary to reach 'arm's-length' agreement in standards setting processes involving organizations (private and public) and the economic issues arising from the production of the quasi-public or public good represented by standards. Quasi-public goods, those available to members of a 'consortium' or similar closed group, are characteristic of various 'proprietary' standards. These 'proprietary' standards include those that are unpublicized and used internally as a means of coordinating and dividing labour among different organizations, defined as 'local' standards in this chapter. At the most basic level of economic analysis, technical compatibility standards provide a means of reusing and hence economizing on engineering design costs.

Before outlining the main arguments of this chapter, it is useful to briefly indicate the relevance of technical compatibility standards to the issues associated with CoPS. Technical compatibility standards are often discussed in relation to mass-production and the large-scale reuse of standards engineering efforts. CoPS, by contrast, are often identified as not involving mass-produced products and systems. What relevance do standards have for CoPS?

In the case of both CoPS and 'complex' mass-produced products, the level of design costs is relatively high. The distinction between them arises from the level of output of similar or identical artefacts expected for the two types of products. In the case of 'complex' mass-produced products, a large scale of output provides a means of amortizing design costs and the principal economic issue is whether market demand will support high levels of output. For mass-produced artefacts, failure to achieve market objectives will result in the abandonment of the product design and serious damage to the originating company. Because of competition between such products, the market for mass-produced products is likely to involve the emergence of a single 'dominant design' (Utterback 1996), which is commercially successful, that is, it amortizes design costs and yields at least a normal rate of return on invested capital. When a dominant design involves a collection of components and subsystems, it is likely that technical compatibility standards will be developed to provide a means of coordinating vertical supplier chains. In this context, technical compatibility standards are closely linked to a massive scale of output and to convergence on a dominant design.

In the case of CoPS, the size of the product market is much smaller and the range of possible substitutes much narrower. This may be the consequence either of market or technological conditions. Market conditions for some types of CoPS, for example, civil engineering projects, naturally limit the quantity output; the Thames, Schuylkill, or other rivers of 100–200 miles in length only require a limited number of bridges and these are likely to be built (and rebuilt) infrequently. For a variety of producer goods, it is technological conditions that influence the total output; maintaining a competitive position requires introducing technological improvements as they become available. Moreover, complex goods are subject to continuous problem-solving and debugging activities, some of which compel major 'model' changes curtailing the 'production run' of previous designs. In effect, dominant designs for CoPS may fail to emerge because technological change continually 'breaks open' incumbent designs.

Unlike mass-produced products, CoPS artefacts are likely to be sold on the basis of pre-negotiated prices with potential buyers or on the basis of continuing relationships with particular customers. Like mass-produced products, however, CoPS may incur engineering costs that require a higher level of market success than can be assured from 'pre-order' processes. In addition, many of the most sophisticated CoPS products, including civil engineering projects, are based upon bidding procedures that involve 'all or nothing' contests between rival companies.

To summarize, the engineering costs of both mass-produced products and CoPS are relatively high. In the case of mass-produced products, a principal objective is to amortize these costs by producing large quantities without incurring further design costs, a process that often leads to the emergence of a dominant design and a series of standards associated with that design that facilitate the coordination of supplier networks and vertical chains of supply. In the case of CoPS, high design costs are persistent, either because of a small potential market for a particular model or because models are frequently altered to embody technological improvements. Regardless of whether the product is mass-produced or is a CoPS, companies have an incentive to reduce the costs of design in order to enhance their competitiveness and profits. These observations serve to emphasize the point made by (Hobday, Rush, and Tidd 2000) that distinctions between mass-produced products and CoPS should not be overstated. Another way of saying this is that the production systems for these two types of artefacts are likely to co-evolve through processes of convergence and cross-fertilization. A key feature of this co-evolution lies in how the process of systems integration is managed.

It is in these processes of co-evolution and cross-fertilization related to systems integration that an examination of 'standards' is particularly useful. The integration of control systems into machinery is as old as the industrial revolution, involving examples such as the use of governors to control the power output of the steam engine. In the language of electronic systems, the steam engine governor is integrated with the steam engine through an interoperable interface, the governor controlling the steam engine, while the output of the steam engine determines the operation of the governor. The nature of the linkage between the two subsystems in this case is mechanical. A key feature of the development of the electronics industry is the analysis of such mechanical interfaces, their 'decoupling' through the introduction of electronic rather than mechanical, hydraulic, or electromechanical linkages. As the introduction of electricity allowed the substantial redesign of factories by allowing electrical motors to substitute for power shafts from a central power drive (DuBoff 1979; Devine 1983; David 1991), the 'decoupling' of mechanical control linkages permits their replacement by digital control pathways using electronics. When considering these elements of technological history, a fundamental point about systems integration emerges. Systems integration possibilities are interdependent, they 'co-evolve' with the means for decoupling linkages that previously were necessary for systems integration.

Some of the concepts and terminology employed to describe compatibility 'integration' drawn from electronics and telecommunication technology are illustrative of these processes of co-evolution and cross-fertilization. In electrical and electronic systems, technical compatibility standards provide a means for creating 'interconnectable' or 'interoperable systems'. Two systems are interconnectable when the outputs of one can be utilized as the input of the other. A simple technical compatibility standard is needed for the design of a voltage converter that transforms alternating to direct current and reduces the voltage to an appropriate value. Such converters are 'connectable' to a wide variety of electrical appliances that require a dc power source.[1] Systems are interoperable when they mutually control each other's operations. For example, a personal computer modem controls and is controlled by the personal computer to which it is attached; the same modem is capable of controlling the modem on the other end of the telephone connection. In both cases, the aim is to synchronize the transmission and receipt of data between devices that are capable of operating at different rates and that must 'adapt' to line conditions and other factors affecting the attainable rate of data transfer.[2]

Technical compatibility standards, interconnection, and interoperability are the building blocks of electronic systems, one of the types of systems that will be examined in this chapter. The means devised for the design of mass-produced electronic products suggests more widespread opportunities for the use of compatibility standards in design processes and is linked to the emergence of the idea of 'modularity'. The discussion is organized around three themes: coordination, negotiation, and memory, each of which constitutes a chapter section. The final section of the chapter recapitulates the highlights of the chapter and suggests a focus for further research.

8.2   Coordination

A major source of the economic value of technical compatibility standards is that they enlarge the market for the supply of compatible components or subsystems, enabling competition and price reduction. However, two other elements of compatibility standards are even more relevant for the production of CoPS.[3] The first is the role of these standards in providing a transitory 'freeze' in the progress of engineering designs and in supporting redirection or redeployment of design resources to other activities. The second element of compatibility standards to be considered is their support of functional specialization within subsystems of larger systems. The process of standards setting usually does not determine how larger systems are to be designed, but it does limit the range of technical decisions that must be made. Both of these elements serve useful purposes in achieving the interorganizational coordination necessary for creating CoPS by creating a 'fixed point' around which coordination can occur.

Compatibility standards define a standard for the interface between components and subsystems. Assuming for the purposes of this section that these standards are 'set' by the systems integrator (further discussion of the negotiation of such standards is the subject of Section 8.3), they serve as a means for defining what is delivered in terms of functionality and performance from a component or a subsystem to other parts of the system. It is useful to consider two extreme possibilities with regard to this interface between the system as a whole and its constituent components and subsystems.

At one extreme is the possibility that the interface completely defines the range of effects that the subsystem may have on the larger system in which it is embedded. In this case, the engineering design of the component or subsystem does not have larger systemic effects. In other words, one may design the system as a whole without taking into account anything but the definition of the interfaces. This possibility gives rise to the idea of 'modular' systems (Robertson and Langlois 1992; Baldwin and Clark 1997).

At the other extreme is the possibility that, regardless of the definition of the interface, the system cannot be designed without taking the design characteristics and performance of the components and subsystems into account. In this case, the design of components and subsystems plays a major role in the integrated design of the system. When integrated design is required, design processes are likely to be more interactive and require, at a minimum, more extensive consultation processes and, more likely, require the construction of prototypes in order to trace overall system functionality and performance.

In practice, actual CoPS projects involve a complex mixture between interfaces that can be taken as a sufficient definition of the component's or subsystem's contribution to the entire system and interfaces that are 'incomplete' in defining or characterizing the overall performance of the system. In the latter case, the definition of a technical compatibility interface is only a starting point for the design of the entire system. It is also not straightforward to assume that the entire system's performance will be predictable even if designers act as if the interface is all that matters.

A common cause of this 'mixture' is that the range of possible effects that the subsystem may have on the system as a whole is not completely captured in the definition of the interface and, as a result, efforts to operate in the first situation (where standards are taken as complete) turn out to involve operation in the second, that is, where the interface is incomplete. In these circumstances, the role of technical compatibility standards is to provide a starting point for the iterative and interactive processes of integrating the entire system.

Because such standards 'freeze' technological capabilities by defining the contributions of the component or subsystem, they provide a first recourse in working through the systems integration problem. They establish priority for the question, is the interface functioning as specified? If it is, then the issue becomes whether the definition of the interface is incomplete for the integration of the system as a whole, that is, whether, inadvertently, there are features of the interface that are propagating effects in the system, or whether it is the interaction between supposedly well-defined interfaces that create effects making it necessary to redefine the compatibility standard of the interface. How these issues are resolved between the systems integrator and components suppliers is a key issue for the technical management of such projects.

A complementary way to conceptualize coordination issues is to begin with the overall architecture of the system and to take the view that its decomposition into subsystems and components is a design choice. In examining decomposition, one may begin with the simple observation that large systems such as CoPS involve interfaces between many different components and subsystems. The interface or joining 'places' in the system are determined by the system's design, which in turn is constrained by the technology employed. Some technologies inherently involve 'tight coupling' in which a component or subsystem strongly influences the performance of other components and subsystems (e.g. internal combustion engines), other technologies support 'loosely coupled' systems (e.g. telecommunication networks), and still other technologies support 'decoupled' systems (e.g. traditional batch manufacturing processes).

It is an interesting historical question with regard to any particular technology to ask how the tightness of component and subsystem coupling was initially specified and how it evolves over time. For many older mechanical technologies, tight coupling between components and subsystems was initially necessary because of the way that control systems operated. For example, the historic multi-stroke engine involved a mechanical coupling between the introduction of fuel, ignition (in petrol systems typically through mechanical rotation of electrical contacts), and exhaust. More recent designs involve separating the control system from mechanical coupling, in effect 'loosening' the connection within the system—a process that requires a different set of capabilities in interface and system design than the older system.[4] Arguably an increasing array of designs involves the separation of control from other parts of the system and the creation of specific control interfaces. The demands that this separation of control places on other components and subsystems depend upon the specific features of the system. It is possible that either looser or tighter coupling, or even decoupling, will result from the separation of control.

This trend towards separation of control systems is particularly apparent in some large technical systems such as telecommunication networks. After the early history of human-switched telecommunication connections, the innovation of mechanical telecommunication switches involved tight coupling between the originating terminal equipment (e.g. the telephone of the calling party) and the switch that set up the path to the receiving terminal equipment (e.g. the telephone of the receiving party). Because of the tight coupling inherent in the design of the system, telecommunication users were dependent upon a particular set of components operating according to design. A call that reached a defective part of the switching network died and had to be reinitiated. Modern electronic switches have the capacity to monitor the switching process and employ error recovery if some part of the network is not operating. The result is a much higher level of reliability and, because the control system is electronic rather than electromechanical, the performance of the system is also much higher.

More generally, loose coupling usually involves some degree of penalty in terms of 'performance', although it is important to distinguish between engineering and economic performance. A tightly coupled telecommunication system such as an undersea cable control system is able to achieve high 'performance' in terms of bandwidth utilization at the cost of denying service when more signals arrive than can be accommodated.[5] Thus, high throughput performance may come at the expense of reduction in connection reliability.

The advent of 'packet' transmission has further loosened the tightness of coupling at higher levels of the telecommunication system, making it possible to 'route around damage', a defining characteristic of the internet and the more general use of internet protocol methods in telecommunication of both voice and data signals. In this case, the 'looseness' of the coupling involves both technical and economic advantages, which is one of the reasons that telecommunication companies are either adopting, or actively considering the adoption of, voice-over packet networks. The growth of the internet has dramatically decoupled a variety of communication processes. For example, while the transmission and receipt of e-mail involves loosely coupled exchange of information, most users prefer to remain 'decoupled' from the receipt of e-mail messages, using the mail server as a decoupled 'store' of messages in their system of communication. In a similar fashion peer to peer exchange of information, audio and video messaging, and other 'background' processes often involve the decoupling of at least one of the communication parties from the need to be connected, that is, coupled into the communication system.

More generally, the case of 'decoupled' systems involves operations in which the connection between parts of the system is only indirectly linked. Traditional methods of manufacture, involving the accumulation of 'work in process' that is entered into an inventory for future assembly, is one example of a 'decoupled' system. Such 'decoupled' systems may generate their own design issues (e.g. how to govern the logistical problems of planning and storing outputs), but it is stretching the idea of 'systems integration' to encompass these possibilities. Instead, it is more useful to analyse 'decoupled' systems as involving a product platform incorporating a number of distinct systems. For example, in the design of an aircraft, the in-flight entertainment system is 'decoupled' from the integrated systems controlling the flight. It would be disconcerting, to say the least, if such systems were made interoperable and the regulations concerning in-flight use of wireless electronic devices is an example of an attempt to maintain the integrity of wireless systems within the aircraft from possible interference with other wireless interfaces (such as those used by mobile phones).

This section has considered the system design problem largely within the framework of a 'master designer', a situation in which the systems integrator not only plans for the implementation of the entire system but also understands the source of all potential problems and their possible resolution. This is a highly idealized model of the actual design of CoPS. Nonetheless, it is a useful starting point as it indicates the processes of systems integration and decomposition as design decisions and highlights the significance of the growing use of electronic control systems to 'loosen' the coupling between components and subsystems. Looser coupling heightens the importance of interface design and implementation and the role of standards, formed either at the level of the industry or locally. In practice, uncertainties about the source of 'bugs' or bottlenecks in the overall system present major technical management problems since in a multi-organizational context knowledge is distributed between different organizations. The distribution of knowledge also makes it unrealistic for the systems integrator to dictate the interfaces between system components and subsystems, at least in an autarkic manner. This is the starting point for the discussion of 'negotiation', the subject of the next section.

8.3 Negotiation

CoPS differ in the extent to which the systems integrator is able to control the overall design and specification of components. The most conspicuous cases where the systems integrator relies upon other companies are particularly important for the analysis of industrial structure. In these cases, there is often an early and thorough partition of subsystem producers, such as the division of labour between aircraft engine and airframe producer (Prencipe and Paoli 1999) or between hardware and software producers (Steinmueller 1996). Such major structural fractures in the division of labour suggest that the benefits of vertical integration are overwhelmed by risks in integrated production and the advantages of competing suppliers.

Economists have argued that the division of labour is related to the size of the market since Adam Smith coined the phrase 'the division of labour is limited by the extent of the market' (Young 1928; Stigler 1951). Nonetheless, how a firm or an industry progresses from integrated production to interorganizational division of labour has not been a central issue in economic analysis. This is largely because economists have encapsulated or 'black boxed' the issue as the outcome of the 'make or buy' decision. Integrated production occurs when the costs of internally coordinating production are lower than the costs of external coordination of production. The costs of interorganizational division of labour are influenced by the potential for economies of scale and specialization in external supply. Although this formulation 'answers' the question of what determines the division of labour, it fails to answer important questions about the pre- and co-requisites for the emergence of an effective supplier industry. Where do such suppliers come from and how do they gain the competencies or knowledge necessary for making effective offers to incumbent integrated producers? More particularly, how might a company that wished to outsource production create the conditions for a supplier industry to emerge?

One possibility is to create technical compatibility standards. However, if systems integrators define standards that are for their exclusive use, there will be a problem in recruiting suppliers whose market opportunities will be limited to the systems integrator. Suppliers' economic prospects will be contingent upon their power to negotiate favourable deals with the systems integrator. Moreover, arrangements of this type are not likely to lead to economies of scale or offer an 'upside' for the supplier, further increasing the costs of this arrangement and diminishing the pool of potential entrants. A solution is to make the technical compatibility generic or industry-wide, so that additional companies may become purchasers. Assuming that other companies do in fact become purchasers, an opportunity for further entry of suppliers is opened and a more complete market may develop. This alternative, however, raises problems for both the systems integrators and suppliers. For suppliers, no company wants to be the producer of a commodity product in which it has no competitive advantage relative to other suppliers. In many cases, this issue can be resolved by learning or other dynamic economies of scale realized by the initial entrant and its immediate followers. For systems integrators, the use of generic standards threatens to provide an advantage to rivals or new entrants. The component or subsystem to be standardized must not be the principal source of competitive advantage for the systems integrator. This issue is often resolved by the complexity of the systems integration and the existence of critical components that are either not outsourced or only outsourced to captive suppliers.

A second possibility is to define supply opportunities in terms of generic industry capacities. For example, the production of die cast metal or plastic parts of a certain order (increasing over time) of complexity at a modest level of specification tolerance is something that is within the competence of hundreds or thousands of suppliers. Components of this type are unlikely to require technical compatibility standards at all and likely to rely on the 'local' specification provided by the engineering drawing and tolerance specifications.

Between the possibilities of captive supply, industry-wide standards, and generic components or subsystems there are many possible arrangements. All of them involve negotiation between the systems integrator and potential suppliers. These negotiations involve the creation of supplier capabilities that are specialized to the needs of the systems integrator, but may also, to varying degrees provide the supplier with the capability of servicing other customers. These capabilities are what Teece (1986) calls co-specialized assets.[6] Because of the specialization of the supplier capabilities to the systems integrator needs, the systems integrator is likely to have to co-invest with the supplier. Although price is an essential part of these negotiations, it is likely that the engineer's idea of 'cost price' rather than the economists' idea of 'market price' will be the principle of negotiation. In situations where the supplier has market power due to unique technological knowledge or intellectual property, the systems integrator's ability to pay may be a 'hidden principle' of the negotiation.[7] The result of such negotiations is a 'local technical compatibility standard', which will meet the needs of the systems integrator and may even be proprietary, but which will also allow the supplier to adapt or reconfigure the design to meet the needs of other customers.[8]

The principal contributions of local technical compatibility standards to the negotiation in these intermediate cases are to reduce the extent of specialization involved in the co-specialization process, thereby creating a more incentive compatible basis for supply. For example, by limiting the product specification to the interface standard, the systems integrator's purchaser need not become involved with how suppliers meet the requirements of the standard. The systems integrator is thus less able to displace the supplier and the supplier is able to maintain knowledge about the 'inner workings' of its component or subsystem as proprietary. This provides a clear incentive for the supplier to agree to a standardization process. The incentive for the systems integrator to utilize technical compatibility standards is that they, in principle, open the market to alternative suppliers who can employ a somewhat different design of the 'inner workings' or the interface to satisfy the needs of other customers. Local technical compatibility standards have some potential to reduce the market power of the supplier in the short run and more potential in the medium term because they are vulnerable to other suppliers devising better ways of meeting the standard. On the other hand, the supplier is able to employ the development resources provided by the systems integrator as a 'subsidy' for their entry into other markets, an advantage that the suppliers' rivals may not have.

If technical compatibility standards are an incentive compatible means of reducing the extent of co-specialized asset negotiation processes, why are they not used more frequently, that is, why are they not a central principle in the operation of CoPS industries? There are at least three reasons.

First, the nature of the technologies employed to make components and subsystems may not offer a realistic possibility for alternative supply.

Without an incentive for the systems integrator, there is no basis for engaging in the costs of standards making, and captive supply (either internal or through exclusive arrangement) will be the prevailing arrangement.

Second, even if standards could, in principle, enable competitive supply, they may be too transitory to serve this purpose. Standards making itself takes time[9] and thus a technical compatibility standard has to be relevant for long enough to enable competitive supply. Rapid technological change, especially in high performance 'state of the art' systems will reduce the relevance of technical compatibility standards for the systems integrator.

Third, the systems integrator may wish to maintain proprietary control over the component or subsystem. A standard not only opens the possibility for alternative suppliers, it also creates the possibility for alternative systems integrators or an externality that can be employed by rivals. Thus, as noted earlier, the systems integrator's competitive advantage must lie outside of the component or subsystem. If it does not, standards are irrelevant and the sole question is whether a supplier is willing to make the buy option in the make or buy decision viable for the systems integrator.

In summary, technical compatibility standards have a role in mitigating the negotiation problems that arise when co-specialized assets are created in the division of labour between systems integrators and component and subsystem suppliers. This role is shaped by several technological and economic influences. A first influence is the consequence of technological opportunities available for producing a particular CoPS. Abundant technological opportunities support rapid technological progress and make standards ephemeral; they also support the creation of alternative suppliers and, possibly, alternative systems integrators. A second influence is whether the component or subsystem is a source of competitive advantage for the systems integrator. When it is, standards are unlikely to be employed because of the risks of creating advantages for rival or new entrant systems integrators. A third influence is whether there are likely to be multiple potential purchasers for the component or subsystem. When there are not, standards are likely to be irrelevant. Fourth, and finally, the technology in question has to be one in which technical compatibility standards are relevant, that is, they can be implemented. Electronic technologies are particularly noteworthy sources of standardization opportunities, subject to the constraints suggested by the other influences. Further assessing this potential in relation to engineering design issues is the subject of the next two sections, the first on the role of compatibility standards in stabilizing design processes and the second on the growing opportunities to employ simulation techniques in the design process.

8.4　Memory

Further inquiry into the processes of division of labour in industries that produce large technical systems or complex products and systems entail examining how capabilities are constructed and retained over time. A useful focus for such examination is the issue of organizational memory, the retention and enhancement over time in the firm's capabilities for problem-solving as well as the replication and enhancement of past performance.[10] In some technological intensive industries, organizational memory is secondary to the ability to engage in rapid *ad hoc* problem-solving and reconfiguration of interorganizational arrangements, see Brown and Eisenhardt (1998) for examples. The role of technical compatibility standards in these industries is often to consolidate the ownership of a market by creating a coterie of complementary products and services, for example, the efforts of Intel and Microsoft to stimulate the development of multimedia standards. In these cases, standards have more to do with enhancing the demand for technology 'platforms' in products that are highly modular than in complex integration processes such as those necessary to construct a large building, the complex producer goods used to make integrated circuits, or produce a flight simulator. In these latter cases, it is often necessary to retain knowledge from one period to another. Moreover, it is common for such systems to be made on a one-off basis, reconfigured with different or additional options to different customers, and upgraded incrementally with modest or no change to some of the components or subsystems.

Under these conditions, it is important to have specific guidance about how changes can be introduced in components and subsystems without the requirement of achieving in-depth knowledge of how these parts of the system work. Local technical compatibility standards generally and interface standards specifically provide this sort of guidance. These standards support the division of labour across time and between organizations by providing a memory of how the pieces of the system fit together. Creating standards is therefore an act of defining what is to be remembered about how the system is constructed. In addition, the collection of interface standards provides a guide to alternative ways that the system might be decomposed into different subsystems; how, for example, a tightly coupled system might be redesigned to employ looser coupling by embedding the critical elements responsible for the tight coupling within a particular subsystem.

Organizational memory and the competences that are linked to it are particular to individual organizations. Divisions of labour that assign responsibility for subsystems and components across organizational boundaries are divestitures of the organizational memory and competences necessary to make these components and subsystems. This process is sometimes viewed with alarm and described as the 'hollowing' out of company competences. There is certainly the possibility that short-term cost minimization in the production of a single generation of products might lead a company to divest the sources of memory and competence necessary for creating the next generation of products. At the same time, however, by divesting itself of accumulated capabilities, a systems integrator attains the freedom to rethink the complex products and systems that it makes. The pressures to respond to the problems and difficulties of external contractors is likely to be lower than the pressures that can be exerted by colleagues operating within the same organization. Of course, it is quite possible that companies may over-estimate their own understanding of the products that they produce and inadvertently sever an arterial source of knowledge in the excision process represented by outsourcing. However, it is also possible that retaining par-ticular competences may bias the design of the entire product to satisfy internal constituencies and lead to disadvantages with rivals, the incumbent or entrant, that take a fresher approach to design issues. In effect, outsourcing is a dialectical process in which the excision of capabilities creates a tension or 'contradiction' between what is internal and external that is resolved through a process of synthesis. In this case, the synthesis involves developing memory and competence around the process of resolving these contradictions, that is, in the problem-solving related to interorganizational coordination rather than processes of design that are based upon internal competences.

What is being synthesized also enters into this process. Outsourcing also sets in motion an independent accumulation of memory and competence in the supplier firms. A key observation as to how this process works was made in Rosenberg's (1976: 9–31) study of the machine tool industry. Rosenberg observed that the technical design of machine tools became more generic when they were produced by an independent sector. In effect, a technological trajectory involving the creation of ever more general-purpose devices replaced a pattern of product specialization in which machine tools were designed around the specific needs of one class of user firms. The exploration of the potential for more generic products in which the supplier can retain competitive competence is the essence of this process. From the supplier's perspective the ideal component or subsystem is one that can be customized to the needs of a variety of systems integrators, affords supplier rivals very little ability for imitation, and is subject to decreasing costs of production.

Electronic components and subsystems meet all of these criteria except for the difficulty to imitate. The capacity for imitation in electronic com-ponents and subsystems creates strong incentives to continuously innovate in, or at least change, the design of the product. It may be responsible for the common observation in industry that modern producer goods are 'over-specified' in terms of the complexity of their control systems (mostly elec-tronic) and thereby are more difficult to maintain and more difficult for human operators to learn to use. These problems can be seen as outcomes of the supplier incentives to set a moving target for rivals while simultaneously creating products that appeal to broader markets (features useless and confusing to some are valuable to others).

Technical compatibility standards have an unexpected role in this context. While suppliers seek to bind their customers closer by better meeting many of their needs (albeit with more complex products that are not necessarily appreciated), systems integrators can discipline this production of variety and the threat of being bound to proprietary standards of the supplier by specifying or agreeing to standards. In doing so, systems integrators may benefit rivals, but failure to do so may incur higher costs in terms of the unwanted proliferation of variety. In this sense, standards serve as a means of simplifying the complexity of producer good systems and thereby limiting the divergence created by dispersing the memory and competence for component and subsystem production.

The purpose of this section has been to examine how technical compatibility standards influence the accumulation of organizational memory and competence as systems integrators operate in an environment characterized by ever-increasing division of labour and knowledge. Interorganizational distribution of knowledge necessarily leads to distribution of memory and competence. It also creates a specific set of incentives for technological improvement and change. By way of example, it has been argued here that these incentives may produce 'excess variety' as suppliers attempt to increase the generic qualities of their products (to enlarge their market), to offer proprietary features (to increase their market power with respect to systems integrators), and to make frequent improvements or changes in their products (to defeat the imitative efforts of rivals). Technical compatibility standards can be seen as a means for systems integrators to govern these incentives and to 'simplify' what might otherwise, from the systems integrator's viewpoint, be seen as the production of excess variety.

8.5 Conclusion

It is now well recognized that technical compatibility standards play an important role in permitting the dis-integration of the development and production of components and subsystems designed to be integrated into complex products and systems (as defined in the Introduction, Section 8.1). Analyses of the processes by which these standards are set have focused on the contrast between *de facto* (market-led) and *de jure* (cooperative standard-setting by voluntary standards organizations) mechanisms. This dichotomy directs researcher attention to the standards-making process itself. This chapter returns to the more fundamental question of why companies have interests in forming technical compatibility standards including those that are 'local' within the networks of firms responsible for the production of complex products and systems.

The discussion in this chapter has emphasized the role of technical compatibility standards in supporting the division of labour by providing a means of defining the interfaces connecting the components and subsystems of large technical systems or complex products and systems. The principal purpose of the section on coordination (Section 8.2) was to assess the constraints including the feasibility of interorganizational division of labour. This investigation of feasibility highlighted the importance of tight and loose coupling in the design of systems and observed the growing use of electronic control systems as a means of creating more flexibility in system design.

While the initial assessment of coordination issues and the feasibility of division of labour were framed in terms of systems integrator (or master designer) control, a deeper analysis involves considering the negotiation (Section 8.3) between systems integrator and suppliers. The limiting cases of captive and generic suppliers were defined and this led to the definition of negotiation problems related to the co-specialization of assets between systems integrators and suppliers of components and subsystems. It was argued that technical compatibility standards provide an incentive compatible means for solving this specific negotiation problem. The relatively modest use of public standards-making processes in complex product and system industries stems from the continuing importance of captive supply, the transitory nature of some designs, and systems integrator desires to maintain proprietary control of component and subsystem designs.

The section on memory (Section 8.4) examines the prospects for extending the use of technical compatibility standards in supporting solutions to interorganizational coordination problems when knowledge is distributed between systems integrators and component and subsystem suppliers. As this (and preceding sections) observe, the disintegration process creates specialized competences with their own trajectories of change and improvement and thus an interorganizational distribution of knowledge-generating and production activities. The process of recalling this knowledge, memory, becomes a central issue in which standards can play a central role.

As Section 8.4 notes, recent history has demonstrated the facility with which design and production of electronic systems using standard defined interfaces can be distributed. This lesson has not been ignored by other industries and has been broadly applied to production in other industries including complex products and systems where reliance on electronic systems for control further supports this growth of interorganizational division of labour.

The issues of memory cannot, however, be disentangled from struggles for control or the emergence of separate lines of initiative within the network of firms involved in knowledge accumulation. The interorganizational division of labour ignites rather than extinguishes further struggles for control and technical compatibility standards can play an important regulatory role in this struggle.

A principal conclusion of this chapter is that technical compatibility standards are as relevant to complex product and system industries as they are to industries that employ mass production. This relevance does not mean, however, that technical compatibility standards are employed to create the same form of competitive selection process or advantages in the industries where complex and flexible systems integration is a central feature as in those industries based on mass production of standardized products. Instead of a competitive process struggling for adoption of a dominant design, the competitive process in the systems integration industries involves implementing design through the processes of coordination, negotiation, and memory. These processes have the capacity to determine competitive outcomes between firms and hence the 'competitiveness' of particular managerial approaches or practices, and merit continued and intensified examination.

Notes

1. A more complex example illustrating the problems of interconnection is the case of alternating current voltage converters such as those used to transform European 220 V power mains for the use of North American and Japanese 120 V equipment. Such devices offer much more limited 'compatibility' due to the more complex characteristics of alternating current compared with direct current. For example, such converters do not typically shift the frequency of the alternating current, which in Europe is 50 Hz whereas in the United States it is 60 Hz. This difference in frequency is enough to defeat interconnection for some types of electrical products.
2. One might think that more complex devices would require more complex compatibility standards. This is not necessarily so, as it is possible to locate the functions of adaptation and interoperability within the device itself rather than within the interface or its implementation. Thus, a computer modem may be used to receive a video transmission without any of its specific features being devoted to the video information itself. This is possible because the data interpretation occurs within the personal computer while the modem is simply passing a bitstream between devices.
3. It is important to note that CoPS may involve large numbers of standardized components. For example, civil engineering projects may involve the use of concrete and steel construction in which both technical compatibility and reference standards are ubiquitous.
4. Early difficulties with the electronic control of fuel injection systems are a historical example of the difficulties in building these new capabilities.
5. While there is currently a surfeit of intercontinental telecommunication capacity, this was not always so.
6. Co-specialization involves the older economic issue of bilateral market power, the case where both supplier and purchaser have market power over each other, that is, the purchaser has monopsonistic power because of the absence of alternative customers and the supplier has monopolistic power because of the absence of alternative suppliers. The textbook solution to this problem is vertical integration. However, this does not address the potential advantages arising from the vertical division of labour between supplier and purchaser.
7. Quite naturally, it is not a very fruitful strategy to adopt 'ability to pay' as an explicit principle in a price negotiation. Instead, the negotiation proceeds from

an alternative definition of 'cost price' in which a full cost rather than an incremental cost accounting principle is employed. Cost plus an allowed profit is a typical implementation of the full cost principle.

8. In the case of proprietary compatibility standards, an accommodation must be made with the systems integrator or the co-specialized asset must be incompletely specialized, that is, it must be sufficiently adaptable that non-infringing products can be produced.

9. The timeliness of standards-making is an important subject—see, for example, Weiss and Sirbu (1990). One source of 'delays' in public standards making is the need to take all stakeholders' interests into account. Increasingly, a variety of standards are quasi-public goods (produced by a 'club' of interested parties). While the private approach may be more rapid, it also may erect barriers to entry by settling on standards that advantage a more limited number of suppliers—see David and Steinmueller (1996).

10. The latter capability is often considered in the evolutionary economics framework of 'routines' as defined by Nelson and Winter (1982). In the case of complex products and systems considered in this chapter, it is common for activities and procedures to be restructured or changed continuously. It is therefore more appropriate to focus on the replication and enhancement of performance (e.g. timely completion of projects within budget and meeting expectations) than routines (e.g. achieving the same outcome using the same activities and procedures).

References

BALDWIN, C. Y. and CLARK, K. B. (1997). 'Managing in an Age of Modularity', *Harvard Business Review*, 75/5: 84–93.

BROWN, S. L. and EISENHARDT, K. M. (1998). *Competing on the Edge: Strategy as Structured Chaos*. Boston, MA: Harvard Business School Press.

DAVID, P. A. (1991). 'Computer and Dynamo: The Modern Productivity Paradox in a Not-too-distant Mirror', in OECD Report *Technology and Productivity: The Challenge for Economic Policy*. Paris: OECD, 315–37.

—— and STEINMUELLER, W. E. (1996). 'Standards, Trade and Competition in the Emerging Global Information Infrastructure Environment', *Telecommunications Policy*, 20/10: 817–30.

DAVIES, A. and BRADY, T. (2000). 'Organisational Capabilities and Learning in Complex Product Systems: Towards Repeatable Solutions', *Research Policy*, 29/7–8: 931–53.

DEVINE, W. D., Jr. (1983). 'From Shafts to Wires: Historical Perspectives on Electrification', *The Journal of Economic History*, 43/2: 347–72.

DUBOFF, R. B. (1979). *Electric Power in American Manufacturing, 1889–1958*. New York: Arno Press.

FARRELL, J. and SALONER, G. (1988). 'Coordination through Committees and Markets', *RAND Journal of Economics*, 197/2: 235–52.

GREENSTEIN, S. and DAVID, P. A. (1990). 'The Economics of Compatibility Standards: An Introduction to Recent Research', *Economics of Innovation and New Technology*, 1/1–2: 3–41.

HAWKINS, R. W., MANSELL, R., and SKEA, J. (eds.) (1995). *Standards, Innovation and Competitiveness: The Politics and Economics of Standards in Natural and Technical Environments*. Cheltenham: Edward Elgar.

HOBDAY, M., RUSH, H., and TIDD, J. (2000). 'Innovation in Complex Products and Systems', *Research Policy*, 29/7–8: 793–804.

MILLER, R., HOBDAY, M., LEROUX-DEMERS, T., and OLLEROS, X. (1995). 'Innovation in Complex Systems Industries: The Case of Flight Simulation', *Industrial and Corporate Change*, 4/2: 363–400.

NELSON, R. and WINTER, S. (1982). *An Evolutionary Theory of Economic Change*. Cambridge, MA: Harvard University Press.

POLANYI, M. (1962). *Personal Knowledge: Towards a Post-critical Philosophy*. Chicago: University of Chicago Press.

PRENCIPE, A. and PAOLI, M. (1999). 'The Role of Knowledge Bases in Complex Product Systems: Some Empirical Evidence from the Aero-engine Industry', *Journal of Management and Governance*, 3: 137–60.

ROBERTSON, P. L. and LANGLOIS, R. N. (1992). 'Modularity, Innovation, and the Firm: The Case of Audio Components', in F. M. Scherer and M. Perlman (eds.), *Entrepreneurship, Technological Innovation, and Economic Growth: Studies in the Schumpeterian Tradition*. Ann Arbor, MI: University of Michigan Press, 321–42.

ROSENBERG, N. (1976). *Perspectives on Technology*. Cambridge: Cambridge University Press.

RYCROFT, R. W. and CASH, D. E. (1999). *The Complexity Challenge: Technological Innovation in the 21st Century*. London and New York: Pinter.

STEINMUELLER, W. E. (1996). 'The US Software Industry: An Analysis and Interpretive History', in D. C. Mowery (ed.), *The International Computer Software Industry*. Oxford: Oxford University Press, 15–52.

STIGLER, G. J. (1951). 'The Division of Labour is Limited by the Extent of the Market', *Journal of Political Economy*, 59/3: 185–93.

TEECE, D. J. (1986). 'Profiting from Technological Innovation: Implications for Integration, Collaboration, Licensing and Public Policy', *Research Policy*, 156: 285–305.

UTTERBACK, J. (1996). *Mastering the Dynamics of Innovation*. Cambridge, MA: Harvard Business School Press.

WEISS, M. B. H. and SIRBU, M. (1990). 'Technological Change in Voluntary Standards Committee: An Empirical Analysis', *Economics of Innovation and New Technology*, 1/1–2: 111–33.

YOUNG, A. (1928). 'Increasing Returns and Economic Progress', *Economic Journal*, 38: 527–42.

9

The Cognitive Basis of Systems Integration
Redundancy of Context-generating Knowledge

MASSIMO PAOLI

University of Perugia and St Anna School of
Advanced Studies, Pisa, Italy

9.1 Introduction

In the last two decades, management literature has mainly focused on such principles as relentless cost controls, lean and flat organization, continuous re-engineering, and continuous rationalization, and a focus on core knowledge. These principles have paved the way to outsourcing and decentralization processes of activities not deemed core, and have led towards mythical hyper-efficient forms of business organization, such as the virtual corporation.

Relying on a totally different approach, the aim of this chapter is to offer some thoughts as to how systems integration can be developed and maintained. The approach is rooted in the concept of *redundancy of knowledge basis*. This concept underlines the role and importance for a firm's systems integration capabilities of (*a*) individuals as bearers of knowledge and (*b*) organizational contexts as containers that enable individuals to develop their knowledge. Systems integration resides in the capability of vision-construction of change.

The chapter argues that the role of systems integrators and systems integration capability involves the dynamic control (i.e. the ability and power to direct) of technological trajectories of the critical components, parts, subsystems, and, above all, of the trajectory of systems integration itself. The assembler and the activity of assembling are not necessarily involved in the control of the systems integration dynamic. I argue that being a mere assembler, may become unsustainable in those environments that are characterized by multi-technological products or processes comprising many parts and complex interrelated dynamics.

In order to develop the argument, the chapter is structured as follows. In the first section, I offer a definition of the traditional model of individual knowledge which is at the basis of the paradigm of 'efficiency without intelligence', and which is still informing managerial common sense.

Section 9.2 provides an outline of a different interpretation of human knowledge. This new point of view on knowledge may justify the passage to a *redundancy of intelligence* paradigm as opposed to an efficiency one, without forgetting the economic reasons for efficiency. Section 9.3 focuses on the concept of systems integration. The last section, using the principle of systems integration control, argues for the superiority of the reasons for the redundancy of intelligence.

9.2   The Traditional Concept of Individual Knowledge

Few mathematical problems remain to be resolved,
in a short time we'll resolve them all. (David Hilbert)

Scientific progress in physics is ended,
we know all, there is nothing left to discover. (William Thompson (Lord Kelvin))

The 'Positive' Concept of Knowledge

The concept of knowledge has long been at the centre of major reflections in various fields. As we have already argued elsewhere (Paoli and Prencipe 1999), management literature is very often based on neoclassical economics' assumptions of individual knowledge, devised in the twentieth century by the epistemology of neopositivism and logic empiricism. The main tenets are as follows, (*a*) knowledge is made up of information, (*b*) information has the same nature as knowledge, even if it is found at different hierarchical levels of the cognitive system, (*c*) therefore, a coherent assembly of information (like the pieces of a jigsaw) forms knowledge. In other words, the result of putting the pieces of a mosaic (information) together will be knowledge.

Some Principles of the Simple Economics of Knowledge—Information

According to the neoclassical approach, knowledge—information is understood to be endowed with three fundamental attributes.

Indivisibility. 'there is no gain to acquire the same information twice...the production of knowledge is thus basically different from the production of goods....' (Arrow 1969: 30). In other words, there is no intrinsic advantage in reproducing a unit of knowledge—information, because there is no economic incentive to do it (Arrow 1962: 609–25), 'the same knowledge that enables the youngest to make the first airplane (of paper) will serve him to make his sixth or twelfth airplane...' (Machlup 1984: 160).

Absence of Rivalry in Use. The same unit of knowledge can be used by more than one subject at a time, that is, one bit of knowledge can be reproduced *ad infinitum* at marginal costs equal to zero.

Non-exclusiveness in Use. This characteristic defines the inappropriability, that is, the impossibility, of the exclusive use of a given bit of knowledge. Possession of the latter does not imply its ownership, and neither of these conditions imply exclusive use. It proves impossible to avoid others utilizing produced knowledge, and it is impossible to enhance its value. In order to determine the value of a given bit of knowledge–information, it is necessary to know its content, but once the latter is known the buyer will lack any incentive to pay a price to purchase what he has already acquired. On the other hand, refusal by the seller to disclose such content would effectively prevent any assessment of its value (estimation of the incentive to buy) on the part of the purchaser. So the market value of a piece of knowledge– information risks being null (with the supply already infinitely elastic as costs approach zero).

Knowledge–information can always be rendered explicit. In this context, the condition of tacitness is essentially concerned with the cost of codifiability rather than with the actual impossibility of knowledge codifiation. In other words, knowledge can be defined as tacit when the cost to codify it is extremely high, but given the right incentives, and the right forecast of benefit expected from the codifying operation, codification can begin immediately. It is not the nature of knowledge–information that prevents its codification: indeed, the opposite is true—its nature always makes codification possible (at worst, with different cost levels).

Perfect Decomposability. If knowledge–information is perfectly codifiable, that is to say, representable through symbols and linguistic expressions, then it can be decomposed at will. Consequently, it will be equally easy to decompose the processes employed to obtain it. And provided that the definition of ownership rights and the elements forming the object of appropriability are clear, this characteristic of decomposability of the object knowledge and of the processes that produce it makes it feasible to devise some efficient form of division of labour in the processes themselves. In the final analysis, this allows for some form of efficient partitioning of innovative labour in general (Arora and Gambardella 1994).

Perfect Transferability/Absorbability. In addition to decomposability, in the light of the completely symbolic nature of knowledge–information, it is also necessary to postulate its perfect transferability. However, for the latter to take place efficiently and effectively, at least two requirements must be satisfied: (*a*) there must be a clear regime of appropriability of knowledge–information, and (*b*) from a cognitive point of view there must be perfect sharing of the syntax through which the bits of knowledge can be assembled into the right meaning. Thus, just like a radio signal, knowledge– information is always ready to be incorporated and absorbed (provided that adequate investments in R&D have been made in the past) on the basis of a model that revolves round the relative costs of production or absorption (and, in any case, this interesting contribution of what is known as absorptive capacity (Cohen and Levinthal 1989, 1990) appears to be more an extension–generalization of the Arrow model than a genuine alternative).

Indistinguishability of the Process from the Linguistic Product. The neoclassical framework has led to the conviction that knowledge is a resource given in every equilibrium state of the system in exactly the same way as other production factors, the only peculiarity being that it constitutes the input for a process whose product is once again (new) information: 'invention and research ... are devoted to the production of information' (Arrow 1962: 614). Thus, the peculiarities of the process whereby knowledge–information is produced ultimately correspond to the peculiar characteristics of knowledge as an economic commodity. In other words, one finds a systematic identification between knowledge as a process (learning) and knowledge– information as the linguistic (symbolic) result of this process.

The Clear-cut Distinguishability Between Scientific Knowledge and Technological Knowledge. While the distinction between scientific and applicational knowledge tends to be somewhat blurred in Arrow, inasmuch as it is 'all' regarded as codified knowledge, the 1959 contribution by Nelson resulted in one of the most lasting classifications in the economics of innovation. 'There is a continuum spectrum of scientific activities. Moving from the applied science end of the spectrum to the basic science end ... the goals become less clearly defined and less closely tied to the solution of specific practical problems or the creation of a particular object' (Nelson 1959: 301). On the one hand, (*a*) there is basic or scientific knowledge–information, which remains a perfect public commodity, 'basic scientific research is ... the best example of pure public good' (Romer 1993: 73), revealing, from the cognitive point of view, a hierarchical super-ordering as compared to technological knowledge, of which it quite frequently acts as an input. On the other hand, (*b*) one finds applied knowledge–information, whose nature is no different from scientific knowledge, but which can be rendered appropriable through exogenous market-regulating policy measures (mainly patents). The impact of such measures (degree of influence and exclusiveness of patents) should derive from a precise definition of the extent of the incentives judged to be applicable or optimal on a case-by-case basis.

The Epistemological Bases of 'Positive' Knowledge

We argue that the previous understanding of knowledge is based on some fundamental assumptions:

1. Reality is outside of us and is accessible—we discover it through observations or experiments.
2. Formal systems (e.g. languages) adopted to represent theories describe reality, and they do so in a way that the first ones to express it do not have syntactical problems.
3. There are no ambiguities in the attribution of meaning to hypotheses, theories, observations, and languages; therefore, there are no problems in attributing common and shared meanings to theories when they become universal truths.
4. From a methodological point of view, it is necessary and sufficient to follow the Aristotelian/Cartesian principles of the distribution of problem-solving, or, in other words, to break up the problem, to start by solving the smallest and easiest problems. When it seems that every problem (or a substantial part of it) has been solved, it is possible to reconstruct, given that the reconstruction process is just the analogous opposite of deconstruction. In other words, there are no differences in the nature of the deconstruction and reconstruction processes.

In the course of the twentieth century, the evolution of epistemology annihilated this explanatory paradigm. Maturana and Varela have fundamentally dismissed the first point by applying the concepts of an autopoietic system and structural coupling, as we shall illustrate in the following section. Gödel (1931) disproved the second point by showing how formal systems that are complete subsequently become contradictory, or when they are not contradictory, then they must be incomplete (Nagel and Newman 1992: 93). Duhem (1914) and Quine (1969) rebutted the third point by indicating the impossibility of singularly heading the theory. The work of Bachelard (1953, 1996) showed the inconsistency of the fourth point. Accordingly, the reconstruction process is not the analogous opposite of the breaking down process, since the former entails the development of new and different meaning. In fact, a problem is broken down in order to solve it. The breaking down process starts when the problem is only identified and not yet solved as known. As a consequence, during the breaking down process, meanings might be lost, while during the reconstruction process, new meanings might well be attributed to the problem at hand. Therefore, once again we are forced to reconstruct a different sense of individual knowledge.

This last point is very important for explaining the cognitive basis of system integration. The process of rebuilding–recomposing is an act of reconstruction. The discipline of paleontology gives us a useful metaphor. In fact, the construction of the external forms of prehistoric animals takes place through a process of recomposition, which is usually based on a few poorly preserved fossils of these animals' internal structures. The recomposition of these external forms is largely 'creative' (especially if there are very few fossils); by using admittedly *ad hoc* solutions, the inevitable gaps in knowledge produced by the reduced availability of fossils (and of their 'internal' character) are filled. Rebuilding is a similar action. To recompose the parts (partial solutions) of a whole (e.g. an undecomposed phenomenon or problem) that was previously decomposed (when we knew nothing about it) means reinventing the missing links and inserting them into the system for the purpose of completing it (of giving sense to it). Bringing a partial solution to another partial solution (maybe in a different field) is therefore an act of construction of sense—which involves certain aspects that are completely invented—and not an act of mere recomposition.

The discussion above explains why there are levels of knowledge basis dedicated to the parts, to the interfaces, to the architecture, and at least one dedicated to the integration of the systems. Moreover, it also explains why the integration process requires the integrator to possess a high variety of knowledge bases:

- to put together the parts;
- to manage the interfaces;
- to organize the architecture;
- to invent the 'missing' links (e.g. to integrate).

The complexity of the role of integrator emerging here explains why such a role has to be a central one.

9.3   Assigning Meanings and the Concept of the Autopoietic System

Everything that is said
is said by an observer. (Humberto Maturana)

the reason sees only
what can produce
according to her design.... (Immanuel Kant)

Some Principles of Cognition in Autopoietic Systems

An important part of modern neurophysiological studies argues that individuals are autopoietic systems (Varela, Maturana, and Uribe 1974; Maturana and Varela 1980, 1987), that is, brains and bodies that can operate only thermodynamic exchanges with each other and with the environment. Brains are connected by filters that select the stimuli that the central nervous system interprets without any possibility of accessing reality (i.e. the environment or the world) or the other autopoietic systems (i.e. the other individuals). According to this view called structural coupling, every perturbation coming from outside may cause changes in the state of an autopoietic system, but the nature of these changes completely depends on the structure of the per-turbed system. Individuals can only exchange thermodynamic expressions, such as vibrations in the air, light in different wavelengths, chemical particles which make up smells, and pressures on the skin. These thermodynamic impulses can be considered supports for languages. In turn, these supports can be considered hand in glove with language only by oversimplification. They are, in any case, significants (i.e. sequences of symbols ruled syntact-ically) that are only linguistic expressions, such as words, images, sounds, behaviour—in other words, vehicles for information.

In this context, knowledge and information do not share the same nature. The former is pure sense and cannot be shared. The latter comprises lan-guage, syntax carried by significants that have no objective sense, symbols (in any form) to which the emitting subject has applied a meaning, and to which each of the receivers will apply his subjective meaning. The word 'red' has one meaning for the emitting individual, and millions of meanings for the millions of potential or actual receivers (e.g. think of a Daltonian); con-sequently, it can have neither one meaning nor a shared meaning (too many senses = no shared sense). Information cannot give sense, it needs sense. Knowledge is one's personal system of meanings. Knowledge is the matrix that allows an individual:

- to recognize that a sequence of symbols is interrelated to each other and that they are not symbols at random;
- to form one or more significants transporting information;
- to apply sense to that information (this process depends on one's capability to interpret, that is, based on what one already knows).

According to the sense that the individual gives to these significants, they may become either the magical atmosphere of Vivaldi's Four Seasons or a tedious noise, the strange look of an anonymous face or the beautiful smile of your son, the sumptuous perfume of a Brunello di Montalcino or an incomprehensible mixture of unknown smells. It is the individual's know-ledge that gives the significants some meaning, and only specific meanings. Individuals produce sense even if they do not want to (they think, they know, they learn even if they do not want to); they survive because they produce sense continuously, though, of course, not necessarily the right sense.

An autopoietic system can never know if it is right or not, because the sense created about any phenomenon it interfaces with is always a hypothesis of the world, and it remains a hypothesis forever. This system is continuous and greatly dependent on will because it serves the continuous action of men and their continuous intervention in the world. In fact, agents always behave, even when they decide not to. Individuals cannot share senses because they can only talk about them, they can emit significants. As a consequence of this regime of exchange, the autopoietic systems cannot measure their semantic distance or proximity from one other and cannot communicate and share any meaning, only information (i.e. linguistic expressions) that does not carry any objective sense *per se*.

Beyond the Vanishing Illusion of Sharing Senses: The Concept of Context

Therefore, the autopoietic systems composing an organization cannot share any rule or any other organizational routine or memory, neither can they share any actual vision of the system (product or process), because they do not share senses. Furthermore, they cannot exchange meanings (not even those related to the syntax of the rules to be shared in order to form an 'organization'). They cannot exchange meanings about the distance or the proximity of their processes of convergence (if there was one), because they only produce languages, syntax, significants, and information, following a strange spiralling cycle in which the more they are aware of the uselessness of the effort to communicate something to someone, the stronger is their effort to communicate. It is not possible to expand here on the consequences on organization, but this phenomenon allows us to introduce the idea that individuals in social systems (systems of individuals, but increasingly systems of contexts too) do not form organizations but systems of actions and relations.[1] And, because they act in contexts, these relations also become interactions among micro–meso–macro-contexts (i.e. physical, sociotechnical, and cultural containers).

The organization implodes into its action.[2] The social system becomes a hierarchical system of continuous 'formatting' patterns of action and not a separate entity that implements such patterns (Argyris and Shon 1978). The social system becomes a hierarchy of what we label contexts in which individuals act: 'context as collective locus for all the events that indicate to the organism–agent the set of options within which the latter must make further choice' (Bateson 1976).

Therefore, a social system is above all a system of contexts. People come into the world, live, learn, work, love, and die in contexts. The nature of the context is somehow generative of the learning.[3] Losing or abandoning a context entails losing its cognitive generative capacity. In this work, we refer to the generative capacity of firms' contexts, but we are fully aware that many other contexts do exist, in every social subsystem, and that they are all generative of learning. In other words, agents remain imprisoned by contexts. Even if they change context, they only pass to another context, either in the same social system or in a different one (hence, all relations are context-dependent).[4]

Within this web of actions and relations, the effort to conform to what each individual believes to be dictated by the necessity of coordinating behaviour often creates the illusion of sharing.[5] Nonetheless, the significances (and behaviours) of individuals are convergent because they are originated by the same context (constructed by each participant on his own, in parallel, but also together with others in the same context). At the most, convergence, and not sharing, is what ensues, but it will be a convergence of languages (e.g. words, behaviours, and so on) and not of meanings. It is the same process with which, for example, paradigmatic languages (Kuhn 1970), or operational slangs[6] emerge, or with which dialects are almost transformed into common spirits—for example, the languages of veterans and the languages of war stories (Cohen et al. 1996).

According to the approach discussed above, therefore, each agent taking part in the systems integration process has a different system in mind and, most of all, has a different vision of its conceptual and technological dynamic. It is important not to confuse the actual sharing of significances with the convergence of linguistic behaviour. Very often, the latter seems to share even some senses or values, but it is a purely linguistic illusion. Language convergence does not entail the sharing of meanings or the sharing of significances related to a process like systems integration (and its dynamic). The system (product or process) realized is not the result of shared meanings and is not an actual common vision. It lies in its specific design: a more or less sophisticated linguistic artefact. Just like any other linguistic artefact, design is a complicated product. Systems integration is a process, and, particularly when firms want to use it as a competitive weapon, it is a dynamic process. Therefore, like the conceptual and technological evolution of the system, it is a complex process.

Knowledge as a System of Senses–Meanings

'Live on the contrary!'
repeated Alice with great astonishment,
'I've never heard such a thing.'
'But it offers a great advantage' said the Queen,
'which is that memory works in all senses.'
'I'm sure that mine functions in only one direction'
Alice noted
'I can't remember things before they happen'
'A memory has little value if it only works for the past'
said the Queen. (Lewis Carroll)

A person's knowledge is a dynamic and complex system, composed of at least four other large systems.

1. The deep system of meanings continually produced and tied to the self-reference of the psyche, in other words, the sense of things with 'us' at the centre. From the moment that we are conscious, we are naturally at the centre of our respective universes (Gregory 1991: 746; Arduini 1998: chapter 2).
2. The system of memory creation–processing–activation processes (use and production of significances).

3. The system of memory processing–activation–creation products (from significances to linguistic expressions/perceptions, and vice versa).
4. The system of relationships among points 1, 2, and 3 above.

When the concept of system is attributed the meaning of a complex unit, because it is intrinsically dynamic, relational (the system emerges from functional relations activated, and is not seen as the static equivalent of its parts or of its structure), and organized (again, held together by processes), then one has a *unitas multiplex* (Angyal 1941). In this case, the foremost and fundamental complexity is created by conjugating, in a dynamic relational perspective, the idea of unity with that of diversity, multiplicity, and irreducibility of its characteristic unitary system properties to component parts; individuality is combined with decomposability (or quasi decomposability). The latter, however, is obtained at the price of decomposing and transfiguring the system itself, despite the fact that such a system cannot be reduced to its component parts. Because, on the one hand, the whole is more than the sum of its parts (refer to 'superadditive composition rule'—Foerster 1962: 866–7; Simon 1962: 468) and, conversely, the parts cannot be reduced to the system, because the whole is actually less than the sum of the parts. In effect, the parts too are constrained within their role to reduce complexity, at least within the confines of the system. This enables the system itself to assume and maintain its own functional identity (Morin 1983: 145–7).

In order to grasp the nature of the complexity we are dealing with, it is indispensable to appeal for what has been termed the concept of emergence as a quality, a property, a product (of the activated functional relations in a system), as globality (since it cannot be dissociated from the systemic unit), event (it arises discontinuously once the system has been formed), novelty (in respect of the parts), irreducibility (it cannot be decomposed without the risk of its own decomposition which, as in system decomposition, is also a transformation into something else), indeducibility (it cannot be deduced from the quality-functions of the parts), and, finally, as implexity (Morin 1983: 139–43; Le Moigne 1990: 48; Churchland and Sejnowski 1992: 13). Emergence, as a phenomenon, is linked to the process of transformation of the parts into a whole which, by this very process, forms, and transforms, maintains and organizes complementary tendencies, creates diversity, forges links between and organizes antagonisms, organizes antagonism within complementarities (Lupasco 1962: 332), and controls organizational entropy (Morin 1983: 156). It allows variety to spread out and repetitive order to be re-established and transformed into organizational reliability, that is, it is the survival capacity (Atlan 1974: 1–9) of the knowledge-system itself.

In simpler words, knowledge is the continuous emerging sense of things, it is meaning with an intrinsic value, independently of how or through what means it is created (it is always an act, a process; it is never a stored file). Sense is the cornerstone that allows the construction of our interpretations of the reality that surrounds us, without which it would be impossible to plan and evaluate our continuous interventions in the world. Sense is continuously rebuilt by means of memory.

9.4   Systems Integration

More the things you know, more the things you have to know. (Leonardo da Vinci)

L'intelligibilité du compliqué se fait par simplification.
L'intelligibilité du complexe se fait par integration
(le simple est toujours le simplifié). (Gaston Bachelard)

Integration of Systems as Integration of Conceptualizations

We contend that systems integration is a meta–super–cognitive–negotiative–dynamic process among individuals distributed throughout the contexts of several firms that are made up of specific physical attributes, combined also with the knowledge of the agents themselves, their linguistic interactions, their organizational rules, incentives, power distribution, beliefs, myths, and cultures. Because of these agents it is possible, at the same time, to construct the system integration process of a multi-technology artefact (process or product) and, as a consequence, its evolutionary path.

The dynamics of the artefact–product/process–system, in fact, arise from the joined and superimposed technological trajectories of the whole and its parts. Moreover, it is the result of the multi-disciplinary convergence–divergence and integration–disintegration, both at the technological and the scientific levels. This phenomenon constitutes a further level of evolution endowed with a remarkable generative capacity of: (*a*) autonomous scientific and technological trajectories–opportunities, and (*b*) continuous reconfiguration of the dependence and influence of relationships between scientific and technological fields. In relation to the latter, it is worth highlighting that to a great extent it affects the dependence and influence that relationships have between system, subsystems, and parts.

In the light of this, evolution of the product/process–system (and therefore the activity of systems integration) can be identified as a continuous destruction–reconstruction of hierarchical and functional orders which over time affect the ways of the conceptual and ideal decomposition[7] of the product–system itself. In this context, systems integration is a macro-process of conceptualization, by which several problems may emerge, related to the design of the product or the engineering of the manufacture. The relationship between the dynamic of conceptualization and the ensuing design problems is, however, the same as that which can be observed between knowledge and the linguistic artefacts called information. Thus, systems integration can never be reduced to a problem of design, even if it can be expressed only by design, just as knowledge can never be reduced to information–language, even if it can only be expressed by language.

Integration: A Complex Process of Modelling

Into this framework we introduce the key distinction between the capacity of designing and producing the product–system, which is at the most complicated, hence conceived and defined, and the effort to master systems integration and its evolutionary dynamics, that is, the complex strategic problem, therefore, non-definable, uncertain, and undefined. The distinction between complicated (or hypercomplicated, like an aero-engine that can have up to 20,000 components) and complex calls attention to the fact that complexity is not in reality, but rather in the constructions built for it at subjective and group levels. These constructions, in fact, change according to the knowledge endowed (Prencipe 2000, 2004; Paoli and Prencipe 2003).

According to Simon (1962), a system can be subdivided into relatively independent parts. That is to say, it is possible to obtain an adequate partitioning of the system allowing most interactions to occur within each individual component part, and not among the parts. Interactions among the parts are weaker than interactions inside the parts. The identification of characteristics of near-decomposability of systems has an important bearing on the issue we are analysing here, because it is linked to innovative typologies of a modular nature, characterized by a degree of design autonomy at the subsystem level (Prencipe 1997, 2004; Brusoni, Prencipe, and Pavitt 2001). The assumption of near-decomposability is linked to how systems knowledge of a separable type is produced, namely to the relative independence and the possibility of decontextualizing the cognitive foundations pertaining to the individual parts within the whole. However, compared to Simon's approach, the point of view developed in this chapter is different because it considers near-decomposability in a more explicit way—not so much as an attribute of the system in itself, but rather as a function of the (subjective) conceptualization of the system.

If it is true that the nature of knowledge influences the decomposability of the system, it is also true that the manner in which the system's conception construes its decomposability influences the nature of the knowledge required for its control. Dominion over the construction of models cannot disregard the environment, and the organizational implications are also relevant. If decomposability is not a function of the system as such, but of its conception, then it is generated in the context of the division of labour. At this point it may be useful to establish a corresponding classification of agents' constructions. More specifically, two contrasting orders of construction/modelling are found for the composition of observed systems (Table 9.1). With disjunction–decomposition, the complicated construction–model obtains a simple view of the fragmented phenomenon.

TABLE 9.1 *Two different orders of constructing (complicated/complex)*

System/phenomenon	Construction	System/phenomenon	Construction
Decomposable	Complicated	Indecomposable	Complex
By disjunction	Application/	By conjunction	Combination/
	decomposition		composition
Decomposed	Simple	Indecomposed	Implex

Source: Le Moigne (1990: 27).

With composition–combination, the complex construction model acquires an implex vision (non-decomposable) of a non-decomposed phenomenon. The former may be decomposed and the job divided (e.g. in order to photocopy a large number of pages), the latter cannot be decomposed and is much better done by oneself (everyone knows the difficulties of writing a co-authored paper or book).

Any process of modelling, however, makes use of sophisticated forms of codification and language. It is an eminently and irreducibly 'personal' process, through which it is possible to create different alternative readings–interpretations of phenomenon. Since complexity is inherent in the construction, that is where it belongs. This means that there are no complex phenomena, but complex constructions of phenomena that have been observed, that is, created (*dans notre tête*). We can outline the creation process as the flow of becoming which relinquishes the idea of analysis of something perceptible with the aim of assuming the idea of intentional constructive conception, which is, in turn, composed of instrumental representations of phenomena created and understood as complex and therefore indecomposable except at the risk of mutilation. Such a process is constituted by transition from the figure of the analyst to that of the conceptualizer–constructor (Le Moigne 1990: 27–8), from the decomposable object to the conceivable project, from decomposition into simple passive elements to the composition of implex actions.

Firms, being social systems composed of autopoietic systems, can deal with the problem of mastering the systems integration process (and its dynamics) only by creating complexity in the constructions[7] that they build, and that in some ways affect the product's path. Such constructions are the result of more or less chaotic/ruled negotiations among the constructions of the agents in an organization that is legitimated to speak of the technological trajectories that the systems (and therefore the systems integration) could potentially assume. Thus, a fundamental, though simplified principle may emerge. The more the knowledge of a group of agents distributed in several contexts is retained, and the more varied it is, the greater the complexity of the model of world, of

change, of new system, of systems integration that the group may construct–
negotiate.

The Imposed Redundancy (Variety) of Knowledge Bases and Contexts

For these reasons, one of the strategic tasks of systems integration firms
is to retain in-house redundant knowledge bases. It is worth underlining, however, that judging the importance of the knowledge basis relies
heavily on the complexity that the systems integrator has been able to create
in the past. We keep referring to the continuous negotiation taking place
among visions of individuals (autopoietic systems) within the organizations
of these firms, and to the continuous dynamic of their knowledge basis.
There are no knowledge bases of 'firm', only the knowledge bases possessed by men. The path to which we are referring is the path of
each of their knowledge bases, and the path of equilibrium points where
the negotiations among these visions into the organizations converged in
the past.

This path, which is *ex ante* uncertain and non-definable, is the process of
the evolution of the artefact envisaged by the systems integrator firm and
selected in the marketplace. Despite the great importance that characterizes
the historical path of the organization and the effectiveness–efficiency
achieved by the organizational mechanisms, the latter has to be differentiated
by the technical–scientific quality of the individuals belonging to the organization. The knowledge basis possessed by individuals, their history, the
history of the organization, found the roots that create complexity. In other
words, the knowledge bases should be considered as generators of the
complexity required to create the evolutionary path (or paths) of the systems
integration. The creation of complexity involves the generation of a greater
number of different potential states of the world, that is, of technological
alternatives for parts, subsystems, and the whole architecture of the system,
and their relationships.

An important part of the knowledge basis is formed by expertise,
namely by theoretical elaboration and hands-on knowledge and, therefore,
is heavily dependent on the generative contexts it refers to. Within this
frame, the distinction between knowledge related to the nature of nature
(scientific knowledge usually deriving from fundamental or long-term
research) and the ways to manipulate it (technologies commonly devised by
applied research and industrial development) tends to blur and, as a consequence, gives rise to unitary and global knowledge which is no longer
decomposable. This process ends up being both the effect and cause of the
emergence of a new concept of integrated and transdisciplinary knowledge,
that originates from the methodologies and the sociology of classic sciences, but that is triggered by applications (Gibbons et al. 1994).

But what does possession of the knowledge basis in order to generate effective competence and specific know-how[8] mean for a business organization? According to the definitions provided in this chapter, it means that:

- in a business organization there are agents with profound knowledge at least of the single and fundamental scientific–technological disciplines necessary for the development of the knowledge basis (of the subsystems, architecture, and interfaces);
- the organization places at their disposal the contexts (laboratories, product processes, organizational machine rules, work methodologies, incentives, languages, schools, economic resources, power and dynamic distributions, paradigms, myths, beliefs, stories, etc.) to be able to express such knowledge.

The typical transition is from (a) individual paths (individuals are called to work alone) to (b) multidisciplinary task forces (individuals are called to work, according to their own knowledge basis in a specific task area, to (c) interdisciplinary teams (everyone's work is to occupy oneself with the entire task, including the integration, which is anticipated as a collective operation undergone by all the participants; everyone is responsible for the task—this set-up generally allows disciplinary fusions), to (d) stable transdisciplinary groups (permanent group–work structures that decide their tasks and the areas of intervention—it also nourishes disciplinary fusions to give life to knowledge bearers who are no longer reduced to discipline).

The following example will better illustrate this process. In a multidisciplinary order, a problem of fluid dynamics can be faced by statistics, physics, chemistry, mathematics, etc., each one dealing with the problem in a separate way. An interdisciplinary approach, however, will see them work together as statistics, physics, and so on, thus sharing the global task. In a transdisciplinary order (following an obvious history of interdisciplinarity), the work group will comprise only fluid dynamics. In any case, the knowledge to support the capacity of systems integration emerges from the application of all knowledge in all effective contexts (not only in R&D, but also in the production of the components and of the system, in the planning, etc.) on the basis of recomposition that we can imagine, given the system's breakdown, carried out to reconstruct it. All these activities can be clearly described as 'situated', in other words, they are the fruit of 'interactions between agents and physical systems and with other people' in a specific context (Clancey 1993: 87–114; Greeno and Moore 1993: 49; Vera and Simon 1993: 7, 46), namely, the one pertaining to the specific agent subject. If the context is a social system, then the overall picture also includes its 'being' history and the developmental path of its routines, of its decision-making mechanisms, and the roles of the different interest or power groups and ideologies present in the organization itself 'Knowledge is about meaning. It is context specific and relational' (Nonaka and Takeuchi 1995: 58).

Thus, if firms do not keep a sufficient number, variety, and redundancy of contexts in-house, then their capability of systems integration drastically diminishes. It is the metaphor of the blind man who does not know what he does not see. So losing contexts means losing knowledge connected to them. Awareness appears individually when someone who we have always beaten (perhaps at chess) finally beats us. It occurs from a social point of view (perhaps when playing football) when the team who has never won before finally beats us. But how many defeats will be necessary for us to become aware that it was not fate or anything else? Particularly in the case of businesses, how many signals will be ignored before an individual within a firm realizes that defeats are the effects of a loss of competitive ability due to a lack of knowledge, to the loss of context?

9.5   Concluding Remarks: Maintaining Control of Systems Integration

We argue that knowledge tends to be increasingly represented in unique (by transcending the classic dichotomy base-applied) and transdisciplinary (by transcending the classic boundaries between disciplines) ways. If the linguistic outcomes of cognitive activities are more or less appropriable in economic terms, the cognitive processes that may lead to those outcomes, that is processes of production of knowledge, are always appropriable because they are agent-specific and therefore firm-specific. In fact, competencies and historical paths of learning are specific to each autopoietic system forming the social group called organization, and they are linked to the evolution of organization and to its settings in terms of number, variety, and redundancy of (cognitive) contexts and their constituents. The latter can be considered as generators of robust views of the world or, rather, of richer constructions of possible options in the evolution. The more the processes have been completely internalized over time, the deeper those possible options are rooted. Bearing these things in mind, we can apply this summarizing scheme to systems integration cognitive strategy that we can put forward as an exemplary case (Paoli and Prencipe 1999).

1. Given a product/process–system or its family.
2. Its systems integration evolutionary dynamics, conceived as an ability to introduce innovations (to be measured not only in quantitative terms— incremental or radical—but also in qualitative terms—modular, interface, architectural, systemic) and, therefore, as a capacity to compete through and by means of innovation, can be described with complex models

(the lower the complexity of the constructions, the greater the loss of competitive capacity through innovation). These models are specific to those particular individuals and, through organizational specifications, to those particular groups in specific organizational contexts in which those particular individuals are working.

3. The degree of complexity of those constructions is a function of processes of relevant knowledge which are absolutely tacit in nature (Crozier 1964; March and Olsen 1976; Pfeffer 1978; Scott 1992); 'enacted environment is not synonymous with the concept of a perceived environment... to emphasize that managers construct, rearrange, single out, and demolish many objective features of their surroundings... the process of enacting is one in which the subject partly interacts with and constitutes the object' (Weick 1969–79: 164–5). Complexity depends on specific situations: (*a*) on the two-way (circular) relationships between scientific (and its state, namely descriptive, predictable, etc.), technological, applied, and integrated knowledge (Reismann 1992: 110); and (*b*) on the elaboration of experience (all contained in contexts).

4. In any case, abandoning activities of support to cognitive processes and contexts (e.g. R&D, but also manufacturing, of components and subsystems), and shifting towards a general assembling organization, entails losing the capacity of modelling the possible evolution of the systems integration. Put differently, this leads to the often irreversible loss of the ability to create complexity in modelling the evolutionary path of the system, and, as a result, to the loss of strategic control of the evolution of its integration. The actual risk is that of losing the role of systems integrator (i.e. the person who decides which evolutionary trajectory the system takes), thus becoming a simple assembler without even realizing that this is happening (e.g. see the evolutionary dynamics of assembler versus componentist relations in the automotive sector).

The Challenge is to Keep a High Capacity to Create Complexity

Of course, other considerations, predominantly economic or strategic in character, may in any case lead to the adoption of different or alternative solutions concerning structure, level, and nature of vertical integration and/or of the various possible internalizations. From the point of view of the knowledge necessary for strategic dominion over evolution of systems integration, however, it may prove extremely dangerous to entertain the illusion that the cognitive results, for example, of research activities, can be systematically purchased. Similarly, it would be equally risky to believe that the division of labour does not need to be systematically considered as the surrender of cognitive processes, a transfer of generative contexts, and the jeopardization of world-creating ability (Paoli and Prencipe 1999). There is no learning without context, because learning is an action which incorporates (it enacts, one might say) the context (which, therefore, is defined in this work as generative). That is to say, there cannot be a learning dissociated from the context in which the operational action–activity will produce learning (Vigotsky 1978; Leontieff 1981; Gardner 1983). A failure to realize the peril inherent to the assignment of contexts would inevitably result in diminished capacity for 'imagination–creation' of alternative paths of opportunity. The costs and strategic implications of such assignments should always be evaluated in and by the decentralizing decision-making processes, in such a way as to mitigate the weight of mere economic evaluations (Paoli and Prencipe 1999).

Looking at the issue from a slightly different perspective, it is precisely due to their ability to create opportunity that many leaders of former technologies substituted by earth-shattering breakthroughs have still managed to retain institutional continuity. In this way, strongly rooted chemicals industries have successfully survived the radically innovative waves of synthetic products (Pavitt 1990), thus becoming leaders of new solutions; and the same process is taking place in biotechnology. This ability to retain institutional continuity depends primarily on learning from experience, in accumulated expertise and capacity for integration of a diverse knowledge basis. Such ingredients make it possible to engage in strategic elaboration in order to overcome the distinction between content–process and context of strategic elaboration itself (Dodgson 1989). This is because learning about the context defines the content of innovative strategic behaviour, while implementation of the latter, with the ensuing learning, redefines, or rather recreates, a new context, thereby blurring the demarcation between definition of the content of technological strategy and its implementation. Without experience, there can be no learning (i.e. non-decomposable and therefore non-sharable unitary processes), and without learning, there is a failure or, at the very least, a decrease in the capability to continually recreate the spectrum of exploitable opportunities along the path that is equally continually recreated. Such a spectrum must possess the breadth required by current competition conditions, or by the strategic position the firm has assigned itself in a more or less illusory fashion.

Notes

1. For more detailed discussions on this issue, see Paoli and Grassi (2000) and Paoli and Prencipe (2003).
2. For a more detailed analysis of organizing, see Weick (1969–79).
3. This is also the concept at the basis of *formative contexts* (Unger 1987; Ciborra and Lanzara 1988; Lanzara 1993).
4. 'The notion of context encompasses the implicit assumption that for an agent the sequence of actions, events and experience is somehow segmented and divided into contexts that can be considered equal or indifferent. The sensitivity to

context, that is, the ability to distinguish and recognize contexts is an essential element of the programme for the action of the actor: it is the base of the action of deciding and controlling its behaviour. If the context is pre-interpreted, then few resources will be mobilized. If, instead, the context is ambiguous, unstable, or too generic, most of the cognitive work of the actor will be aimed to "build meaning", to decode and define the context in order to guide the action' (Lanzara 1993).

5. A more in-depth (and probably disruptive) line of thinking emerges from the reasoning above. Individuals, as parts of social systems, have 'intentions' (Searle 1992). A financial vice-president wishes to become a CEO, an important politician, a rich man, but (at the same time) also a member of the 'Buena Vista Social Club'. It is worth noting that this feature of 'having intentions' within a social system has never been taken into consideration by the social sciences. The concept of system, in fact, has been used as a simple analogy borrowed from physics or biology. However, while physical or biological systems are composed of parts that might be other things (i.e. play other roles in different systems), and are assigned to and constrained by specific tasks (our liver does not wish to be the brain), how many other roles in how many other social subsystems does a financial vice-president wish to interpret simultaneously? And now, in this moment, while he is talking with our clients, to which role in which social system is he responding?

6. Obvious examples of slang are easily found in nearly all specialized magazines, even in those designed for a popular readership; for instance, magazines dealing with microelectronics, computer science, or the internet, which have become practically incomprehensible to anyone who does not have a minimal familiarity with these technologies.

7. In this chapter the notions of programme (only indirectly considered) and representation–conception–construction do not share the common meaning of cognivitism (Craik 1943; Bartlett 1961; von Wright 1972; Elster 1983; Haugeland 1985, 1989; Minsky 1989; Cummins 1993; Lanzara 1993; Oliviero 1995). In this work the terms representing–conceiving–constructing mean bringing to the mind–consciousness. They do not refer to images, schemes, or models of a perceived external environment, but to cognitive structures that build the external environment by associating meaning with perceptions that they do not have by themselves. Our concept of construction draws heavily on the idea of knowledge-as-action (Piaget 1967), on the notion of knowledge-in-action, and on the considerations about representation that are not based on symbolic systems (Kosslyn and Hatfield 1994), the so-called learning without representation approach (Maturana and Varela 1980, 1987; von Foerster 1987).

8. I do not have here the opportunity to develop deeply the articulation of knowledge (i.e. knowledge basis, competence, expertise, skill), but I do argue that without a knowledge basis we cannot aspire to systems integration. Perhaps for operations such as 'editing' or assembling, only operative competence and know-how without complete theoretic reference are required — for example, for the bricklayer who knows nothing about construction science in order to build a good, straight wall, it is enough to know the 'plumbline'. For the guide of the evolutionary dynamics of systems integration a deep theoretical understanding—

which means being able to conceive new forms of wall, as well as new alternatives to what forms it—is indispensable. In simple terms, since only operative competence and know-how are available, there would not be sufficient complexity in the constructions of the modality of alternative systems integration.

References

ANGYAL, A. (1941). *Foundations for a Science of Personality*. Cambridge, MA: Harvard University Press.

ARDUINI, A. (1998). *Fondamenti della Psiche*. Pisa: ETS.

ARGYRIS, C. and SCHON, D. A. (1978). *Organisational Learning: A Theory of Action Perspective*. Reading, PA: Addison Wesley.

ARORA, A. and GAMBARDELLA, A. (1994). 'The Changing Technology of Technological Change: General and Abstract Knowledge and the Division of Innovative Labour', *Research Policy*, 23: 523–32.

ARROW, K. J. (1962). 'Economic Welfare and the Allocation of Resources for Invention', in R. R. Nelson (ed.), *The Rate and Direction of Inventive Activity: Economic and Social Factors*. Princeton, NJ: Princeton University Press, 609–25.

—— (1969). 'Classificatory Notes on the Production and Transmission of Technological Knowledge', *American Economic Review*, 59/2: 29–35.

ATLAN, H. (1974). 'On a Formal Definition of Organization', *Journal of Theoretical Biology*, 45: 295–304.

BACHELARD, G. (1953). *Le Matérialisme Rationnel*. Paris: PUF.

—— (1996). *Le Nouvel Esprit Scientifique*. Paris: PUF.

BARTLETT, F. C. (1961). *Remembering*. Cambridge: Cambridge University Press.

BATESON, G. (1976). *Verso un'Ecologia della Mente*. Milan: Adelphi.

BRUSONI, S., PRENCIPE, A., and PAVITT, K. (2001). 'Knowledge Specialization, Organizational Coupling, and the Boundaries of the Firm: Why do Firms Know More than they Make?', *Administrative Science Quarterly*, 46: 597–621.

CARROLL, L. (1975). *Alice in Wonderland*. Milan: Garzanti.

—— (1975). *Behind the Looking Glass*. Milan: Garzanti.

CHURCHLAND, P. S. and SEJNOWSKI, T. J. (1992). *The Computational Brain*. Cambridge, MA: MIT Press.

CIBORRA, C. and LANZARA, G. F. (1988). 'I Labirinti dell'Innovazione, Routines Organizzative e Contesti Formativi', *Studi Organizzativi*, 19.

CLANCEY, W. J. (1993). 'Situated Action: A Neuropsychological Interpretation. Response to Vera and Simon', *Cognitive Science* (Special Issue: Situated Action), 17/1: 87–115.

COHEN, W. A. and LEVINTHAL, D. A. (1989). 'Innovation and Learning: The Two Faces of R&D', *The Economic Journal*, 99: 569–96.

—— —— (1990). 'Absorptive Capacity: A New Perspective on Learning and Innovation', *Administrative Science Quarterly*, 35: 128–52.

—— BURKHART, R., DOSI, G., EGIDI, M., MARENGO, L., WARGLIEN, M., and WINTER, S. (1996). 'Routines and other Recurring Action Patterns of Organisations: Contemporary Research Issues', *Industrial and Corporate Change*, 5/3: 653–98.

CRAIK, K. J. W. (1943). *The Nature of Explanation*. Cambridge, MA: Cambridge University Press.

CROZIER, M. (1964). *The Bureaucratic Phenomenon*. Chicago, IL: Chicago University Press.

CUMMINS, R. (1993). *Significato e Rappresentazione Mentale*. Bologna: Il Mulino.

DODGSON, M. (1989). 'Introduction: Technology in a Strategic Perspective', in M. Dodgson (ed.), *Technology Strategy and the Firm: Management and Public Policy*. London: Longman, 1–10.

DUHEM, P. (1914). *La Théorie Physique: Son Object et sa Structure*. Paris: Rivière.

ELSTER, J. (1983). *Ulisse e le Sirene*. Milan: Feltrinelli.

FOERSTER, H. VON (1962). 'Communication amongst Automata', *American Journal of Psychiatry*, 118: 865–71.

—— (1987). *Sistemi che Osservano*. Rome: Astrolabio.

GARDNER, H. (1983). *Frames of Mind: The Theory of Multiple Intelligence*. New York: Basic Books.

GIBBONS, M., LIMOGES, C., NOWOTNY, H., SCHWARTZMAN, S., SCOTT, P., and TROW, M. (1994). *The New Production of Knowledge*. London: Sage.

GÖDEL, K. (1931). 'Über Formal Unentscheidbare Sätze der Principia Mathematica und Verwandter Systeme', *Monatshefte für Mathematik und Physik*, 38: 173–98.

GREENO, J. G. and MOORE, J. L. (1993). 'Situativity and Symbols: Response to Vera and Simon', *Cognitive Science* (Special Issue: Situated Action), 17/1: 49–59.

GREGORY, R. L. (1991). *Enciclopedia Oxford della Mente*. Florence: Sansoni.

HAUGELAND, J. (1985). *Artificial Intelligence: The Very Idea*. Cambridge, MA: MIT Press and Bradford Books.

—— (1989). 'Meccanismi Semantici (Semantic Engines)', in J. Haugeland (ed.), *Progettare la Mente. Filosofia, Psicologia, Intelligenza Artificiale*. Bologna: Il Mulino, 7–42.

KOSSLYN, S. and HATFIELD, G. (1984). 'Representation Without Symbol Systems', *Social Science*, 51: 1019–45.

KUHN, T. (1970). *The Structure of Scientific Revolutions*. Chicago, IL: University of Chicago Press.

LANZARA, G. F. (1993). *Capacità Negativa*. Bologna: Il Mulino.

LE MOIGNE, J. L. (1990). *La Modélisation des Systèmes Complexes*. Paris: Dunod.

LEONTIEFF, A. N. (1981). 'The Problem of Activity in Psychology', in J. V. Wertsch (ed.), *The Concept of Activity in Soviet Psychology*. Armonk, NY: Sharpe, 37–71.

LUPASCO, S. (1962). *L'Energie de la Matiere Vivante: Antagonisme Constructeur et Logique de l'Hétérogène*. Paris: Julliard.

MACHLUP, F. (1984). *The Economics of Information and Human Capital*. New York: New York University Press.

MARCH, J. G. and OLSEN, J. P. (1976). *Ambiguity and Choice in Organization*. Bergen: Universitetsforlaget.

MATURANA, H. and VARELA, F. (1980). *Autopoiesis and Cognition: The Realization of Living*. Dordrecht: Reidel.

—— and VARELA, F. (1987). *The Tree of Knowledge*. Boston, MA: Shambhala.

MINSKY, M. (1989). *La Società della Mente*. Milan: Adelphi.

MORIN, E. (1983). *Il Metodo: Ordine, Disordine, Organizzazione*. Milan: Feltrinelli.

NAGEL, E. and NEWMAN, J. R. (1992). *La Prova di Gödel*. Turin: Bollati Boringhieri.

NELSON, R. R. (1959). 'The Simple Economics of Basic Scientific Research', *The Journal of Political Economy*, 68: 297–306.

NONAKA, I. and TAKEUCHI, H. (1995). *The Knowledge-creating Company*. New York: Oxford University Press.

OLIVERIO, A. (1995). *Biologia e Filosofia della Mente*. Bari: Laterza.

PAOLI and GRASSI, M. (2000). 'Caught in the Middle: An Investigation of Three Recurrent Controversies in the Management of "Organizational" Knowledge'. Paper to the International Meeting on Organization, Business Processes Resource Centre, University of Warwick, Coventry, UK; February.

—— and PRENCIPE, A. (1999). 'The Role of Knowledge Bases in Complex Product Systems: Some Empirical Evidence from the Aero-engine Industry', *Journal of Management and Governance*, 3: 137–60.

———— (2003). 'The Relationships between Individual and Organisational Memory: Exploring the Missing Links', *Journal of Management and Governance*, 7/2: 145–62.

PAVITT, K. (1990). 'What we know about the Strategic Management of Technology', *California Management Review*, 32: 3–26.

PFEFFER, J. (1978). *The External Control of Organizations*. New York: Harper & Row.

PIAGET, J. (1967). *Biologie et Connaissance*. Paris: Gallimard.

PRENCIPE, A. (1997). 'Technological Capabilities and Product Evolutionary Dynamics: A Case Study from the Aero Engine Industry', *Research Policy*, 25: 1261–76.

—— (2000). *Competenze Tecnologiche Divisione del Lavoro e Confini d'Impresa*. Milan: Franco Angeli.

—— (2004). *Strategy, Systems and Scope: Managing Systems Integration in Complex Products*. London: Sage.

QUINE, W. V. O. (1969). *Ontological Relativity and Other Essays*. New York: Columbia University Press.

REISMANN, A. (1992). *Management Science Knowledge*. Westport, CT: Quorum Books.

ROMER, P. M. (1993). *Two Strategies for Economic Development: Using Ideas vs. Producing Ideas* (World Bank Annual Conference on Developments Economics). Washington, DC: WBP.

SEARLE, J. R. (1992). *The Rediscovery of the Mind*. Boston, MA: MIT Press.

SCOTT, R. W. (1992). *Organizations*. Englewood Cliffs, NJ: Prentice Hall.

SIMON, H. A. (1962). 'The Architecture of Complexity', *Proceedings of American Philosophical Society*, 106: 467–88.

UNGER, R. M. (1987). *False Necessity*. Cambridge: Cambridge University Press.

VARELA, F., MATURANA, H., and URIBE, R. (1974). 'Autopoiesis: The Organization of Living Systems, Its Characterization and a Model', *Currents in Modern Biology*, 5/4: 187–96.

VERA, A. H. and SIMON, H. A. (1993). 'Situated Action: A Symbolic Interpretation', *Cognitive Science* (Special Issue: Situated Action), 17/1: 7–48.

VIGOTSKY, L. S. (1978). *Mind in Society*. Cambridge, MA: Harvard University Press.

WEICK, K. E. (1969–1979). *The Social Psychology of Organizing*. Reading, PA: Addison Wesley.

WRIGHT, G. H. VON (1972). 'On So-called Practical Inference', *Acta Sociologica Finnica*, 15: 39–53.

10

Towards a Dynamics of Modularity
A Cyclical Model of Technical Advance

HENRY CHESBROUGH

Haas Business School, University of California, Berkeley, USA

10.1 Introduction

The literature on modularity (or more precisely, of what Schilling terms 'product modularity')[1] documents a close correspondence between the technical structure of a complex good, and the organizational structure of the firm producing that good (Simon 1962; Garud and Kumaraswamy 1995; Sanchez 1995). Economic theories have shown how standards can emerge out of a competition between rival standards (e.g. Farrell and Saloner 1986; Katz and Shapiro 1986), and the process of competing within standards fosters focused competitive strategies (Rotemberg and Saloner 1994; Baldwin and Clark 2000). This leads to vibrant innovation within the industry, with thousands of companies all competing within the modular structure of the industry.

These accounts certainly help to explain the external basis of innovation within industries such as the personal computer industry (Langlois 1992; Langlois and Robertson 1995). Other work has documented increasingly modular technologies and organizations in aircraft engines and chemical engineering (Brusoni and Prencipe 2001), aerospace (O'Sullivan 2001), disc drives (Christensen and Chesbrough 1999; Chesbrough and Kusunoki 2001), and consumer electronics (Sanchez 1995). A recent integrative treatment showed the effect of modularity on industry structure, positing a progression from vertically integrated structures to horizontally organized, modular players (Baldwin and Clark 2000).

While we have certainly made real progress in opening the 'black box' of modularity (Brusoni and Prencipe 2001), much remains to be done. This chapter will focus on some areas where our understanding is underdeveloped, and where the conclusions reached to date raise important issues that have not been addressed. It will attempt to lay some groundwork for advances in those areas, and offer an empirical analysis that might motivate additional empirical work in future.

The first distinction is one of dynamics. In these works, there is a fundamentally static perspective to the analysis. The modules that comprise 'modularity' are treated as artefacts, and the process from which they emerge is left unexplored. As a result, the predictions tend to be one-sided: every technology will proceed from a less modular, more integrated state towards a more modular state (Baldwin and Clark 2000). This is incomplete; every technical architecture has inherent performance limits. Sooner or later, the linkages among components that comprise the architecture constrain the further advance of the system. In order for the system to advance, a new architecture must be found. That is a fundamentally different task from the task of innovating *within* a given architecture.

A second critical issue that I believe has been insufficiently developed is the relationship between modularity within the firm, and modularity in the market. While these can go hand in hand (Sanchez 1995) they need not do so. And it is important to understand the conditions under which one does or does not lead to the other. In particular, the issue of systems integration figures prominently, and how integration occurs within the firm differs substantially from how it emerges through the market.

Once we consider dynamics, the process of advancing to a new, better architecture is a third area that needs much more analysis. An industry that has experienced extensive modularity in its market is now populated by a myriad of participants, who coordinate through the interfaces of the current architecture. These participants' activities function as complements to one another. Yet, our understanding of systems with highly evolved complementarities tells us that these systems are hard to advance. How do the parties engaged in the current architecture evaluate whether and when to participate in the new architecture? How do systems architects credibly commit to new interfaces, so that modular complementors can make specific investments in support of the new architecture?

The rest of the chapter is structured as follows: The next section examines the sources of internal modularity, and the conditions under which that leads to market modularity. The third section develops a dynamic cyclical model of how the technical architecture of a system evolves, and presents some empirical evidence of component performance in the hard disc drive (HDD) industry. The fourth section discusses the question of systems integration within an architecture, and how market leadership is required to spur a further round of the cycle. Relatedly, the question of who makes rents, and how, figures importantly in the evolution of the industry. Concluding remarks follow.

10.2 Internal Modularity and Market Modularity

In the early stages of a new technology's development, there are enormous technical uncertainties to manage. The technology itself is highly immature, and unable to perform any useful task very effectively. In order to advance the technology to become economically useful, the developer must select a focus for development. In any reasonably complex system, there are a large number of components and subsystems to coordinate, and myriad possibilities for how best to connect these disparate elements together (Ulrich 1995).

Here, the requisite information of how the different elements function together is not well defined, and interactions between elements are poorly understood. This is a condition of technological interdependence. As Ulrich and Eppinger's Design Structure Matrix (DSM) has shown, tightly interdependent technologies can achieve better product performance (albeit at the expense of flexibility), relative to more modular architectures. While the system may function well, changes to one part of the system can have effects in many other parts of the system in non-obvious ways (Ulrich and Eppinger 1995).

In this early stage of technology evolution, managerial coordination, rather than markets, provides the most effective mechanisms to coordinate the relationships between elements of the system. The comparative benefits of internal coordination arise from Williamson's (1975, 1985) concepts of markets versus hierarchies. Due to the complexities inherent in interdependent technologies, their numerous technical interactions cannot be fully characterized, and are only poorly understood. Under these conditions, markets do not function effectively and can even be hazardous. A customer cannot fully specify his requirements to a buyer, and cannot predict how the component or subsystem will affect his system. When these problems arise, bargaining costs ensue.

The usual recourse in the market would be to switch suppliers. Because the interdependencies are poorly understood, though, bringing in another supplier may only introduce new technical problems, which again may be viewed differently by the different parties to the transaction. Technological interdependence undermines the ability to discipline one supplier by switching to another. To achieve the close coordination and to facilitate rapid mutual adjustment between interdependent technologies, administrative coordination outside of the market is required to develop the technology effectively.

As the technology begins to mature, other possible uses of the technology are contemplated. Research on technical problem-solving has shown that engineers do not—indeed, they cannot—evaluate all of these possible combinations of technology. Instead, they attempt to partition the problem into more specific tasks (Simon 1962; von Hippel 1990, 1994; Kogut and Zander 1992), and employ heuristics to connect components together to form a subsystem (Henderson and Clark 1990). These subsystems in turn are connected to create systems. So a system is built out of a series of nested subsystems (Simon 1962).

This partitioning and architecting reduces the complexity of technology development dramatically. It is a necessary and beneficial strategy to get products to market on a timely basis, within a reasonable budget. Once deployed and launched, however, the connections between components, subsystems, and systems become difficult to adjust. They take on a life of their own, as past, present, and future elements all target the connection interface, in order to perform their function without disrupting the rest of the system.

One of the paradigmatic examples of this partitioning process that ushered in more internal modularity in a systems architecture is the IBM System 360 development (Fisher, McGowan, and Greenwood 1983; Pugh 1995). IBM took a major step toward a modular architectural design in 1964, at the same time as it designed its first modular mainframe computer, the IBM Series 360 (Pugh, Johnson, and Palmer 1991; Baldwin and Clark 2000). However, while the technical design of the 360 was far more modular than earlier IBM designs, there were no external markets for components to supplant managerial coordination across the interface between components and product design. The supply of components in system 360 and 370-class mainframes remained almost entirely captive.

Another example of internal modularity arose in Xerox's copiers and printers. Xerox created a communications protocol, known as Ethernet, to allow the company to 'mix and match' different combinations of document-feeding modules into the copy engine, and employ a variety of document-sorting, -collating, and -stapling modules at the back end of the copier (Pake 1986; Chesbrough 2002). This greatly increased the number of equipment configurations that Xerox could offer to its customers, without a con-comitant expansion in the number of products it had to manufacture and stock in inventory. As with IBM, however, these standards did not usher in a plethora of external companies to offer competing components to plug into Xerox copy engines.

This is because at the outset the interface standards amongst the modules were internal and proprietary. Under such conditions of 'internal modu-larity', companies such as IBM and Xerox could simplify their engineering tasks and expand the scope of their offerings to consumers, without fear of having their profits competed away by third parties seeking to connect to those same interfaces. Indeed, they could even subcontract the design and manufacture of components to third-party suppliers, while its competitors could not use those same unmodified components from those suppliers.

This raises an important question that has been neglected in the modu-larity literature to date: what are the conditions under which internal mod-ularity can lead to external or market-mediated modularity?[2] While the partitioning of a complex system into an architecture of more manageable modules is necessary, it is by no means sufficient. The analysis of Baldwin and Clark (2000) skips over this crucial intermediate step, in tracing the evolution of modularity within an industry.

It is likely that the answer to this question will also depend on environ-mental conditions surrounding the industry and the technology. Sako

(Chapter Twelve, this volume) analyses the conditions under which modularity can influence the structure of an industry and the location of firm boundaries. She found that labour markets and capital markets play an important mediating role, in determining whether a modular product leads to a modular organization or industry. This mediating role for labour and capital markets was also found by Chesbrough (1999) to be a critical variable in the presence or absence of startup firms in the United States or Japan, respectively during various technology transitions in the HDD industry.

Sufficient Conditions for Market Modularity

If a systems technology has matured to the point where the relationships among its elements have been partitioned, and the interactions between those partitions are now well understood, we have achieved some necessary conditions for modularity. What more is needed to enable markets to take over the coordination tasks of innovation to advance that system?

The answer draws on the institutional conditions that markets need to be able to function, such as property rights (North 1990). Of more particular interest here are the informational conditions needed to enable the transaction costs within the markets to be low enough to permit effective market exchange (Williamson 1975). Below are four criteria that must be satisfied, in order for markets to manage effectively the further innovation of a system:

(*a*) First, the interactions between the components in the architecture are well understood by numerous parties within an industry and the effects of changes to components upon the system can be predicted. This implies that the knowledge of internal modularity achieved by one firm must now be diffused outside the firm into its surrounding environment.

(*b*) Second, the required attributes of components in the system must be able to be clearly specified. This implies that the features and functions of components are unambiguous, and that transacting firms can clearly communicate their requirements. This also implies that concepts and codes are widely shared within the environment (Brown and Duguid 2000).

(*c*) Tools and equipment exist to verify that the required attributes of components have been met. In complex components and subsystems, advanced tools and equipment are often needed to be able to satisfy the information needs of customers and suppliers. They also help to codify information that was previously tacit (Monteverde 1995). These tools are powerful enablers of modularity.[3]

(*d*) A capable supplier base exists, such that a firm can credibly invoke the possibility of switching suppliers to discipline any current supplier from holding up the firm, in resolving issues of technical integration of components or modules into the system.

These conditions greatly improve the information available outside the firm in the market, so that outside firms can now opt to provide some portion of the system, without fear of disrupting other parts of that system. Supplying firms can choose which systems to support, and which elements within the system to provide. Buying firms can discipline suppliers by switching to other suppliers, without fear of disrupting the functioning of their systems.

For example, a modular interface within a system exists when clear, explicit interfaces exist, that document the connection between the sub-system and the system. In HDDs, for example, if a read–write head (itself a complex system, including the head, the air bearing to fly the head, the arm to support the head, and so on) can be used with multiple discs, and if multiple heads can be used with a given disk, then this interchangeability means that modularity exists in the design of a disc drive. Modularity at this interface enables an arm's-length relationship between the suppliers of heads and discs, and the disc drive companies. It can enable an intermediate market, usually termed an 'OEM market' in industry parlance, to emerge at this interface. This can deconstruct a previously internal supply chain into a network of suppliers and buyers (Langlois 1992; Christensen and Rosenbloom 1995). Entry can occur on both sides of the interface, as new suppliers compete to sell components, while new disc drive companies outsource critical components in their drive, and compete on time to market with new drive designs.[4]

Technological interdependence, by contrast, exists when such an interface does not exist. Here, the use of a different component in a system can result in many non-obvious problems. Lacking a clear interface, product designers would not know which of the many attributes of a component need to be specified to particular tolerances, in order to have the product perform as expected when the components are assembled together. Unambiguous methods to measure these attributes may not exist ('is the component bad, or is our test for it bad?'), and engineers may be unable to predict or model how variation in the attributes of some components will affect the required design of other elements of the product. Here, an intermediate market will be thwarted, due to the information problems and bargaining costs that arise. Companies cannot easily switch suppliers in their design.

In Kaufman's (1993) lexicon, these interdependent conditions create a 'rugged landscape' that complicates the development of solutions to improve the product.[5] Under conditions of high technological interdependence, optimal component designs and the product architecture can only be defined iteratively and interactively by an integrated development organization. Much of the knowledge of effective integration may be tacit in form, making it hard to transmit within the firm, and even harder to share across firms (Monteverde 1995). These conditions make it difficult, if not impossible, for firms to enter the intermediate markets as suppliers. This is often the case with scale-up situations in many process-based industries (Pisano 1996).[6]

Once buyers and suppliers can utilize exchange to develop a system, and withdraw from exchange with little or no penalty, the discipline, incentives, and market aggregation features of market exchange overtake the earlier advantages of internal coordination (Williamson 1975). Here is where the power of markets powerfully advances modular systems (Baldwin and Clark 2000). Pure modularity and pure technological interdependence are, of course, extreme boundary conditions. Most products and technologies exist somewhere along a continuum between these extremes (Brusoni and Prencipe 2001).

10.3   A Dynamic, Cyclical Model of Modularity

Once the conditions for market modularity are satisfied, analysts like Baldwin and Clark (2000) predict an inevitable progression towards a modular industry structure, which industry practitioners sometimes term 'the horizontalization of the industry' (Grove 1996).

I wish to suggest, though, that this cannot be the end of the story. Once a modular industry has emerged, it has within it a highly elaborated structure of complementary providers, whose goods complement and extend the value of the system. However, our knowledge of systems with high degrees of this complementarity tells us that such systems are hard to advance (Milgrom and Roberts 1990; Kaufman 1993). While component innovation within the system can continue to occur so long as the boundaries of the component's relation with the rest of the system are respected, innovation at the systems level becomes increasingly problematic.

Every architecture has its performance limits. As an industry evolves, it will eventually reach the limits of what the present architecture can achieve. The technological yield of a system's components will approach their theoretical limit (Iansiti 1997). The connections between components and subsystems that enabled them to interoperate earlier, now place increasingly severe restrictions on the speed and method of their operation. The architectural yield achieved from a given relationship of components will also approach its limit (MacCormack 2001). Thus, the very partitioning of the system that enabled market modularity to develop, later turns into a restriction upon that system's further evolution.

To provide two examples of the performance constraints of a given architecture, consider the word length of a microprocessor, or the system bus within a personal computer. The original IBM PC had an 8-bit word length, meaning that 'words' or instructions of 8 bits could be processed at one time. Later on, this word length was increased to 16 bits. While old software and hardware could run on this new processor, the full benefit of the processor could only be realized if new complementary goods exploited the full 16-bit word length. How to address, index, error-detect-and-correct, and store these additional bits, though, was not initially standardized. Each complementor had to rearchitect its product for the new, ill-defined word length. The complementary goods manufacturers, in turn, were unsure of whether the benefits of rewriting their products for this new word length would be justified. Moreover, they wanted to wait until others had done so as well. This created an additional 'chicken and egg' inertia that held up the supply of new complements.[7]

A second example of this architectural limit is the PC system bus. The original IBM PC's bus ran plenty fast for add-in hardware products ca. 1981. And its interface was well documented and understood, so thousands of products were introduced that could plug into the expansion bus. But by the late 1980s, the bus itself became the bottleneck that limited the performance of the system and these add-on products. Then, no fewer than three alternative bus architectures arose to ease this bottleneck. Each was incompatible with the other, and the nuances of each took time to figure out. It took the industry many years to sort this out. Intel ended up forward integrating into the design of the system bus, and supplying the PC motherboards to its customers, in order to gain sufficient industry momentum for its bus architecture over the rival alternatives (Gawer and Cusumano 2002).

To advance beyond the limits of a given architecture, a new architecture must be established. The earlier relationships between the elements of the system, which were stable, broadly understood, and supported by a large number of market participants, now breaks down. A new partitioning of a new system must be developed. This new architecture, in turn, is not fully characterized at its inception. As before, there are a myriad number of ways that the system could be constructed. Only now, are there many actors with vested interests, specific investments, and strong incentives to have that system evolve in certain directions, and not others. The complementarities among these participants that created and extended the value of the earlier architecture now create rigidities that impair evolution at the systems level.

This can lead to a modularity trap (Chesbrough and Kusunoki 2001). Within the firm, the focus on developing products to compete within the standard eventually erodes the amount of system-level knowledge within the firm. While focused firms are effective in linking to the established architecture, they lack the knowledge to envision how best to connect to a new architecture. Within the industry, the collection of focused competitors that modularity enthusiasts celebrate (Rotemberg and Saloner 1994; Baldwin and Clark 2000) now lack the collective knowledge of how to evolve the system. They may also lack the ability to take collective action, necessary to coordinate a shift from one system of highly interconnected parts to a new system of connections.

This raises important issues again not discussed in the modularity literature to date. How do highly modular industries evolve beyond the limits of their architecture? Where does the knowledge come from to direct the evolution of the system? Who has the incentive and the ability to lead such a transition? Under what conditions will others follow the leader?

I suggest that the pattern of industry evolution shifts, from its well elaborated modular state back to an interdependent state. Only in the interdependent state can the broad systems architecture be revisited, and rearchitected. This heightens the uncertainty, ambiguity, and tacitness of information involved in this phase of the innovation process. Internal coordination within the firm again rises to the fore in negotiating this advance, while firms who continue to rely upon the market to make the advance will be frustrated by the market's inability to coordinate this type of innovation challenge. The source of rents within the industry also shifts, from focusing within a single layer of the system, to an additional source of rents for the overarching architecture of the system. This cyclical model of evolution will be illustrated with data from the disc drive industry below.

The Evolution of Disc Drive Components—1980–95[8]

Hard disc drives are complex marvels of technology that have advanced in density and in cost-per-megabyte even faster than Moore's law in semiconductors. They are used to provide storage to computers and other devices that employ microprocessors. They consist of many complex elements, but for present purposes, the critical subassemblies in a disc drive are the heads, the discs, and the electronics. The heads detect the presence of a magnetic field on a rotating disc by flying at a very small height over the disc. The disc stores magnetic domains, which are activated by the flying head that 'writes' the domain with a current in the head. The electronics translate these fields into '1s' and '0s', as well as managing the movement of the heads and discs.

When HDDs were initially introduced, they employed iron oxide heads and discs. While these technologies advanced nicely for many years, they later began to reach theoretical limits of their capability (Christensen 1993). These limits, in turn, were constraining the advance of HDDs, in terms of the cost per megabyte of these drives. If the HDDs did not continue to improve in cost, then other storage technologies would overtake them, and drive them out of the market.[9]

IBM responded to the approaching performance limit of oxide heads and discs by developing components based on thin film materials. These thin film heads and discs provided a ten-fold improvement in cost per megabyte, though they experienced significant problems in getting into high volume manufacturing. However, the merchant suppliers of oxide heads and discs confronted problems in shifting to the new thin film components. The head producers in particular confronted new interdependencies between the head and the rest of the disc drive. The earlier 'mix and match' that allowed merchant head suppliers to sell their products to disc drive manufacturers broke down. The integrated head manufacturers (i.e. the firms that made drives, as well as heads) were able to adopt the thin film heads years ahead of the merchant suppliers, precisely because they could employ internal administrative means to coordinate the interdependencies between the heads and the drive design. It took many years for merchant head producers like Read-Rite and AMC to create viable thin film head products to sell to independent drive makers.

Interestingly, the movement to thin film discs did not prove nearly so troublesome. Startup companies that pursued thin film discs found that their superior performance did not require the same drive redesign that was required of firms wishing to use thin film heads. Thin film discs could be used with oxide heads, metal in gap (MiG) heads, and thin film heads, with little cost in switching between them. Thin film discs soon developed a healthy merchant market, and independent suppliers like Komag were able to sell to independent drive manufacturers like Maxtor.

A decade after their introduction to the market, thin film heads themselves began to reach diminishing returns in their ability to advance. In 1992, IBM announced that its researchers had developed another new and very different type of recording head technology, called *magneto-resistive* (MR) heads, which offered another ten-fold improvement over the performance of thin film heads. The complexity and tacitness of the MR heads was well illustrated by an IBM engineer's statements at its announcement: 'We don't fully understand the physics involved, but we can replicate the event.' As was the case with thin film heads, the MR heads were an interdependent technology. The design of the discs, actuator mechanisms, and read–write channels depended upon the design of the head—and vice versa.

While the creation and development of the MR head was a technical achievement in itself, its incorporation into disc drive designs required other breakthroughs in the design of the drive. MR heads that passed incoming inspection would be placed in established disc drive designs, and those drives would fail final inspection. Identifying the sources of failure was a difficult and time-consuming task. The established design rules and models that connected the heads with the associated discs and electronics technologies had to be thrown out. The ultimate solution to using MR heads in drives that could pass final inspection required redesign of the head–disc interface, the electronics, and the manufacturing process to assemble the drives.

Integrated manufacturers who made their own heads such as IBM, Hitachi, and Fujitsu, could sort out these interdependencies, and figure out feasible solutions to these problems. Their integration, and their continued investments in research and advanced engineering, enabled them to maintain a high level of systems integration capabilities for how the different subsystems in disc drives interacted. In the event, they were years ahead of non-integrated drive manufacturers in getting MR-based disc drives to market. In fact, Quantum and Seagate, the largest OEM drive makers, were each subsequently forced to integrate into making their own MR heads, and to engage in the research and technology development efforts required to support the creation, integration, and manufacture of drives with advanced components.

Non-integrated disc drive companies such as Western Digital and Maxtor in the United States, and NEC and Toshiba in Japan, struggled mightily, working with their independent head suppliers to keep up with the pace of density improvement that IBM forged. All fell behind. These non-integrated firms found themselves in an organizational trap, where they lacked the internal systems integration capabilities of MR's technical interdependencies to extricate themselves (Chesbrough and Kusunoki 2001).

Later in the 1990s, MR technology became better understood and hence more modular. Independent head makers could now offer MR heads. At the same time that MR heads were becoming well understood, and intermediate markets were taking over the coordination of that technology, a new GMR (giant magneto-resistive) head technology came to the market out of IBM's research labs. And again, the integrated drive manufacturers with internal R&D capabilities in materials, heads, electronics, and disc drives were better able to incorporate the new head technology into their drive designs.

Empirical Evidence of Cyclical Nature of HDD Evolution

The evidence presented so far has been limited based upon earlier papers, utilizing data from managers at a few salient firms in the disc drive industry. To examine my arguments in detail across the entire industry, I have constructed an analysis of 3894 individual disc drive models that shipped in the disc drive industry from 1980 to 1995.[10] This analysis examines the shift in the industry from iron oxide heads to thin film heads to MR heads, and from iron oxide discs to thin film discs. The first transition, from iron oxide heads and discs to thin film heads and discs, occurred in the 1980s. In what follows, I have chosen 1987 as the dividing year, since that is the year in which volume shipments of thin film components began in the merchant market. The later transition to MR heads arose in 1994, when IBM began its shipments of products with this type of head.

My claim in this chapter is that technology advance will cycle between periods of interdependence and periods of modularity, and that firms and markets respectively will outperform the rival type of organization in each mode. When technologies are interdependent, internal organization can better sort out these complex technical interactions than market-mediated transacting, due to the lower coordination costs of internal organization in dealing with interdependent technologies. This internal advantage goes away when technologies' interrelationships become better understood. Once the sufficient conditions for market modularity above are met, the incentives available within the market elicit greater innovation, and spread the costs of innovation across a wider market, relative to internal organization. At some later time, though, once these well-understood, modular technologies hit their performance limits, an interdependent technology phase arises anew.

To assess this claim, I will examine the pattern of disc drive component performance over the period of 1980–1995. From the above casual empirical evidence, I assume that there were periods where internal integration of heads was a superior approach, and there were periods where modularity conditions developed, and market coordination was superior. Given these assumptions, I now examine whether in fact the disc drive components, particularly disc drive heads, cycle between better performance from integration, to better performance through the market, and back. In the early period, from 1980 to 1986, I expect strong advantages to internal supply of HDD heads. I would then expect a period where thin film heads become widespread, from 1987 to 1993, such that the internal organizational advantage dissipates. But once MR heads arrive on the scene, in 1994 and 1995, I would expect internal organization to again make better use of them initially. Though my data end in 1995, I would also expect the performance of drives with MR heads to become less associated with internal heads within a few years after 1995, as the intricacies associated with these components become better understood.

My dependent variable is a measure of what I term the 'architectural performance' of each disc drive. This is the amount of storage realized in the disc drive in comparison to the components that went into that drive model. Intuitively, this measure captures the ability of drive makers to achieve high-density designs out of their individual disc drive components. Higher densities reflect greater technical efficiencies, because the same technical components yield higher amounts of storage.

I defined architectural performance to be the actual areal density achieved by each disc drive, relative to a predicted average areal density achieved by all firms utilizing the same underlying components in the drive, designed in the same year. Areal density is measured in millions of bits per square inch.

The predicted average areal density measure for all drives using those components is derived from compiling data on all the Disk/Trend measures of product parameters for each year from 1980 through 1995. The relationship of each of these components and the resulting areal density of the drive model is estimated for each year, which generates coefficient estimates for the individual components (such as the types of heads or types of discs used in all the drives shipped that year), in the population of disc drive models. These coefficient estimates are then applied to the actual component specifications of each individual disc drive model, to determine a predicted average areal density for each model.

With these two measures in hand, I then divide 'predicted areal density' into the *actual* areal density of each product model, to create the 'architectural performance' measure.

$$\text{Architectural performance} = \frac{\text{actual areal density in that specific drive model}}{\text{calculated average areal density from those components}}$$

An example might help to illustrate the concept. The IBM 2.5″ Travelstar LP 2360 (code named 'Bolero') shipped in 1995. It incorporated IBM's MR head in its design, along with a thin film disk, run length limited (RLL) code, and other component features. Its actual areal density was 644 million bits per inch. We calculate the average areal density for these components by regressing the areal density of all products in the sample in 1995 by the components that they use. We then apply these estimated coefficients to the actual components used in a given drive model to arrive at the estimated areal density for that model. The average areal density for products with these same components as the IBM Travelstar was calculated to be 390 million bits per square inch. We construct the measure of architectural efficiency by taking 644 million bits per inch, and dividing that by the calculated average. In this case, the model's architectural efficiency was 1.651, meaning that IBM was able to achieve 65 per cent more areal density than the average of drives with the same components that shipped in 1995.

Disc drive firms during this period varied in whether they made the heads and media themselves or not, and my analysis above suggests that this difference ought to matter in periods where the technology was inter-dependent. If this is so, then I should be able to observe differences in their architectural performance, that is, in the areal density they actually achieve in the products they ship. During periods of high interdependence, drive models with internal head production ought to fare better. Their advantage ought to disappear, though, once the interdependencies are understood, and intermediate markets for the components have arisen. One might even conjecture that independent suppliers might then achieve higher density, relative to internal sources of components.

Table 10.1 describes the correlations of the variables in the analysis. The explanatory variables are all dummy variables for the type of component technology used in the drive model, and whether that component came from an internal source or an external source. The final three measures are inter-action terms, which measure subsets of internal and external sources for different head and disc technologies. Note the high correlation between models with internal heads and models with internal discs. Note also the high degree of correlation between the thin film discs, and the internal source of discs (0.502), as well as the similarly high correlation between thin film heads, and the internal source of heads (0.585). This suggests that thin film heads and discs may exhibit similar effects in their impact on architectural perfor-mance. This would contradict at least part of the story above, which argued that thin film discs were not an interdependent technology at the outset.

Table 10.2 shows the results of regressing architectural performance for 3894 disc drive product models that shipped from 1980 through 1995. The

TABLE 10.1 *Summary statistics and correlations of HDD components*

Variable	Definition and construction	Number of observations	Mean	SD	Min	Max
Archperf	Architectural performance, actual areal density divided by predicted density	3,894	1.052	0.329	0.096	3.132
TF head	Thin film head, dummy variable	3,894	0.315	0.464	0	1
MR head	Magneto resistive head, dummy variable	3,894	0.035	0.185	0	1
TF disc	Thin film disk, dummy variable	3,894	0.664	0.472	0	1
own head	Internally supplied head, dummy variable	3,894	0.382	0.486	0	1
own disc	Internally supplied disk, dummy variable	3,894	0.496	0.500	0	1
own tfdsk	Interaction term, of own disk and thin film disk	3,894	0.333	0.471	0	1
own tfhd	Interaction term, of own head and thin film head	3,894	0.136	0.343	0	1
own MRhd	Interaction term, of own head and MR head	3,894	0.035	0.185	0	1

	Archperf	TF head	MR head	TF disc	own head	own disk	own tfdsk	own tfhd
Archperf	1.0000							
TF head	− 0.0411	1.0000						
MR head	0.0731	− 0.1299	1.0000					
TF disc	− 0.0476	0.3214	0.1363	1.0000				
own head	0.0878	0.0700	0.2440	− 0.0480	1.0000			
own disc	0.0736	0.0570	0.1683	0.0137	**0.7127**	1.0000		
own tfdsk	0.0302	0.1850	0.2450	**0.5020**	0.4610	**0.7117**	1.0000	
own tfhd	− 0.0043	**0.5853**	− 0.0760	0.1376	0.5047	0.3398	0.3692	1.000
own MRhd	0.0731	− 0.1299	1.0000	0.1363	0.2440	0.1683	0.2450	− 0.0760

coefficient for thin film discs is significant and positive in the first model for the overall sample, and in three partitioned samples for 1980–6, 1987–93, and 1994–5 that follow. Not shown in this table are annual year dummies, to control for time trends (since disc drives advance in areal density each year). Drive models with thin film discs achieved higher architectural performance in these data, both overall and in each period. This means that products that

TABLE 10.2 *Regression analyses of heads and discs upon architectural performance*

	All models (1)	1980–6 (2)	1987–93 (3)	1994–5 (4)
Constant	1.003**	1.020**	0.793**	1.249**
	0.033	0.043	0.031	0.040
TF head	−0.001	0.139*	−0.013	−0.074
	0.016	0.063	0.016	0.042
TF disk	0.116**	0.109*	0.153**	dropped[+]
	0.021	0.053	0.025	
MR head	−0.028	NA	NA	0.158*
	0.034			0.072
Own head	0.089**	0.088*	0.102**	−0.233**
	0.018	0.041	0.020	0.085
Own disc	0.012	−0.033	0.076*	0.150**
	0.022	0.039	0.032	0.042
Own thin film head	−0.022	−0.057	−0.015	0.099
	0.024	0.091	0.024	0.090
Own thin film disc	0.002	0.157	−0.081*	dropped
	0.023	0.087	0.031	
Year dummies	included			
Number of Observations	3894	979	2502	413
Chi-square	19.94	4.86	13.27	5.77
Adjusted R-squared	0.10	0.04	0.06	0.06

*$p < 0.05$,
**$p - 0.01$
{+} By 1994, all disc media was thin film.

employed thin film discs exhibit enhanced architectural performance, and this performance benefit persists throughout each period, except for the last period, where every product in the sample utilized a thin film disc.

The behaviour for thin film heads in Table 10.2 differs from that of thin film discs, in contrast to their similar correlations in Table 10.1. The estimated coefficient for thin film heads is insignificantly related to architectural performance overall; however, the behaviour of this variable changes markedly over the three periods. Drive models with thin film heads initially achieve a significantly higher architectural performance in the period from 1980 to 1986. As discussed above, this is the period when thin film heads were almost exclusively captive. From 1987 to 1993, and 1994 to 1995, however, the influence is insignificant. As discussed above, this is when thin film heads transitioned to become less interdependent and more modular, and drive makers could incorporate merchant thin film heads into their designs.

The architectural performance of drive models with MR heads also is not significant in the overall sample. However, MR heads only entered into the Disk/Trend specification tables in 1994. In the subsample of drives in the last 2 years, its usage is significantly and positively related to architectural performance.

Separate from the performance effects of including the components themselves in each model, is the question of whether there is a performance benefit from supplying the component internally or not. Table 10.2 shows a statistically significant effect for firms that make their own heads, and to a lesser extent for firms that make their own discs. Firms who make their own heads appear to enhance the architectural efficiency of their product designs. This effect is positive in the first two periods, and negative in the third period, when MR heads emerged. In this third period, though, MR heads are associated with a significantly positive effect on architectural performance. Since all MR heads during these 2 years were internally supplied,[11] I interpret this to mean that making thin film heads internally in 1994 and 1995 had a negative effect on architectural efficiency, while making MR heads internally had a positive one. Making one's own discs also enhances the architectural efficiency of the models using those discs, in the latter two periods. (Interaction terms for making one's own thin film heads and thin film discs, are not significant. However, the degree of correlation of these interaction terms with whether or not firms make their heads and discs is high, 0.505 for heads, and 0.712 for discs, as shown in Table 10.1. Thus, the interpretation of the variables for making one's own heads and discs is hard to disentangle from the interaction terms.)

These results are generally supportive of my cyclical model. I expected the degree of interdependence in a component like thin film heads and MR heads to evolve over time. The behaviour of the thin film head variable performs very much as I would predict. In the 1980–1986 period, there appears to have been a performance advantage to using thin film heads, and a further advantage to using one's own thin film heads. By the 1994–5 period, though, as thin film heads are widely available and MR heads enter the scene, the thin film head is *negatively* associated with architectural performance. The MR head, by contrast, now is associated with superior performance. In this last period, models with internally supplied discs and MR heads are associated with a performance advantage, relative to models where these components are outsourced.

Firms making drives that utilize a more modular component (here, thin film discs) ought not to realize an architectural performance benefit, since there are equivalent components available in intermediate markets that can substitute for the internal discs at little or no switching cost. This appears to be the case: thin film discs are associated with higher architecture performance, regardless of whether one makes them, or buys them. Indeed, in the 1987–93 period, there was a performance disadvantage associated with making one's own thin film discs, likely due to the wide assortment of merchant discs available, and the ability to plug and play different discs into each drive model.

Alternative Explanations and Interpretations

There are other interpretations possible for these results. Companies choose whether or not to make their own components for other reasons beyond improving the areal density of their designs, such as reducing the cost of the components or assuring the supply of critical components on reasonable terms. I did not have any reliable measures of production volumes by model and costs by component that could isolate these issues from the question of technical design performance.

However, any alternative theory must account for the varying influence of thin film heads over time. An alternative theory must also explain why making heads internally is associated with greater architectural performance, while making discs is not. Both were important component technology advances that arose from similar materials science at approximately the same time in the industry. Both components were supported by startup companies seeking to create merchant markets for these components.[12] Yet, the two components exhibit quite different effects on architectural performance.

10.4   Systems Integration, Rents, and Systems Advance

If modularity is not the stable end state of industry evolution, and if my claim of cyclicality in the evolution of technology from interdependent to modular and back is plausible, then the question of how the system itself evolves beyond modularity becomes crucially important. Within an architecture, the market can itself coordinate advances of the myriad components and subsystems that comprise the architecture. Yet, advancement beyond the current architecture reintroduces the complexity at the systems level that modularity was intended to manage. Who now possesses the systems integration knowledge (Brusoni and Prencipe 2001) to evaluate how best to advance, across the myriad possible combinations?

As argued above, markets alone cannot manage the coordination of such an advance, owing to the complex, poorly understood, and tacit nature of the coordination challenge, and the associated bargaining costs that arise from this. In fact, the relentless pressure of markets in modular technologies impose a further dilemma: how can firms retain their systems-level knowledge in a modular world, when they must compete against highly focused, narrow business strategy firms, who consciously choose not to incur the costs of developing and maintaining the systems level knowledge?

This requires us to consider how innovating firms can earn rents throughout the innovation cycle. In the cyclical model sketched above, the source of rents varies over time. In the early interdependent phase, firms create and capture value in two discrete ways: one through the use of superior components, and the other through superior architectural combinations of those components. In the disc drive case above, IBM profited not only from its use of a more advanced component, it profited as well from its ability to manage the interactions of that advanced component with the rest of the system. With the advent of modularity, though, the latter source of value-added is obliterated. Firms can only expect to profit from their value-added within their level of the technology, and cannot expect to recover any value from their systems integration capabilities. So IBM can still profit from a more advanced thin film head (and today, an MR head), but cannot now profit from its ability to integrate that head into its drives.

Once the advance of modularity has obliterated the rents from architectural knowledge, there is a real question of how a firm may sustain its systems integration capabilities in the absence of being able to profit from that knowledge. In the case of microprocessors and operating systems, for example, both Intel and Microsoft respectively have accumulated substantial market power. It is not surprising that each firm is able to retain systems integration capabilities, even as they offer products that serve only a portion of that system. In other areas, such as consumer electronics, there seems to be no equivalent concentration of market power, which raises the question of how systems level knowledge is developed and maintained there. While both the computer and consumer electronics industries utilize components that are driven by the economics of Moore's Law, there seems to be far less systems level innovation in consumer electronics than in personal computers and workstations. This could be due to the loss of systems integration capabilities in the former industry.

If this systems level knowledge is absent from a modular industry, that industry may be chained to the current architecture that underlies its technologies, and unable to evolve beyond that. In Kaufman's (1993) terms, they may be confined to climbing a local peak, while never leaping to a more global peak (see also Gavetti and Levinthal 2000). Ethiraj and Levinthal (2001) utilize simulations to probe for conditions under which modularity can enable actors to scale higher peaks, and find that interdependence is often useful in jumping to a new peak.

Even with extensive systems integration capabilities and at least some degree of market power, the evolution of modular industries remains problematic. Gawer and Cusumano (2002) describe the activities of firms seeking to build 'platform leadership'. Yet, their account demonstrates the difficulty of advancing architectures in an industry, precisely because so much modularity has developed. In Gawer and Cusumano's account, for example, Intel is apparently terrified that, after investing billions of dollars to design and launch a new generation processor in a new fabrication facility, few people in the market will feel a strong need to buy the new, improved product. Until the complements that exploit the new generation emerge, the value of the new generation processor is rather marginal. Complementors, in turn, do not wish to commit to the costs of rewriting a new generation of products unless and until the new processor is well established in the market.

To overcome this coordination problem, Intel has to build a coalition of third parties, to incur the costs and take the risks to make new products that complement the new architecture. This includes bribing the companies (Intel underwrites half or more of the development cost of some key complements), building alliances with leading firms, and even selecting a 'rabbit' who in return for early access to Intel's technology, will pioneer a particular complementary product (Gawer and Cusumano 2002: 39–76).

These complementor firms are themselves taking real risks. Intel could decide to enter into manufacture of the complement itself (something that Microsoft apparently does with some frequency, according to Gawer and Cusumano).[13] Or Intel could abandon a new architecture, if it was not being well received in the market. This would strand the complementors, and cost them all specific investments they had chosen to make to support the new architecture.

So, to understand how and when technical advance over generations of modular architectures can occur, we will need to utilize theories of alliance formation, competition between alliances, and credible commitments to third parties. These topics have not been incorporated in most work on modularity to this point in time. But once we take the problem of systems advance seriously, they must be added to the research agenda.

10.5   Conclusion, and Directions for Further Research

Modularity is not an end-state of technological evolution. Every architecture contains a technical performance limit. I think that the recent enthusiasm for modularity (e.g. Baldwin and Clark 2000) pays insufficient attention to the dynamics of technical advance. At some point, that architecture must be transcended, if technical advance is to continue. Analysis of components in the HDD industry suggests that technological architectures may cycle between modular and interdependent states in order to advance. The latter state of evolution implies that organizations must retain a high level of systems integration capabilities, even when they procure (or supply) components in intermediate markets (Brusoni and Prencipe 2001).

Failure to retain the systems integration capabilities could result in a 'modularity trap', where the buying firm no longer possesses the systems integration capabilities to incorporate new (interdependent) component technologies effectively into their systems (Chesbrough and Kusunoki 2001). Note how previously decentralized firms that prospered during the modular phase of technology in their industry, such as Microsoft and Intel, are now making substantial investments in basic research on systems architectures themselves. Such investments would make little sense if each firm expected its core architecture to remain modular indefinitely. They make eminent sense, though, as mechanisms to create the systems integration capabilities needed to pursue, and profit from, more interdependent technological architectures, when such technology shifts occur.

This may smack of perfect hindsight. How can one know *ex ante* when such a shift is imminent? More study along the lines of Monteverde (1995) and Jacobides (2002) is needed of the key constituent elements in intermediate markets, such as studying the effect of improving test equipment, or advances in design tools. These act to codify the interactions within elements of a complex system. If my model is correct, there may be powerful predictive information available from closely studying these enabling advances. The emergence of these artefacts may presage a shift towards greater technological modularity.

The boundary of the firm may need to adjust as these shifts arise. Novak and Eppinger (2001) have found that automotive manufacturers vary in their choice of architecture, and that their choice influences their decisions of whether or not to vertically integrate. Their data may enable them to conduct tests of the dynamics of this decision, to determine whether it varied over time for individual firms. If a firm chooses a modular approach, Gawer and Cusumano's (2002) work on platform leadership points the way forward for further work on how modular systems advance, and how the system architects lead this advance, given the substantial inertia that develops in systems with strong complementarities.

We need much more empirical work in this area, since most of the evidence supporting the importance of modularity utilizes only qualitative data (Schilling 2002). As with the evidence above, it will be challenging to design an empirical study that effectively controls for alternative explanations. But such evidence could elaborate on the main case, and establish conditions for when we would—or would not—see modularity take hold. And this does not even touch on the issue of how intellectual property is managed in the task of launching a new architecture. Gawer and Cusumano's (2002) account of platform leadership suggests that this is another important and neglected determinant of the conditions under which modular systems can advance.

This is important because our current theories of modularity predict too much. With few exceptions (such as Ethiraj and Levinthal 2001), the prediction of technology evolution towards modularity is unqualified in most accounts. Yet limits to modularity surely exist, and these need to be understood. Why, for example, is the personal computer industry and the stereophonic industry modular in structure, while the computer game industry remains an industry of proprietary architectures vying for the market (e.g. Nintendo, Sega, PlayStation, Xbox)? After all, these systems all use very similar components in their architectures, and all of these components are advancing on the trajectory of Moore's Law. Relatedly, why did 3DO's attempt to establish a horizontal standard through its own operating system within the game industry in the early 1990s (which would have created a modular architecture for the industry) come to naught? Why did 3DO fail where Microsoft succeeded?

My model of a cycle of technological evolution, from modular to inter-dependent (and back), would benefit greatly from careful historical analysis of other technologies, and the organizational response of firms to the different states of characterized knowledge of the technology over time. Brusoni and Prencipe (2001) offer two brief histories of aircraft engines and chemical engineering. Each history shows the enduring value of retaining systems integration knowledge, even if some portions of the value chain are outsourced. Interestingly, they do not observe the saliency of intermediate markets in those settings that I report here in the HDD industry. We still have much to learn about when and why technical modularity leads (or does not lead) to modularity in the market. And we need to think hard about whether and how those modular industries subsequently advance.

Notes

1. Schilling (2000) explores modularity in numerous contexts, from mathematics, linguistics, biology, and sociology. However, the bulk of her analysis is restricted to product modularity, in the field of innovation management. This chapter follows her in restricting attention to this area within the larger domain of 'modularity'.
2. Schilling (2000: 315) defines modularity to be a condition where components in a system can be disaggregated and recombined into new configurations with little loss in functionality. This is a definition of technical modularity, which says nothing about market modularity.
3. Gawer and Cusumano (2002) identify the importance of tools for Intel and Microsoft in promoting their respective 'platforms' within the industry. These tools lower the costs of adoption for third parties who wish to make complementary products that support the platform. They also provide critical information that markets need, in order to coordinate exchange within an architecture.
4. An example of modularity in production comes from the rise of 'interfaces' known as design rules in the semiconductor industry. There, the use of design languages in ASICs, such as Verilog, map circuit designs directly to chip layout and eventual fabrication. The advent of these languages has helped to facilitate the emergence of the so-called 'fabless' semiconductor design firms, and the emergence of independent production foundries that are dedicated to the production of other firms' chip designs. This has deconstructed the vertically integrated design and manufacturing model of semiconductor manufacturing into a more modular industry—at least in ASICs.

5. More formally, greater interdependence among 'n' different components implies a higher value for 'k', the measure of the interactions among the 'n' components.

6. Pisano's notion of 'learning before doing' corresponds closely with the idea of modularity, since learning before doing presumes the existence of well characterized models of how interactions will likely behave when put into higher volume manufacturing. 'Learning by doing', on the other hand, fits well with interdependency, in that significant trial and error is required before processes can be scaled up.

7. This situation arose again with Intel's Pentium processor, which had a 32-bit word length, and confronts the industry today with the 64-bit word length Itanium processor. In both transitions, the complements that took advantage of the additional word length were slow in coming. This is a critical reason that Intel has decided to pursue corporate venture capital—to spur the more rapid introduction of new applications to reduce the lag in time for complements to come into the market. See Chesbrough (2002) and Gawer and Cusumano (2002).

8. The evidence reported below is taken from Christensen and Chesbrough (1999) and Chesbrough and Kusunoki (2001). See those references for a more detailed account of the facts presented in brief form here.

9. During the period of 1980–95, there were a number of rival storage technologies to hard disc drives. Bubble memory in the early 1980s utilized semiconductor fabrication technologies to store data. By the mid-1980s, optical technologies posed a threat to hard disc drives as well. Flash memory arose as a viable storage alternative by the early 1990s. The ability of hard disc drives to see off these challengers was due primarily to the continued improvements in cost per megabyte of hard disc drives, improvements that occurred at a faster rate than Moore's Law (Disk/Trend, various years; Chesbrough 1999, 2003).

10. I am indebted to Clay Christensen for the suggestion to perform this analysis, and I am grateful to Matt Verlinden and James Porter of Disk/Trend, Inc. for access to the data used in this analysis.

11. The interaction term for making one's own MR heads (not shown in the regression model) is 1.000, reflecting the lack of an effective merchant market for MR heads in 1994 and 1995.

12. Read-Rite and Applied Magnetics were merchant head suppliers in the thin film head transition, and Read-Rite later attempted the MR head transition. Komag was a leading merchant thin film zzdisc manufacturer.

13. In a new platform area for Microsoft, some of its chickens may be coming home to roost. Its X-box gaming system is struggling against the Sony Play-Station and Nintendo systems, primarily due to a lack of cool games from independent third parties. Given Microsoft's predatory behaviour towards complementors in the PC software market (where it frequently competed with them, according to Gawer and Cusumano), third parties in the game industry understandably may worry that Microsoft may behave similarly with them as well, and therefore choose not to invest in the X-box platform.

References

BALDWIN, C. and CLARK, K. B. (2000). *Design Rules: The Power of Modularity.* Cambridge, MA: MIT Press.

BROWN, J. and DUGUID, P. (2000). *The Social Life of Information.* Boston, MA: Harvard Business School Press.

BRUSONI, S. and PRENCIPE, A. (2001). 'Unpacking the Black Box of Modularity: Technologies, Products, and Organizations', *Industrial and Corporate Change*, 10/1: 179–205.

CHESBROUGH, H. (1999). 'Arrested Development: The Experience of European Hard Disk Drive Firms in Comparison with US and Japanese firms', *Journal of Evolutionary Economics*, 9/3: 287–330.

—— (2002). 'Making Sense of Corporate Venture Capital', *Harvard Business Review*, 80/3: 90–9.

—— (2003). 'Environmental Influences upon Firm Entry into New Sub-markets: Evidence from the Worldwide Hard Disk Drive Industry', *Research Policy*, 32/4 659–78.

—— and KUSUNOKI, K. (2001). 'The Modularity Trap: Innovation, Technology Phases Shifts and the Resulting Limits of Virtual Organizations', in I. Nonaka and D. Teece (eds.), *Managing Industrial Knowledge*. London: Sage Press, 202–30.

CHRISTENSEN, C. M. (1993). 'The Rigid Disk Drive Industry: A History of Commercial and Technological Turbulence', *Business History Review*, 67/4: 531–88.

—— and CHESBROUGH, H. (1999). 'Technology Markets, Technology Organization, and Appropriating the Returns to Research', *Working Paper 99–115*, Boston, MA: Harvard Business School.

CHRISTENSEN, C. M. and ROSENBLOOM, R. S. (1995). 'Explaining the Attacker's Advantage: Technological Paradigms, Organizational Dynamics, and the Value Network', *Research Policy*, 24: 233–57.

ETHIRAJ, S. and LEVINTHAL, D. (2001). 'Modularity and Innovation in Complex Systems', *Working Paper*, 25 September, Philadelphia, PA: The Wharton School.

FARRELL, J. and SALONER, G. (1986). 'Installed Base and Compatibility: Innovation, Product Preannouncements and Predation', *American Economic Review*, 76: 940–55.

FISHER, F., McGOWAN, J. J., and GREENWOOD, J. E. (1983). *Folded, Spindled and Mutilated.* Cambridge, MA: MIT Press.

GARUD, R. and KUMARASWAMY, A. (1995). 'Technological and Organizational Designs to achieve Economies of Substitution', *Strategic Management Journal*, 16: 93–110.

GAVETTI, G. and LEVINTHAL, D. (2000). 'Looking Forward and Looking Backward: Cognitive and Experiential Search', *Administrative Science Quarterly*, 45: 113–37.

GAWER, A. and CUSUMANO, M. (2002). *Platform Leadership.* Boston, MA: Harvard Business School Publishing.

GROVE, A. (1996). *Only the Paranoid Survive.* New York: Doubleday.

HENDERSON, R. M. and CLARK, K. B. (1990). 'Architectural Innovation: The Reconfiguration of Existing Systems and the Failure of Established Firms', *Administrative Science Quarterly*. March: 9–30.

IANSITI, M. (1997). *Technology Integration: Making Critical Choices in a Dynamic World.* Boston, MA: Harvard Business School Press.

JACOBIDES, M. G. (2002). 'Where do Intermediate Markets Come From?', paper presented at the Academy of Management Meeting, Denver, Colorado.

KATZ, M. and SHAPIRO, C. (1986). 'Technology Adoption in the Presence of Network Externalities', *Journal of Political Economy*, 94: 822–41.

KAUFMAN, S. (1993). *Origins of Order: Self-organization and Selection in Evolution.* New York: Oxford University Press.

KOGUT, B. and ZANDER, U. (1992). 'Knowledge of the Firm, Combinative Capabilities, and the Replication of Technology', *Organization Science*, 3: 383–97.

LANGLOIS, R. N. (1992). 'External Economies and Economic Progress: The Case of the Microcomputer Industry', *Business History Review*, 66/1: 1–52.

—— and ROBERTSON, P. (1995). *Firms, Markets, and Economic Change: A Dynamic Theory of Business Institutions.* London: Routledge.

MACCORMACK, A. (2001). 'Developing Complex Systems in Dynamic Environments: A Study of Architectural Innovation' (HBS Working Paper 02–035). Boston, MA: Harvard Business School.

MILGROM, P. and ROBERTS, J. (1990). 'The Economics of Modern Manufacturing', *American Economic Review*, 80: 511–28.

MONTEVERDE, K. (1995). 'Technical Dialog as an Incentive for Vertical Integration in the Semiconductor Industry', *Management Science*, 41: 1624–38.

NORTH, D. C. (1990). *Institutions, Institutional Change, and Economic Performance.* New York: Cambridge University Press.

NOVAK, S. and EPPINGER, S. (2001). 'Sourcing by Design: Product Complexity and the Supply Chain', *Rand Journal of Economics*, 47/1: 189–204.

O'SULLIVAN, A. (2001). 'Achieving Modularity: Generating Design Rules in an Aerospace Design-build Network', paper given at the Academy of Management 2001 Meeting in Washington, DC.

PAKE, G. (1986). 'From Research to Innovation at Xerox: A Manager's Principles and Some Examples', in R. Rosenbloom (ed.), *Research on Technological Innovation, Management and Policy.* Greenwich, CT: JAI Press, 1–32.

PISANO, G. (1996). *The Development Factory: Unlocking the Potential of Process Innovation.* Boston, MA: Harvard Business School Press.

PUGH, E. (1995). *Building IBM: Shaping an Industry and its Technology.* Cambridge, MA: MIT Press.

——JOHNSON, L., and PALMER, J. (1991). *IBM's 360 and Early 370 Systems.* Cambridge, MA: MIT Press.

ROTEMBURG, J. and SALONER, G. (1994). 'Benefits of Narrow Business Strategies', *American Economic Review*, 84/5: 1330–49.

SANCHEZ, R. (1995). 'Strategic Flexibility in Product Competition', *Strategic Management Journal*, 16: 135–9.

SCHILLING, M. (2000). 'Towards a General Theory of Modularity', *Academy of Management Review*, 25: 312–34.

—— (2002). 'Modularity in Multiple Disciplines', in R. Garud, R. Langlois, and A. Kumaraswamy (eds.), *Managing in the Modular Age: Architectures, Networks and Organizations*. Oxford: Blackwell Publishers.

SIMON, H. (1962). 'The Architecture of Complexity', *Proceedings of the American Philosophical Society*, 106/6: 467–82.

ULRICH, K. (1995). 'The Role of Product Architecture in the Manufacturing Firm', *Research Policy*, 24: 419–40.

—— and EPPINGER, S. D. (1995). *Product Design and Development*. New York: McGraw-Hill, Inc.

VON HIPPEL, E. (1990). 'Task Partitioning: An Innovation Process Variable', *Research Policy*, 19: 407–18.

WILLIAMSON, O. E. (1975). *Markets and Hierarchies: Analysis and Antitrust Implications*. New York: The Free Press.

—— (1985). *The Economic Institutions of Capitalism*. New York: The Free Press.

PART III

Competitive Advantage and Systems Integration

11

The Geography of Systems Integration

MICHAEL H. BEST

Center for Industrial Competitiveness, University of Massachusetts,
Lowell, USA

> For the pattern is more than the sum of the threads; it has its own symbolic
> design of which the threads know nothing.
>
> (Arthur Koestler[1])

11.1 Systems Integration as a Principle of Production and Organization

In 1987, America's Defense Science Board, a governmental advisory board of distinguished scientists, claimed that the United States was in the lead in only three of more than a dozen critical semiconductor technologies (*Economist* 1995: 4). America's semiconductor industry was suffering. It was symbolic. The loss in industrial leadership was not expected in high-tech industries. Scientific research in the great industrial laboratories of AT&T, DuPont, General Electric, IBM, and Xerox was not being converted into a stream of commercially successful products. Many warned of a 'hollowing out' of American industry given the capability of the Japanese model to engage in rapid new product development, absorb technologies, diffuse innovations, and achieve new comprehensive production performance standards. Manufacturing firms that had built American industry, such as General Electric and Westinghouse, were downsizing and outsourcing manufacturing and diversifying into financial services and the media.

But by 1996, the United States had established a dominant position in microprocessor chips (the most technologically complex semiconductor) and a strong leadership position in personal computers, telecommunications including internet-related activities, and software. Sales of US information and communication technology (ICT)-related industries increased by four times more than that of Japanese ICT-related industries between 1990 and 1995 (*Economist* 1997).[2] Similar tales of new or renewed industrial leadership can be told of the life sciences complex of sectors including biotech and medical devices, advanced materials including nanotechnology, and

201

complex product systems including factory automation systems, testing, and measurement equipment.

In this chapter, the technological resurgence is explained in terms of the creation of a new competitive advantage anchored in the innovative dynamics of regional clusters. In recent years Paul Krugman (1991), Michael Porter (1990), and AnnaLee Saxenian (1994) have spurred renewed interest in industrial districts, clusters, and regional competitive advantage.[3] I propose an alternative conceptual framework, the capabilities and innovation perspective, for understanding changes in regional industrial success in terms of underlying principles of production and organization.[4]

Uncovering the underlying but unifying principle clarifies the sources of success, the challenges, and strategic opportunities confronting both enterprises and policymakers within the global economy. The resurgence of American technological leadership in the 1990s can be explained as a transition to systems integration, a new principle of production and organization.

The term systems integration as applied in this chapter means the capacity of a system to be redesigned, or to redesign itself, to take full advantage of design changes in subsystems or elements within the system. The idea of 'full advantage' includes accounting not only for the direct, one-way effects of design improvements on system performance, but also the interactive, feedback effects made possible by a redesigned system.

An example of 'full advantage' or systems integration thinking is captured in the following quotation about the product redesign implications of an innovation in carbon fibre on aircraft construction: 'The real pay-off is when the design is rethought to take full advantage of the composite's properties—not just its strength to weight superiority' (*Economist* 2002: 27). In fact, taking full advantage of a technical innovation may involve rethinking not only product design but also the plant layout, production system, and business organization.

The purpose of this chapter is to apply the concept of systems integration to better understand the regional concentration of industry. Geographical specialization has always been a feature of industrial organization. A short list of examples of 'industrial districts' includes Sheffield (England) steel and cutlery, Philadelphia (Pennsylvania) and Lowell (Massachusetts) textiles, Grand Rapids (Michigan) office furniture, Dalton (Georgia) rugs, Providence (Rhode Island) jewellery, Connecticut River Valley precision machining, New York City finance, New Jersey pharmaceuticals, Bangalore (India) software, Sassuolo (Italy) ceramic tiles, and Baden-Württemburg (Germany) car components.

The claim is that such industrial districts or regional clusters benefit from mutual adjustment processes that facilitate increased specialization in capabilities and skills, the sources of regional competitive advantage. Regional specialization patterns are like 'symbolic designs', which express hidden processes of capability and skill development that are the threads that successive generations of a region's business enterprises weave together to form a distinctive industrial tapestry. Such patterns of regional specialization are not centrally managed. The idea of systems integration suggests a self-organizing capacity with the potential to reconfigure the regional collectivity of capabilities and skills towards new industrial purposes. The analogy applied here is that a regional collectivity of firms can exhibit self-organizing properties like that exhibited in many biological and human institutions, including language itself. In such cases individuals mutually adjust into self-organizing families, neighbourhoods, and cultures.

The reconfigurations may not be smooth, but they are ongoing. The 'geography of systems integration' points to enterprise interfaces in the form of regional networks and institutions that facilitate processes of mutually interactive capability specialization among constituent firms. Where a supportive regional environment for systems integration prevails, we find networks of firms with specialized and complementary capabilities.

The starting point is the capabilities perspective of the firm. In fact, the idea of 'geography of systems integration' is itself an example of taking 'full advantage' of a design change in a subsystem. The capabilities theory of the firm anchored in the growth and innovation dynamics of the 'Penrosian enterprise' offers a rethinking of conventional approaches to business and industrial organization.[5]

In the following sections, I explore the transition to the new principle as manifested in organizational, production, and technological capabilities.

11.2 Systems Integration and Business Organization

A striking example of systems integration as a principle of business and industrial organization is captured by the comparison of the minicomputer and PC industries in Figure 11.1. The minicomputer industry was dominated by vertically integrated enterprises and autarkic or 'integral product architectures'. In contrast, the PC industry is an illustration of 'open systems' constituted by networked groups of enterprises, each pursuing a business strategy of focus and network: focus on a core capability and network for complementary capabilities.

The minicomputer industry was concentrated along Route 128 in Boston, Massachusetts. The PC industry was centred in Silicon Valley. But the competition between the two regions was not simply between computer sizes. Route 128 had the technical capacity for transition to PCs and most of the minicomputer companies did make PCs. The problem was that the technical capabilities of the Route 128 region were bottled up in vertically integrated business models, which limited the regional processes of increasing specialization and innovation. Collectively, the Route 128 enterprises could not compete against the focus and network, open-systems business model that prevailed in Silicon Valley. In effect, Silicon Valley enjoyed a superior

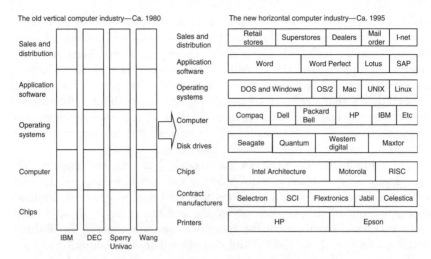

Fig. 11.1 Competing business models
Source: Adaptation from *Only the Paranoid Survive* by Andrew Grove, 1996. Used by permission of Doubleday, a division of Random House, Inc.

regional technology management capability. The decentralization and diffusion of design within the region facilitated rapid technological development in response to market opportunities.

The idea of regional competitive advantage presupposes a role for business and industrial organization in explanations of regional economic success. Alfred Marshall (1920, originally published in 1890) elaborated the idea of 'industrial districts' in which enterprises enjoy the benefits of collectively sharing a pool of 'special skilled labor', 'subsidiary industries devoting themselves each to one small branch of the process of production', and the collective effect of new ideas ('if one man starts a new idea, it is taken up by others and combined with suggestions of their own; and thus becomes the source of further new ideas'). Marshall's formulation remains highly relevant. Unfortunately, most modern treatments of Marshall reduce his concept of the benefits of localization to internal and external economies of scale, and thereby lose sight of the role of increasing specialization, specialist skill formation, and new ideas.[6] But while Marshall's formulation is highly suggestive, it has room for improvement.

Technology and innovation are either missing or exogenous to the Marshallian, post-Marshallian, and conventional cluster perspectives on regional specialization. The reason can be located in a shared implicit assumption about business organization. Each perspective populates a theory of localization with shadow-deep, 'representative' firms in which organizational, production, and technological capabilities have no force.

Instead of capabilities, the firm is defined in terms of costs of production. The role of firms in post-Marshallian accounts is to substitute managerial hierarchy for the market as a coordinator of 'predesigned' economic activities; in the capabilities perspective, firms are central to the process of advancing a region's unique technological capabilities.

The capabilities theory of the firm replaces the cost of production theory. The starting assumption of the capabilities and innovation perspective is that firms seek to compete on the basis of establishing a unique, hard to imitate capability in the marketplace. Capabilities (unlike 'factors of production') cannot be purchased in the marketplace; they are defined as activities that require experience at working together: they cannot be done alone and they take time to develop.[7] Firms that seek to establish a unique technological capability can be called entrepreneurial firms. For entrepreneurial firms, the pursuit of a unique technological capability is an endless iteration from technological capability to market opportunity, and from market opportunity back to technological capability. Products are continuously redefined in the process.

Two dynamic and mutually reinforcing capability development processes are brought into focus. The first is the technology capability and market opportunity dynamic internal to the firm; the second is inter- and intra-firm dynamic. Each requires further elaboration.

Developing unique capabilities demands specialization: enterprises cannot specialize in multiple capabilities without losing focus. But the benefits of investing in the specialization of unique capabilities depend upon simultaneous investments in complementary capabilities. Markets can efficiently coordinate the various 'branches of the process of production' if numerous suppliers of the same product exist for each branch. But the very idea of the entrepreneurial firm is to develop unique and hard-to-imitate capabilities. Hence, the process of increasing capability specialization militates against the relevance of the assumptions of the representative firm and price competition under which market regulation works best.[8] As the theory of market failure holds, the introduction of monopoly elements—in this case a capability development process—creates problems for market coordination. Each enterprise runs the risk of opportunistic behaviour by suppliers of complementary capabilities. Historically, this risk was reduced by vertical integration, the defining organizational characteristic of American Big Business.

Two forms of inter-firm networking offer an alternative to either vertical integration or market coordination (make or buy) of complementary capabilities in a production system. The first is closed-system networking as exemplified by the Japanese *keiretsu*. The closed-system networking model fostered the principle of multi-product flow and the associated leap in performance standards (cheaper, better, faster) that underlay the New Competition of the 1970s and 1980s.

The second type is open-systems networking as exemplified by the PC industry. Open-systems networking is also referred to as horizontal integration, multi-enterprise integration, inter-firm cooperation, networking, loose coupling, or affiliated groups of specialist enterprises. Specialist companies within a regional system of enterprises can integrate, dis-integrate, and reintegrate with other companies as technologies and market opportunities change.[9] This is the domain of systems integration and reintegration.[10]

The competitive advantage that systems integration enables is based on the sustained refinement of capabilities offered by a dynamic between capability development internal to the firm and the composite capability of a system or critical mass of capability-networked enterprises. Thus, the existence of an open-systems PC industry enables individual firms to pursue highly specialized capability development and network for the complementary capabilities. The resulting decentralization and diffusion of design enhances capability specialization, capability development, and innovation potential of the system of enterprises.

The organizational advantage of an open-system's industrial district is that the pursuit of diverse technological capabilities and market opportunities by business enterprises involves endless reconfigurations of enterprise networks and capabilities. The reconfiguration of networks is the means by which clusters are redesigned to capture the 'full advantage' offered by technological advances in elements within the cluster. At its best, it is a self-assembling or self-organizing mode of regulation.

The 'churn' of enterprises in an industrial open system is an enabler of Schumpeterian creative destruction that, in turn, facilitates technological change and industrial transition.[11] Churn enhances the capacity of a regional system of enterprises to reconfigure in response to the inherent fallibility of even brilliant innovators to predict the technological future, on the one hand, and the inherent uncertainty of technological change, on the other. The dilemma is captured by Paul Severino, a serial entrepreneur in Boston's Route 128 region: 'Ken Olsen [founder of DEC] was and is brilliant but one man cannot always guess right about the future.'

Network reconfigurations are reinforced by spontaneous regroupings of skills across enterprises in an open-system (Saxenian). New product development can involve inter-firm, virtual technology teams or 'communities of practice' (Brown and Duguid 2000). Regional economies that have the capability to rapidly reconfigure networks of enterprises and to spontaneously regroup skills to take advantage of innovations in subsystems can be said to have systems integration and reintegration capabilities. Such a region, if not all of the firms within it, is an infrastructure for rapid new product development involving multiple technologies.

The potential for network reconfigurations and spontaneous regroupings of technology teams depends upon an open-system model of industrial organization and cross-firm project teams. But the existence of 'open systems' not only fosters reconfigurations and regroupings, it creates an industrial infrastructure that acts back on capability specialization within and among the constituent enterprises. This specialization, in turn, fosters technological innovation and the potential for yet more new enterprises and new configurations of enterprises.

But open systems on the organizational side are closely linked to open systems on the technological side. The idea of system integration suggests a common design principle that enables the integration of independently designed components. Here, the term 'open system' suggests that the system design rules are openly published. A closed system, in contrast, suggests the challenge of integration is achieved by an overarching design principle which leaves no space for independently designed components. The IBM 360 computer, for example, was a closed system before an antitrust ruling forced the publication of the system design principle and thereby began a process that led to an open system. The embedded and private operating system of Massachusetts minicomputer companies is another example.

The internet is a facilitator of open-systems networking. In fact, the internet is an archetypal open-systems technology. It embodies interface rules that enable design modularization. The internet facilitates communication in the management of supplier relations by seamlessly integrating information across different computer systems, parts lists, and even design programmes. But the internet should not be confused with the advances in productivity that come from capability specialization. The development of specialist capabilities is a management-intensive process that takes teamwork, time, and enterprise partnering.

Open-systems networking offers greater flexibility for new product development and innovation than does vertical integration. While a vertically integrated company operates under a single hierarchy that can direct departments to cooperate, it does so with a commitment to a particular set of technologies. It has simultaneously to place bets on technological trajectories for each. Furthermore, the vertical integrator has legacy subsystems in multiple capabilities and related skills. This creates barriers to iterative reconfigurations of capabilities to exploit improvements in subsystems.

Once capability becomes the unit of analysis, technology becomes central to explanations of industrial development and competitive advantage. Firms seek to establish unique technological capabilities within a context of iterative capability/opportunity process within firms and the internal/external dynamic between individual and networked groups of firms. Technology capability development is cumulative both within firms and across networked groups of firms. The cumulative and collective features of technology capability development have important implications for the 'geography of systems integration'.

11.3   Systems Integration and Production Capabilities

Henry Ford and Systems Reintegration

Systems integration, as a one-off activity, is not new. Henry Ford, for example, was acutely aware of the opportunities offered by redesigning a whole system to take full advantage of a technological innovation in a component part. In this, Ford and his chief engineer, Charles Sorensen, understood the challenge, and rewards, of *systems* integration. Ford redesigned the car production system to take full advantage of electric power. The dynamo, for Ford, was not simply a means to reduce the cost of power but a means to redesign production and manufacturing itself to apply the production principle of flow. This meant an order of magnitude increase in productivity and performance standards.

Electricity, like information technology, is often given credit for fostering a leap in productivity. This is wrong. Both, however, can act as enabling technologies for business enterprises to make a transition to a more advanced production system. But it is the redesign of the system that lies behind the advance in business performance, not the technology. In the case of Ford, electricity was critical to applying the principle of flow, but without the principle of flow Ford would not have ushered in a new industrial age.

The 'full advantage' effect of the innovation in electric power depended upon the transition from batch to mass production. The critical role of designing production according to the logic of continuous flow is captured by one of Ford's most successful students, Taiichi Ohno, creator of the Toyota just-in-time system:

> By tracing the conception and evolution of work flow by Ford and his associates, I think their true intention was to extend a work [read material: MB] flow from the final assembly line to all other processes.... By setting up a flow connecting not only the final assembly line but all the processes, one reduces production lead time. Perhaps Ford envisioned such a situation when he used the word 'synchronization'. (Ohno 1988: 100)

Ohno identifies the single term that makes operational the principle of flow and the revolution at Ford Motor company: synchronization. In the words of Charles Sorensen (1957), Ford's chief engineer: 'It was ... complete *synchronization* that accounted for the difference between an ordinary assembly line and a mass production one.'

Henry Ford's assembly lines can be seen in this light. It was not economies of scale or the speed of the line that was revolutionary in *concept*; it was the idea of synchronizing production activities to successively identify and eliminate bottlenecks to flow. Electric power was not new, nor was the assembly line. Ford's innovation was to use the former to rethink the latter.

Flow meant redesigning machines to incorporate unit drive motors. The electric motor freed plant layout and machine location from the dictates of a central power system and the location constraints of the associated shafts and belts. Power, for the first time, could be distributed to individual machines, the speeds and feeds of the machines could be individually adjusted, and machinery could be arranged on the factory floor according to the activity-sequence logic of product engineering and material flow.

Ford's assembly line was simultaneously a self-organizing signalling device to identify bottlenecks to flow. Inventory built up in front of bottleneck machines and activities. The engineering task was to sequentially revamp bottleneck operations into conformity with the standard cycle time.[12] Every time a bottleneck was removed, productivity and throughput advanced.[13]

Scheduling, too, was decentralized and self-organizing in Ford's system. The idea that Ford's plants could indeed operate without chaos would have seemed, understandably, far fetched. At an output rate of 8000 cars per day, production of the Model A, with 6000 distinct parts, involved 48 million parts in motion. A huge planning and scheduling department would seem to be necessary. But instead of chaos, Ford's plants were orderly. Schedules were met and order was achieved by the application of the synchronization rule: equalize cycle times.

From Vertical to Systems Integration at Intel

Intel is representative of systems integration in production as Ford was for the introduction of mass production. In fact, Intel's process integration challenge is reminiscent of Ford's. But whereas Ford pursued process integration and synchronized a range of machines, Intel pursues systems integration and integrates over 600 activities embodying an array of technologies with deep roots in various technology and science research programmes being conducted outside the company. The new production system involves deepening systems integration internally and extending it externally.

The production challenge addressed by Intel is not to achieve economies of scale for a given technology, but to achieve continuously higher productivity and lower costs by sustained technological change. The historic productivity curve for chips has doubled every 18 months for three decades, following Moore's Law. The challenge is to manage manufacturing processes involving a range of technologies to satisfy productivity advances of this dimension. It demands integrating and reintegrating technologies which are themselves being independently redefined, and on a continuous basis.

The development of systems integration in production was the real innovation in production capabilities in recent decades, although attention has been focused on process integration. Process integration or lean manufacturing does not capture Intel's uniqueness. Process integration is a static concept with respect to component design rules; it does not imply organizational openness to innovation or technological change. Worse, the challenge of process integration exerts pressure to freeze technological change. *Kaizen*, or continuous improvement management, pursues experimentation and technological improvement but holds basic technology design rules constant.

Intel's integrated manufacturing focus requires the construction of full-scale experimentation plants.[14] For Intel, new product development is simultaneously new process development. Experimentation is carried out in full-scale manufacturing facilities under actual, not simulated, operating conditions. In the words of Moore (1996):

With a product as complex as semiconductors, it is a tremendous advantage to have a production line that can be used as a base for perturbation, introducing bypasses, adding steps, and so forth. Locating development and manufacturing together allows Intel to explore variations of its existing technologies very efficiently. (p. 168)

Intel's concept of integrated manufacturing in which research experimentation and manufacturing are co-located is a response to the challenge of (complex) systems integration: changes in individual components will have system altering effects, some of which cannot be identified or measured except in actual operating conditions.

Applying the principle of systems integration has external as well as internal implications. Systems integration pulls into the production organization the challenge of ongoing integration of technology design rules at both component and interface levels.

Lean manufacturing methods internally and closed inter-firm networks are mutually reinforcing; so, too, are systems integration precepts internally and open inter-firm networks. For lean manufacturers, we think of inter-firm relations in terms of vertical networks of firms along a tightly linked 'production chain'; for systems integrators, the image is of horizontal networks fostering increasing capability specialization among an ever greater spectrum of specialist enterprises.

Intel is also adept at networking to tap existing technology bases in the integrated process of pulling technologies into the production system. Instead of designing its own equipment or complimentary components for the various uses of microprocessors, Intel establishes and publicly discloses parameters for makers of chip-making equipment and for users of Intel chips for the next generation of microprocessors. Following the precepts of design modularization, equipment manufacturers build to published interface design rules and performance requirements established by Intel. Equipment makers, in turn, independently and privately design machines that will be inserted into Intel's chip fabrication plants. The challenge is to meet interface design rules, which themselves incorporate in Moore's Law rates of performance improvement.

The challenge of rapid technological change continually generates technical challenges and the search for solutions. Teams 'dip-down' into the scientific and technological bodies of knowledge that are available in universities and 'industrial districts'.[15] This involves identifying where specialized knowledge and expertise can be located. Companies form long-term relationships with university research groups and other technology-oriented firms to access it.

The 'systems integration model of innovation' is distinguished from 'science push' and incremental innovation models in Figures 11.2 and 11.3. The 'science push' model of American Big Business is a one-way process that starts with basic research in the lab and ends with new products. The incremental model is an interactive process designed to pursue a competitive

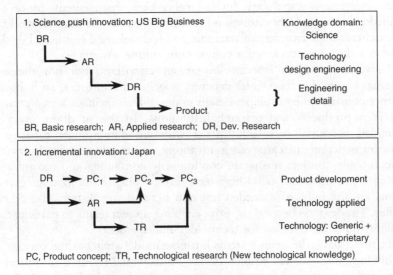

Fig. 11.2 Two models of innovation
Source: Adapted from David Methé (1995), *Engineered in Japan.*
Oxford University Press.

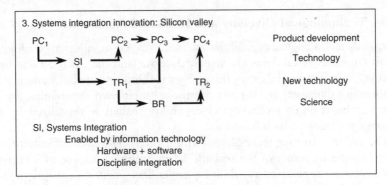

Fig. 11.3 Regional systems of innovation

strategy of leadership in new product development cycle times. New products and production processes are designed concurrently and developmental research is focused to incorporate technological advances in harmony with new product introduction cycles.

The systems integration model, shown in Figure 11.3, also starts with product concept development, but involves systems integration in both technology development and business organization. Two conditions are required. The first is the formation of technology integration teams with the capacity to communicate across multiple technology domains and associated disciplinary languages.[16] The second is networking. As a feature of its systems integration capability, Intel's technology management process is embedded in virtual laboratories in the form of broad and deep networks of researchers at the frontiers of scientific and technological research. For this, Silicon Valley has developed a unique competitive advantage.

University research laboratories are an important, but not the only external knowledge base. Intel depends upon, and reinforces, an industrial district constituted by multiple design nodes, which includes a vast array of specialist producers and research institutions. In this, it draws upon an extended industrial high-tech district with an extraordinary capacity to conduct experiments, carry out innovations, and conduct research. In fact, Silicon Valley project teams are continuously combining and recombining within a population of 6000 high-tech firms. Thus, technology integration teams are the hubs of extended research networks in districts like Silicon Valley. They extend beyond the firm, enabling project teams to participate in a highly innovative milieu for technology management.

In these ways, the open-systems business model stretches the concept of technology management to incorporate fundamental research into production, not as a driver but as a servant of technological advance. A virtual regional technology management encompasses the pursuit of breakthrough innovations in technological knowledge.

11.4   Technological Diversity and Industrial Speciation

A region's technological capabilities are like a seabed or industrial ecology, in which entrepreneurial firms are spawned, grow, and die. At the same time, however, entrepreneurial firms, driven by a technology capability and market opportunity dynamic, are forever advancing their own capabilities. In the process, the region's technological capability seabed is revitalized by the ongoing activities of its inhabitants.

The variation among technologies within a regional system of enterprise is critical to the fecundity of the seabed. Adam Smith's principle of increasing specialization, applied to capabilities, engenders greater variation of capabilities within a system of networking enterprises.

Greater technological diversity is particularly relevant to innovation in the form of industrial speciation, or the creation of new industrial subsectors. Speciation, a metaphor borrowed from natural science, refers to innovation that emanates from new combinations of technologies that lead to new product applications and industrial classification categories.[17]

The tendency to speciation or the creation of new industrial subsectors and technological combinations is an extension to the region of the internal growth dynamics of the 'Penrosian' firm. The very process of successfully developing new capabilities to address market opportunities creates new, unused resources for the next technology capability and market opportunity cycle. It also opens market interstices or new market niches and thereby the opportunity for new firm creation. But the act of filling the market interstice or niche creates yet new niches; the process is potentially never ending.

Speciation is a consequence of increased specialization. Greater specialization leads to increased variation of capabilities within a system of networking enterprises. Variety fosters ingenuity and innovation. Sometimes the variation fosters a metamorphosis of the district itself as new species of technologies emerge with new product applications. These become, in turn, market opportunities for refining technological capabilities and, perhaps, further specialization and variation.

An industrial district, unlike any single firm, offers the potential for new and unplanned technology combinations that tap a variety and range of research- and production-related activities. This protean character of technological capability, particularly evident in high-tech sectors, is a feature of industrial change, even in the oldest sectors. The electronics industry metamorphoses into, for example, an information and communications sector. Furniture becomes interior design and furnishing. In most cases, the process of industrial speciation cannot be done within a single firm. Speciation involves new combinations of technologies.

Thus, a region's technological capabilities are an outcome of a cumulative and collective history of technological advances embedded in entrepreneurial firms. Just as individual entrepreneurial firms develop unique technological capabilities, a virtual, collective entrepreneurial firm extends a region's unique technological capabilities. The regional process of technology capability advance will likely involve a succession of firms, with new firms building on advances made by previous innovators. Regional specialization, in the form of industrial districts or clusters, is the outcome of the technology/market dynamic played out at the level of the collective entrepreneurial firm.

Cluster dynamics and the development of regional technological capabilities are not limited to high-tech regions. They lie behind the competitive advantage of 'low-tech', high-income industrial districts common to the 'third Italy'. Such districts have developed a competitive advantage in design capabilities that have fostered industrial leadership in a range of design-led and fashion-oriented industries. In fact, the existence of cluster dynamics addresses the anomaly of high-income and 'mature' industry regions.

Systems Integration and Biotech in Massachusetts

According to a recent report, New England has the highest concentration of biotechnology companies in the United States, with 456 bioscience companies employing 26,000 people.[18] Thus, the region employs roughly 1 in 6 biotechnology employees in the country, nearly 10 times its population ratio.

The application of biology to production can be traced back to the fermentation of yeast to make bread and beer in ancient times and the selective breeding of crops and animals in past centuries. But modern biotech stems from the discovery in 1953 of the structure of DNA, the molecule that contains the genetic information for making proteins, by James Watson and Francis Crick; followed by the demonstration in 1973 of recombinant DNA technology by Stanley Cohen and Herbert Boyer. The associated set of tools meant that genetic material in DNA could be manipulated and for the first time, cells could be turned into factories for making unlimited supplies of proteins (and even whole organisms). Thus, the recombinant DNA technology that defines the modern biotech industry is only about three decades old.

Why has the modern biotech industry grown so fast in Massachusetts? The Massachusetts location is certainly linked to the collection of world leading universities and research hospitals and to federally funded research laboratories in the region. But strong R&D is not sufficient to explain industrial growth.[19] Many regions in the United States, Europe, and Japan had a similar set of research institutions in the early days of modern biotech, but few have enjoyed the extent of enterprise development and employment growth as Massachusetts.

A basic research capability is an important element in a region's innovation system, but the relationship between R&D and regional industrial success is neither direct nor one-way. From the capabilities and innovation perspective, Massachusetts' rapidly growing biotech industry is an ongoing process of increasing capability specialization and cluster reconfiguration.

To elaborate, a region's innovation capability is embedded in its specialized and diverse technological capabilities, primarily in enterprises, and the dynamics of mutual specialization associated with cluster reconfiguration processes. While a full analysis is not available, we can highlight a number of characteristics and processes that have been established in Massachusetts and, together, suggest the relevance of the 'geography of systems integration'.

The starting point for understanding cluster dynamic processes is a region's technology genealogy. But sustained regional industrial success depends upon a combination of continuity and change in core technological capabilities over time. To understand regional technology capability development, we look to a 'productivity triad' of business organization, production including technological capabilities, and skill formation. These are the three critical subsystems in the geography of systems integration.

Business Organization: Entrepreneurial Firms, Old and New.   In a vibrant regional ecology of innovation, entrepreneurial firms, old and new, are advancing specialist technological capabilities internally, triggering techno-diversification, and partnering for complementary capabilities. The early stages of a new industry, in particular, are marked by the rapid growth of entrepreneurial firms. The existence of networks of specialist enterprises is pivotal to reducing the entry barriers to new firm creation and to the mutual adjustment processes that pull more enterprises into the dynamic processes on increasing capability specialization.

Biotechnology is a new industry compared with the PC industry. It may never have as wide a spectrum of specialist enterprises. Nevertheless, the biotech industry of Massachusetts has a number of features of an open-systems geographical cluster.

First, Massachusetts companies are represented in all of the diverse collection of interrelated product-application segments that make up the biotech industry. These include medical therapeutics, human diagnostics, genomics, medical devices, agribusiness, scientific equipment supplies, scientific services, and others (Massachusetts Biotech Council 2000). Many of these firms predate the revolution in science that established modern biotech.

Second, Massachusetts is home to previously existing specialist companies that have redefined their mission to capture opportunities from biotechnology. Many of the companies that are members of the Massachusetts Biotechnology Council were established long before the biotechnology industry appeared (2000). Examples include: Advanced Instruments (1955), Corning (1904), Honeywell (1904), Harvard Apparatus (1904), Instrumentation Laboratory (1959), Micro Video Instruments (1964), Orion Research (1964), Osmonics (1969), VWR Scientific Products (1854), Abt Associates (1965), and Charles River Laboratories (1946).

Third, the region is marked by a rapid turnover of firms, both entering and exiting.[20] This churn, as noted, is an enabler of Schumpeterian creative destruction that, in turn, facilitates the conversion of new technologies into product applications.[21]

Fourth, Massachusetts has a unique collection of specialist 'tools' companies.[22] In the words of Jim Vincent (chair and CEO of Biogen Inc.) and Henri Termeer (chair and CEO of Genzyme Corp.): 'many of the tools revolutionizing the pharmaceutical discovery and development process—genomics, bioinformatics, and combinatorial chemistry—have been invented and *continue to flourish in this region*' (2000. Italics added). They add 'it is no wonder that a number of the world's major pharmaceutical companies have chosen to locate research and development facilities in the Boston area.'

Technology Capabilities: Specialization and Convergence.   The economic development role of entrepreneurial firms is to drive the cumulative and collective advances that propagate a unique cluster of regional technological capability. Technological capabilities are often subtle and complex. Capabilities, by definition, are organizational in character; they take time and teamwork to develop and cannot be bought and sold in the marketplace.

The biotechnology industry is not a single technology but a cluster of related technological capabilities. Massachusetts has business enterprises that are driving the whole range of generic technologies that have come to constitute the biotech industry. This includes the following (Biotechnology Industry Organization 2001: 1):

- Monoclonal antibody technology
- Cell culture technology
- Cloning technology
  - Molecular cloning
  - Cellular cloning
  - Animal cloning

- Genetic Modification technology
- Protein engineering technology
- Hybrid technologies
  - Biosensor technology
  - Tissue engineering technology
  - DNA chip technology
  - Bioinformatics technology

New technology combinations are a feature of the geography of systems integration. A regional pool of diverse technologies offers greater potential for new combinations. The development of biotechnology in Massachusetts has been marked by a high degree of technology convergence in a number of industries, most notably with information technology, medical devices, and nanotechnology.

The leading example is the convergence of biotech with IT. While the integration of software and hardware is the centre of new product development in virtually all modern industries, the frontier of information technology today is being pushed by life science research. The computational requirements required to store and analyse the information on the human DNA sequence, for example, are an order of magnitude higher than the data requirements in circuitry design and other information-intensive electronics activities.

Information technology was the fastest growing Massachusetts industry in the 1990s. Between 1989 and 1996, Massachusetts software companies, output, and employment nearly tripled: companies increased from 800 to 2200, revenues from $3 billion to $7.8 billion, and employment from 46,000 to 130,000 (Rosenberg 1997). While IT companies with product and service applications in biotechnology are a small proportion of the total, 'bioinformatics' is a rapidly growing new industrial subsector and a prime example of industrial 'speciation'.

Many of the leading computer companies have invested in bioinformatics. Compaq's Cambridge research laboratory, for example, has long had a focus on bioinformatics and, in 1999, Compaq created a Bioinformatics Expertise Center in Marlboro (Aoki 2000). Corning, which developed computational capabilities for the ICT industry, has a $10 million deal with Whitehead Institute of Biomedical Research to develop 'DNA chips' that will give pharmaceutical and biotech companies a new way to test drugs on 10,000 human genes (Aoki 2000).

A second example is the convergence of biotechnology and nanotechnology. Massachusetts' companies have been on the leading edge of driving down critical size dimensions since the refinement of the machining and tooling industries that began with the application of the principle of interchangeability along the Connecticut River Valley early in the nineteenth century (Best 2001). The genomics and proteomics revolutions have created demands for miniaturization to match the magnitudes at which nature constructs, the domain of nanotechnology (a nanometer = one billionth of a meter, or 3–4 atoms in width). Nanotechnology is used to create micro devices such as gene chips or embedded drug delivery devices.[23] Nanotechnology is about structures that self-assemble, which is fostering advances in fabrication techniques. But the computational complexity of DNA reactions may one day be mimicked in the form of biological computers.

The convergence of biotechnology and medical devices is a third case of technology convergence. Biopolymers, for example, are used in drug delivery. Medical device companies represent 7 per cent of biotechnology companies in Massachusetts. But the region has one of the biggest concentrations of medical device companies in the United States.

The vibrancy and extent of technological convergence fostered by entrepreneurial firms in each of these areas reinforce the theme that it is misleading to think of regional innovation capability in terms of technology transfer from research institutes and universities (and the associated linear or science-push model of innovation). Nevertheless, skill formation institutions play an equally important role in the geography of systems integration as business organization and production capabilities.

Skill Formation: Industry and Education Interaction. Identify any successful firm in global competition and behind it will be a history of interactions with regional education institutions that contributed to the shaping of a core technological capability. The role of skill formation institutions is partly to partner in R&D projects, but more critically it is to develop a curriculum that is responsive to the generic technologies being pursued by the region's technology-led companies. Individual firms can grow by attracting the requisite skilled personnel from other companies, but a region cannot grow without a complementary expansion in the skill profiles needed to advance the region's technological capabilities.

In an era of systems integration, the range of disciplines that is required for new product development is considerable. Even small firms engaged in new product development require the integration of mechanical, electronic, software, and production engineering disciplines. Many biotech companies demand a wide range of specialist skills. The multidisciplinary R&D group at Randox, a small biotech company in Northern Ireland, requires the following occupational specialties: biologists, synthetic chemists, physical chemists, neural network specialists, polymer chemists, mechanical engineers, electrical engineers, software programmers, physicists, molecular biologists, biochemists, and immunologists (Best 2001: 197).

Evidence of an alignment of skill formation and biotech skill demands can be found at the website of the Massachusetts Biotechnology Council. While the region faces a shortage of highly educated people, the region's educational institutions are part of an informal manpower development process with the potential to reconfigure the skill formation system to coordinate demand for skills with graduates and training programmes.

As we shall see next, regions that fail to align skill formation with local technological development will lack the knowledge base to sustain cluster dynamic processes. Industrial districts will likely be established elsewhere.

In answer to the question, 'why was a biotech industrial district established in Massachusetts?', we can conclude: Greater Boston enjoyed a heritage of a critical mass of relevant systems integration capabilities. Few regions had the same capacity for techno-diversification, integration, and speciation, particularly in biotech. Systems integration, in this case, is not about modularization, but about a new model of technology management and a new regional ecology of innovation.[24] The cluster dynamic processes have converted a collectivity of disconnected old and new firms into a higher level, self-reinforcing, inter-firm macro-level organization that has constituted a 'regional innovation' system (see Figure 11.3). Cluster dynamics collectively drive a technology and establish a regional competitive advantage. The regional competitive advantage is interrelated with basic research within the context of a productivity triad that links the open-systems business model, production capabilities, and skill formation. Without all three elements of the triad, basic research would not to be integrated with production capabilities in the region.

11.5   Regional Technology Genealogy and Skill Formation

Here, too, we can apply the idea of a system's capacity for redefinition or reconfiguration to take full advantage of innovations within elements of the system. While whole regions can undergo periods of decline, successful regions are those with the capacity to combine continuity and change in the underlying technology capabilities and associated skill sets, even while product applications and industrial subsectors may be historically short-lived. For example, innovations in turbine technology were central to the powering of the textile mills and, today, the New England region is a centre for jet engine turbine technology.

Thus, many regions have endured as industrial centres even while suffering periodic and often severe losses of markets and jobs, and business bankruptcies. How and why? The answer is that firms, as individual members of regional groups of firms, can play an often unnoticed role in fostering regional competitive advantage, even though individually they may not survive technology and market shifts. Cumulatively and collectively, 'entrepreneurial' firms contribute to the upgrading of a region's technological capabilities, its knowledge base, and skills even as (and sometimes because) they have failed to survive individually. The idea is that a region's unique technological capability is both relatively independent of and advanced by a region's entrepreneurial firms.

We can now draw links between cluster growth and skill formation, the third interactive domain in dynamic regional economies. Moving up the value-added scale and developing regional innovation capabilities is not a matter of business organization and production capability alone; it is simultaneously an investment, private and public, in the region's knowledge base, particularly engineering education. Skill formation is the process of replenishing the knowledge base that supports a region's entrepreneurial firms. While individual firms can grow without the support of regional policies to advance skills, the growth of a networked system of enterprises will be quickly choked by the lack of a skill formation system that is in sync with the skills needed to fuel the region's expanding technology base. Specialized skill formation is critical to sustaining a region's particular technology genealogy. Thus, a region's unique technology capabilities and its skill formation system are mutually reinforcing.

As shown in Figure 11.4 and Table 11.1, regions of the world in which electronics has achieved the goal of driving value-adding growth for a sustained period have simultaneously undergone a transition in skill formation capability at the graduate engineering and science level.[25] The internationally successful electronics regions all have over twenty scientists and engineers per 10,000 of population (National Science Board 1996; 1998; Best 2001: 188). Poor countries rarely have one-tenth of this level. The major policy implication is that success in the electronics and electronics-derived industries involves the decentralization and diffusion of new product development, and innovation capabilities that in turn depend highly on graduates in natural science, engineering, mathematics, and computer science.

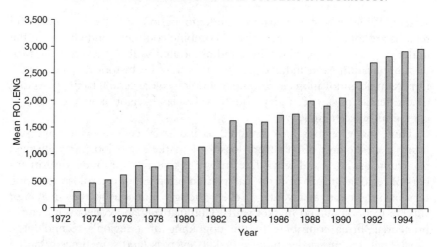

Fig. 11.4 Republic of Ireland engineering graduates
Source: National Council for Educational Awards (1995)

	1975 NS&E	1975 M&CS	1995 NS&E	1995 M&CS
Ireland	706	NA	5,456	NA
Singapore	702	NA	2,965	NA
South Korea	10,266	0	47,277	12,351
Taiwan	6,700	1,200	15,170	2,818

Table 11.1 Growth in engineering and science graduates, 1975–95
Source: National Science Boards (1996, 1998)

The critical role of skill formation brings regional policymaking into the geography of systems integration. The capabilities and innovation perspective focuses attention on three interrelated policy domains: first, entrepreneurial firms and inter-firm networking; second, a range of production-related capabilities for new product development, technology management, anticipating technology transitions, and innovation; and third, a skill formation system that supplies the technology-driven enterprises with the appropriate range and level of skills. But the mutually interactive feature of these three domains suggests that rapid productivity-led growth does not come from policy changes in one domain alone. While entrepreneurial firms are the agents of innovation, productivity-led growth involves alignment of step-changes in business organization, production capabilities, and skill formation. The interlocked aspect of the three domains underlies the idea of a productivity triad. Making changes in any one domain, on its own, may not impact on productivity; policy changes must be integrative across the three domains. For this reason, regional governance structures that foster alignment of policies in the three domains are critically important to the growth process.

11.6   Summary: Regional Innovation Systems

In Sections 11.2–11.5, systems integration is used as a conceptual tool to expand on the industrial district and cluster approach in two ways. First, we characterized a range of cluster dynamic processes that drive innovation and productivity-led growth in the world's most successful electronics enterprises and regions. We focused attention on interactive links between 'entrepreneurial firms', the drivers of technological advance, and inter-firm networks. Networking systems and capabilities foster the decentralization and diffusion of design within a region and become not only a conduit for innovation, sectoral transition, and value-adding growth, but also a source of new entrepreneurial firms. Second, we gave special attention to the role of technology management capability within companies and networked groups of companies. Open systems in the technological and organizational domains were seen to be mutually reinforcing and to set a new performance standard for innovation over both vertically integrated (and integral product architecture—its technical counterpart) and closed network systems. Entrepreneurial firms were seen as critical to a range of cluster dynamic processes that include techno-diversification; technological integration, dis-integration, and reintegration; and industrial 'speciation'. Third, we tied in the skill formation side of innovation and regional growth. These processes underlie 'regional systems of innovation'.

While the high-tech industrial districts are unique in terms of research intensity, they exhibit regional innovation characteristics in an exaggerated form that are common to early stages in the development of mid-tech industrial districts apparent in the illustrations of Alfred Marshall. These include the following.

First, the technology/market dynamic of the entrepreneurial firm drives the 'Silicon Valley effect', a *new firm creation process* which produces yet more entrepreneurial firms. The regional capability to create new firms can be measured in terms of the ratio of new to total number of firms. One study estimates that nearly three-quarters of Silicon Valley firms have been created in the last 15 years compared with less than one-quarter in German 'high-tech' regions (Kluge, Meffert, and Stein 2000: 100).

New firms enhance an industrial district's capacity for reconfiguration and thereby the Schumpeterian process of 'creative destruction'. In the process, new firms engender regional techno-diversification that increases technological specialization and the variety of distinctive technology capabilities within a region. As noted, this is an extension of Adam Smith's fundamental principle of increasing specialization from skills to capabilities.

Second, an open-system industrial district is, as well, a collective experimental laboratory. Networked groups of firms are, in effect, engaged in continuous experimentation as the networks form, disband, and re-form. Both the ease of entry of new firms and the infrastructure for networking facilitate the formation, demise, and re-formation of technology integration teams. However successful the industrial district as a mode of economic coordination has been in international competition, up to now it has been considered appropriate only to 'light' industry, such as the design-led fashion industries of the 'third Italy' and the machine tool and metalworking regions of Baden-Württemberg in Germany.

Third, an open-system district expands the number of simultaneous experiments that are conducted. A vertically integrated company may carry out several experiments at each stage in the production chain, but a district can exploit dozens simultaneously. In this way, a district counters the barriers to introducing new ideas in firms that already have well developed capabilities around competing technologies.

Fourth, an open-system district fosters the decentralization and diffusion of design capabilities. Design modularization in the personal computer industry is an example. IBM got the process underway in response to an antitrust ruling to publish its system design rules. This was greatly enhanced when Microsoft and Intel developed the design modules for the operating system and the microprocessor. The resulting standards have created enormous market opportunities for specific applications software. But, in addition, the concept of design modularization combines common interface design rules with decentralization of component design. This diffusion of design capability increases collective innovation capacity. It can also strengthen the district model of industrial organization, and even encourage conversion from a closed to an open system.[26]

Fifth, the diversity of technologies within a dynamic district creates potential for innovations as a consequence 'unplanned confluences of technology from different fields' (Kostoff 1994: 61).[27] In a survey of innovation, Ronald Kostoff finds that the first and most important factor associated with innovation is a broad pool of advanced knowledge. In Kostoff's words 'an advanced pool of knowledge must be developed in many fields before synthesis leading to innovation can occur'. This advanced pool of knowledge is the critical factor, not the lone entrepreneur:

The entrepreneur can be viewed as an individual or group with the ability to assimilate this diverse information and exploit it for further development. However, once this pool of knowledge exists, there are many persons or groups with capability to exploit the information, and thus the real critical path to innovation is more likely to be the knowledge pool than any particular entrepreneur. (1994: 61)

The knowledge pool is developed through non-mission oriented research in a range of fields 'by many different organizations'. Kostoff does not underestimate the role of planned research, but stresses the combination: 'mission-oriented research or development stimulates non-mission research to fill gaps preceding the innovation'.[28]

From this perspective, an industrial district, unlike any single firm, offers the potential of a technological full-house with a variety and range of research and production-related activities, which can foster creativity, fill gaps, replenish the knowledge pool, link needs to research, and incite an unplanned confluence of technologies. The innovation opportunities of specialist regions act as a magnet for entrepreneurial firms headquartered in other regions. For example, just as hundreds of Silicon Valley information and communications technology firms have established a presence by acquiring Boston area firms, dozens of Irish and Israeli software, and biotech firms have offices in the Greater Boston area.[29] The innovation potential that attracts firms from around the world into Massachusetts is the skill base, the diversity of technologies that are potential inputs to systems integrators, and the time compression facilitated by the wide and deep supply base for doing new product development.

The industrial district is a regional organizational capability anchored in a region's technology genealogy that is the outcome of endless iterative processes between technological capabilities and market opportunities of the region's enterprises. It is also an application of the principle of systems integration to geographical regions. We can say that the geography of systems integration is about the application of systems integration to the sub-systems that constitute regional economies. Advances in technology have made systems integration an operational principle in many production units, just as the open-systems business model has fostered the decentralization and diffusion of design and thereby fostered regional innovation capabilities. Ironically, in an age of globalization, the forces of localization in regions where systems integration is a principle of production and organization may never have been stronger.

Notes

1. Cited in Faulks (1996).
2. US sales in ICT industries grew from $340 billion in 1990 to $570 billion in 1995 and those of Japanese ICT industries from $450 billion to $500 billion over the same period.
3. For a review of the literature, see Martin (1999).
4. I have drawn from a fuller development of the capabilities and innovation perspective in Best (2001).
5. The capabilities perspective, is derived from Penrose (1995; originally 1959) and owes much to Lazonick (1991). Penrose's distinction between resources and the

services of resources is the starting point; Lazonick's account of industrial development, in which organizational capability is the central variable, extends the scope from growth of the firm to growth of industries. Other scholars who have proposed a capability-based approach include Teece and Pisano (1994) and Grant (1995). See Pitelis (2002) for an assessment of Penrose's legacy.

6. Marshall himself was partly to blame. His metaphor of supply and demand as two blades of the scissors, each playing a role in the determination of price, focused attention on a static conception of production at the expense of the dynamic processes he introduced to explain industrial districts.

7. The unit of enterprise specialization is not a component, part, or product, but a unique or distinctive capability. Unique capabilities may express themselves in a range of products and/or services in single or multiple industrial sectors.

8. The 'representative' or textbook firm is a carbon copy of every other firm in the industry. Representative firms are without distinctive capabilities. In terms of the efficiency criterion of neoclassical economics, the more isomorphic firms that produce the same product, the greater the price competition and closer the economy to achieving allocative efficiency.

9. This process of combining, constituting, and reconstituting offers an explanation of high value-added regions such as Singapore and Hong Kong associated with integration and packaging capabilities (Enright, Scott, and Dodwell 1997).

10. Such serial partnering is unique to open-system networks.

11. This churn of enterprises counteracts the 'innovator's dilemma' of single companies as described by Clayton Christensen (1997), but only if the region is populated by the 'open-system' or focus and network business model. Regional technology capabilities are secure if the regional system of enterprises includes both incumbents and attackers. In contrast, a region in which free entry is limited risks blocking the entry of firms with disruptive technologies, much like the Upas tree poisons the seedlings of other species of plants around it; for the example of heavy engineering killing off alternative technologies and regional growth in Glasgow, Scotland, see Checkland (1981).

12. Equal cycle times does not mean each machine is operating at the same pace, but that just the right amount of parts for each car are made in each time cycle.

13. The principle of flow yields a simple rule to concentrate the attention of engineers: equalize cycle times. Optimally, every operation on every part would match the standardized cycle time, the regulator of the pace of production flow. Failure to synchronize appears as inventory buildup in front of the slower operation. Any activity that takes more time does not meet the condition and requires engineering attention. The way to increase the flow of material is not to speed the pace of the conveyor belt but to identify the bottleneck, or slowest cycle time, and develop an action plan to eliminate it.

14. For details on Intel's approach to technological development, see Iansiti and West (1997).

15. Intel divides research into two types: research that 'require[s] integrated manufacturing capability to examine' and 'chunks' that do not require state of the art semiconductor technology (Moore 1996: 72). Intel focuses on the former and networks with universities for the latter.

16. Each engineering and scientific discipline has a distinctive 'language'. Mechanical, electrical, and software engineering methodologies, for example, are based on different units of analysis and measurement. Systems integration involves technology teams that can combine the strengths of the disciplines to develop and produce new product concepts. Internal training programmes at companies like Intel rely on software tools developed for each discipline to facilitate interdisciplinary communication. Nevertheless, no functional equivalent short of experience and teamwork has yet been discovered to Douglas Adams' 'Babel fish', a device used to enable intergalactic communication in *A Hitchhiker's Guide to the Galaxy* (1989: 42).

17. Stephen Jay Gould (1996) argues that progress comes from variety not complexity. Gould uses the analogy with a full house in poker to make the point that excellence is a property of all parts together. Trends are better read as variation within full systems rather than 'things moving somewhere'.

18. Ernst and Young (2000) reported that more than 1200 biotechnology US companies employed 153,000 workers, up 42 per cent from 108,000 in 1997.

19. Over the years Massachusetts has suffered through economic downturns, even while basic research has flourished.

20. New business incorporations in Massachusetts increased through much of the 1990s, from 15,000 in 1991 to 18,500 in 1999 (Massachusetts Technology Collaborative 2001: 37).

21. Patent activity by new firms in the US pharmaceutical and biotechnology industries outstrips other nations. Henderson, Orsenigo, and Pisano (1999: table 7.3: 291) report that 43 per cent of patent activity in the United States was from new firms and 34.5 per cent from established companies (22 per cent was from Universities), whereas many countries had 80 per cent from established companies, including Japan, Germany, Switzerland, Denmark, and Italy.

22. 'Tools' companies can be found in each of the seven commercial market sector categories in Massachusetts. Examples include Genomics Collaborative, Phylos, Surface Logix, Alkermes, Millenium, and ArQule.

23. 'Both nanotechnology and molecular electronics researchers have made use of the technological developments in the life sciences, including the use of enzymes, proteins, and small organic molecules in the synthesis and assembly of very small scale materials. These approaches could lead to new ways to design and fabricate extremely small information-processing and mechanical devices.' Ernst and Young (2000: 29)

24. As the biotech industry evolves, regional clusterization may give way to modular clusterization and geographical separation. We may find that the 'geography of systems integration' is particularly relevant to examining the early stages in the development of clusters. However, I would suggest that, even though biotech is perhaps as research-intensive as any industry, the focus on entrepreneurial firms and technology capabilities is equally relevant to high- and medium-tech industries.

25. Electrical engineering graduates increased from 600 to 1600 per year between 1978 and 1988, fueling the 'Massachusetts Miracle' (Best 2001: 155). The expansion in graduates is probably most important in the earliest stages of cluster dynamics; once a region attains critical mass or 'criticality' in its

knowledge base, it has greater potential for enterprise 'churn' associated with the transition to new technological and product applications.

26. The regional innovation processes can be referred to as the 5Ds: disruptive (internal/internal dynamic), dip-down (fast new product development), design diffusion (leveraging creativity), dispersed (laboratories for experimentation), and diversity (new technological combinations).

27. Kostoff's survey supports Rosenberg's historical research on the inherently uncertain dimension of innovation and the role of confluence of trends in shaping the effects of any specific innovation on productivity and growth (1976, 1982). The point here is that an open-systems model of industrial organization counters the inherent uncertainty of technology with the potential for the confluence of trends.

28. Following the broad pool of advanced knowledge, the second critical condition identified by Kostoff is recognition of technical opportunity and need. 'In many cases, knowledge of the systems applications inspires the sciences and technology that lead to advanced systems.' The third, fourth, and fifth critical factors are a technical entrepreneur who champions the innovation, financial support, and management support. The final, sixth factor is continuing innovation and development over many fields. In the words of Kostoff: 'additional supporting inventions are required during the development phase preceding the innovation'. At least three of the six critical factors for innovation success identified by Kostoff point to networking capabilities.

29. Some 60 Republic of Ireland and Northern Ireland high-technology companies are scattered throughout the Greater Boston region (Bray 2002). Michel Habib, Israel's economic consul in Boston, estimates that the number of Israeli technology firms in the Boston area grew from 30 in 1997 to at least 65 in early 1999. The Israeli companies span a range of technologies, including optical inspection machines, medical lasers, digital printing equipment, scanning technology, and biotech. In the words of one Israeli manager 'There are a lot of technological resources and knowledge in the area we can take advantage of.' (Bray 1999)

References

ADAMS, D. (1989). *The More Than Complete Hitchhiker's Guide*. New York: Wings.

AOKI, N. (2000). *Boston Globe*, 8 November.

BEST, M. (1990). *The New Competition*. Cambridge, MA: Harvard University Press.

—— (2001). *The New Competitive Advantage: The Renewal of American Industry*. Oxford: Oxford University Press.

BIOTECHNOLOGY INDUSTRY ORGANIZATION (2001). 'Editors' and Reporters' Guide to Biotechnology', 3 June. www.bio.org

BRAY, H. (1999). 'Hub's High-tech Allure Drawing Israeli Firms', *Boston Globe*, 7 April.

—— (2002). 'Irish Invasion', *Boston Globe*, 30 September.

BROWN, J. and DUGUID, P. (2000). 'Mysteries of the Region: Knowledge Dynamics in Silicon Valley', in C.-M. Lee, W. Miller, M. Hancock, and H. Rowen (eds.),

The Silicon Valley Edge: A Habitat for Innovation and Entrepreneurship. Stanford, CA: Stanford University Press, 16–39.

CHECKLAND, S. G. (1981). *The Upas Tree: Glasgow 1875–1975.* Glasgow: Glasgow University Press.

CHRISTENSEN, C. (1997). *The Innovator's Dilemma: When New Technologies Cause Great Firms to Fail.* Boston, MA: Harvard Business School Press.

THE ECONOMIST (1995). Survey. 16 September.

—— (1997). 'Silicon Valley: The Valley of Money's Delight'. 29 March.

—— (2002). 'Desperately Seeking Lightness'. 21 September.

ENRIGHT, M., SCOTT, E., and DODWELL, D. (1997). *The Hong Kong Advantage.* Hong Kong: Oxford University Press.

ERNST and YOUNG (2000). *Convergence: Biotechnology Industry Report, Millennium Edition.* Thirteenth Annual Report, October. www.ey.com/global/gcr.nsf/International/Knowledge-Center

FAULKS, S. (1996). *The Fatal Englishman.* London: Hutchinson Radius.

GOULD, S. (1996). *Full House: The Spread of Excellence from Plato to Darwin.* New York: Random House.

GRANT, R. (1995). 'A Resource-based Theory of Competitive Advantage', *California Management Review,* 33/3: 114–35.

HENDERSON, R., ORSENIGO, L., and PISANO, G. (1999). 'The Pharmaceutical Industry and the Revolution in Molecular Biology,' in R. Nelson and D. Mowery (eds.), *Sources of Industrial Leadership: Studies of Seven Industries.* Cambridge: Cambridge University Press, 267–311.

IANSITI, M. and WEST, J. (1997). 'Technology Integration: Turning Great Research into Great Products', *Harvard Business Review,* May–June: 69–79.

KLUGE, J., MEFFERT, J., and STEIN, L. (2000). 'The German Road to Innovation', *McKinsey Quarterly,* 2: 99–105.

KOSTOFF, R. N. (1994). 'Successful Innovation: Lessons from the Literature', *Research – Technology Management,* March–April: 60–1.

KRUGMAN, P. (1991). *Geography and Trade.* Cambridge, MA: MIT Press.

LAZONICK, W. (1991). *Business Organization and the Myth of the Market Economy.* Cambridge: Cambridge University Press.

MARSHALL, A. (1920). *Principles of Economics* (8th edn.; original 1890). London and New York: Macmillan.

MARTIN, R. (1999). 'The New "Geographical" Turn in Economics', *Cambridge Journal of Economics,* 23: 65–91.

Massachusetts Biotechnology Council (2000). *Massachusetts Biotechnology Directory: A Guide to Companies, Careers and Education.* Cambridge, MA: Massachusetts Biotechnology Council.

Massachusetts Technology Collaborative (2001). *Index of the Massachusetts Innovation Economy.* Westborough, MA: Massachusetts Technology Park Corporation.

MOORE, G. (1996). 'Some Personal Perspectives on Research in the Semiconductor Industry', in R. Rosenbloom and W. Spencer (eds.), *Engines of Innovation.* Boston, MA: Harvard Business School Press, 165–74.

NATIONAL COUNCIL FOR EDUCATIONAL AWARDS (1995). *Twenty-Second Report, 1995.* Dublin: National Council for Educational Awards.

NATIONAL SCIENCE BOARD (1996, 1998). *Science and Engineering Indicators*. Washington DC: US Government Printing Office.

OHNO, T. (1988). *Toyota Production System: Beyond Large-scale Production*. Cambridge, MA: Productivity Press.

PENROSE, E. (1995; originally 1959). *The Theory of the Growth of the Firm*. Oxford: Oxford University Press.

PITELIS, C. (ed.) (2002). *The Growth of the Firm: The Legacy of Edith Penrose*. Oxford: Oxford University Press.

PORTER, M. (1990). *The Competitive Advantage of Nations*. New York: Macmillan.

ROSENBERG, N. (1976). *Perspectives on Technology*. Cambridge: Cambridge University Press.

——(1982). *Inside the Black Box: Technology and Economics*. Cambridge: Cambridge University Press.

——(1997). 'Software: Fastest Growing Industry', *Boston Globe*, 5 June.

SAXENIAN, A. (1994). *Regional Advantage: Culture and Competition in Silicon Valley and Route 128*. Cambridge, MA: Harvard University Press.

SORENSEN, C. E. (1957). *Forty Years with Ford*. London: Cape.

TEECE, D. and PISANO, G. (1994). 'The Dynamic Capabilities of Firms: An Introduction', *Industrial and Corporate Change*, 3: 537–56.

VINCENT, J. and TERMEER, H. (2000). 'New England's Important Role in the Biomedical Revolution', *Boston Globe*, 25 March: A15.

12

Modularity and Outsourcing
The Nature of Co-evolution of Product Architecture and Organization Architecture in the Global Automotive Industry

MARI SAKO

Saïd Business School, University of Oxford

At a juncture when the outsourcing of modules has become a panacea for all sorts of problems in the car industry, it is worthwhile taking a sober look at what can, and cannot, be expected from it. Recently, both original equipment manufacturers (OEMs) and suppliers have been interested in capturing value from vertical dis-integration of a modular sort, but neither side appears to know fully what costs and gains are involved in pursuing a specific path to outsourcing modules. Baldwin and Clark (1997, 2000) clearly laid out the 'power of modularity' using the US computer industry and its one-time, near-monopolist IBM as evidence. But in many other sectors where the industry structure has been more fragmented from the start, such as the car industry, there is a choice of paths to be taken in order to 'go modular'. Depending on the path chosen, as this chapter will show, technological know-how and capabilities end up being distributed quite differently between OEMs and suppliers. While the scope for choice of different paths is limited to an extent by the existing industry structure and initial conditions in organizational capabilities, much of it is in the hands of the companies involved in the supply chain. As Starr noted over three decades ago, 'turning to the modular approach produces a great deal of unplanned obsolescence' and 'the design and engineering costs of entering into such production configurations can be exceptionally high' (Starr 1965: 139). The question is whether there is enough will power within leading car companies to incur this necessarily high set-up cost of going modular. This strategic choice, in turn, will determine the future of the industry structure, and in particular the power dynamics between the OEMs and suppliers. This chapter analyses how strategic considerations moderate the way product architecture affects organization architecture and vice versa.

The chapter is structured as follows. The first section provides a definition of modularity in product architecture and organization architecture. Three distinct paths to achieving the outsourcing of modules are identified by separating outsourcing and modularization. The second section examines the mixed motives of OEMs and suppliers wishing to 'go modular'. It is argued that different combinations of these motives predispose companies to choose a different path to outsource modules. Lastly, the chapter considers the implications of these different paths for industry dynamics and supplier relationships. Although the empirical details of this paper are largely about the car industry, much of the findings have relevant implications for any industry that designs, produces and distributes a complex product involving multiple technologies.

12.1   Modularity in Product Architecture and Outsourcing in Organization Architecture

Modularity, be it in product or organization architecture, is a bundle of characteristics that define (*a*) *interfaces* between elements of the whole, (*b*) a function-to-component (or task-to-organization unit) mapping that defines what those elements are, and (*c*) hierarchies of decomposition of the whole into functions, components, tasks, etc. Much of the existing literature addresses some, but not all, of the characteristics that are relevant to defining modularity. This section outlines these characteristics first in product architecture, before moving on to a discussion of their links to organization architecture. This section concludes with three basic implications. First, it is argued that ranking the bundle of characteristics into a unidimensional integral–modular spectrum is difficult. Second, a move towards a modular product architecture gives scope for reconsidering the corresponding organization architecture, but there is no simple deterministic link between the type of product architecture and organization architecture. Third, the added value of employing the term 'architecture', rather than 'design' (namely 'product architecture' rather than 'product design', and 'organization architecture' rather than 'organization design') lies in the explicit recognition of the existence of an architect. What distinguishes an architect from a designer is the former's knowledge of the entire system, which is a precondition for executing systems integration effectively. In theory, modularity captures the notion of a clear division of labour between the architect with architectural design knowledge and designers with knowledge of each module. In a dynamic world of technological change, however, such a division of labour appears to be neither feasible nor desirable. Hence the importance of architects as 'systems integrators', where systems in question are both products and organizations.

Modularity in Product Architecture

A starting point for defining modules, for many scholars and practitioners, is the notion that there exhibit strong interdependence within, and independence between, them (Ulrich 1995; Baldwin and Clark 2000). A sole focus on interfaces leads to a definition of product architecture as 'a complete set of component interface specifications' (Abernathy and Clark 1985). In management literature, more than in the engineering literature, there is a tendency to home in on interface specification as an important feature of modularity. Most recently, Baldwin and Clark (2000) devoted much of their seminal book to elaborating various ways in which partitioned chunks of a product can be mixed, matched, and reused, using different operators, such as splitting and substituting, augmenting and excluding, and inverting and porting. Similarly, Pine (1993), following Ulrich and Tung (1991), identified different ways in which modules can be connected, for example, by component swapping and sharing. Less sophisticated discussion of modular interfaces has focused on a binary contrast between standardized versus customized interfaces, or between open and closed (i.e. proprietary) interfaces. In this interface-focused perspective, modularity is often identified with standardized and open interfaces, not least because they enhance the possibility of mixing and matching. Nevertheless, there are other interface characteristics, such as reversibility (i.e. ease with which chunks can be disconnected, by plugging or bolt–nut connection rather than welded connection), that mitigate the absence of interface standardization. Thus, modularity in interface specification is itself a bundle of characteristics that enhances the independence between modules as physical chunks (Fixson 2002). As noted later in this section, the relevant features of such independence differ when we consider modules in the arena of design, production, or use and reuse.

The fact that specifying the nature of interfaces is a necessary but not a sufficient condition for defining modularity becomes obvious when one poses the question: what is the boundary of the modules for which the interfaces apply? One answer is provided by Ulrich (1995) who defines the product architecture as 'the scheme by which the function of a product is allocated to its physical components.' He goes on to define modularity in terms of both elements and interfaces: 'a modular architecture includes a one-to-one mapping from function elements in the functional structure to the physical components of the product, and specifies decoupled interfaces between components. An integral architecture includes a complex (non one-to-one) mapping from functional elements to physical components, and coupled interfaces between components' (Ulrich 1995: 422). This modular–integral dichotomy is conceptually powerful, particularly as it points to function containment within a chunk as an operational guideline for defining the boundary of a module. But once any deviation takes place from a 'purely modular' case (i.e. functional containment in each component, with decoupled interfaces), it is difficult to rank different combinations of characteristics along a modular–integral spectrum. For instance, is a product architecture with a one-to-one mapping from functions to components but without decoupled interfaces more or less modular than a product architecture with a many-to-one mapping from functions to components with decoupled interfaces?

Any complex product may be decomposed into hundreds or thousands of elementary components, and a bundle of components may be a module, but it is not at all evident how large a bundle should constitute a module. One partial solution to this question is to introduce the notion of nested hierarchies, in which components and functions are simultaneously part of a higher-level system and consist themselves of multiple subsystems. As Simon noted 40 years ago, complex systems tend to organize themselves in hierarchies (Simon 1962). Hierarchies solve the problem of complexity by enabling a repeated decomposition into smaller elements. Following Clark (1985), Fujimoto (1997), and Takeishi and Fujimoto (2001) identified multiple hierarchies linked to product and process technology, and those linked to customers and markets. Specifically, we might compare corresponding levels in two hierarchies, for instance, a hierarchy of product functions (as identified by customer needs) and a hierarchy of product components. Then, the function-to-component mapping at each level in the hierarchy may exhibit varying degrees of modularity or 'integrarity' (à la Ulrich). For a product like computers, the mapping might be quite modular (i.e. more like one-to-one than one-to-many or many-to-one) at a relatively high level in the hierarchy (e.g. data input function in keyboards). For cars, it seems that whilst some large chunks (such as engines and seats) exist, they tend to contain multiple functions (e.g. comfort, safety, etc. for seats), and modularity in the sense of a simpler function-to-component mapping may exist at lower levels in the hierarchy.

Any product has to be designed, produced, and used by explicitly recognizing the hierarchy of components and functions. But different phases of the product life cycle demand different objectives, and the need to coordinate between them imposes another layer of complication in attempting a single optimal decomposition of products. For modularity-in-design (MID), product designers are interested in reducing lead-time and cost for design and development. One way of achieving this objective is to engage in parallel development of modules by independent design teams. By making sure that design tasks are independent between modules, one module can be redesigned without affecting other modules. In modularity-in-production (MIP), production managers are interested in increasing operational efficiency. Modules are normally interpreted here as subassemblies that are easy to test (an idea of function containment is evident here) and install (i.e. with a small number of fixing points). But at a lower level in the product hierarchy, modular subassemblies themselves are used as a way of postponing customization, by mixing and matching standardized components. Operational efficiency, therefore, results from both component interchangeability, late customization and the resulting inventory reduction, in order to meet the demand for product variety. Lastly, in modularity-in-use (MIU), consumers are interested in ease-of-use (including compatibility and upgradeability) and ease of maintenance (including minimizing the cost of repair and recycling). For this, easy disconnection between modules and even within modules is essential. Taking account of these three phases in the product life cycle means that competing demands are likely to be put on what is a module. For instance, a high degree of design integration within a cockpit module—for example, by making the casing of the heating, ventilation, and air conditioning (HVAC) unit be a carrier for wiring harnesses—conflicts with the MIU objective of minimizing the cost of repair and reuse. Relevant interface characteristics are also different: function containment for designers, ease of installation for producers, ease of disconnection and reuse for consumers. Hence, it would be rare for modular boundaries to be optimized with respect to every phase.

To summarize, modularity as a concept can only be defined as a bundle of characteristics concerning module interfaces, the function-to-component mapping, and hierarchies in different phases of the product life cycle. In a 'pure modular' case, interfaces are standardized and reversible, there is a one-to-one mapping of all functions and components, and mapping at each level between any pair of hierarchies is also one-to-one. In the absence of such product architecture, it is no wonder that systems integration (in the sense of ensuring that the whole product, when put together, works well) is necessary in nearly all cases. A systems integrator may be a centralized coordinator with architectural knowledge, that polices and adjusts the design rules that define interconnections amongst interfaces. In the course of iterative adjustments, however, local knowledge from module teams is necessary to make the adjustments. A good example in the car is the achievement of a particular noise/vibration/harshness (NVH) level at different maximum speeds, as engineers develop their understanding of the subtle linkages between the body, chassis, engine, and drive-train. A whole workable car continues to rely on such systems integration know-how.

Given the continued importance of system integration in designing and producing cars, it is not surprising that the two modules studied by the author, namely cockpits and door inners, exhibit different boundaries from model to model in Europe. Figure 12.1 gives a schematic sketch of the sort of components that may be included in the cockpit module, containing at a minimum the instrument panel (or dashboard) and the cross car beam. In reality, a variety of other parts—such as an instrument cluster, the HVAC unit, the steering column and wheel, and airbags—may be assembled by suppliers before the subassemblies leave the suppliers' site (as shown in Figure 12.2). Similarly, a door module typically contains, at a minimum, the carrier plate with a window regulator, window motors, and a locking mechanism. But other components, such as loudspeakers, fasteners, wiring harnesses, and glass guidance mechanisms may be added in some cases

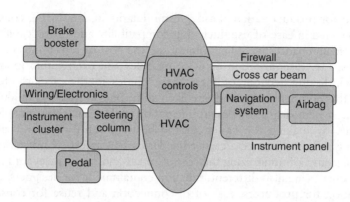

Fig. 12.1 Cockpit module boundaries

	A	B	C	D	E	F	G
IP/dashboard	x	x	x	x	x	x	x
Cross car beam	x	x	x	x	x		x
Instrument cluster				x	x	x	x
Centre displays/dials							x
Switches				x	x	x	x
Centre console				x			x
Radio/I.C.E.					x	x	x
Globe box	x	x	x	x	x	x	x
Air ducts		x		x	x	x	x
Bezels/vent control		x	x	x	x	x	x
HVAC system				x	x		x
Steering column				x	x		x
Steering wheel				x			
Driver airbag				x			
Passenger airbag		x		x	x	x	x
Pedal box							x
Wiring harness				x	x	x	x
Firewall							x

Fig. 12.2 Cockpit module boundaries for European car models
Source: IMVP European Module Supplier Survey 2000.

(see Figure 12.3). These figures give systematic evidence for Europe, that the product architecture of a car differs substantially from model to model, and that the notion of mixing and matching, or sharing and reusing modules across models, never mind across OEMs, is not generally possible due to large variations in modular boundaries.

Outsourcing in Organization Architecture

Modularity is a concept that has been applied to a wide range of fields that deal with complex systems (Schilling 2000). Organizations are such complex systems that may be modularized, by developing well-defined interfaces

	A	B	C	D	E	F	G
Carrier plate		x	x	x	x	x	x
Window regulator	x	x	x	x	x	x	x
Window motors	x	x	x	x	x	x	x
Electronic control box	x	x	x				
Internal locking		x	x	x	x	x	x
External locking					x		x
Latch		x	x	x	x	x	x
Water seal	x	x	x	x	x	x	x
Side impact padding							x
Wiring harness		x	x	x		x	x
Loud speaker		x	x	x			x
Door trim							
Fasteners				x	x	x	x
Structure frame	x						
Glass	x						
Division car	x						
Power support		x					
Glass guidance				x	x	x	
Inside handle				x	x	x	

Fig. 12.3 Door module boundaries for European car models
Source: IMVP European Module Supplier Survey 2000.

between organization units, and a clear task-to-organization unit mapping at various levels in organizational hierarchies. By analogy to product architecture, organization architecture may be defined as a scheme by which tasks are allocated to organizational units and by which those units interact and coordinate with each other. Task allocation as the main starting point for designing an organization reveals the rationalist bias in organization analysis (in the sense employed by Scott 1998). If we start with the notion of 'strong interdependence within and independence between', then an organization is modular if it consists of units with people whose tasks are interdependent within, and independent between, the units, be they teams, departments, or divisions.

As with modular product architecture, interfaces between modular organization units must be well defined. Standardization is one of the several ways in which interfaces can be well defined. For example, a production team that works according to standard operating procedures may be considered to have more standardized organizational interfaces than a team of craftsmen each with their own way of doing things. The notion of standardized rules concerning how tasks are coordinated between organization units has led some management scientists to focus mainly on interfaces, rather than a task-to-organization unit mapping, to define organizational modularity. For instance, Fine employs the term 'supply chain architecture', and calls it modular when the architecture is characterized by geographical, organizational, cultural, and electronic distance (Fine 1998: 136). The implicit assumption made here is that with these characteristics, tasks which pass between modular organization units have to be necessarily well defined (i.e. explicit and codified). Also, this definition indicates that interface characteristics for organization architecture, just as for product architecture, are multiple, and different aspects matter more for different tasks or phases in the product life cycle (see later discussion in this section).

Apart from a focus on interfaces, organization architecture may also be characterized mainly with hierarchy in mind. All organizations consist of some sort of hierarchy, with various possible ways in which tasks are decomposed and allocated to smaller organization units. Hierarchy in organization architecture, in our current context, may be manifested in both an internal authority structure of a company and the tiering of suppliers in the supply chain. In all vertical relationships, task delegation without meddling is a mark of autonomy. Thus, for both horizontal and vertical links within, and between, organization units, modularity may be characterized by a relative absence of the need for interaction. Task containment within an organization unit, rather than task sharing between units, is one way to achieve independence or autonomy. As an example, a project team that undertakes all phases of a project, or an autonomous work group that can assemble an entire car, may be considered more independent from the rest of the organization, than a functional team that has to coordinate with other functions in the organization. But within the development function, a development team that has a clearly defined set of tasks that do not depend on the completion of tasks by other teams is autonomous and therefore modular.

In economics, Langlois (1999) goes as far as to argue that the price system in well functioning markets is the standard interface that allows modular organization units to coordinate with one another without communicating except on one dimension, the price. Here modularity in organization negates the need for hierarchy completely. But at the same time, when this happens, it becomes rather nonsensical to talk about a modular 'organization' coordinated by the invisible hand. If interfaces are defined solely by the price system, there is no role for an organization architect. It is precisely because both the internal organization and the supply chain are coordinated by price and other mechanisms that it makes sense to separate the role of an organization architect and organization designers.

Interfaces for organization architecture are more difficult to specify, as compared with those for physical product architecture, for another reason. This is due to the view of organizations as a process or as a natural system (Scott 1998), rather than as a rational Weberian structure with a clearly defined set of goals. Many classics in organization theory have struggled with competing conceptualizations of organizations as technical versus institutional, or as closed versus open systems. More specifically, in dealing with the contradictory pull of autonomy and interconnectedness, Burns and Stalker (1961) assigned connectedness to the mechanistic organization and autonomy of components to the organic organization. Similarly, Lawrence and Lorsch (1967) argued that differentiation within an organization could be compensated for by integrative mechanisms such as cross-functional committees. Thus, whilst mechanistic organizations and differentiation may be associated with modularity in organization architecture, these organizational characteristics are also associated with the integrative mechanisms that bind an organization together. Thus, in a rational perspective of an organization, modularity may be characterized by decoupling, that is, by two organization units that are independent and do not respond or interact to each other at all. But in alternative perspectives of an organization, decoupling negates the essence of an organization, and therefore there is no such thing as a decoupled organization architecture. This leads us to take note of the concept of loose coupling (Orton and Weick 1990), to preserve the notion of an organization as a simultaneously rational and indeterminate system. In decomposing and integrating a product, we relied on the notion of an architect with an architectural design knowledge. In differentiating and integrating an organization also, we need the notion of an organization architect who can design an organization and adapt both spontaneously and deliberately to demands for changes in organization design. The visible hand, therefore, has to be alive and well.

Outsourcing is basically the reallocation of tasks from within an organization unit to another unit, normally separated by ownership. In the context of the outsourcing of modules, OEMs may consider outsourcing design and development only, production and assembly only, or both. In the design and development phase, a module supplier may be given full responsibility in developing the module, or it may co-develop the module with the OEM in a co-located design team. Thus, module design may not happen within an organization with unified ownership, but both cultural and geographical proximity is important for the success of co-development. In production and assembly, the development of supplier parks and modular consortia indicate that the outsourcing of modules goes hand in hand with the development of a more 'integral' organization, with geographic proximity facilitating much interaction and communication. In this case, although ownership is separate, proximity is a necessity and a manifestation of the importance of organizational integration.

OEMs' decision on the sequencing of various tasks for outsourcing has implications for organization architecture. In Figure 12.4, there is a presumption of a well-defined evolutionary path, with an OEM outsourcing the logistics and assembly of modules first, before it gives greater responsibility in the form of quality assurance, purchasing, and sourcing of components that go into the module (i.e. control over second-tier suppliers), and eventually engineering and development. Incentives for OEMs and suppliers are compatible if this evolution is followed through; for OEMs, gradual outsourcing with an increase in the confidence level in the relationship is supposed to minimize the chances of being captured or held up by suppliers; suppliers can earn greater value-added eventually with design integration

	Logistics and module assembly		Purchasing and quality management		Development and sourcing	
	OEM	Supplier	OEM	Supplier	OEM	Supplier
Logistics		O		O		O
Assembly		O		O		O
Quality	△	△	△	O		O
Purchasing	O			O		O
Sourcing	O		O			O
Engineering	O		O			O
Development	O		O		O	O

Fig. 12.4 Sequencing of tasks for outsourcing to module suppliers

	A	F	G	H	I	J	K	L	M
IP/dashboard	△	X	X	X△	X△	X△	X	△	X
Cross car beam	△	X	X	O	X△	O	O		△
Instrument cluster	△			△	△	△	△	△	X
Central displays/dials				△					X
Switches	△			O	△	△	△	△	△
Centre console	△			X	△				X
Radio/I.C.E					△		△	△	X
Sat navigation etc.					△	△			
Glovebox	△	X	X	X△	△	X	X	△	O
Airducts	△	△		XO	△	X	X	△	O
Bezels/vent control	△	△	△	O	△	O	X	△	O
HVAC system	△			△	△	△	△		X
Steering column	△			△	△	△	△		X
Steering wheel	△			△					
Driver airbag	△			△					
Passenger airbag	△	△		△	△	△	△	△	X
Pedal box					△	△			△
Wiring harness	△			X	△	△	X	X	X
Other wiring				X					
Firewall					△				△
Keyless entry				△					
Steering column shroud				X△	△				
Sound insulation				△					

X, Produced in-house by module supplier; O, bought from suppliers selected by module supplier; △, bought from suppliers nominated by OEM.

Fig. 12.5 Control over components for cockpits
Source: IMVP European Module Supplier Survey 2000.

work, making them willing to buy into low-margin assembly-only business in the first instance. In reality, however, in some emerging market locations like Brazil, it is never intended that locally based suppliers go much beyond doing the assembly of modules designed elsewhere. At the same time, some global modular suppliers, such as Intier (the car wing of Magna), are investing heavily in systems knowledge about the whole car, so that they can win from the start a business to design and develop a module.

Figure 12.5 gives evidence of which party, the OEM or the module supplier, has control over selecting second-tier suppliers of components that go into cockpit modules produced in Europe. It indicates how extensive the practice of OEMs nominating component suppliers is, and how far this reality is from the rhetoric as gauged through the author's interviews, that OEMs control only strategically important parts such as airbags. Supplier interviewees also spoke derisorily about the OEMs' reluctance to let go, as captured by the term 'shadow engineering'. But this seemingly wasteful overlapping in design and supplier selection tasks is an attempt by OEMs to retain their systems integration capability. Thus, Figure 12.5 may be interpreted in a number of ways. One possibility is that this is a transition towards a situation in which OEMs will focus purely on styling and marketing, withdrawing from manufacturing and assembly altogether. In this scenario, some OEMs would wish to delegate systems integration tasks to powerful suppliers that can design a whole car. Another possibility is that the table portrays a more static picture of the state of play, with OEMs wishing to retain systems integration knowledge in-house.

Three Paths to Outsourcing Modules

Once we recognize that the outsourcing of modules requires a sequencing of different tasks for outsourcing, the picture becomes quite complex. However, let us simplify for analysis by assuming that there is only one set of tasks—either design only, or production only, or a package of design and production—to be outsourced. Take an OEM which has a non-modular product design and whose organization is highly vertically integrated in-house. The OEM has a choice of three trajectories for moving from the initial position to the ultimate position of the outsourcing of modules by: (*a*) designing modules and producing them in-house first before outsourcing them; (*b*) outsourcing non-modular components before moving towards modular design; and (*c*) simultaneously implementing modular design and outsourcing (Figure 12.6).

In the first path, modular design is likely to be adopted only if it brings about significant performance improvements and solutions to problems arising from design integration, ergonomics, or complexity. By the time modules are outsourced, OEMs would be in a position to teach suppliers, and much of the module design as well as architectural knowledge would remain with OEMs. In the second path, outsourcing rather than modularization is the initial driver, and benefits of modularity may take some time to emerge when outsourcing runs ahead of modularization. This is not least because it is unclear whether the OEM or the supplier will end up taking a lead in proposing modular design and the integration of components. In the third case, a simultaneous implementation of modularization and outsourcing is possible if there are capable module suppliers already in the marketplace. OEMs can achieve a faster pace of innovation but face the danger of losing in-house capability and control. At the same time, suppliers

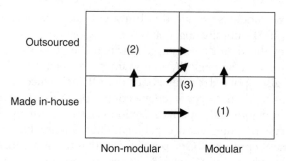

Fig. 12.6 Three paths to outsourcing modules

face an opportunity to influence the direction of technological innovation, and to capture a greater share of returns to R&D. Thus, the path followed to outsource modules has a clear implication for the ultimate distribution of capabilities and know-how between OEMs and suppliers.

Moreover, the overall level of complexity in the supply chain may, or may not, decline depending on this distribution of capabilities. Specifically, an OEM that produces modules in-house or has suppliers with solution is likely to benefit from an overall improvement as a result of modularization. By contrast, an OEM which outsources modules without an in-house set of solutions may end up not improving the amount of complexity in the total supply chain and therefore pay more dearly for the modules than if they were produced in-house.

Implications for the Link Between Product Architecture and
Organization Architecture

A predominant view of the link between product architecture and organizational architecture in engineering science is to start with product architecture and to work out a corresponding organization design. A specific example of this rational organization design that follows from product architecture is the derivation of the task structure matrix (TSM) from the design structure matrix (DSM) (Baldwin and Clark 2000, following Eppinger). With a slightly different concern, Sanchez and Mahoney (1996), in discussing strategic use of modularity in product design, contend that products design organizations. Thus, non-modular products are best produced in non-modular organizations. But modular products call for modular organizations, and this correspondence is beneficial for enhancing organizational flexibility, eliminating the need for hierarchical coordination.

This chapter takes a different stance. First, modularity in product architecture gives greater scope for choice in organizational design, thus giving an opportunity to trace 'path dependence' at the juncture at which such choice exists. Second, organization inertia may well make the reverse causal direction (from organization architecture to product architecture) important. Thus, product architectural choice influences organizational design, but pre-existing organization structures and capabilities also influence product design (Gulati and Eppinger 1996). To be fair to Sanchez and Mahoney, they too recognize this two-way causation: 'although organisations ostensibly design products, it can also be argued that *products design organisations*' (Sanchez and Mahoney 1996). It is then an empirical question to gauge which causal direction has been stronger over a particular period of time.

Given the above perspective, the notion that product architecture causes organization architecture is not so deterministic. In the car industry, product modularization may be considered to go together with outsourcing, if not straightaway but ultimately, because open and well-defined interfaces lower barriers to entry. But the fact that IBM adopted a distinctly non-modular organizational structure to manage its System 360 mainframe computer, doing its best to keep interfaces proprietary to prevent others from supplying compatible modules indicates clearly that a decision over product modularity is separate from a decision over outsourcing.

Moreover, there is evidence in other industries that the reverse causation of organizational architecture affecting product architecture may be quite strong and significant. Certainly, experience in the disc drive industry suggests that, at least for a period, an industrial organization of small, highly specialized firms was closely linked to within-module innovation (Chesbrough and Kusunoki 2001). These specialist firms had limited incentives for changing the product architecture because they had particular skills within narrowly defined domains. Thus, at least in the short-run, product architecture was constrained by organizational architecture. Similarly, Henderson and Clark (1990) have shown that in the photo-lithography industry, few firms successfully weathered the shifts in archi-tectural innovation rather than within-module innovation. These examples suggest that far from optimizing organizational architecture to capitalize on the specialization of the element of a given product architecture, the organization in fact seems to constrain shifts in product architecture. When these shifts do take place, they are likely to be slow and meet with internal organizational resistance because of the effect that they have on labour, capabilities, and power.

If there is a two-way relationship between organizational architecture and product architecture, then we would expect that a range of product archi-tectures emerge depending on organization history. For instance, those firms with a highly integrated supply chain architecture might be expected to retain a more integral modular product architecture. If so, integral product archi-tecture is likely to persist in Japan even in the presence of modular design by some non-Japanese manufacturers, unless a radical solution is proposed for a module whose technical and economic benefits outweigh the well-established advantage of integration exploited by close coordination in the supply chain.

Likewise, firms that have made a significant investment in both deep and diverse technical knowledge are unlikely to promote modular product architecture that provides competitors with advantages within modules and renders their integrative skills less valuable.

By contrast, the popularity of the notion of modularization in the United States and Europe may in part be due to the hope that it might enable the retention of, or reversion to, arm's-length trading with suppliers without being locked into any committed relationships. Then we would expect a greater move towards modularization where supplier relations are market-based than where they are long-term and obligational. There is some evidence in the car industry that US and European OEMs are ahead of Japanese OEMs in thinking about modular product architecture, and one may conjecture that one reason for this is the pre-existing organization architecture of OEMs and their supply chain. However, apart from the pre-existing organization architecture, there is also a difference in the mix of strategic drivers that predisposes certain OEMs to be more interested in outsourced modules than others. The next section discusses these drivers which are relevant to the global car industry.

12.2   Modular Strategies: Why are OEMs and Suppliers Interested in 'Going Modular'?

The car industry has been the source of innovative management practices in production in the twentieth century. After the 1910s, Ford's moving assembly line, making use of standardized and interchangeable parts, revolutionalized the way cars were made, leading to mass production supplanting craft production in most locations. A second paradigm shift occurred with the advent of the Toyota Production System and its diffusion in the form of lean production that emphasized the elimination of waste and good functional quality. Now, the focus of many OEMs and suppliers is on so-called modular strategies in product design and production. What opportunities and threats are driving OEMs' and suppliers' wish to 'go modular'? This section identifies four strategic drivers, and discusses their implications for OEM–supplier relations. Wherever appropriate, a comparison with the computer industry is made. It is evident that modularity in the car industry is not just an engineering principle but part of corporate strategy. OEMs' motives for adopting modules are multiple, and different motives lead to a varying degree of push for outsourcing modules.

Marketing Strategy

Perhaps the most topical driver for going modular is manifested by some OEMs' interest in benchmarking Dell Computers Inc. Dell represents 'best practice' in combining the power of the internet with 'Build to Order'

(BTO) and mass customization (Pine 1993). Mass customization enables the assembly of a great variety of products by standardizing components that can be mixed and matched. Postponing customization until end-users specify the exact mix and match enhances operational and logistical efficiency.

No OEM is yet to host a Dell-like website that enables the final purchaser to track the car being built in the factory. In reality, 'BTO' is still a long way from being implemented in its true form, because paint defects give unpredictable variability in production, and make it difficult to assign a specific customer to body-in-white (BIW) (Holweg and Pil 2001). Cars are also a much more complex product than computers, typically containing 4000 components compared with 50 or so components for computers, potentially enabling much greater product variety. Despite these complications, major OEMs are exploring ways of improving their ability to 'BTO' with a view to serving consumer demand for a highly sophisticated car that is individualized through factory-installed options. And if consumers demand delivery with a short lead-time (say within a week from the order date), having modules with standardized interfaces becomes an essential complement to 'BTO'. In this sense, the demand for BTO may drive the implementation of modular design and production.

Nevertheless, BTO is much easier when parts are compact, lightweight, and easy to ship. This condition is violated in the case of large chunks of a car, such as seats and front ends. That is why product variety in cars is likely to be pursued, not by decomposing the car into large chunks and mixing and matching them, but more by specifying colour, trim, and options such as wheel hubs, mirrors, audio units, and navigation systems. Personalization and the retention of a distinct look-and-feel of a car may therefore be pursued by mass customization of specific components at a low level in the product hierarchy, combined with a fairly integral product architecture that addresses 'drivability' and other desirable functions that users look for in the total car.

The electronification of the car, particularly after the advent of telematics, may make cars more similar to computers in their need for upgrading and compatibility. Just as computers require software upgrades, cars require more frequent upgrades in navigation systems than in BIW shells. This demand for upgradeability may promote standardization in software for cars, but not necessarily in physical modular chunks.

Mass customization is not a new idea, but B2C e-trading may make it more popular and possible, as OEMs accumulate systematic information about consumer tastes, typically retained by dealers to date. The potential for using this information to enhance customer loyalty is vast. But there is no evidence so far that if offered the choice, consumers would wish to mix and match large chunks of the car—for example, retain a Mazda engine and seats and slot them into a Jaguar.

Production Strategy

Attaining operational efficiency on the factory floor has been a longstanding objective of the car industry. In fact, as a principle of production, modularity has a century-old tradition dating back to the so-called American Production System, in which the core idea of interchangeable parts preceded the advent of mass production (Best 1990). Eventually, mass production, typified by Ford's moving assembly line, led to standardizing work methods through time and motion study. Standardization means that the sequence in which each detailed production task is to be carried out is specified, as is the exact time taken for each task. In fact, 'product architecture' is defined by major OEMs today as the 'build sequence', indicating how important the assembly process is in car manufacturing.

Standardizing task time allows assemblers to meet mass production's basic requirement, which is to balance the line. When standardization is difficult to achieve, complex and ergonomically difficult tasks are taken off the main line, and it is those subassemblies made off the main assembly line, that came to be called modules. In the 1980s, Renault conducted an ergonomic review and ended up taking difficult tasks off the main assembly line, organizing in-house subassembly lines for powertrain, dashboards, front ends, and doors. Around the same time, it was extensive automation at the Cassino plant that led Fiat to rethink its organization of assembly. Automation necessarily introduced a degree of inflexibility, and Fiat responded by replacing a very long final assembly line with a shorter one fed with multiple subassembly lines. In such a context, a module came to be defined as 'a set of components assembled, which can be checked and tested before final assembly'. At this stage, modules were assembled in-house by OEMs, and there was no notion of outsourcing.

A more recent initiative in the 1990s to introduce production modules is associated with the OEM's wish to cope with in-line complexity due to ever-increasing product variety. Product variety requires manufacturing flexibility, which is often equated with the flexibility of the process equipment in the plant (e.g. CNCs (Computerized Numerically Controlled) and robots) and low set-up times. But as Ulrich argues, 'much of a manufacturing system's ability to create variety resides not with the flexibility of the equipment in the factory, but with the architecture of the product' (Ulrich 1995: 428). For flexibility, the product architecture must allow for the use of a relatively small number of building blocks in different permutations. This permutation process is none other than assembly, and this enables firms to postpone some of the final assembly for customization. The reliance on assembly rather than parts fabrication to engender product variety is essential in a product such as the car, which has many metal parts requiring unavoidable tooling and set-up costs (Whitney 1993).

However, in order to understand why this later phase of introducing production modules in the 1990s is associated with outsourcing, we must turn to the next driver in finance.

Financial Strategy

Since the 1990s, some major OEMs began to speak of modularization to mean the outsourcing of modules. 'Being assembled and tested outside our facilities' was added to the definition of a module at Fiat, while Ford reported rather sensationally its intention to outsource key parts of its final assembly operations, which 'could signal the company's gradual withdrawal from final assembly as a core activity—transforming Ford from a carmaker into a global consumer products and services group' (*Financial Times*, 4 August 1999).

Outsourcing has always been associated with the exploitation of lower wages either in emerging markets or in non-unionized workplaces. This is borne out by the fact that the simultaneous implementation of modularization and outsourcing has occurred most frequently in the context of greenfield site investment projects. But there is wide recognition that lower wage rates in themselves are a limited and short-lived source of competitive advantage (Rommel et al. 1996). Either the wage gap may be eroded over time, or lower productivity may offset the wage advantage. Module suppliers are typically expected to locate very close to the final assembly plant, either on a supplier park or as part of a modular consortium. This geographical proximity, combined with tight synchronization of operations between the assembler and suppliers, put pressure on wage differentials to close.

A much more powerful force sustaining the interest in modularization even where it faces scepticism in operational and labour terms is the goal of moving assets off the books of OEMs to suppliers. Outsourcing of modules in greenfield sites enables OEMs to shift initial investment costs and risks to suppliers. This is said to enhance return on assets (ROA) for OEMs, which would in turn assist them in raising their shareholder value. This belief in the need to go on an 'asset diet' was heightened by the decline in the valuation of automotive firms in the midst of the dotcom boom, reaching a mere 2.5 per cent of the total market capitalization in Europe and 1.2 per cent in the United States in mid-2002. Nevertheless, the direction of causation and the exact mechanism for asset diet to lead to shareholder value enhancement are open to question.

There is some evidence from our study that OEMs with a lower return on assets are keener on modularization (although this is different from claiming that modularization leads to better ROA). They also tend to face severe financial pressure from low profitability of small car segments (particularly in B and C classes). The predominance of small passenger cars in European, relative to US, markets may also explain why European-based OEMs have started showing interest in outsourcing modules earlier than their North American counterparts. Nevertheless, at least two reasons caution against the viability of this financial strategy for OEMs.

First, in existing assembly sites, outsourcing has been quite slow, not least due to union opposition to it. General Motors' Yellowstone Project had to be abandoned after UAW opposed it fiercely, creating a notion that modularity is a dirty word and a euphemism for outsourcing and undercutting of union labour rates. It has not been possible, therefore, to simply go for 'downsize and distribute' (Lazonick and O'Sullivan 2000), even if management wanted to proceed faster.

Second, one implication of shifting the burden of capital investment to suppliers is a higher overall cost of capital, assuming that suppliers with their smaller size face a higher cost in raising capital than OEMs. Those higher capital costs must be absorbed somehow, possibly by returning to OEMs in the form of higher prices for the modules they buy. Alternatively, suppliers may attempt to lower their cost of capital by continuing to grow and consolidate in a wave of mergers and acquisitions. Either way, OEMs are beginning to turn the logic of transaction cost economics upside down, by making suppliers bear the cost of investing in customer-specific assets (e.g. in the form of supplier-owned tooling) (Williamson 1975). This necessarily enhances suppliers' incentive to make the tooling as general and reusable as possible.

Technological Strategy

The last strategic driver for going modular is technological. The car has always been a complex multi-technology product. But the range of new technologies captured by the car has increased over time, with greater electronics content, new materials (aluminium, magnesium, and plastics being candidates for an alternative to steel), and new energy sources (notably LPG, electricity, and fuel cells). Some OEMs, even devoid of the aforementioned financial pressure, are reacting to this phenomenon by redefining their core competence and by shifting more and more responsibility for R&D to suppliers. By making suppliers bear the upfront cost and risk of R&D, OEMs hope to ease access to supplier-developed technologies by making them engage in design or concept competition. But as the outsourcing of R&D proceeds, suppliers would naturally wish to implement a tighter appropriability regime by patenting previously unpatented ideas.

Whether or not new technology enhances modularity or integrality in product architecture depends on whether the value of innovation is seen to lie within the module, across systems or at the component level. If there is a degree of stability in product architecture, innovation may be spurred by parallel processing of modular design teams each free to adopt new technology within the module without affecting the other modules (Tomke and Reinertsen 1998). Even here, there is an issue around which supplier is best appointed as first-tier supplier to play the role of a within-module design integrator. For example, for a historical reason, the dashboard supplier (with plastics technology) is normally the first-tier supplier of a cockpit module, which requires other technologies in instrumentation and electronics. To enhance the design integration of the cockpit, it may be better to appoint a supplier with an electronic and electrical capability to be a first-tier module supplier.

In a more dynamic setting, modularity is often only a short-run solution to product architecture. Under uncertainty, it is better to err on the side of integrality than on modularity in product architecture to promote innovation (according to a simulation by Ethiraj and Levinthal 2002). Moreover, if technological change may shift between modularity and integrality, it may be better to err on the side of integrality in organization architecture to avoid what Chesbrough and Kusunoki (2001) call a 'modularity trap'. In such a trap, benefits from a shift in an industry from a modular to a more integral phase of technological development cannot be exploited fully by firms due to inertia in organization structure more suited to serving modular product architecture. One solution to avoiding the modularity trap is to follow the prescription of Brusoni, Prencipe, and Pavitt (2001): multi-technology firms need to have knowledge in excess of what they need for what they make, to cope with uneven rates of change in technologies on which they rely. The unevenness of technical change renders systems integration capability all the more important, as it requires addressing unpredictable inter-module or inter-system interdependencies.

For this reason, OEMs may well choose to outsource production or assembly, but not outsource technological knowledge. But this latter is a matter of strategic choice. OEMs face a choice between remaining a product architect (thus retaining technical leadership in all sorts of technologies as well as total product architectural knowledge), and becoming a modularizer that follows the architectural decisions of other OEMs. Sustainable profits come in the former case from architectural and technological innovation, whilst the source of competitive advantage in the latter is likely to lie in other areas such as brand management.

The above analysis is somewhat at odds with the traditional transaction cost explanations of the boundary choices of firms since these choices are generally not thought of as strategic, but rather arising in response to operational costs associated with asset specificity and opportunism. In a study of the auto industry, Monteverde and Teece (1982) suggest that 'assemblers will vertically integrate when the production process, broadly defined, produces specialized, nonpatentable know-how'. However, the creation of even patentable know-how could be undertaken either within, or outside, the firm, depending upon strategic considerations of whether or not OEMs remain product architects.

Linking Strategic Drivers to Outsourcing of Modules

To summarize, OEMs' incentives to modularize are multiple, driven by changing phenomena in marketing, production, financial markets, and technology. It was shown that in the car industry, thinking about modules has had the longest history in the production area, whilst the other three drivers are of more recent import. Also, financial incentives seem to be of utmost importance in many OEMs' 'modular strategies' in the 1990s and beyond.

Nevertheless, a different mix of the four drivers gives rise to a different choice in the path to outsourcing modules. As we saw, production strategy may lead to more use of modules in the sense of subassemblies, but in itself is neutral to whether or not these modules are outsourced. A financial driver in itself will predispose OEMs to outsource first and foremost. But without an accompanying logic in production, marketing, or technology, they may not get to switching from outsourcing components to outsourcing modules.

Outsourcing is a decision about organization architecture, and about the drawing of the boundary of the firm. It has shown that such a decision is a matter of strategic choice. But this choice is commonly mediated by labour and capital market conditions, as Baldwin and Clark (2000) show in the case of computers. They argue that with IBM's System 360, some design teams internal to IBM decided to spin-out as independent firms, while other design teams emerged outside of IBM to compete head-on. Baldwin and Clark attribute this deverticalization of the US computer industry to a combination of the modular design principle and the availability of venture capital to finance modular design teams.

Given this analytical framework, we can account for differences between the evolution of modules in the computer industry and the car industry, and between firms in different countries within each industry (see Figure 12.7 for a summary of computers versus cars comparisons). The trigger for the use of modules in the computer industry was user demand for compatibility. This starting point with MIU meant that for MID, global design rules were consciously created for modular plug-able computers. A modular product architecture led to a modular organization with independent design teams but within a single corporation. The eventual dis-integration of the industry into modular suppliers in the United States, but not in Japan, may be accounted for by the inter-firm mobility of technical labour and the availability of venture capital for start-ups in the United States and their relative absence in Japan.

	Computers	Automobiles
Catalyst for modularity	MIU→MID	MIP→MID
Organizational adaptation	Modular design teams and start-ups first, outsourcing later	Outsourcing, tiering and consolidation of suppliers
Labour markets	Mobility of technical labour	Wage differentials between OEM and suppliers
Capital markets	Venture capital for start-ups	Investment banking advice for M&A

Fig. 12.7 Computers and autos compared

In the car industry, the starting point for adopting modularity was in production, specifically in assembly involving complex and ergonomically difficult tasks. MIP, initially undertaken by OEMs themselves, enabled the outsourcing of modular assembly to first-tier suppliers. But unlike in the computer industry which saw many spin-outs and start-ups in the process of adopting modules, the car industry faces excess capacity, slow growth, and globalization. It is not surprising, then, that in the labour market, savings on operator wage costs rather than the mobility of technical labour is at issue. In the capital market, rather than venture capital assisting the process of vertical dis-integration, investment banking advice has led to much consolidation of suppliers wishing to remain, or become, module suppliers. New opportunities for saving on labour costs and M&A are both less common in Japan than in Europe or the United States. These differences contribute to the reasons why modularization is pursued more keenly in Europe and the United States than in Japan.

12.3   Conclusions

This chapter has had two major aims: a clarification of the concept of product architecture and organization architecture, and understanding how strategic considerations mediate the way product architecture affects organization architecture and vice versa. Empirical evidence focused mainly on the car industry with some comparisons with the computer industry. Modularity as a key concept in product architecture, and outsourcing as a counterpart in organization architecture, have been discussed in relation to the notion of systems integration, where systems are both products and organizations.

In relation to the first aim, product or organization architecture was identified as a bundle of characteristics that define (*a*) interfaces between elements of the whole, (*b*) a function-to-component (or task-to-organization unit) mapping that define what those elements are, and (*c*) hierarchies of decomposition of the whole into functions, components, or tasks at different stages in the product cycle. Multiple dimensions exist, even in defining interfaces, and this makes it impossible to rank different types of architecture along a uni-dimensional integral–modular spectrum. In both the product and organization realms, an explicit recognition of hierarchies of decomposition helps clarify the analysis. In product architecture, different stages in the product cycle put different demands on modularity. In particular, MID, MIU, and MIP are three arenas, each with a different set of objectives, demanding different degrees of integration and modularity at varying levels of the product hierarchy. Choosing optimal module boundaries is not straightforward also when facing technological change because a modular product architecture requires considerable stability over time rather than a different set of module boundaries for each time period. For all these reasons, the role of the product architect, with a product-wide systems knowledge, continues to be important in the car industry.

The chapter has also discussed how the relationship between product architecture and organizational architecture is tenuous for a number of reasons. The pre-existing organizational architecture may act as a hindrance to changing product architecture, thus making the causation in changes between product architecture and organizational architecture two-way. Three distinct paths to outsourcing modules were identified, with each path resulting in a different distribution of know-how and capabilities between OEMs and suppliers. The choice of a path depends, in part, on the initial organization architecture. The Japanese penchant for sticking to an integral product architecture, as compared with the US/European OEMs' keen endorsement of outsourced modules, is explained in terms of the greater organizational integration that already exists in Japanese OEMs and suppliers.

Moreover, a mix of strategic drivers was identified as mediating the link between product architecture and organizational architecture. First, in marketing, OEMs' policy to pursue BTO may encourage product modularity, but leaves the question of outsourcing (i.e. organizational modularity) unaffected in theory. Second, a policy to improve production efficiency may lead to the creation of subassembly lines, but whether or not they are retained in-house or outsourced is indeterminate solely with this strategy in mind. Third, in technological strategy, a choice to remain a product architect, rather than a 'modularizer' (that follows the architectural decisions of other OEMs), is likely to lead to changes in product architecture (from integral to modular and back to integral) without much change in organization architecture that continues to 'know more than it makes' (Brusoni, Prencipe, and Pavitt 2001). Lastly, financial strategy to enhance shareholder value via asset reduction is associated with outsourcing (i.e. changes in organizational architecture) without necessarily any shift in product architecture. A comparison between the car and computer industries also points to the importance of labour and capital market conditions as factors mediating the outsourcing decision. It is no wonder that a difference in the mix of these strategic drivers, combined with pre-existing architectural differences, has led to a diversity of product and organizational architecture amongst car manufacturers.

To conclude, this chapter went beyond the pre-existing general discussion of the influence of product modularity on organization design, specifically by using evidence in the car industry to discuss what changes modularity might bring to the organization of design, development and production. Modularity in product architecture gives greater scope for choosing among alternative organization architectures. But the exact choice of organizational form and boundaries depends on corporate strategy, factor conditions, and the existing distribution of capabilities.

Acknowledgement

The author gratefully acknowledges funding by, and valuable discussion within, the International Motor Vehicle Program (IMVP). This paper incorporates insights gained through interviews carried out at OEMs and module suppliers in Europe and North America. I wish to thank all those who gave generously of their time in answering my questions.

References

ABERNATHY, W. J. and CLARK, K. B. (1985). 'Innovation: Mapping the Winds of Creative Destruction', *Research Policy*, 14: 3–22.

BALDWIN, C. Y. and CLARK, K. B. (1997). 'Managing in the Age of Modularity', *Harvard Business Review*, September–October: 84–93.

————, (2000). *Design Rules: The Power of Modularity*. London: MIT Press.

BEST, M. (1990). *The New Competition: Institutions of Industrial Restructuring*. Cambridge, MA: Harvard University Press.

BRUSONI, S., PRENCIPE, A., and PAVITT, K. (2001). 'Knowledge Specialization, Organizational Coupling, and the Boundaries of the Firm: Why Do Firms Know More Than They Make?', *Administrative Science Quarterly*, 46: 597–621.

BURNS, T. and STALKER, G. M. (1961). *The Management of Innovation*. London: Tavistock.

CHESBROUGH, H. and KUSUNOKI, K. (2001). 'The Modularity Trap: Innovation, Technology Phase Shifts, and the Resulting Limits of Virtual Organizations', in I. Nonaka and D. J. Teece (eds.), *Managing Industrial Knowledge: Creation, Transfer and Utilization*. London: Sage, 202–30.

CLARK, K. (1985). 'The Interaction of Design Hierarchies and Market Concepts in Technological Solution', *Research Policy*, 15/5: 235–51.

ETHIRAJ, S. K. and LEVINTHAL, D. (2002). *Modularity and Innovation in Complex Systems* (mimeo). Philadelphia, PA: Wharton School.

FINANCIAL TIMES (1999). 4 August.

FINE, C. H. (1998). *Clockspeed: Winning Industry Control in the Age of Temporary Advantage*. New York: Perseus Books.

FIXSON, S. (2002). 'Linking Modularity and Cost: A Methodology to Assess Cost Implications of Product Architecture Differences to Support Product Design', Doctoral Dissertation, MIT.

FUJIMOTO, T. (1997). *The Evolution of a Manufacturing System at Toyota*. New York: Oxford University Press.

GULATI, R. K. and EPPINGER, S. D. (1996). *The Coupling of Product Architecture and Organizational Structure Decisions*. (Working Paper 3906), Cambridge, MA: MIT International Center for Research on the Management of Technology.

HENDERSON, R. M. and CLARK, K. B. (1990). 'Architectural Innovation: the Reconfiguration of Existing Product Technologies and the Failure of Established Firms', *Administrative Science Quarterly*, 35: 9–30.

HOLWEG, M. and PIL, F. (2001). 'Successful Build-to-Order Strategies start with the Customer', *Sloan Management Review*, Fall: 74–83.

LANGLOIS, R. N. (1999). *Modularity in Technology, Organization, and Society* (mimeo). Storrs, CT: University of Connecticut.

LAWRENCE, P. R. and LORSCH, J. W. (1967). 'Differentiation and Integration in Complex Organizations', *Administrative Science Quarterly*, 12: 1–47.

LAZONICK, W. and O'SULLIVAN, M. (2000). 'Maximizing Shareholder Value: A New Ideology for Corporate Governance', *Economy and Society*, 29/1: 13–35.

MONTEVERDE, K. and TEECE, D. (1982). 'Appropriable Rents and Quasi-vertical Integration', *Journal of Law and Economics*, 25: 321–8.

ORTON, J. D. and WEICK, K. E. (1990). 'Loosely Coupled Systems: A Reconceptualization', *Academy of Management Review*, 15/2: 203–23.

PINE, B. J. (1993). *Mass Customization: The New Frontier in Business Competition*. Boston, MA: Harvard Business School Press.

ROMMEL, G., BRUCK, F., DIEDERICHS, R., KEMPIS, R.-D., KAAS, H.-W., FUHRY, G., and KURFES, V. (1996). *Quality Pays*. London: Macmillan Business.

SANCHEZ, R. and MAHONEY, J. T. (1996). 'Modularity, Flexibility, and Knowledge Management in Product and Organization Design', *Strategic Management Journal*, 17: 63–76.

SCHILLING, M. A. (2000). 'Towards a General Modular Systems Theory and its Application to Interfirm Product Modularity', *Academy of Management Review*, 25/2: 312–34.

SCOTT, R. (1998). *Organizations: Rational, Natural, and Open Systems* (4th edn.). Englewood Cliffs, NJ: Prentice Hall.

SIMON, H. (1962). 'The Architecture of Complexity', *Proceedings of the American Philosophical Society*, 106/6: 467–82.

STARR, M. K. (1965). 'Modular Production—A New Concept', *Harvard Business Review*, 43/(November–December): 131–42.

TAKEISHI, A. and FUJIMOTO, T. (2001). 'Modularisation in the Auto Industry: Interlinked Multiple Hierarchies of Product, Production and Supplier Systems', *International Journal of Automotive Technology and Management*, 1/4: 379–96.

TOMKE, S. H. and REINERTSEN, D. (1998). 'Agile Product Development: Managing Development Flexibility in Uncertain Environments', *California Management Review*, 41/1: 8–30.

ULRICH, K. (1995). 'The Role of Product Architecture in the Manufacturing Firm', *Research Policy*, 24: 419–40.

ULRICH, K. T. and TUNG, K. (1991). *Fundamentals of Product Modularity.* (Working Paper WP3335–91-MSA), Cambridge, MA: MIT Sloan School of Management.

WHITNEY, D. E. (1993). *Nippondenso Co. Ltd: A Case Study of Strategic Product Design* (mimeo). Cambridge, MA: C.S. Draper Laboratory.

WILLIAMSON, O. E. (1975). *Markets and Hierarchies: Analysis and Antitrust Implications.* New York: Free Press.

13

Modularization in the Car Industry
Interlinked Multiple Hierarchies of Product, Production, and Supplier Systems

AKIRA TAKEISHI

Institute of Innovation Research, Hitotsubashi University, Tokyo, Japan

AND

TAKAHIRO FUJIMOTO

Faculty of Economics, University of Tokyo, Tokyo, Japan

13.1 Introduction

The concept of 'modularization' has attracted increasing attention in the car industry in the last few years. The meanings and purposes of modularization in this industry vary between regions and companies. There is no clear-cut definition of the term shared by the whole industry. Yet, there is a relatively common feature across various practices of modularization in the industry. It entails having larger units in subassembly and also often involves outsourcing these subassemblies to suppliers (as most frequently observed in the European car industry).

This fact suggests that there are at least three facets in the phenomenon called 'modularization': (*a*) 'modularization in product architecture' (modularization in design) which has often been discussed in the field of technology management; (*b*) 'modularization in production'; and (*c*) 'modularization in inter-firm system' (outsourcing subsystems in larger units to outside suppliers). These three facets are often confused when discussing modularization. While the European car industry has been interested mainly in outsourcing, the Japanese industry has focused on modularization in production. Neither has addressed 'modularization in product architecture'. As we look further into the ongoing practices in the car industry, however, we can detect some changes that may lead to modularization in product architecture.

In the car industry it is possible to observe such complicated, multi-faceted, and sometimes confusing processes of modularization. If we could present a single conceptual framework within which all trends in the industry can be analysed somehow consistently, it would contribute to a better understanding of the concept of modularization. This chapter therefore focuses on the car industry and attempts to provide a framework for understanding the modularization processes in the industry. This chapter also aims to probe into dynamic interactions and architectural changes between three systems—product, production, and inter-firm systems. Since modularization in the car industry is still in a fluid, transitional stage at the present time, the industry provides us with a particularly interesting field where we can witness in real-time such dynamic interactions and architectural changes.

The next section of this chapter sets out a conceptual framework that sees development and production activities for cars as multiple hierarchies of product, production, and inter-firm systems. This framework serves as a platform for subsequent analysis. The following section describes modularization in the car industry. We investigate what is actually happening in the industry and the rationales behind these changes, while comparing the practices of modularization in the Japanese, European, and US car industries.[1] We then discuss how some changes in production and supplier systems could lead to changes in product architecture. The chapter concludes with a summary of our analysis and we discuss some implications for the future of the car industry.

13.2 Analytical Framework: Development/Production Systems for Cars as Multiple Hierarchies

Before investigating the actual practices of modularization being implemented in the car industry, we would like to propose a conceptual framework as the premise for the analysis. One of this chapter's aims is to discuss the concepts of 'modularization in product system', 'modularization in production system', and 'modularization in inter-firm system' within the same framework, and identify the differences and linkages between them. This framework is based on the concept of 'multiple hierarchies'. It sees development–production activities for cars as multiple, interlinked hierarchies. It contends that the hierarchies in product, production, and inter-firm systems make up one complex system, where the three systems are related to each other (this framework is based on Fujimoto 1999).

Architecture is the basic design concept of an artificial system. As Simon (1996) pointed out long before, a complex system in general could be described as a hierarchy, which is composed of interrelated subsystems, each of the latter being in turn hierarchical in structure, until we reach some lowest level of elementary subsystem. Firms' developmental–productive systems are no exception.

The development–production activities of cars can be understood as information circulation processes from development to production to

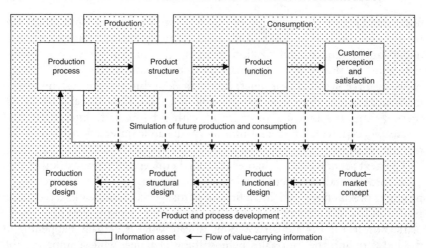

Fig. 13.1 Information circulation in product development, production, and consumption
Note: For visual simplicity environmental uncertainty, supplier systems, and sales
systems were omitted from the chart.
Source: Adapted and modified from Fujimoto (1989) and Clark and Fujimoto (1991).

marketing to consumption, and finally back to development (Figure 13.1).
Value-creating information assets at each stage of product–market concept,
product functional design, product structure design, product process
design, production process, and product structure can be regarded as what
Penrose (1959) called 'productive resources'. How these resources are divided
and coordinated among carmakers and suppliers (first-, second-, and lower-
tier) defines inter-firm, or supplier, systems for car development and
production.

As Figure 13.2 depicts, each of these production resources takes the form
of a hierarchy, composed of subsystems. Therefore, car development and
production systems could be described as multiple hierarchies, consisting of
market–need hierarchy, product–function hierarchy, production–process
hierarchy, and so on, with each hierarchy interrelated with one another. We
could then define the architecture of a product or process as interrelations
among these hierarchies.

Let us explain each of the three facets of modularization (modularization
in product, production, and inter-firm systems) with this concept of 'multiple
hierarchies'. First, 'modularization in product' is defined in terms of the
interrelation between the product–function hierarchy' and the 'product–
structure hierarchy'. We can illustrate such an interrelation with diagrams like
those shown in Figure 13.3(a) (e.g. Göepfert and Steinbrecher 1999). The left
diagram is a schematic representation of the so-called 'integral' product.
Since the elements making up the product function (the left triangle) are
interrelated with those making up the product structure (the right triangle) in

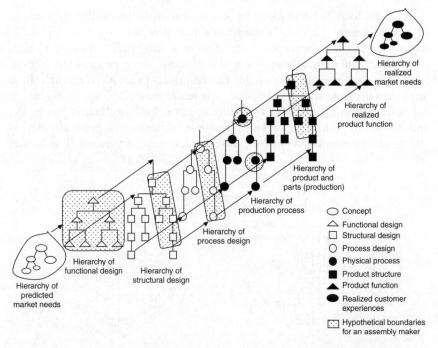

Fig. 13.2 Multiple hierarchies in automobile product development, production, and consumption. Note that the connection between the functional hierarchy and the structural hierarchy is usually more complicated than the one that this diagram indicates

a complex manner, the designer of subsystem [S1] has to take the following factors into account:

(*a*) Functional interdependence with the other subsystems (such as s1←f1←s2, and s1←f2←s2);

(*b*) Structural interdependence with the other subsystems (physical interference, for example, s1←s2);

(*c*) Interdependence with the design of the entire system (consistency with the design of the whole system, s1←S1←S);

(*d*) Interdependence between the subfunctions (such as f1⇔f2, and F1⇔F2).

'Modularization in product' decreases such interdependence between the concerned elements. It allows one-to-one correspondence between the subsystems and their functions, and enables, for example, the designer of subsystem [S1] to focus solely on subfunction [F1] and [S] (the structure of the product as a whole). The subsystem becomes a 'module with a self-contained function', which can be designed more autonomously. Remaining interdependence after modularization can further be reduced if the interfaces between the elements are simplified and standardized as much as possible.

We can illustrate 'modularity in production' with the similar diagrams as shown in Figure 13.3(b). It comprises the 'product–structure hierarchy' (right triangle) and the 'product–process hierarchy' (left). In order to simplify our explanation, among the whole manufacturing processes, we focus here only on assembly work in the 'product–process hierarchy'. It is important to note that the 'product–structure hierarchy' in this figure, as part of 'multiple hierarchies of product structure and production processes', and its counterpart in the previous 'multiple hierarchies of product function and product structure' might have different hierarchical patterns. The former

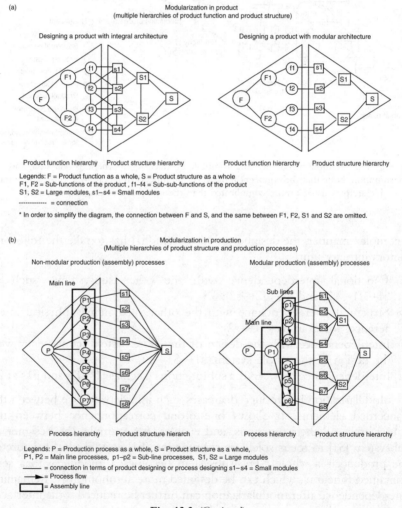

(a)   Modularization in product
(multiple hierarchies of product function and product structure)

Designing a product with integral architecture   Designing a product with modular architecture

Product function hierarchy   Product structure hierarchy   Product function hierarchy   Product structure hierarchy

Legends: F = Product function as a whole, S = Product structure as a whole
F1, F2 = Sub-functions of the product , f1–f4 = Sub-sub-functions of the product
S1, S2 = Large modules, s1–s4 = Small modules
-------------- = connection

* In order to simplify the diagram, the connection between F and S, and the same between F1, F2, S1 and S2 are omitted.

(b)   Modularization in production
(Multiple hierarchies of product structure and production processes)

Non-modular production (assembly) processes   Modular production (assembly) processes

Main line   Sub lines

Main line

Process hierarchy   Product structure hierarch   Process hierarchy   Product structure hierarchy

Legends: P = Production process as a whole, S = Product structure as a whole,
P1, P2 = Main line processes, p1–p2 = Sub-line processes, S1, S2 = Large modules
——— = connection in terms of product designing or process designing s1–s4 = Small modules
——▶ = Process flow
▭ = Assembly line

Fig. 13.3 (*Continued*)

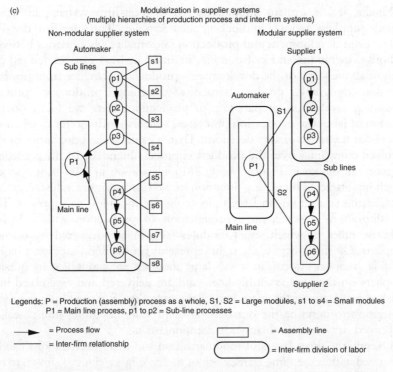

(c)   Modularization in supplier systems
                              (multiple hierarchies of production process and inter-firm systems)

Legends: P = Production (assembly) process as a whole, S1, S2 = Large modules, s1 to s4 = Small modules
         P1 = Main line process, p1 to p2 = Sub-line processes

——▶   = Process flow   = Assembly line
———   = Inter-firm relationship   = Inter-firm division of labor

Fig. 13.3 Multiple hierarchies of product, production, and supply systems

hierarchy is built up in pursuit of 'functional independence' of each sub-system (i.e. the degree to which a function of the product is achieved by a single subsystem), while the latter is made up of 'structural cohesiveness' (i.e. the degree to which a collection of parts can be physically handled as one unit). The latter hierarchy is intended to contribute to 'structurally cohesive modules', which make it easier to manage material handling and quality control. The difference between these two hierarchies can be understood by observing the parts list for the product design, which is not the same as that for production management.

The left diagram represents non-modular production processes. Without any 'structurally cohesive large modules', the product has to be assembled from eight small modules (s1–s8) at the same hierarchical level on one long main assembly line. On the contrary, in the right diagram, there are two structurally cohesive modules 'S1 and S2' on the right, and two subassembly lines to build them and one short main line for finished products on the left (remember the famous watchmaker story in Simon 1969). It can be said that the 'product–structure hierarchy' with cohesive modules is translated into the 'product–process hierarchy' with one main line and two subassembly lines.

Finally, let us explain 'modularization in inter-firm system', in which outside suppliers conduct and deliver subassemblies. The inter-firm division of labour in development and production (a carmaker's boundaries between in-house operations and outsourcing, or make-or-buy) can be defined for each of all the steps of the development–production activities from product function designing, product structure designing, production process designing, production preparation, to production. Here we focus on the division of labour in production processes, which we often refer to when we talk about the make-or-buy decisions. That is to draw the boundaries of the involved companies over the production process hierarchy of the preceding diagram, as shown in Figure 13.3(c). 'Modularization in inter-firm system', which has attracted increasing attention in the European car industry, entails outsourcing subsystems in large units (cohesive modules) to suppliers. The left diagram is a schematic representation of production with a higher in-house ratio, in which small modules (s1–s8) are delivered by outside suppliers. On the contrary, the right represents production based on a highly modular supplier system, in which large modules are assembled by outside suppliers on their subassembly lines, and are delivered and assembled into finished products on the main line of the carmaker. We can apply the same illustration to describe the outsourcing of product designing (the so-called 'approved drawings' or 'black-box components').

Overall, the three facets of modularization and their interrelations can be illustrated within the same framework of multiple hierarchies as shown in the three pairs of diagrams. Product engineers, process engineers, and purchasing managers must make decisions about the product and process hierarchies and the inter-firm boundaries, while securing close coordination between them. It is obvious that these three facets of modularization must not be mixed up. At the same time, it is also clear that these decisions are interrelated with each other. They are the processes of making decisions about interrelated hierarchies of product functions, product structure, and production processes. There is always a possibility of some inconsistency or conflict between the decisions. In a sense, the most critical challenge in modularization is how to avoid or overcome such inconsistency and conflict through coordination.

We have discussed the three decision-making processes from a rather static point of view thus far. Such decisions, however, in reality, are probably being made in a cumulative manner over time in most cases. We therefore have to take 'path-dependency' into account—the outcome may depend on the specific sequence of decision-making.

The following section probes into the actual practices of 'modularization' in both Western and Japanese car industries. Let us briefly summarize our analysis beforehand. Western carmakers have a strong inclination toward 'modularization in inter-firm system', or outsourcing, which has stimulated 'modularization in production'. One of their challenges is to cope with the inconsistency or conflict created between such 'modularization in procure-ment/production' and 'modularization in product architecture'. Japanese car-makers, on the contrary, have focused on in-house 'modularization in production' thus far and have been relatively quiet about aggressive out-sourcing adopted by Western counterparts. Carmakers in Japan instead seem to seek for 'modularization in product architecture' facilitated by the need for the functionality and conformance quality of modules assembled on in-house subassembly lines. Since Western and Japanese car industries have been following different paths in implementing modularization, their pro-duct architectures, production process hierarchies, and boundaries between in-house operations and outsourcing could be diverse, as they emerge.

13.3   Modularization in the World Car Industry

European and US Car Industries

It is two German carmakers, Volkswagen and Mercedes-Benz (presently Daimler-Chrysler), that geared up the car industry's modularization in the mid-1990s. Their new assembly plants, which started production in 1996 and 1997, introduced modularization on a large scale, specifically at Volkswagen's plants in Resende (Brazil), Boleslav (Czech), and Mosel (former East Germany), and Mercedes-Benz's plants in Vance (United States) and Hambach (France).

These plants share two characteristics. One is that they have assembled cars from relatively large subassemblies. A car is a system made up of numerous components. There is a wide choice of managerial units at the intermediate stage in the process of putting them into a car. These plants have departed from the conventional way of assembling cars. At conven-tional plants, individual components—for example, instrument panels, gauges, and wire harnesses—are fixed one by one to a vehicle body on the final assembly line. Instead, at these new plants, these individual components are subassembled on a separate line, and then installed as a module into a body on the final assembly line. In the framework we discussed in the previous section, this is to redesign the hierarchy in production processes by setting a new intermediate layer to it (as shown in the right diagram of Figure 13.3(b)). Carmakers in the world have divided cars into many parts in order to make development and production processes manageable. As some carmakers have drastically redesigned the hierarchies in their development and production processes through modularization, others have also begun exploring new hierarchies.

The second characteristic shared by these plants is that they have let outside suppliers develop and assemble subassemblies. In the previous fra-mework, this means to narrow the scope of in-house operations in the hierarchy of the inter-firm system (moving the inter-firm boundaries up to a higher hierarchical level), as shown in the right diagram of Figure 13.3(c). MCC's plant in Hambach is a typical example of such outsourcing. MCC is a joint venture of Mercedes-Benz and SMH (a Swiss watch manufacturer), which assembles a two-seater small-sized car called 'Smart'. A group of suppliers known as 'system partners' surround MCC's assembly plant. They build large modules such as cockpit modules, rear axle modules, and door modules, and deliver them directly to MCC's final assembly line. MCC even outsources body welding and painting, which traditionally carmakers carry out in-house. Carmakers in the United States have not yet become as aggressive in pursuing modularization as these German companies. However, they have indicated their intention of letting their so-called 'full-service' system suppliers handle larger sets of components in development and production.

There are three main reasons why Western carmakers have been expanding the scope of outsourcing. First, they want to take advantage of the suppliers' lower labour costs. Second, they can cut investment costs and risk by giving more important responsibilities to the suppliers.[2] Third, these moves toward modularization have also been accelerated by their policy of reducing the number of first-tier suppliers. This idea was originally taken from the Japanese carmakers' approach (Clark and Fujimoto 1991; Cusumano and Takeishi 1991; Nishiguchi 1994). However, compared to their Japanese rivals, European manufacturers are already letting their suppliers handle larger modules. It seems that a strong sense of crisis underlies their aggressive outsourcing because it has been difficult to make profits from their car business. In other words, they have been seeking outsourcing as part of an attempt to redesign 'business architecture' (Fujimoto, Takeishi, and Aoshima 2001).

Responding to and promoting such demand from manufacturers, there has been a growing number of mergers and acquisitions among suppliers in the United States and Europe. They aim at establishing themselves as module suppliers and expanding business with major carmakers by becoming qualified to manage the development and production of a larger set of components as a module.[3]

There are, however, some cases where module suppliers are assigned only to subassemble the components, each of which is still manufactured and designed by the incumbent suppliers. In these cases, carmakers still maintain control over the choice of suppliers for the individual components, as well as the management of their prices, quality, and design. Carmakers have chosen to do so partly because they think that module suppliers are not capable of handling all aspects of the module. They are also concerned that extensive outsourcing to a limited number of suppliers may make the costs and technology of components unknown to themselves, reduce competitive pressure for suppliers, and thus weaken their own negotiating power. Nevertheless, such limited outsourcing probably only offers the limited advantage of cheap labour. It does not appeal to suppliers either, because they are treated only as simple subcontractors with little added value while asked to invest lots of money and take risks. Carmakers are still in the process of exploring where they should draw the boundaries in their development and production activities.

Japanese Car Industry

Unlike the US and European car industries, the Japanese car industry has shown few visible initiatives toward modularization. But when we looked closely into what Japanese companies are doing, through interviews and a questionnaire survey, we found out that they were dealing with the issue in a different way with different aims.

First, let us look at the results of our questionnaire survey.[4] We conducted a questionnaire survey with 153 first-tier suppliers in February and March 1999. In this survey, the term 'modularization' was not used because there was no commonly shared definition of it. Instead, a number of questions about several important aspects of modularization were asked to capture recent changes in the industry. The respondents were asked about the degree of changes over the last 4 years (a typical model changeover cycle) in nineteen measures regarding design and production processes of their components.

A factor analysis of the responses has identified the following four factors: (*a*) component standardization, (*b*) shift to integral architecture, (*c*) functional independence/interface simplification, and (*d*) expansion of the subassembly scope. The results of this factor analysis suggest that it is difficult to generalize what is meant by modularization because it involves multiple dimensions.[5]

Table 13.1 shows the average answer scores. The biggest change over the last four years has been 'shift to integral architecture'. The functions assigned to individual parts had become more complex (item 17), and the need for structural or functional coordination with other components had increased (items 18 and 19). These changes were in an opposite direction to modularization. Note that we see signs of modularization in architecture in the increase of component sharing within each customer (carmaker) (items 6, 7, 13, and 14). Yet, the scope of component sharing was quite limited among variations of a particular model, or at most, among different models of carmaker. There had been almost no attempts for component sharing across different carmakers (items 8 and 15). Further, there had been only little progress in the functional independence of components and the simplification of interfaces (items 11, 12, and 16). There had been a very small number of cases where carmakers had asked their suppliers to subassemble a larger set of components (items 2–4).

To sum up, the product architecture had become more integral, although some carmakers had shown some interest in the use of standardized

TABLE 13.1 *Recent changes of component and production in the Japanese car industry (results of a questionnaire survey with first-tier suppliers)*

	Standardization of component design within an automaker	Architectural integrality	Functional independence/ interface rationalization	Expansion in subassembly scope	Score
1 Size of the component reduced with the same basic structured			●		0.31
2 Number of parts making up the component increased				●	0.02
3 Number of assembly process steps for the component increased				●	0.09
4 Component has been incorporated into another assembly component					0.07
5 Process steps and costs to assemble the component decreased with the adoption of integrally-molded parts					0.47
6 Component design was shared by different models of the same automaker	●				0.44
7 Component design was shared between different variations of the same model	●				0.57

8 Component design was standardized across different automakers		0.19
9 Component design was shared by the current and earlier models		−0.11
10 Number of variations within a vehicle model decreased	•	0.19
11 Number of interfaces (such as contact points) with other components decreased	•	0.13
12 Designs of interfaces (such as contact points) with other components were simplified		0.19
13 Designs of interfaces (such as contact points) were standardized within a model	•	0.28
14 Designs of interfaces (such as contact points) were standardized between different variations of a model	•	0.40
15 Designs of interfaces (such as contact points) were standardized across different automakers		0.09

TABLE 13.1 (*Continued*)

	Standardization of component design within an automaker	Architectural integrality	Functional independence/ interface rationalization	Expansion in subassembly scope	Score
16 Function of the model became more self-contained (independent)			●		0.11
17 Function of the model became more complex (with more functions required)		●			0.62
18 Need for functional coordination with other components increased		●			0.62
19 Need for structural coordination with other components (such as checking, matching, and interferences)		●			0.63
Average Score	0.42	0.62	0.19	0.05	0.28

Note: This table is based on the results of a questionnaire survey with 153 Japanese first-tier suppliers, which was conducted in February and March 1999, in Japan. The respondents answered the degree of changes in each item. Scores were: 'changed' = 2, 'no changes' = 0, 'changed adversely' = − 2. Columns are the four factors identified by a factor analysis. ● indicates that the item had a strong correlation with the corresponding factor. The scores in the bottom rows are the average scores for the items with a strong correlation with the factor. See Fujimoto, Matsuo, and Takeishi (1998) for the details of the questionnaire survey, and Ku (2000) for the results of the factor analysis.

Source: Questionnaire survey with first-tier suppliers in Japan (1999).

components and interfaces. On the other hand, there had been almost no progress in the type of modularization prevalent in the European and US car industry, namely outsourcing of subassemblies in larger units to suppliers.

However, the above survey tells only about what component suppliers saw. If we look at what is happening inside carmakers, a different picture appears. Figure 13.4 shows the results of our interviews (conducted from March to July, 1999) with eight Japanese carmakers, about to what extent components around the instrument panels were subassembled before being installed on the main assembly line for some of their models. It plots the

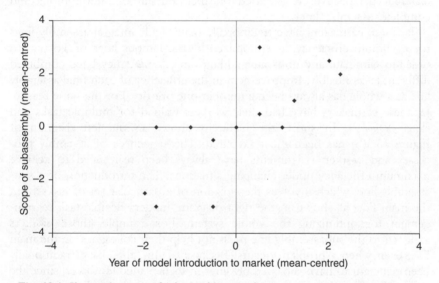

Fig. 13.4 Changes in scope of subassembly around instrument panels at Japanese car-makers' assembly plants. This figure plots the relationship between the number of components subassembled around the instrument panels, and the year in which the model in question was introduced to the market. The scores are all mean-centred within each carmaker. For the year of market introduction, the score measures a difference between the year in which the model in question was launched and the average year in which the carmaker's sample models were launched. The higher the score, the newer the model, among the carmaker's models in the sample. For the scope of subassembly, the score measures a difference between the number of components subassembled for the model in question and the average number of components subassembled for the car-maker's sample models. The higher the score, the larger the scope of subassembly, among the carmaker's models in the sample. Components examined for subassembly include: instrument panels, gauges, meter panels, glove compartments, wire harnesses, air conditioner switches, air conditioner units, air conditioner blowers, air conditioner ducts, air vents, audio systems, and navigation systems, steering shafts, steering columns, steering switches, ignitions, column shifts, airbags (for drivers), airbags (for passengers), cup holders, ashtrays, pedals, and cross members (twenty-three components)

Source: Interviews with eight Japanese carmakers (conducted in Spring and Summer, 1999).

number of component types subassembled for the model (vertical axis) and the year in which the model in question was introduced to the market (horizontal axis). The scores were all mean-centred for adjustment across carmakers. We could see a positive correlation. The newer the model, the wider the scope of the subassembly. In other words, there has been some progress in having subassemblies in larger units inside car assemblers.

Then, why have Japanese carmakers promoted the in-house use of sub-assemblies? They have done so partly because they were stimulated by American and European rivals who have been actively adopting modular-ization. However, some carmakers are interested in modularization with a different perspective. It is based on their pursuit of 'autonomous and complete' assembly lines.

Japanese carmakers have traditionally built highly integral assembly lines for maximum efficiency, as epitomized by the famous lines of Toyota. In order to eliminate any non-value-adding time, '*muda*', they have combined different tasks flexibly. Improvement in the efficiency of each final assembly line as a whole has always been a number one priority. For the same reason, Japanese carmakers have had their workers trained for multiple tasks and skills ('*tanoko*'). In short, the hierarchy shown in the left diagram of Figure 13.3(b) has been most favoured. The sequences of assembly pro-cesses and worker assignments have always been rearranged to achieve maximum efficiency under changing situations. The introduction of a sub-assembly line, which involves the isolation of a particular set of tasks from the main line, as shown in the right diagram, hinders flexible task rearran-gement for optimizing the whole system. For example, those workers assigned to the subassembly line must not help their colleagues on the main line, even when a problem occurs. Because of this, they have traditionally been reluctant to have subassembly lines in their plants. However, since the early 1990s, they have begun changing their views for several reasons.

First, carmakers have placed a greater importance on employee job satisfaction. This change of attitude originated from a serious shortage of workers during the bubble economy (Fujimoto and Takeishi 1994). It has also been influenced by the necessity of dealing with the growing number of female and elderly workers. The adoption of subassembly lines improves the workers' satisfaction in two respects. First, working for a subassembly line allows workers to maintain a comfortable working position (better ergo-nomics). Suppose your job is to attach various components around the instrument panel. If you work on a main line, you may have to stand in a torturous position, leaning over the panel in the car. By contrast, if you work on a subassembly line, you can maintain a relatively comfortable working position, standing while attaching all the components to the panel. In addition, it is considered that handling a functionally related set of tasks helps you understand the significance of your work. This would motivate and satisfy workers.

Second, they have placed greater importance on a self-contained quality control system. According to this idea, the quality of each subassembly is inspected upon completion, not on the final line as part of a finished product, in order to find defects at the earliest stage possible. The adoption of self-contained quality control has facilitated the adoption of subassemblies to be inspected upon completion. This is closely related to the significance of work mentioned above. If you can check the quality of a subassembly you have just completed, you can gain a sense of your work's significance and accomplishment.

With increasing emphasis on worker satisfaction and self-contained quality control, Japanese carmakers have been replacing their conventional integral lines with new self-contained lines, and thus adopting more and more subassemblies.[6] However, they have been reluctant to outsource the subassemblies to outside suppliers, as confirmed in the results of the previous questionnaire survey as well as our interviews with carmakers. This is a big difference compared to the European car industry, where modularization often proceeds with outsourcing.

There are some reasons for this reluctance. First, the cost advantage in outsourcing modules is not so great in Japan because the wage gap between carmakers and the first-tier suppliers is narrow compared to Western counterparts. Second, in order to have outsourced subassemblies delivered in sequence to the main line on short lead-times, the suppliers' shops should be located within a very short distance of the assembly plants. Yet, investment opportunities for building such new facilities are currently quite limited in Japan. Even if this is possible, carmakers are concerned that each plant might rely too much on the particular suppliers selected, and thus its competitive pressure toward them might be reduced. Third, carmakers have been doubtful about the capability of suppliers to handle a larger scope of tasks since Japanese suppliers have long specialized in the development and production of individual functional components. It is also true that Japanese carmakers have a dislike of losing knowledge about the technology and costs of any parts involved. The absence of those component suppliers who have proactively had mergers and acquisitions in order to develop and produce larger modules as emerging in the United States and Europe, has also kept Japanese carmakers primarily focused on in-house subassemblies.

13.4 Redefining Product Architecture

As we have discussed thus far, modularization in the car industry has centred upon the redefinition of hierarchies in production system and inter-firm system. The former entails the expanded use of subassemblies, the change common in the Japanese, European, and US car industries. The latter involves the expanded use of outsourcing, which has been prevalent in Europe and the United States, but inconspicuous in Japan.

The redefinition of hierarchies in production and inter-firm systems is essentially different from modularization in product system (as shown in Figure 13.3). In the first place, cars are usually categorized as relatively integral products in terms of product architecture (Fujimoto 2001), and thus are difficult to be modularized further. But if we probe into what is happening in the industry, we observe some movements in which the redefinition of hierarchies in production and inter-firm systems may lead to modularization in product architecture.

Among such movements is the redesigning of the components necessitated by the adoption of subassemblies, which has been addressed by Japanese carmakers. The use of subassemblies has some disadvantages. A subassembly built from many components is difficult to handle because of its size and weight. Such a subassembly is also difficult to fit perfectly onto other subassemblies or the body. Accuracy in assembly work is more difficult to achieve with subassemblies than with smaller, individual components. If some additional parts or fixtures are needed only to ensure ease of handling and accuracy, it would result in an unacceptable increase in costs and weight. Furthermore, unless the assignment of functions to some components is redefined, it may often be impossible to check the quality of a subassembled module.[7]

In order to solve these problems brought about by modularization, Japanese carmakers have placed great emphasis on redesigning the components within a subassembly module. Such efforts include the integration of some components into others for reduced cost and weight, and the reassignment of functions to realize self-contained quality control (e.g. making the functions of an instrument panel module more independent so that the quality of its electrical system can be tested independently). These attempts are nothing but the redefinition of product architecture. The integration of some components into others involves making the product architecture of certain sets of components more integral. Making the function of a set of components more independent entails the modularization of the set.

Such attempts to redesign have been triggered by the redefinition of the hierarchies in production systems, and may lead to the redefinition of organizational boundaries (following the path: 'modularization in production system' → 'modularization in product architecture' → 'modularization in inter-firm system') (see Figure 13.5). According to Fujimoto and Ge (2001), the 'approved drawings' (or 'black-box components') are more likely to be adopted for certain parts for which the responsibilities for quality control can be clearly defined. In other words, such parts can be outsourced because the functions assigned to them can be managed by outside suppliers as independent, self-contained units. If the redefinition of product architecture allows us to redefine the scope of quality control responsibilities in larger units, development and production within that scope could be outsourced

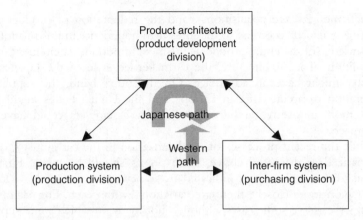

Fig. 13.5 Dynamics of modularization in the auto industry

more easily to outside suppliers. As a result, outsourcing of development and production would be further promoted.[8]

Some Western carmakers include 'a testable set of components' as an important condition for modularization. This suggests that the assignment of independent (testable) functions has been treated as an important requirement for outsourcing. This implies the sequence that 'modularization in inter-firm and production systems' facilitates 'modularization in product architecture' (Figure 13.5).

Probably the most outstanding example of products developed in this manner is 'Smart' being manufactured in the aforementioned MCC plant. This car is made up of a highly unique body frame called a TRIDION cell and plastic body panels. Unlike the integral architecture of ordinary passenger cars with a mono-cock body, Smart's product architecture was designed to be built from modules. Bosch, one of the largest component suppliers in the world, once pointed out that one of the requirements for successful modular production was to design a car optimized for modules, and cited Smart as an example. The development of such a car can be described as a process in which the division of labour with outside suppliers expedites the redefinition of the relationships between functions and structures to define explicit conditions for contract and evaluation measures, and, as a result, the architecture of the product becomes modularized.

Product architecture could be redefined in the process of modularization in both the Japanese and European car industries. But the difference in the paths they have followed might make their new architecture different in nature (Figure 13.5). In Japan, the redefinition of product architecture has been addressed under the leadership of carmakers in cooperation with multiple suppliers.[9] In Europe, carmakers have often outsourced a large set of components to a single supplier (who has become a module supplier through mergers and acquisitions), and the redefinition of product architecture is pursued according to the inter-firm boundaries in this relationship. If knowledge of the entire product is the most important requirement for the redefinition of its architecture, the carmaker-led style of the Japanese car industry might have an advantage. On the other hand, the supplier-led redefinition of architecture in Europe and the United States might bring about more innovative architecture that any assemblers could have ever recognized.

While the recent processes of modularization in the car industry can be summarized as discussed above, three points should be made. First, the regional differences we have indicated are somewhat simplified. If we look at each region more closely, there are variations within each. For example, in Japan, we observe some cases, although not many, in which some suppliers are merged and try to provide modular products to carmakers. This is an attempt at supplier-led modularization. Some European carmakers emphasize in-house production. For example, Audi, a company of the Volkswagen Group, focuses on in-house production at its Ingolstadt Plant, Germany. It outsourced some subassemblies to outside suppliers, but plans to have them back to in-house operations, a strategy similar to many Japanese carmakers. Some other European carmakers have also become more sceptical about the benefit of outsourcing the production and development of a larger set of components to suppliers. How the path will evolve in each region has yet to be seen.

Second, modularization in this industry is basically adopted for individual models. Even Western carmakers use particular modules for particular plants or models. There has been no case of adopting the same modules across different models or plants. The same applies to subassemblies and design rationalization in the Japanese car industry. In this sense, the modularization in the car industry is closed modularization. It is essentially different from open modularization observed in personal computers, bicycles, and stereo component systems, where standardized interfaces and components are widely shared across companies. If a carmaker outsources design tasks in very large units to one particular supplier, the free hand given to the supplier might allow it to pursue the component sharing and standardization to a certain extent. However, since the optimization of components and modules for each model's better product integrity is of great importance in the industry, we have not seen any extensive attempt toward the commonalization and standardization of interfaces across different carmakers.[10]

Third, for optimization close coordination between a carmaker and its suppliers is still critical and the carmaker's capability and knowledge for effective coordination are needed (Takeishi 2001, 2002). It is not unlikely that the modularization of inter-firm system would harm the optimization. For example, modular suppliers with more negotiating power against carmakers may not respond to their customers' request for optimization. Or by outsourcing a larger set of components, carmakers may lose their own knowledge about the components, without which they cannot achieve better coordination and integration for individual models. In such cases, the modularization in inter-firm systems would then be slowed down or reversed to maintain product integrity and customer satisfaction. The role of car-makers, or 'systems integrators', is very important in examining and deciding how far inter-firm modularization should proceed. Any systems integrator that makes poor judgements would easily lose competitive advantage.

13.5   Discussion: Dynamics of Modularization in the Car Industry

Modularization in the car industry is still in the trial and error stage. The industry began addressing the issue only a few years ago. The contexts and purposes of modularization vary across regions and companies. So it is still quite uncertain and unpredictable how it will evolve and what impacts it will have. Our argument is therefore no more than speculation. Yet, it would be safe to say that ongoing processes concerning modu-larization provide us with some interesting cases to explore the dynamics surrounding architectural changes based on our proposed framework of multiple hierarchies.

What lies at the centre of the dynamics is interactions between production system, inter-firm system, and product architecture. Changes in the hier-archies in production system and/or inter-firm system cause tension in their relationships with product architecture, and thus encourage the redefinition of product architecture.

Baldwin and Clark (2000) pointed out that the issue of modularization involves 'modularity in design', 'modularity in use', and 'modularity in pro-duction' (though their discussion primarily focused on 'modularity in design'). Sako and Murray (1999) argued that each of these has its own optimal architecture, and thus well-balanced relationships among them should be maintained in the process of modularization. This suggests that these three aspects of modularization are correlated with each other and close coordination among them is necessary. Sako and Murray further pointed out that coordination must be secured between product architecture and organizational architecture (intra- and inter-firm organizations) as well. Echoing their argument, this chapter suggests that changes in inter-firm system might lead to changes in product architecture. It is well known that modularization in product architecture sometimes changes the structure of the division of labour in the industry (from a vertical industry structure to a horizontal industry structure) (Fine 1998). This chapter suggests that the relationship between product architecture and inter-firm system is two-way—not only the former influences the latter, but also the latter has some impact on the former.

As argued in Section 13.2 on the analytical framework, the hierarchies in product system, namely hierarchies in product structure and product function, correspond to those in production system and inter-firm system. The hierarchical structure of a complex system is formed as a method to rationalize the division of labour (Simon 1969). Each product, production, and inter-firm system has its own logic for the division of labour. Hierarchies in production system and inter-firm system change in their own contexts (e.g. the improvement of worker satisfaction, the utilization of the wage gap between different companies, the reallocation of risk and investment burden, and so on). And such changes in production and inter-firm systems would demand changes in product architecture. Conditions within design activities are not the only factor for changes in product architecture. European carmakers, for example, are exploring new architectures across inter-firm, production, and product systems in the search for a more profitable business model (although the outcomes are yet to be seen).

Modularization in the car industry seems to proceed with hierarchical changes in each of the product, production, and inter-firm systems in its own context and with its own logic, and at the same time evolving through dynamic interactions among these multiple systems of hierarchies. If this is the case, the key to successful modularization for carmakers probably lies in close cooperation and coordination between their development, production, and purchasing functions, as well as with their suppliers. That is what carmakers are expected to do as a systems integrator.

Given different business environments, different capabilities and strategies, and different paths toward modularization, we might see the coexistence of various patterns of modularization in the world car industry. Also, there could be a scenario for multiple patterns of modularization being used for different product lines and market segments. Or, if any particular pattern could command outstanding competitive leadership, the entire industry might be converged into that pattern of modularization. The future of modularization depends on which pattern allows carmakers to design and produce cars with the greatest benefits for consumers.

The future of technological innovations in the medium- or long-term is also important. The urgent need to protect the environment has accelerated the competition for a new power source (such as hybrid engines and fuel cells) to replace the conventional internal-combustion engines. With rapidly advancing information and communication technologies, the development of an Intelligent Transportation System (ITS) has also been progressing. The growing importance of information technologies in vehicles has made the role of software much more important, and thus may facilitate a kind of modularization through the separation of hardware and software. When these new technologies are put into practical use, the architecture of cars will need to be totally redesigned and such changes will inevitably influence production, and inter-firm systems as well. It is anticipated, under such circumstances, that new architectures (for product, production and inter-firm systems) of the car industry will be established through dynamic interactions between ongoing attempts at modularization and emerging new technological innovations.

While we have thus far focused on the car industry, our framework of multiple hierarchies should be applicable for other industries. Any industry or business involves product, be it physical or service, process, and inter-firm systems. It is the architecture of each hierarchical system and interactions among them that determine the competitive climate and dynamics of the industry. We hope this chapter provides a valuable framework for further research across different industries.

Acknowledgement

We would like to express our sincere appreciation to the interviewees and the participants of the supplier questionnaire survey for their collaboration. We also thank Seunghwan Ku for his assistance and contribution in data analysis. This research was financially supported by a grant from Research for the Future Program of Japan Society for the Promotion of Science (JSPS), a Grant-in-Aid for Scientific Research of JSPS, and the MIT International Motor Vehicle Program.

Notes

1. This chapter is based on the results of a series of interviews with carmakers and component suppliers in Japan and other countries that was carried out between 1999 and 2000 as part of a research project on 'Modularization and Outsourcing' in the International Motor Vehicle Program at MIT. We also conducted a questionnaire survey of Japanese component suppliers.

2. It is said, for example, that assembly plants actively outsourcing larger modules to suppliers could pay back from their investment even on a relatively small scale of production. However, some interviewees at European and American carmakers pointed out that saving of labour and investment costs would not necessarily be very important advantages of modularization. Labour costs do not account for such a large portion of total production costs in car manufacturing. Further, if suppliers' subassembly plants are adjacent to a carmaker's final assembly plant, there is a strong chance for the wage gap between the assembler and suppliers to be narrowed. It is also true that investment costs shared by suppliers would be reflected in the prices of their parts. For suppliers whose scale of business is relatively small, it is more likely that they have to pay higher capital costs than their customers.

3. See, for example, *Automotive News* (22 June 1998). Lear Corporation is among such suppliers. Originally a seat manufacturer, the company acquired Ford's seat production division in 1993. Since then the company has branched out

into new component areas by buying twelve suppliers, and has grown into a leading supplier whose products cover entire car interiors, including seats, instrument panels, door trims, roof trims, rearview mirrors, carpets, and air conditioners.

4. For details of the questionnaire, see Fujimoto, Matsuo, and Takeishi (1999).
5. Factor analysis was performed by Ku and is reported in Ku (2000).
6. Some carmakers have also tried to divide their main lines into some self-contained sub-blocks. For this new assembly system, see Fujimoto (1999).
7. It is also true that Japanese-style production, which often uses mixed-model assembly lines (in which different models are assembled on the same line), prevents carmakers from adopting subassemblies. Suppose it was decided to use subassemblies for the production of a certain model, then assembly work on the main line would be quite uneven between different models, making the operation inefficient. Note, however, that this problem will be solved over time.
8. It should be noted that historically, Japanese carmakers outsourced more in development and production, using 'black-box parts', than European and US carmakers, as discussed before. How did the 'black-box parts procurement system' emerge and evolve in Japan? According to Fujimoto (1999) one factor, among others, was that in the 1960s and 1970s, carmakers outsourced engineering activities more to suppliers due to the shortage of in-house engineers at model proliferation time. It means that the architecture of the inter-firm system in component development was redefined to reduce carmakers' excessive engineering workload. How this change in the inter-firm system affected product architecture and process architecture in consequence is an intriguing question yet to be analysed.
9. Since suppliers have extensive knowledge of individual components, their cooperation is indispensable for the development of any modules, even if subassembly is done in-house by a carmaker. There is a unique approach called '*kyogyo*' in the Japanese car industry in which a number of suppliers work together to develop sets of components in larger units, under the leadership of a carmaker. For examples of design streamlining through '*kyogyo*', see *Nikkei Mechanical*, January 1999.
10. The car industry's resistance to standardization has a long history. In 1910, the Society of Automotive Engineers (SAE) proposed the standardization of parts across the industry. It wanted to make assembly work more efficient by ensuring compatibility between different parts from different carmakers. While relatively small-sized carmakers supported the proposal, it did not become a reality due to resistance from major assemblers such as Ford and GM. They did not want to lose the strong position they had established (economy of scale) and stuck to their own standards (Langlois and Robertson 1992).

References

AUTOMOTIVE NEWS (1998). 22 June.

BALDWIN, C. Y. and CLARK, K. B. (2000). *Design Rules: The Power of Modularity*. Cambridge, MA: MIT Press.

CLARK, K. B. and FUJIMOTO, T. (1991). *Product Development Performance: Strategy, Organization, and Management in the World Auto Industry*. Boston, MA: Harvard Business School Press.

CUSUMANO, M. A. and TAKEISHI, A. (1991). 'Supplier Relations and Management: A Survey of Japanese, Japanese-transplant, and US Auto Plants', *Strategic Management Journal*, 12/8: 563–88.

FINE, C. H. (1998). *Clockspeed: Winning Industry Control in the Age of Temporary Advantage*. Reading, MA: Perseus Books.

FUJIMOTO, T. (1999). *The Evolution of a Manufacturing System at Toyota*. New York: Oxford University Press.

——(2001). 'Akitekucha no Sangyoron' [Industry Analysis by Architecture], in T. Fujimoto, A. Takeishi, and Y. Aoshima (eds.), *Bijinesu Akitekucha: Seihin, Soshiki, Purosesu no Senryakuteki Sekkei* [*Business Architecture: Strategic Design of Products, Organizations, and Processes*]. Tokyo: Yuhikaku (in Japanese), 3–26.

——and GE, D. S. (2001). 'Jidosha Buhin no Akitekuchateki Tokusei to Torihiki Hoshiki no Sentaku [Architectural Characteristics of Auto Components and Choices of Transaction Systems]', in T. Fujimoto, A. Takeishi, and Y. Aoshima (eds.), *Bijinesu Akitekucha: Seihin, Soshiki, Purosesu no Senryakuteki Sekkei* [*Business Architecture: Strategic Design of Products, Organizations, and Processes*]. Tokyo: Yuhikaku (in Japanese), 211–28.

——MATSUO, T., and TAKEISHI, A. (1999). 'Jidosha Buhin Torihiki Patan no Hatten to Henyo: Wagakuni Ichiji Buhin Meka heno Anketo Chosa Kekka wo Chushin ni [Development and Transformation of Car Component Transaction Patterns: Results from a Questionnaire Survey with Japanese First-tier Suppliers]', Discussion Paper CIRJE-J-17, Faculty of Economics, University of Tokyo (in Japanese).

——and TAKEISHI, A. (1994). *Jidosha Sangyo 21-seiki heno Shinario* [*The Automobile Industry: A Scenario Towards the 21st Century*]. Tokyo: Seisansei Shuppan (in Japanese).

——and AOSHIMA, Y. (eds.) (2001). *Bijinesu Akitekucha: Seihin, Soshiki, Purosesu no Senryakuteki Sekkei* [*Business Architecture: Strategic Design of Products, Organizations, and Processes*]. Tokyo: Yuhikaku (in Japanese).

GÖEPFERT, J. and STEINBRECHER, M. (1999). *Modular Product Development: Managing Technical and Organizational Independencies* (mimeo).

KU, S. (2000). 'Nihon Jidosha Sangyo ni Okeru Mojuraka no Doko to Kigyokankei ni Kansuru Kenkyu: Mojuraka ni Taisuru Hihanteki Kento wo Chushinni' [A Study of Modularization and Inter-firm Relationships in the Japanese Automobile Industry: A Critical Examination of Modularization], Unpublished Master's Thesis, Faculty of Economics, University of Tokyo (in Japanese).

LANGLOIS, R. N. and ROBERTSON, P. L. (1992). 'Networks and Innovation in a Modular System: Lessons from the Microcomputer and Stereo Component Industries', *Research Policy*, 21: 297–313.

NISHIGUCHI, T. (1994). *Strategic Industrial Sourcing: The Japanese Advantage*. New York, NY: Oxford University Press.

PENROSE, E. T. (1959). *The Theory of the Growth of the Firm*. Oxford: Basil Blackwell.

SAKO, M. and MURRAY, F. (1999). 'Modules in Design, Production, and Use: Implications for the Global Automobile Industry', paper submitted to MIT IMVP Annual Sponsors Meeting, Cambridge, MA.

SIMON, H. A. (1996 (1969)). *The Science of the Artificial* (3rd edn.). Cambridge, MA: MIT Press.

TAKEISHI, A. (2001). 'Bridging Inter- and Intra-firm Boundaries: Management of Supplier Involvement in Automobile Product Development', *Strategic Management Journal*, 22/5: 403–33.

—— (2002). 'Knowledge Partitioning in the Inter-firm Division of Labor: The Case of Automotive Product Development', *Organization Science*, 13/3: 321–38.

14

Systems Integration in the US Defence Industry
Who Does It and Why Is It Important?

EUGENE GHOLZ

Patterson School of Diplomacy and International Commerce,
University of Kentucky, Lexington, USA

Modern systems integration techniques were developed in the cold war American defence establishment (Sapolsky, Chapter Two, this volume). They were aggressively applied, largely successfully, to develop technology for that conflict. Now, the American military again intends to improve its capabilities radically, presumably augmenting America's national security, by capitalizing on the information revolution. Each of the military services (Army, Navy/Marine Corps, and Air Force) has developed its own particular version of information-enhanced operations, and they are working together (called 'the jointness') to conduct warfighting experiments and to set overarching objectives for the so-called Revolution in Military Affairs. The realization of the vision in part depends on organizational changes in the armed forces to help them fight in new, information-oriented ways, but it also depends on the acquisition of new weapons and communication technologies. The first key step in transformation—defining the way in which scientific advances will be applied in the military context and thereby converting technical progress into innovation—relies on America's unique capabilities in systems integration.

The information revolution in military affairs is, in fact, the apotheosis of the 'systems approach' to warfare, on which the US military embarked in the early days of the cold war. During the Second World War, land forces learned the advantages of combined arms, melding infantry, artillery, and armour into a system for overcoming defensive obstacles; later in the cold war, aviation became truly integrated into that force package, improving combined arms capabilities still further (Herbert 1988). Similar advances were made, also drawing on the Second World War antecedents, in anti-submarine warfare, using aviation, surface, and subsurface platforms and independent sensors like the SOSUS network in a system approach (Sapolsky and Coté 1997). Forces for air defence, over-the-horizon strike targeting, strategic ballistic missiles, and many other categories drew from the cooperative use of many different weapon and support systems

279

(Michel 1997; Hughes 1998; Friedman 2000). In modern militaries, and especially in the American military, heterogeneous types of forces cooperate to achieve levels of combat power greater than the sum of the combat power of the parts. Today, advocates of network-centric warfare (NCW), which has spread beyond its roots in the US Navy to all of the services, believe that improved communications networks and sensor technologies will allow new, more decentralized American forces to work together as a system, increasing their effectiveness at traditional missions and allowing them to prosecute post-cold war missions that would otherwise be too difficult or too dangerous.

The network-centric transformation vision relies heavily on the ability of various platforms to share information in real time using a range of interconnected networks. Achieving the NCW vision will require lashing networks together, maintaining networks in the face of constant change, making intelligent tradeoffs amongst competing system designs, and tasking various platforms with their operational roles. Transformation, thus, places a high premium on systems integration skills and the organizations that possess them.

A basic definition of systems integration emphasizes interoperability—the requirement that each military system works in concert with other systems based on sufficient communication across well-defined interfaces (Johnson 2003, Chapter Three, this volume). The NCW concepts obviously stress such inter-system compatibility, and casual discussions of systems integration in the context of transformation often refer only to interoperability requirements (Svitak 2002). However, ensuring interoperability is only one part of the systems integrators' task.

Systems integrators are responsible for a number of key roles during the overall acquisition process, beginning with translating objectives derived from military doctrine into technical requirements suitable for launching acquisition programmes. The key part of this process is making tradeoffs of capabilities among various systems—given a set of desired capabilities, which component of the system of systems should perform each of them? In the current, early stages of thinking about NCW, systems integration will define the nodes that make up the network, the capabilities that will be essential for each type of node, the number of nodes that must participate in various operations, etc. Later in the acquisition process, systems integrators will maintain control of technical standards and interfaces (ensuring inter-operability), manage the cooperation among contractors and subcontractors, test products and their subcomponents, and support the users' efforts to customize and modernize products as missions and technologies evolve.

This chapter will argue that the military needs to exploit certain organizational innovations that facilitate systems integration as the first step in its broader transformation effort. The first section defines systems integration in the defence sector. The second describes the set of organizations that currently provide systems integration capability to military customers. The third section reviews the key issues in successful systems integration performance—the key measures by which systems integration organizations can be evaluated for their potential contribution to military transformation. Finally, the fourth section discusses organizational changes that might be necessary early on in transformation to nurture sufficient systems integration and to focus systems integrators' efforts on the key tasks to promote the information technology revolution in military affairs. These organizational changes are not the ones on which apostles of transformation usually focus: they normally discuss changing the military's operational chain of command and its promotion patterns. (For good evaluations of these concerns, see Harknett et al. 2000; Stanley-Mitchell 2001). These concerns are very real for the long-term ability of the military to augment its combat power using network-centric systems. However, to even acquire those systems, the military needs to begin by investing in systems integration organizations that will define the network itself.

14.1 Systems Integration in Defence

There are several levels of systems integration in the defence sector, all of which involve decisions among technical alternatives and linking disparate equipment so that heterogeneous parts can operate together (for a summary, see Table 14.1). First, at the 'lowest' level, weapon systems integration ties various components, often supplied by subcontractors, into a single product (e.g. a surface-to-air missile or a fire-control radar).[1] Some key facilities owned by the prime contractor segment of the defence sector specialize in this type of systems integration (e.g. Raytheon in Tucson, Arizona, for missiles or Northrop Grumman in Linthicum, Maryland, for radars). Second, platform integration combines various types of equipment (weapons, propulsion, sensors, communications, etc.) into a mission-capable form like a fighter aircraft. It is not necessarily more or less complex than weapon systems integration, nor is it necessarily a higher or lower value-added activity; different types of systems integration must be analysed on a case-by-case basis. But again, some prime contractors (Lockheed Martin Aeronautics in Fort Worth, Texas, or General Dynamics' Bath Ironworks in Bath, Maine) define this capability as one of their core competencies.

The real emphasis in transformation—and the level of systems integration that is now most ardently pursued by defence-oriented organizations—is 'system of systems integration' or 'architecture systems integration'. It connects different types of platforms to facilitate cooperative military operations, providing the technical counterpart to the military services' operational expertise (knowledge of how to fight). It essentially translates doctrine-writers' statements of objectives into sets of requirements that can be written into the acquisition community's contracts with industry. It involves broad

TABLE 14.1 *Summary of the levels of systems integration in the defence industry*

	Component systems integration	Platform systems integration	Architecture systems integration
Distinguishing skills	Technical capabilities in specific core areas	Project/subcontractor management	System definition
Key implementing tasks	Engineering development, component production	Production, system assembly	Tradeoff studies, customer interface
Example organizations	Subcontractors like Northrop Grumman Electronic Systems and Raytheon Missile Systems	Prime contractors like Lockheed Martin Aeronautics and General Dynamics' Bath Ironworks	Technical advisors like MITRE and SAIC

Note: The skills, tasks, and organizations listed in this table are not exclusive; the entries simply highlight the different emphases of the various levels of systems integration. For example, platform systems integration surely involves many technical capabilities that overlap with those of subcontractors, and component systems integration often involves some assembly tasks and core competencies in project and subcontractor management.

tradeoffs among different technical approaches—for example, hardware versus software solutions, or the decision whether to transmit raw or processed data across the network. Historically, system of systems integration has been accomplished by organizations within the military services (e.g., the laboratories that support systems commands, like the Naval Surface Warfare Center, Dahlgren Division) or closely allied to them (specialty organizations, including Federally Funded Research and Development Centers (FFRDCs) like MITRE). NCW's emphasis on simplified platforms, distributed capabilities, and interconnection of military assets via advanced communications networks will force the acquisition community to rely more than ever on first class system of systems integration.

Military-oriented systems integration skill is based on advanced, interdisciplinary technical knowledge—enough to understand all of the systems and subsystems well enough to make optimizing tradeoffs. It also requires detailed understanding of military goals and operations, and a sufficient reservoir of trust to bridge military, economic, and political interests. Even if some systems integration organizations also have some production capabilities (which may be either an advantage or a liability to the integration process), systems integration is a separate task from platform building and subsystem development and manufacturing. Systems integration is an independent sector of the defence industrial base, but one with porous boundaries that sometimes allow members of other sectors (e.g. platform builders) access to the systems integration task. Different combinations of systems integration capabilities are found in traditional defence industry prime contractors, specialized systems integration houses, FFRDCs and other quasi-public organizations, and the military laboratories. Because all of those types of organization understand the crucial role of systems integration in transformation, most are manoeuvring to establish their credibility as systems integrators: for example, prime contractors justify acquisitions of other firms on the grounds that they contribute to a 'systems integration capability', and military laboratories have rewritten mission statements to emphasize systems integration (Chuter 2002; Tumpak 2002).

Organizations that can provide systems integration services have a key, early role in implementing transformation. Objectives for projects in other sectors of the defence industry—for example, for platform-makers like shipbuilders—will flow down from the overall definition of the network-centric system of systems. Early in transformation, systems integrators need to determine what capabilities are necessary for each type of node in the network, considering technical, operational, and economic implications of how capabilities are distributed. This job is one for which the massive, complex cold war defence effort left the United States well prepared. Organizations that specialize in system of systems integration were established as part of the cold war ballistic missile and air defence programmes, and in cooperation they also played vital roles in developing equipment for maritime strategy, missile defence, and other systems-type missions. Transformation advocates need to recognize and exploit the established systems integration skills at the front end of the process.

14.2 The Landscape of System of Systems Integration Organizations

Many organizations have at least some expertise that might contribute to system of systems integration for the American military. Table 14.2 lists a set of examples drawn especially from organizations that support naval acquisition.

As the customer, the military services must define projects' objectives, but the actual technical system of systems integration task is very difficult for the military itself to accomplish. The acquisition community's core competencies,

TABLE 14.2 *Examples of navy-related system of systems integration organizations*

	Government	Private, non-profit	Private, for-profit
Policy analysis	System commands (SPAWAR, NAVSEA, NAVAIR)	Center for Naval Analysis, Institute for Defense Analysis, Rand	ANSER, TASC, Booz-Allen
Scientific research	Naval research laboratory, SPAWAR Systems Center—San Diego[a]	APL, Lincoln Laboratory, SEI	
Technical support	SPAWAR Systems Center—San Diego[a]	APL, MITRE, Aerospace Corporation	SAIC, SYNTEK
Production			Lockheed Martin— Naval Electronics and Surveillance Systems, Raytheon Command Control Communications and Information Systems
Testing and fleet support	SPAWAR Systems Center—San Diego[a]		

Note: Some organizations have additional small-scale activities that give them limited capability in other boxes in the above matrix—for example, SPAWAR Systems Center—San Diego manufactures Link 16 antennas for surface combatants. The above designations are intended to capture organizations' core competencies rather than ancillary work.
[a] Each of the Navy's acquisition system commands has related technical organizations equivalent to the SPAWAR Systems Center—for example, the Naval Air Warfare Center—China Lake and the Naval Surface Warfare Center—Dahlgren.

resident in the system commands, are in understanding government regulations and monitoring suppliers' compliance with cost, schedule, and other contractual terms; acquisition agents are usually not expert in understanding state-of-the-art technologies and the innovative capabilities of various firms. The military's strong in-house technical support—for example, the Navy's old technical bureaus—was phased out during the second half of the cold war, and technical tasks were increasingly outsourced to private industry (Sapolsky, Gholz, and Kaufman 1999). Systems commands can still draw on expertise from subsidiary laboratories (for example, SPAWAR Systems Center—San Diego for C^4ISR), which maintain important niche capabilities, research expertise, and key physical assets required to develop and test new designs end to end (e.g., model basins). Unfortunately, the relationship between science-oriented military laboratories and regulation-oriented system commands is normally tense. Scientists often feel that the continuity of their research and their technical skills are undermined by frequent 'cherry-picking' of researchers out of the laboratory and into the system command itself. For their part, systems command personnel tend to believe that scientists should support their immediate need for technical advice and technologies rather than pursue research projects that may or may not pay off in the future.

This difficult interface between 'pure' science and system acquisition is a challenge for all forms of technical advisory organization—not just for the military's in-house laboratories—but the difficulty is magnified within the military chain of command. Internal technical capabilities are on the one hand constrained by civil service rules, which prevent the military from competing to employ many of the top scientists and engineers. On the other hand, those very same rules also protect internal technical staff from competitive and budgetary threats. For example, the operational Navy often perceives the Navy laboratories and technical advisors as less cooperative than the highly responsive private defence industry, whose scientists and engineers can be induced to work hard for the military through appropriate contractual compensation. As a result, the operational Navy often fails to support the Navy laboratories aggressively.[2] This tension may be exacerbated by 'industrial funding', which forces laboratories to seek 'business' from within other parts of the Navy, other government agencies, and even private industry by drumming up external contracts and participating in various project 'teams', usually with specific, short-term deliverable products.

Warfighters do support the laboratory system, but only in a particular way that undermines the labs' ability to conduct analyses of alternatives and to make high-level tradeoffs among technical approaches. The Navy's system centres are very good at fleet support. But those close ties to quick-reaction demands of the fleet undermine the standardization and interface stewardship role of the systems integrator, and the skills that enable fast, in-the-field fixes—especially fixes of particular systems or subsystems—are not the same as the skills that enable thoughtful optimization of the system of systems.

The emphasis in the laboratories is on testing system performance, confirming that prototypes meet specifications and determining which of several submissions best meets military acquisition criteria. This emphasis permeates these organizations so strongly that in interviews several scientists from military laboratories even defined systems integration in terms of testing performance and interoperability. While they understand the importance of technical advice during the analysis of alternatives before projects' performance evaluation criteria are defined, laboratory personnel emphasize the value of feedback from testing physical systems in improving the ability to define later projects. On the other hand, organizations other than in-house labs do extensive testing and prototype evaluation as part of system development, even though they do not do the final stage of customer acceptance tests. If in-house scientists are right that testing can help maintain technical skills and reveal important lines of evolutionary research, it might be desirable to sell the major testing facilities—the remnants of the unique intellectual and physical capital inside the military—to the organizations that can act as full system of systems integrators. The goal would be to leave the systems commands with enough technical competence to act as 'smart buyers', who could react to technical advice and choose among systems integration proposals developed by outside organizations with the full range of facilities and skills at the system of systems level.

With the services' increasing emphasis on high-level systems integration in their visions of the future, traditional prime contractors that specialize in platform design and production have begun to try to supply architecture systems integration. Firms with core competencies in electronics and network-oriented activities are also angling for platform systems integration work, arguing that inter-platform integration (interoperability) is becoming ever more important in the design of the platforms themselves. Prime contractors have focused for years on understanding the unique demands of the military customer, including hiring retired military officers for important positions in the businesses' strategic planning departments. The private firms are also largely exempt from civil service rules, allowing them the flexibility to hire top technical talent when necessary,[3] and for those scientists who crave equity compensation, private firms can also offer stock options.[4] If, on the other hand, technical team members develop a particular rapport with each other that generates extra value from synergies or experience, private firms have an incentive to support that built-up human capital. Managing technical personnel is a core competency of technology-dependent private firms, including defence industry prime contractors.[5]

However, platform systems integration and system of systems integration are not the same task, and it is not even clear that developing skill at one helps very much in developing skill at the other. Platform integrators may improve their performance through any of a number of different activities: repeated design or prototype development experience; production experience; and maintenance of close relationships with applied technical laboratories, basic science research establishments, academic institutions, and/or the operational user community.[6] Their unique advantage is in linking systems engineering capability with intricate knowledge of the manufacturing process, allowing them to take advantage of production efficiency advantages in the design process. Naturally, prime contractors emphasize the importance of production capability in their discussions of systems integration—just as military laboratories emphasize the importance of full-scale system testing. However, while this advantage surely carries some weight, it is likely to be relatively small in the defence sector, where production runs are often short and very close tolerance production processes are often craft-like, minimizing the potential for major savings. Such production issues should consequently receive a relatively low weighting in the system of systems integration trade space, although system of systems specialists should still strive to consider platform-makers' concerns when they do their overall analyses and requirements definitions. System of systems concerns about platforms' interfaces with the network should take precedence in transformation planning and acquisition.

Moreover, the potential for conflicts of interest—or at least for the appearance of conflicts of interest, the more stringent standard that has been deemed appropriate for government organizations—mandates a separation between architecture systems integration and production in the defence industry. Production prime contractors have the technical capability to scan subcontractors' products, including the offerings of innovative commercial firms, for likely partners in the network-centric defence industry—that is, they can fulfil one of the key technical and management requirements of a systems integrator. They can also make technical decisions about interfaces, network standards, and other requirements definitions; by vertically integrating to combine platform- and components-oriented design and production organizations, large prime contractors might provide technical systems integration services with minimal transaction costs. But expanding the roles of established prime contractors faces a crucial non-technical barrier: lack of trust. Manufacturers certainly test their products before delivery to the customer, but the customer also needs an independent ability to verify product performance—just as military laboratories emphasize. Moreover, the customer might reasonably fear that a manufacturer's tradeoff analysis might be biased in favour of the sort of alternatives that the manufacturer is expert at making—even unintentionally biased, perhaps, by the production contractors' better technical understanding of particular systems and solutions.

This bias problem was first manifest in the defence industry in a 1959 Congressional investigation of the relationship between Thompson–Ramo–Wooldridge (TRW)'s satellite and missile production businesses and the

TRW-owned Space Technology Laboratory (STL), which played a technical direction role on Air Force development and production projects—including some for which TRW submitted proposals. Neither protectors of the government trust nor members of the defence sector that competed with TRW on those space systems contracts would accept the situation, even though no specific malfeasance was uncovered or even alleged. STL was essentially split off from TRW to become Aerospace Corporation, an independent, non-profit, non-production, systems integration specialist, later called an FFRDC (Baldwin 1967: 45–6, 138–9; Dyer 1998: 225–39).[7]

That organizational innovation, which spread with the establishment of other FFRDCs and the similarly organized University Applied Research Centers (UARCs), allowed the military's acquisition organizations to outsource the technical advisory role during the cold war in a way that was protected from conflict of interest scandals (Smith 1966: 18).[8] Some FFRDCs like MIT Lincoln Laboratory specialize in particular kinds of military-oriented research (advanced electronics, in that case), comparable in some ways to the in-house military laboratories but more closely tied to frontier academic research. While the core tasks of various FFRDCs overlap to some extent, Aerospace Corporation (space systems), MITRE (air defence), and APL (naval systems) are the ones that specialize in architecture systems integration.[9]

The historical strength of FFRDCs has been their reputation for high-quality, objective advice. Through flexibility in salary negotiations and quasi-academic status, FFRDCs have been able to attract high-quality personnel. Their promise not to compete for production contracts and to provide equal access to all contractors while safeguarding proprietary information has given them unique, independent technical capabilities (US General Accounting Office 1986: 4). However, they have frequently been criticized as inefficient and relatively expensive: while leaders of FFRDCs frequently claim that their non-profit status allows them to charge less than a hypothetical technically equivalent for-profit technical advisor, many others (notably leaders of for-profit firms like SAIC) allege that the lack of a profit motive in FFRDC work leads to inefficient performance and the potential for feather-bedding (Office of Technology Assessment (OTA) 1995: 28–33; US General Accounting Office 1996: 5–6).[10] Congressional legislation currently limits the budget available to FFRDCs and prevents the military from establishing any new FFRDCs.[11]

For-profit, non-production firms might be able to offer the benefits of FFRDCs while avoiding the controversies linked to non-profit status. Small engineering companies like SYNTEK can offer technical advice to the military with a credible promise not to engage in production, but it is difficult to imagine such a firm nurturing a major laboratory with an independent research capability and agenda, at least under current procurement rules. Without direct access to such scientific assets, it is reasonable to question the ability of a consultancy to maintain top-level system of systems integration skills.[12] Larger for-profit firms like SAIC, which owns Bellcore, the former research arm of the Regional Bell Operating Companies (a partial descendant of Bell Laboratories), offer to fill this niche, but to cover the overhead cost of such laboratories they resist promising to abstain from all production work. Although for-profit firms in the defence industry have learned to form teams to develop major systems and sometimes even join a team on one contract with a firm against which they are competing on another contract, real questions persist about how much proprietary data the for-profit contractors are willing to share with one another. Although a promise not to engage in production would allay some of the fears that prevent platform firms from becoming architecture systems integrators, major for-profit advisory firms are still limited by customers' and competitors' scepticism about their true, long-term independence.

14.3   Systems Integration Performance Metrics

So far, the metrics available to compare systems integration capabilities are limited, so project managers may have difficulty selecting sources for technical advice and deciding how much investment in up-front systems integration work is enough. Carnegie Mellon University's Software Engineering Institute (SEI), a research FFRDC, has developed a rating system for several computer-related skills, including software engineering and systems engineering. The ratings assigned according to the SEI 'Capabilities Maturity Models' are based on a business commitment to follow certain procedures designed to manage complex projects: specifically, they emphasize maintaining control of documentation and interfaces to ensure system-wide performance as components and subsystems are improved in parallel. These software-oriented procedures are at least related to the broader systems integration task, and they may provide a useful model for further work defining metrics for overall systems integration capabilities.[13]

For a broad discussion of the relationship between systems integration and transformation, however, such detailed metrics for evaluating systems integrators are not necessary. The key questions are which of the established systems integration organizations can provide the support required to implement transformation and how can the military services best stimulate that system of systems integration.

Technical Awareness

The bedrock of systems integration is familiarity with the technical state-of-the-art in the wide range of disciplines that contribute to the components of the system. Systems integrators must be able to set reasonable, achievable goals for the developers and manufacturers of the components even as they 'black box' the detailed design work for those components. Sometimes one component maker may have a problem that it can solve only at great expense but could be solved much more easily by shifting the requirements of a different component or by altering the interface standard in a way that would cost other component manufacturers less. It is the responsibility of the systems integrator to understand and implement the necessary tradeoff in the various component specifications in that case. The more access the systems integrator has to technical knowledge of subsystems, the better it will be able to perform that role. There are many ways that a systems integrator can obtain this technical knowledge, including systematically and continuously training and educating critical engineers, hiring personnel from subsystem contractors, and seconding employees to other organizations to work in all phases of component design and production.

Transformation is unlikely to change the role of technical awareness as a systems integration performance metric. To the extent that NCW draws on unfamiliar component systems, it may strain the technical awareness of established systems integration organizations. For example, emerging unmanned vehicle technologies may take over a number of tasks previously assigned to manned systems, requiring systems integrators to be familiar with the state-of-the-art in unmanned vehicles to make tradeoffs between manned and unmanned systems. However, the systems integrator need not have the capability to actually design and build either the manned or the unmanned systems: the specific technical knowledge is not the core competency for the systems integrator; instead, the ability to gain access to that knowledge by working with subsystem contractors, academic experts, and/or in-house researchers is the sine qua non of systems integration.

Developing new sources and kinds of technical awareness may be the core competency of a systems integrator, but it is only natural that the less familiar the component technologies of a particular project are to a systems integrator, the less suited that integrator is to work on it. Even the organizations with the broadest architecture systems integration capability have specialties—Aerospace Corporation in space systems, for example, or MITRE in command and control.

It is by no means obvious, however, that NCW demands new specialties. Instead, it seems to involve the advanced application of a combination of established ones—reliance on space systems for surveillance and communications relays, on intensive exploitation of command and control networks and battle management computation, etc. If a new focus on the network characterizes the systems integration task for NCW, surely MITRE, APL, and for-profit firms like Logicon and SAIC have the necessary technical awareness. Perhaps even the SEI's foray into integration offers a basis for a transition from a pure research FFRDC into a research and systems integration combination that specializes in network technology (akin to APL).[14] Although the commercial internet has burgeoned well beyond its defence origin, the ARPANET, the original DARPA programme has been cited as a classic example of the military's 'systems approach' to advanced technology (Hughes 1998).

The organizational framework through which established organizations' specialties should be applied to the new problems of NCW, however, remains an open question. Various systems integrators might offer competing technical proposals, each offering its best system solution to NCW challenges and pointing out flaws in alternative proposals. American pluralist government is built on the principle that the clash of ideas yields the best policy solutions, and that clash of ideas might help to compensate for each existing organization's implicit biases in favour of its technical specialties. APL (Applied Physics Lab) might point out any pitfalls of Aerospace Corporation's space-based solutions, while Aerospace could reciprocate by illuminating the risks of APL's hypothetical bandwidth-consuming approach. Still, it remains the responsibility of the customer/buyer to evaluate competing claims in order to make decisions in the corporate interest of the Navy or, better yet, the US military as a whole.

Alternatively, a team combining the relevant technical groups from the established systems integrators might be able to offer a comprehensive technical base for network-centric systems integration. Ten FFRDCs and national laboratories combined to provide technical support to the Ballistic Missile Defense Organization (BMDO) through a teaming arrangement called the POET.[15] A full evaluation of the technical performance of the POET is beyond the scope of this chapter, but some preliminary observations are relevant. On the one hand, the POET clearly provided access to an exceptional breadth of technical talent.[16] On the other hand, the participant organizations retained their traditional customers, missions, and cultures, such that they may not have invested their best resources or their full attention in the missile defence effort.[17] A systems integration team to support the information technology revolution in military affairs would gain similar advantages and would face similar limitations.

To apply the full resources of the established systems integrators to the new challenges of NCW, it might be best to create a new systems integrator with a new bureaucratic identity. But it would not be necessary to create such an organization from scratch—and it would be very costly to replicate the investment in human capital that has already been made by established organizations. When MITRE was created as the systems integrator for the SAGE air defence system, its core was formed from Division 6 of Lincoln Laboratory, which chose at that point to focus on research rather than systems integration. MITRE then proceeded to expand its technical awareness into new areas, integrating air defence missiles like the BOMARC into an air defence system initially designed to cue fighter interceptors (Baum 1981: 38–9; Jacobs 1986: 131; Hughes 1998: 62). Today, it might be possible to blend various technical groups spun off by the established organizations, again forming a new FFRDC. The new institution would maintain the well-understood core competency in nurturing technical awareness but would do so in the service of a new customer and organizational mission.[18]

Each of these three candidate organizational forms to supply systems integration to transformation—competition among existing technical advisors, teaming among existing technical advisors, and establishing a new technical advisor—relies on the built-up skills of established institutions: they are evolutionary changes required to proceed with sustaining innovation along the technical awareness performance metric. The financial ownership structure of the technical advisor is less important than its underlying skill base, which can be derived from existing systems integration groups.

Project Management Skill

Efficiency has rarely if ever been the only goal of military acquisition programmes. In addition to serving economic goals, the projects need to meet military requirements and to satisfy political constraints (McNaugher 1989a: 3–12). Nevertheless, efforts to control costs have been a continuous feature of defence policy, because warfighters always have more systems that they would like to acquire, technologists can always use additional resources to push the performance envelope further, and politicians always have non-defence priorities including pressure to lower taxes. All three groups also try to plan their expenditures as part of the budgeting process, and so they need estimates of projects' cost and schedule that are as accurate as possible.

For complex acquisitions with numerous, heterogeneous components—a system of systems—reliable estimates are difficult to come by, due to the vast amounts of information that must be managed to describe the current and projected state of progress. Participants also have incentives to hide some information from oversight efforts. Sometimes they believe setbacks to be temporary (that they will get back on schedule, the promised performance trajectory, or the estimated cost projection before they have to report problems), and sometimes they fear the full disclosure will aid competitors or will lead to pressure to renegotiate fees and expropriate profits. Managers learn to report data in favourable ways, almost always without real malfeasance, that can give a biased picture of progress that protects ongoing projects from oversight (Sapolsky 1982).[19] They also enthusiastically adopt acquisition reform efforts and management fads that promise to reduce costs in the future. Those fads help politicians to vote for projects now, whether or not the efficiency benefits of the reform ever actually materialize (Williams 2001).

System of systems integrators have the expertise to manage projects as well as possible in the face of these constraints. The better a given systems integrator performs in that project management task—setting accurate schedules, projecting attainable technical goals, and minimizing transaction costs among the many organizations that have to contribute to a systems contract—the greater the incentive the buyer has to hire that systems integrator. Project management skill is a key performance metric for systems integration organizations.

Transformation calls for sustaining innovation in project management. Ultimately, for NCW to be useful to the warfighter, a number of different programmes (ships, aircraft, unmanned vehicles, munitions, sensors, etc.) need to deliver compatible systems to the military in the correct order; the schedules need to be timed so that the various deployment dates form the network. Cold war programmes like the Polaris fleet ballistic missile programme, which required tremendous innovation in missiles and guidance, in communications and navigation, and in submarine platforms, faced the same sort of management and scheduling problems. System of systems integration was effectively invented precisely for the purpose of managing such massive, heterogeneous acquisitions (Sapolsky 1972). NCW may require integration of an even broader array of components, making the system of systems integration task even more difficult. But systems integrators are already applying modern information technology to manage complex subcontractor networks, to scan for technological leads that might contribute innovative solutions to military problems, and to interact with potential new suppliers, innovating to support this core task.

At the platform integration level, the project management task under transformation will be little changed from its previous incarnations. Whether any given platform integrator is well positioned to participate in transformation will depend on the demand for its technical skills—whether NCW calls for sustaining or disruptive innovation in that sector of the defence industry. The platform integration task will continue to include management of subcontractor relationships and the detailed design of military systems. In sectors dominated by sustaining innovations, platform integrators' databases of successful subcontractors and procedures for working with the social and political constraints of the government contracting environment will contribute to successful acquisition programmes. Despite acquisition reform advocates' appropriation of phrasing from transformation advocates—the 'revolution in acquisition affairs' or 'revolution in business affairs'—the quest for acquisition reform is separate from military transformation.

At the architecture systems integration level, transformation's biggest challenge in project management will stem from the need to integrate plans and schedules of several powerful customer organizations. The mechanism by which a technical direction agent for NCW can assert control of the technical aspects of project management may change (changes in the customer relationship will be discussed below, in the section on Customer Understanding). But the core project management task will not change much: system of systems integrators will have to integrate some new technical tasks into military systems development, but the disruptive innovations, if any, will fall at the platform or component level rather than in the techniques for organization and management of the system of systems project.

Transformation requires high-level systems integration to evolve along a familiar performance trajectory, contributing as much efficiency and scheduling accuracy to major systems acquisition as possible. The core of the cold war system of systems integration sector—meaning FFRDCs and for-profit systems integration specialists, at least with respect to transaction costs in architecture integration—can provide the necessary technical support to transformation efforts.

Perceived Independence

The key role of a system of systems integrator in defining the technical requirements of various system components (and hence of the system as a whole) requires that it be able to make tradeoffs in the interest of system performance rather than in the interest of the organizations that design or make the system. The architecture systems integration task is tremendously complicated, because military systems have multiple goals—peak warfighting performance, sustained political support for the acquisition programme and for the national security strategy, and minimal expenditure of resources for acquisition, maintenance, training, and operations.[20] That complexity, along with the requisite technical expertise, essentially guarantees that detailed decisions in system of systems integration will not be completely transparent to military customers, congressional appropriators, or defence industry prime and subcontractors that supply components of the system. All of those groups must trust that the systems integrator has considered and protected their interests in making its architecture definition decisions, and any organizations that feel that their trust has been violated have an opportunity to create a scandal by complaining publicly. They are constrained by the understanding that complaining too often or too loudly can subvert the entire process of providing for the national defence. They cooperated in the cold war evolution of system of systems integrators that minimize the problem of bias in system definition, and that lack of bias as a result is a key performance metric for system of systems integrators.

The difficulty in maintaining independence for architecture systems integration is compounded by the pecuniary incentives in defence acquisition. Like all organizations, systems integrators have an incentive to favour solutions that maximize their own organizational rewards, maintaining and exploiting their position as a key node connecting customers and producers in the organizational network of the military–industrial complex.[21] This bias may be purely tacit, as scientists propose certain types of technical solutions based on their particular expertise, thereby reinforcing the value of that particular expertise. Moreover, profits in the defence industry have disproportionately accrued to production rather than research or technical advisory organizations, in large part because profits are regulated, formally and informally, to remain at a certain percentage of projects' revenue, and the bulk of the acquisition spending is concentrated during the procurement rather than the systems development phases of acquisition (McNaugher 1989*b*; Rogerson 1998). In the post-cold war threat environment where the United States faces no peer competitor, those firms with a critical mass of workers, generally production rather than technical organizations, have been able to add considerable political weight to their pleas for financial support from Congressional appropriators (Gholz and Sapolsky 1999). Consequently, the financial prospects for pure system of systems integrators are weak, and they face pressure to vertically integrate systems integration with production capability. Freedom to choose optimal technical solutions is constantly threatened at the margin by pressure from the bureaucratic interests of the services and the political power of platform producers. Because this pressure is well known, trust from the customers that the systems integrators will steward the military's interests and not simply the venal interests of the systems integrators themselves is also threatened.

Even organizations designed to preserve decision-making independence, like most of the established systems integration houses, had some bias built in to their very make-up. They served a particular customer, and the needs of that customer were well known. Perceived independence therefore meant within their own issue domain, where they might rightfully be expected to play honest broker. In turf battles with external forces, however, they might favour particular types of solutions. Thus, the Aerospace Corp. might be unbiased in telling the Air Force about how to organize and equip its own space capabilities, but it would be less so when arguing for space-based solutions rather than non-space-based solutions proposed by other government entities. Outside its immediate area of expertise, solutions proposed by Aerospace must be weighed carefully against alternatives proposed by rival organizations working for rival customers.

By and large, the FFRDC/UARC system of non-production technical advisors functioned successfully during the cold war (OTA 1995). The FFRDCs and UARCs promise as part of their contractual relationship with the government not to engage in production. Some tensions inevitably remain between the producer firms and the FFRDCs, who insist that they need to engage in some prototype building that is quite similar to production in order to maintain their systems integration skills. These tensions may be particularly likely to escalate in the software industry, where the development and production phases of a code-writing project frequently overlap.

For example, APL has been criticized strongly for mixing production with systems integration, specifically in the current dispute over the best technology for the Navy's Cooperative Engagement Capability (CEC). Solipsys, a software firm founded recently by disenchanted former employees of APL, has created a rival system, the Tactical Communications Network (TCN). Solipsys claims that it has not had a fair hearing within the Navy, at least in part because APL is both the technical advisor to the Navy and the developer of CEC. Regardless of the technical merits of CEC versus TCN, and here opinions vary widely,[22] the controversy would be less bitter if APL were not exposed to charges that it favours one solution over the other because it developed that alternative and would participate in its production. The Navy, which will have to decide between the two approaches for its Block 2 acquisition of CEC in 2004, has a real problem evaluating the technical claims of the competing organizations, because its usual technical advisor for this sort of systems integration competition, APL, has a stake in the outcome of the competition (Rotnam 2002).[23] Even if the Navy finds a way to make the technically correct decision, conflict of interest claims will arise—as they already have—and the likely outcome will be to cause extra oversight of the CEC programme, increasing costs and undermining political support for that key early procurement step in developing the Navy's 'Common Operational Picture' that is required for NCW.

Scandals, alleging 'waste, fraud, and abuse' and cost and schedule failures have derailed military investment in the past, and conflicts of interest might be a threat to the move towards NCW. The peaks in the major cycles of the US cold war defence budget were associated with procurement scandals, which at least superficially played a role in reversing the defence budget trend. Even if structural factors like the changing threat environment or the completion of a generational change in the service's key equipment were bringing the procurement cycle to an end, calls to rein in abuse in defence acquisition generally contributed as the proximate cause that determined the timing of the downturn in the defence budget (McNaugher 1989; McKinney et al. 1994). The Future Years Defence Budget now calls for a major increase in procurement spending for the next several years—the defence budget's new cycle. To the extent that the military leadership hopes to use that spending to acquire the systems to implement transformation, the cycle must not end prematurely due to scandal.

Customer Understanding

The military with all its communities (primarily the three services and their major subcomponents like the Navy's aviators, submariners, and surface warfare officers) is a complicated organization with a long institutional history, unique traditions, and organizational biases developed from generations of operational experience. More formally, there is a large body of strategy, tactics, doctrine, and training processes that distinguish the Navy from the other Services and from other government and private sector organizations. The other Services and supporting intelligence organizations have similarly developed their own organizational identities and perspectives on warfighting and national security strategy (Builder 1989). The success of each system of systems integrator depends on its deep understanding of the military environment, because the integration organization's architecture definitions and project management decisions must serve its customer's true goals, which can be difficult to articulate in a simple, programme-specific, written 'statement of objectives'. Navy-oriented systems integrators (e.g., APL, SYNTEK, and Lockheed Martin Naval Electronics and Surveillance Systems) have built up a great deal of tacit knowledge about how and why the Navy operates, without which they would not be trusted to perform the system of systems integration service. While customer understanding is important for any organization, it is a uniquely vital performance metric for architecture systems integration organizations.

Customer understanding is a moving target. On this metric, long experience alone is insufficient. A systems integrator must commit to investing continuously in its military-operational knowledge base. It must monitor lessons learned from recent exercises and operational deployments and changes in military doctrine and national grand strategy in order to keep up with the 'right' kind of technical awareness. Ideally, members of the systems integration organization should participate in war games and exercises where the military services test new operational concepts and introduce virtual prototypes of future platforms and subsystems. Teaming in various forms can only help personnel and organizations develop a greater appreciation for mutual idiosyncrasies. A large part of customer understanding is the maintenance over time of interorganizational relationships that transcend individuals and projects.

Unfortunately, 'customer understanding' might reinforce institutional inertia and reify the status quo; in many ways, this is an analogue to bureaucratic 'capture' where the regulator sees things from the perspective of industry rather than the public interest. Yet, these dangers are best avoided not by creating firewalls or by artificially introducing change from the outside. Rather, both the customer and the systems integrator must self-consciously distinguish between customer understanding for the sake of overall success and close relationships for the sake of blocking change or protecting institutional interests. In short, the systems integrator must be free (and protected) to resolve tradeoff in ways that may harm short-term customer interests but guard the long-term health of the organization as a whole.

The need to make tradeoffs and provide analyses of alternatives that threaten the existing programmes and short-term plans of system of systems integrators' customers puts the organizations in a delicate position. Individual services are wary of criticism and fear losing ground in budgetary competition with other services, just as individual platform makers may resent the oversight that an independent systems integrator provides on particular projects even while understanding that the systems integration role is essential for maintaining the overall success of national defence investment. System of systems integrators' customers must trust that the systems integrator has the customers' true interests at heart.[24]

At the architecture systems integration level, transformation's biggest challenge is its requirement that the system of systems cross many organizational boundaries. This requirement is especially severe in the more expansive visions of transformation that emphasize cooperation of forces from all of the military services rather than networking forces within each service. The different communities within the services have strong, independent identities, ideas about how wars should be fought, and priorities for setting schedules and allocating funding. Each service will try to influence the course of transformation—and to influence the definition of the system of systems—by pushing preferred definitions of the systems integration trade space and by defending and funding particular programmes that the overall systems integrator will then be forced to integrate into the network-centric force structure. Architecture systems integrators will have to understand and balance the conflicting motivations of the several customer organizations.

Most organizations have great difficulty incorporating multiple goals into their organizational identity (Wilson 1989). This problem suggests that a shift to a truly joint systems approach, incorporating all of the nation's military assets, as part of transformation may require establishment of a single, joint acquisition agency to which a single system of systems integrator could be attached. On the other hand, added organizational layers between system of systems integrators and their service customers, who will actually operate military systems, might degrade the level of customer understanding, reducing the integrator's effectiveness in the analysis of alternatives role. Adopting a single buyer for transformational systems might also threaten the diversity of approaches that inter-service rivalry could otherwise provide, stifling innovation and/or increasing the vulnerability of the 'strategic monoculture' to technical failures and adversaries' research (Coté 1995).

Service visions of transformation will require system of systems integration organizations' in-depth customer understanding. Their technical advice must build on established communications channels to all parts of the military, specifically including the several communities of warfighters and the systems commands that specialize in managing the acquisition process. System of systems organizations that find their institutional home serving a particular subset of the military—for example, supporting only space systems in an environment where space and terrestrial systems now need to be analysed as alternatives within the network—may have difficulty developing a contact network and perfecting customer understanding at the 'higher' level system of systems integration environment. However, much as established architecture systems integrators have the skills to expand technical awareness into new areas, those organizations also have the skills to focus on developing customer awareness as a key means of staying in business. Transformation does not change the organizational goal of customer understanding, but organizational boundaries will be at least as difficult—and likely will be more difficult—to overcome than interdisciplinary boundaries in technical awareness.

14.4 Organizing for Systems Integration's Contribution to Transformation

Transformation relies explicitly on intense interoperability, one of the key components of system of systems integration, so transformation and systems integration have become tied together in a very public way. At this early stage of transformation, however, another component of system of systems integration is even more important: tradeoff studies are needed to establish the objectives and requirements for the component systems that will be acquired as nodes and network elements.

Certain established systems integration houses like APL and the MITRE Corporation clearly have expertise that is closely related to the plans for NCW, and those established organizations should play a major part in defining the future IT-based military. Similarly, some of the production-oriented prime contractors have high-level systems integration groups that on technical awareness and project management grounds might join the nucleus of competitive suppliers of architecture systems integration. However, in the face of commitments to the perceived independence and customer understanding performance metrics, the prime contractors' skills are more likely to be optimally applied in the service of platform rather than architecture systems integration. For example, Lockheed Martin has a large systems integration group in Valley Forge, Pennsylvania, with specific expertise in satellites and intelligence collection. Lockheed Martin, of course, would need to keep some proprietary systems integration capability, even if it were clear that the military did not plan to delegate high-level systems integration/technical decision-making to the production prime contractors. Each member of the defence industrial base would then have to make a business decision about what level of in-house funding to allot to systems integration, given that the main institutional home of that core competency would not be with production firms.

There is no reason to invite platform-making prime contractors into the system of systems integration business as part of transformation. The primes want in, because they perceive that systems integration is 'where the money is', at least in the short term, and they perceive it as the level of greatest responsibility in the future defence industry. Moreover, with political pressures building in support of transformation, and with projects that are not perceived as transformational vulnerable to cancellation (like the Army's Crusader self-propelled howitzer), prime contractors are looking for ways to link their activities to transformation. The logic for the primes is the same as it always has been: if a particular kind of acquisition reform is popular, your programmes should be 'demonstrators' of the new technique; if systems analysis and PERT charts are the way to show budget and schedule control, then your programmes should use them; if the military is pursuing an IT-based revolution in military affairs, then your programmes should emphasize their connectivity to the military's burgeoning information network.

Acting as a systems integration agent might be the best protection of all for a prime contractor's business base. Production firms in the defence sector should be expected to complain about outside systems integration houses' role on particular projects, because the advisor's job includes raising awkward criticism of the prime contractors' technical approach and production skills. One way to avoid such criticism would be to make systems integration part of the prime's job. However, given the importance of independence for quality systems integration, and given that up-front technical advice and coordination will help to keep transformation programmes on schedule and budget, production contractors should find it in their interest to support systems integration organizations (especially if paid for mostly from the military infrastructure budget rather than from specific projects' budgets).

On the other hand, it remains very difficult for military services to choose technical advisors for system of systems integration, because systems integration performance metrics are difficult to operationalize and tie to the traditional framework for defence contracting. No top-down metric that is developed for systems integration skill will be able to substitute for organizational competition. The various systems integration organizations can offer a diversity of technical approaches and system of systems proposals, and they can offer technical commentary on and critiques of each other's proposals, giving the military customer enough advice to make informed choices early in the transformation process.

Competition for the system of systems integration role can also help alleviate any resource limitations imposed by pressures to spend the entire defence budget on current operations rather than on technical advice and longer term investment. The consolidation of the defence industrial sector through mergers and the reduced post-cold war demand for long production runs has limited competition for production contracts; the overhead cost of maintaining multiple production lines for each weapon system is also unacceptably high in the current defence budget environment. However, competition among technical advisory organizations—each with a different design philosophy or technical focus—is relatively inexpensive to sustain, and those dedicated systems integrators should be able to help monitor technical efficiency during the production phase of the acquisition process. Meanwhile, in competing for their shares of the technical advisory role during the upcoming military transformation, these organizations will monitor each other's performance, point out technical flaws in competitors' proposals, and help to solve the policy problems of deciding how and how much to invest in systems integration. Exploiting competition among dedicated systems integration organizations should be a relatively low-cost response to the tension between budgetary pressure and the high resource demand of investing in military transformation.

In the end, however, the buck must stop somewhere. Competition among systems integration organizations may keep everyone honest and allow ideas to be triaged, but with regard to individual decisions, the military itself must sort through competing claims and make decisions.

Major acquisition projects or groups of related projects often spawned new procurement and advisory organizations during the cold war. A new acquisition organization–systems integrator partnership might facilitate the transformation effort. Advocates of NCW frequently note that the current acquisition system is organized on a platform by platform basis, which naturally de-emphasizes crucial network investment. The potential problem is very much akin to the barriers to investment in missile defence through traditional acquisition channels that led in the 1980s to the creation of the Strategic Defense Initiative Office, predecessor of the BMDO. The Secretary of Defence or the service secretaries should consider giving NCW a similar home in a new acquisition organization that will develop a bureaucratic interest in acting as the budgetary advocate for transformation. Because the network is intended at least to link systems from many warfighting communities (e.g., surface ships, aircraft, and space systems), this new organization should report directly to the highest relevant echelon of acquisition decision-making.

The new organization could also take responsibility for supporting a new technical advisory organization that will develop expertise specifically in the network and node requirements for future military. This organization will, in all likelihood, borrow personnel and even intellectual capital (e.g., lessons learned databases) from existing systems integrators as well as develop new competencies necessary to handle the complexities of the network-centric environment. Any such new systems integrator would need a high-level sponsor, a reasonable budget, insulation from the inevitable bureaucratic infighting, and, most of all, time to develop the trusted relationships and track record of success that characterize all systems integration houses. The political pressure behind transformation may not be able to wait for those conditions. In the case of the Reagan-era surge in funding for missile defences, a new acquisition organization was organized, because the bureaucratic identities of the services' systems commands diverted their efforts from missile defences into traditional systems; however, technical support for the missile defence systems' diverse components fundamentally relied on the same systems integration skills that were available from established organizations. As a result, the POET team, comprised of the established systems integration houses, successfully provided technical support.

In the current policy environment, the balance is tipping away from dedicated systems integration houses like FFRDCs and the technically skilled professional service corporations and towards prime contractors that build platforms. If the military services succeed in reversing that trend and creating a team of non-production system of systems integrators, perhaps that should be considered enough of a victory. It would provide at least minimal protection from scandal that might derail the trajectory of the information technology revolution in military affairs. Despite the questions that some have raised about whether the POET has optimized technical support for missile defence, a POET-like team for NCW might well make important strides towards improving the technical future of the American way of war. Regardless of the particular institutional form that transformation advocates ultimately adopt, access to first-class systems integration capability will continue to be a hallmark of the American military's acquisition establishment.

Acknowledgement

Some of the research for this chapter was supported by the 'Military Transformation and the Defense Industry after Next' project at the Naval War College. The author would like to thank Peter Dombrowski and Harvey Sapolsky for helpful discussions on systems integration.

Notes

1. Other prime contractors perform a similar, product-specific kind of systems integration for sensor equipment, propulsion equipment, and other major platform components.
2. For a related discussion of the tensions between operational Navy commanders and research scientists at the Office of Naval Research, see Sapolsky (1990: 86, 89, 96–8).
3. The defence business remains a political one, and it is unrealistic to believe that efficiency will ever be the only or even the paramount goal. Defence contracts impose certain social goals on the defence industry labour force, like a preference for mentoring small, minority-owned, or disadvantaged subcontractors.
4. Although this issue was recently highlighted by defence industry leaders' complaints about their firms' stock prices during the late 1990s tech bubble, it is actually a timeworn issue for high-end engineering workers in the defence sector. See, for example, Baum (1981: 129–31).
5. Private firms are sometimes accused of under-valuing research staff continuity in the face of investor pressure for short-term earnings. It is not clear why investors should be expected to make systematic mistakes in valuing research teams: they can simply discount future payoffs of research investment back to a net present value for comparing investments. In the 1990s, investors tended to overvalue the promise of technological progress, including in the defence industry (expectations for which were briefly confused with those for the 'dot com' companies (Gholz 1999).

6. Each of these sources of systems integration skill was cited in one or more interviews—usually in self-serving ways. That is, a systems integration organization with close academic ties would emphasize the importance of access to basic scientific research, while an organization with ties to a major defence production organization would emphasize production experience as a key underpinning of systems integration skill.

7. A similar situation led to the creation of the MITRE Corporation. See Jacobs (1986: 137–41).

8. Smith predicted that the FFRDC role would fade as the military improved its in-house technical capabilities. But for the reasons discussed in the text—and because the FFRDC's success, which Smith underlines in his report, reduced the demand for in-house systems integration capability—the military services never developed sufficient expertise to replace the FFRDCs. For-profit systems integration contractors (e.g., SAIC) have proven to be a bigger threat to the FFRDCs than any resurgent government laboratories.

9. Johns Hopkins University APL is not technically an FFRDC at present (it was until 1977), but it remains a non-profit systems integration organization with a long-term contractual relationship with the US Navy. Like an FFRDC, APL does not primarily engage in production, and it sometimes acts as the technical direction agent on major naval systems contracts. For present purposes, APL can be grouped with MITRE and Aerospace as a systems integration FFRDC, although it also has a strong research programme analogous to Lincoln Laboratory.

10. SAIC specifically acknowledges the technical skills of FFRDCs and actually tried to purchase the Aerospace Corporation in 1996—claiming that they could maintain the skills while adding efficiency due to the profit motive. Air Force resistance blocked this controversial move; many scientists at Aerospace were also sceptical of the acquisition and report that they would have considered leaving the company if the SAIC deal had gone though. See John Mintz (1996).

11. Some people involved in these Congressional decisions believe that the perceived high cost of FFRDCs was the crucial issue in establishing these limits; others see the effects of a lingering controversy over missile defence. The most recent proposal to establish a new FFRDC would have created a Strategic Defence Initiative Institute to support the missile defence effort.

12. SYNTEK, for example, has benefited by hiring a number of technical experts who gained experience working in military laboratories at a time (in the 1960s and 1970s) when laboratories had a stronger role in architecture definition. SYNTEK executives fear that their skills will be hard to maintain in future generations of technical staff. Author interviews, September 2000.

13. The SEI has begun to develop a new Capabilities Maturity Model to evaluate 'Integration' skills: at the direction of OSD (the Office of the Secretary of Defense), they are trying to apply software systems engineering procedures to software–hardware integration. The goal is to develop best practice methodologies for reducing the rate of failures in complex projects. Even this ongoing broadening of the SEI's research remains at a 'lower' level than overall system of systems integration.

14. In interviews, several respondents noted that the Capabilities Maturity Model—Integration (CMM-I) project is causing tension between the SEI and MITRE as they both clamour for the attention of their key customers at the Air Force Electronic Systems Command at Hanscom Air Force Base.

15. The reorganization of the BMDO into the Missile Defense Agency has been accompanied by the creation of a 'National Team' to provide technical support and systems integration for missile defence. The National Team involves prime contractors that produce platforms—specifically including platforms that will be deployed as part of the tiered missile defence system of systems.

16. Author interview, August 2001.

17. Author interview, July 2002.

18. A similar idea was proposed to provide technical support to the missile defence programme: either personnel from established FFRDCs would have been reassigned to the new Strategic Defence Initiative Institute (SDII) or a new division of one of the established FFRDCs would have been created. This approach was rejected in favour of the POET, arguably because the new FFRDC approach was perceived as too slow to set up and too costly. Others suggest that the SDII proposal was blocked by political opponents of missile defence, who hoped to hamstring the effort by denying high-quality technical advice to the Strategic Defense Initiative Office. See Baucom (1998).

19. On rare occasions, oversight officials and/or firms have been known to falsify reports, but those cases are truly the exception rather than the rule (Wall 2001).

20. Conflicts among those tasks have been barriers to the successful application of the systems approach outside of the acquisition environment (Rosen 1984).

21. For a general discussion of this form of organizational behaviour, see Pfeffer (1987).

22. See Balisle and Bush 2002 and the responses in the July and August 2002, issues of *Proceedings*.

23. Author interviews, May 2002.

24. This requirement is another reason that it is difficult for government agencies to perform systems integration in-house: subordinate project managers in the systems commands might not risk criticizing their bosses or their bosses' preferred programmes (OTA 1995: 5). Quasi-public FFRDCs face similar pressure not to criticize their customer too much, but their support and promotion prospects do not come in as direct a chain of command from the potential targets of their technical advice. The position of for-profit systems integration houses is similar to that of the FFRDCs: they are perhaps more responsive to short-term budget pressures from sponsoring organizations than FFRDCs are, but on the other hand, they may have more independence to seek alternative customers if their relationship with a particular contracting command temporarily sours.

References

BALDWIN, W. L. (1967). *The Structure of the Defense Market 1955–1964*. Durham, NC: Duke University Press.

BALISLE, P. and BUSH, T. (2002). 'CEC Provides Theater Air Dominance', *US Naval Institute Proceedings*, 128/5: 60–2.

BAUCOM, D. (1998). 'The Rise and Fall of the SDI Institute: A Case Study of the Management of the Strategic Defense Initiative', Incomplete Draft, August.

BAUM, C. (1981). *The System Builders: The Story of SDC*. Santa Monica: System Development Corporation.

BUILDER, C. H. (1989). *The Masks of War*. Baltimore, MD: Johns Hopkins University Press.

CHUTER, A. (2002). 'Honeywell Eyes FCS Systems Integration', *Defense News*, 29 July–4 August: 4.

COTÉ, Jr., O. R. (1995). 'The Politics of Innovative Military Doctrine: The US Navy and Fleet Ballistic Missiles'. PhD Thesis, Massachusetts Institute of Technology.

DYER, D. (1998). *TRW: Pioneering Technology and Innovation Since 1900*. Boston, MA: Harvard Business School Press.

FRIEDMAN, N. (2000). *Seapower and Space: From the Dawn of the Missile Age to Net-centric Warfare*. Annapolis, MD: Naval Institute Press.

GHOLZ, E. (1999). 'Wall Street Lacks Realistic View of Defense Business', *Defense News*, 20 December: 31.

——— and SAPOLSKY, H. M. (1999). 'Restructuring the US Defense Industry', *International Security*, 24/3: 5–51.

HARKNETT, R. J., and THE JCISS STUDY GROUP (2000). 'The Risks of a Networked Military', *Orbis*, 4/1: 127–43.

HERBERT, P. (1988). 'Deciding What Has to be Done: General William E. DePuy and the 1976 Edition of FM 100-5, Operations', *Leavenworth Papers*, No. 16. Fort Leavenworth, KS: Combat Studies Institute, US Army Command and General Staff College.

HUGHES, T. P. (1998). *Rescuing Prometheus: Four Monumental Projects that Changed the Modern World*. New York: Vintage Books.

JACOBS, J. F. (1986). *The Sage Air Defense System: A Personal History*. Bedford, MA: MITRE.

McNAUGHER, T. L. (1989a). *New Weapons, Old Politics: America's Military Procurement Muddle*. Washington, DC: Brookings Institution.

——— (1989b). 'Weapons Procurement: The Futility of Reform', in M. Mandelbaum (ed.), *America's Defense*. New York: Holmes & Meier, 68–112.

E. McKinney, E. Gholz, and H. M. Sapolsky (eds.), *Acquisition Reform* (MIT Lean Aircraft Initiative Policy Working Group Working Paper #1). Cambridge, MA: MIT Press.

MICHEL III, M. L. (1997). *Clashes: Air Combat over North Vietnam 1965–1972*. Annapolis: Naval Institute Press.

MINTZ, J. (1996). 'Air Force Halts Merger of 2 Companies', *Washington Post*, 16 November: D1.

OFFICE OF TECHNOLOGY ASSESSMENT (OTA), US CONGRESS (1995). *A History of the Department of Defense Federally Funded Research and Development Centers* (OTA-BP-ISS-157). Washington, DC: US Government Printing Office.

PFEFFER, J. (1987). 'A Resource Dependence Perspective on Intercorporate Relations', in M. S. Mizruchi and M. Schwartz (eds.), *Intercorporate Relations: The Structural Analysis of Business*. New York: Cambridge University Press, 25–55.

ROGERSON, W. (1998). 'Incentives in Defense Contracting'. Paper presented at the MIT Security Studies Program, October, 1998.

ROSEN, S. P. (1984). 'Systems Analysis and the Quest for Rational Defense', *Public Interest*, Summer: 3–17.

ROTNAM, G. (2002). 'US Navy to Set New CEC Requirements', *Defense News*, 22–28 July: 44.

SAPOLSKY, H. M. (1972). *The Polaris System Development: Bureaucratic and Programmatic Success in Government*. Cambridge, MA: Harvard University Press.

—— (1982). 'Myth and Reality in Project Planning and Control', in F. Davidson and C. L. Meadow (eds.), *Macro-engineering and the Future*. Boulder, CO: Westview Press, 173–82.

—— (1990). *Science and the Navy: The History of the Office of Naval Research*. Princeton, NJ: Princeton University Press.

—— and COTÉ Jr., O. R. (1997). 'The Third Battle of the Atlantic', *Submarine Review*, July: 40–2.

——, GHOLZ, E., and KAUFMAN, A. (1999). 'Security Lessons from the Cold War', *Foreign Affairs*, 78/4: 77–89.

SMITH, B. L. R. (1966). *The Future of the Not-for-Profit Corporations* (P-3366). Santa Monica, CA: RAND Corporation.

STANLEY-MITCHELL, E. (2001). 'Technology's Double-edged Sword: The Case of US Army Battlefield Digitization', *Defense Analysis*, 17/3: 267–88.

SVITAK, A. (2002). 'Disjointed First Steps: US Services' Transformation Plans Compete, Don't Cooperate', *Defense News*, 19–25 August: 1.

TUMPAK, S. (2002). 'Limit Super Primes', *Defense News*, 15–21 July: 23.

US General Accounting Office (1986). *Strategic Defense Initiative Program: Expert's Views on DoD's Organizational Options and Plans for SDI Technical Support* (GAO/NSIAD-87–43). November. Washington, DC: US General Accounting Office.

—— (1996). *Federally Funded R&D Centers: Issues Relating to the Management of DoD-Sponsored Centers* (GAO/NSIAD-96–112). August. Washington, DC: US General Accounting Office.

WALL, R. (2001). 'V-22 Support Fades Amid Accidents, Accusations, Probes', *Aviation Week and Space Technology*, 29 January: 28.

WILLIAMS, C. (2001). 'Holding the Line on Infrastructure Spending', in C. Williams (ed.), *Holding the Line: US Defense Alternatives for the Early 21st Century*. Cambridge, MA: MIT Press, 55–77.

WILSON, J. Q. (1989). *Bureaucracy: What Government Agencies Do and Why They Do It*. New York: Basic Books.

15

Changing Boundaries of Innovation Systems
Linking Market Demand and Use

MAUREEN MCKELVEY

School of Technology Management and Economics,
Chalmers University of Technology, Gothenburg, Sweden

15.1 Introduction

This chapter focuses on the changing boundaries of innovation systems, in order to understand how system integrators need to link innovation and development to market demand and use. Focusing on these changing boundaries implies a focus on the overall changes in the innovation system over time. These changes in boundaries are visible in actors, relationships, forces that create momentum for additional development, etc. Much of this chapter focuses on two empirical examples—pharmaceuticals and open source software. The two empirical sections present material in such a way as to embed theoretical and analytical points in the empirical evidence. This chapter demonstrates that innovation systems offer a useful tool for understanding which possible future trajectories exist, in terms of sketching how changing boundaries affect the possibilities to integrate the component services, goods, and knowledge into a system.

This chapter argues that the boundaries of innovation systems shift over time. This means that new actors may join and old actors may exit or that new types of actors (such as universities or venture capitalists) may, at certain times, become important for innovation processes. This idea that the boundaries of the innovation shift over time has implications for how, why, and who can influence the integration of all the components into a system. At some points, certain firms can act as systems integrators (Davies, Chapter Sixteen, this volume; Prencipe, Chapter Seven, this volume; Sako, Chapter Twelve, this volume). At other points, however, the activities of all the various actors need to be coordinated through more distributed coordination mechanisms. One example is coordination through market transactions which provide price signals to influence many distributed individuals. Another example is more loosely coordinated networks, such as communities of developers or informal relationships. This implies that if the boundaries shift, then the types and relative importance of these different ways of coordinating activities within the innovation system may also shift. If that happens, then it implies that the firm as systems integrator may be replaced by distributed coordination mechanisms—or vice versa.

Analyses of systems and networks have been quite popular within social science, in general and in relation to innovation studies. A general 'system' or 'network' definition includes the interlinked components and network linkages, which enable, facilitate, or hinder actors to reach some goal. An innovation system, for example, refers to information structures, organizations, institutions, and firms which enable innovation to occur within a defined population of firms (McKelvey 1997a). In the innovation system literature, the economic aspects of novelty such as impact on economic growth, productivity or firm survival can be emphasized (Lundvall 1992; Nelson 1993; Edquist 1997; Edquist, Hommen, and McKelvey 2001)—but are not always done so (Edquist and McKelvey 2000). A network approach from sociology (Powell and Smith-Doerr 2000) and economics (Orsenigo, Pammolli, and Riccaboni 2001) analyses the network in order to relate the frequency and intensity of network relationships to outcomes. Do networks affect economic growth and business survival? Much of the systems integration literature, such as that on complex product systems (CoPS), focuses on the complex and systemic nature of the technology and on the possibilities for firms to compete in such areas (Prencipe 1997; Brusoni, Prencipe, and Pavitt 2001). Similarly, these interactions may be approached through analysing technologies, products, and organization in innovating firms (Pavitt 1998).

The two empirical cases presented here focus more on the process of linking the risky and costly search for innovation and development—with current and expected/future market demand and use.[1] These innovation processes will be characterized as innovation systems, using the concepts of actors, relationships, and systemic outcomes, following Malerba (2002). These three variables give us a platform for comparing what happens in different systems over time—and which roles different actors may play. Despite these similarities, the analysis in the two cases are at somewhat different levels of aggregation, and illustrate different points. These differences are useful for our overall objectives here, for example, establishing how and why the boundaries of innovation systems change over time—and linking such shifts to implications for a systems integration firm.

This chapter thus focuses on the innovation and development process—in this case, in pharmaceuticals and an open source operating system—to see how actors' choices, network relationships, and systemic outcomes are linked to expectations about future returns. In drawing out implications for understanding systems integration, one contribution here is to provide an insight into the fundamental impacts of innovation on industry, and vice versa. Firms have to innovate to keep up—and the same seems true of societies. A second contribution is to thereby make the analysis of systems integration more dynamic. The chapter identifies explanations for different momentum and direction of search activities within innovation systems—which thereby result in different future outcomes, or trajectories. This is done in terms of markets, users, and technology—for example, future markets (for pharmaceuticals) and future users (software) as well as future technological development (for pharmaceuticals and software). This implies that technological change and market change are closely related.

Each actor has expectations about the future—about innovation opportunities, risks, costs, possible markets, etc. The reason for linking the outcomes of innovation system to actors' expectations is that the incentive structure as well as access to information strongly influence the rate, direction, and outcome of search activities (McKelvey 2001d). The search activities carried out by various firms, organizations, and individuals affect, in turn, the outcomes of the innovation and development process. This leads to a focus on system coordination—and actors within it. Hence, in these terms, coordination of the system here implies that the individual decisions of the actors are to some extent influenced by higher level, socioeconomic structures, which influence incentives as well as the rate and direction of search activities.

In examining this specific issue, this chapter focuses on the shifting boundaries of the innovation systems—rather than focusing on a specific firm which acts as a systems integrator. In some literature, 'coordination' is primarily discussed in terms of which types of firms are involved—for example, vertically integrated manufacturing firm versus multiple small firms linked through collaborative arrangements. Here, coordination of the innovation system instead refers to the links between micro-level behaviour and outcomes in relation to the broader socioeconomic structure. A sectoral system of innovation helps us characterize the changing actors, relationships, and systemic outcomes over time. These characteristics of the system are analytical tools, which help link firm choices to internal and external sources of information about novelty of potential economic value.

The first point—shown through pharmaceuticals in Section 15.2—is that the changing boundaries of an innovation system influence how, why, and whom may be involved as a systems integrator versus a component supplier. As such, shifting boundaries affect the innovation opportunities for incumbent and entrant firms as well as the dominant patterns of network relationships, including access to information. The relative impact of an innovation system on a specific firm may be different in different time periods and geographic locations. The overall sectoral system of innovation contains some firms which design and sell components, and other firms which act more to integrate the various fields of knowledge and various goods and services into a final product. However, the firm which was a systems integrator in one time period may be challenged by entrant firms, shift to become a component supplier and/or attempt to collapse the system to a firm-controlled process.

The second main point—shown through open source computer software in Section 15.3—is that the influence of users and/or buyers on the innovation process is partly dependent upon their role as developers and partly on the possibilities for firms to gain economic returns. Their role as developers—and thereby their involvement in a more complex organization of innovation processes—can affect the types and characteristics of products developed. In doing so, the potential opportunities for whether—and what types of actors—can integrate may differ. Market mechanisms as an incentive to promote development activities may function in parallel with other ways of organizing innovative activities among societal actors.

Due to the reasoning presented in the introduction about markets as one form of coordination mechanisms, this distinction between users and buyers matters when we analyse the innovation process and resulting products. Having users who are not buyers affects the incentives to innovate in the first place—in the sense that the market as a coordination mechanism is providing incomplete signals. When understanding innovation processes, other coordination mechanisms also exist, such as incentives which stimulate firms to develop R&D or universities to develop scientific, engineering, or other technical knowledge. Thus, we can argue that the innovation system is at times more oriented towards the development of new ideas—while at other times, market signals through sold products have a larger effect on actors' decisions and behaviour. If the boundaries of an innovation system change, then the coordination mechanisms and the role of systems integrator firms change.

The chapter is organized as follows. Section 15.2 examines the links between modern biotechnology and pharmaceutical companies, from the perspective of how and why the changing knowledge and changing drug demand affects incumbents and entrants to the global pharmaceutical industry. Section 15.3 examines the development of open source software, specifically Linux, in order to examine the impacts of different possible sets of incentives and different ways of organizing search activities on software development. These two sections thus present snapshots of case studies, which are based on other empirical and theoretical work by the author and co-authors. The cases are presented here to emphasize a few principle features of the economic transformation and shifting system boundaries. Section 15.4 concludes and returns to the theoretical arguments for understanding the impacts of changing demand for complex, knowledge-intensive products, such as bundling of goods and services, on the roles of buyers, sellers, and other societal actors.

15.2 Changing Boundaries in Modern Biotechnologies and the Pharmaceutical Industry

The pharmaceutical industry is a large, high-growth, globalized, and innovation-intensive industry. Its products—drugs—are directed to satisfy consumer needs in an area—healthcare—whose importance for society is fundamental and rapidly increasing. Delivery of healthcare and therapeutics requires innovations in various combinations of goods and services, thereby clearly making it a complex product system. Usually, however, no one actor takes on the whole task of systems integration in healthcare. Instead, such actors can be found around the pharmaceutical industry. Pharmaceuticals are in themselves a vital and quite visible part of the healthcare sector. Pharmaceuticals as a product are basically goods, made within a manufacturing sector.

Rather than examining the manufacturing and sales part in detail, however, this section focuses mainly on issues which relate the search activities in discovery—as linked to expected future returns from products. Finding and launching new drugs require high costs of search activities, new medical and biological knowledge, and up to date knowledge of the market. McKelvey and Orsenigo (2001a,b) and McKelvey, Orsenigo, and Pammolli (2003a) analysed the European pharmaceutical sector and the convergence between pharmaceuticals and the new biotechnology through the lens of a sectoral system of innovation. This work addresses issues about how, and why, we can use and develop evolutionary concepts and theories in parallel with an analysis of changes in a specific sector over time. Of these articles, McKelvey and Orsenigo (2001b) provided the basis of the current section. This article argued how and why to analyse populations of pharmaceutical firms in particular national contexts in combination with theoretical explanations about the effects of dynamic selection environments on the innovation strategies—and hence competitiveness—of firms. In doing so, particular attention is paid to mutual impacts of dynamic selection environments on firms, as related to (a) the firms' learning regimes, (b) university–industry relations, and (c) the formation of demand through regulation and markets.

Ever since the last century, pharmaceuticals used to be a traditional stronghold of European industry and still provides by far the largest contribution to the European trade balance in high-technology sectors. However, over the past two decades, the European pharmaceutical industry has been losing ground *vis-à-vis* the United States. Moreover, significant changes have also been occurring within European countries (Gambardella, Orsenigo, and Pammolli 2000). Indeed, over the last two decades, the world pharmaceutical industry has undergone profound transformations. The industry has been experiencing a series of technological and institutional shocks that have affected all stages of the value chain. These shocks have led to deep changes in firm organization and in market structure, within domestic markets, regionally, and globally.

At one extreme of the value chain, the advent of what is now known as the 'molecular biology revolution' and the emergence of biotechnology have radically transformed the prospects and the processes of drug discovery. At the other extreme, the rise of healthcare costs and prescription drug spending has induced a series of cost containment policies. In between, increasingly stringent requirements for the approval of new drugs have implied larger, more costly, and internationally based clinical trials. Developments in legislation and in courts' interpretation of issues concerning intellectual property rights, as well as increasing openness of domestic markets to foreign competition are also having significant impacts on patterns of competition and industrial evolution.

Taken together, these tendencies have implied a sharp increase in the resources needed to develop new drugs. At the same time, they have led to a redefinition of the nature of competition among firms. In fact, the fundamental source of competitive advantages lies in the integration of R&D, marketing, and distribution capabilities. The integration of these different complementary capabilities presents new challenges to individual firms.

Faced with these challenges, both individual firms and national industries have reacted quite differently. Companies have had to redesign their capabilities and strategies. In particular, the rising costs and the new logic of R&D and marketing have induced processes of Mergers and Acquisitions (M&A), increasing concentration, and globalization of the industry. At the same time, new patterns of division of labour and collaboration among firms and other institutional actors like universities and public research centres, are emerging. Key competitive assets for individual firms and countries are increasingly related to knowledge structures as well as to the degree of competitiveness and internationalization. These competitive assets include—but are not limited to—the availability of first-rate scientific research within universities and other public research centres, the structure of the systems of biomedical research, the patterns of inter-firm alliances in marketing and research. These changes in the pharmaceutical industry in the past decades can be analysed as developments which affect the distribution of knowledge capabilities and of economic value among the existing and the potential actors in the system.

Intuitively, the pharmaceutical industry quite naturally lends itself to be analysed as a Sectoral System of Innovation (SSI) or as a network (Galambos and Sewell 1995; Powell, Doput, and Smith-Doerr 1996; McKelvey 1997*b*). Concepts about systems of innovation arise from evolutionary and institutional economics (see Edquist and McKelvey 2000). The innovation systems literature has been analysed at national, regional, sectoral, and technological levels. More importantly, the system of innovation literature emphasizes the importance of interactive learning and knowledge, in order to explain the relative competitiveness of sectors, nations, and regions. For this chapter, Malerba's (2002) definition of a Sectoral System of Innovation (SSI) is a useful starting point:

A sectoral system of innovation and production is composed by the set of heterogeneous agents carrying out market and non-market interactions for the generation, adoption and use of (new and established) technologies and for the creation, production and use of (new and established) products that pertain to a sector ('sectoral products'). (p. 248)

This SSI definition thereby defines the overall industry system in terms of three elements, namely (*a*) actors, (*b*) types of interactions, and (*c*) the outcomes or functions of the system. These three elements of the SSI provide an analytical tool which is useful for understanding and redefining the nature of competition in specific sectors.

The recent changes outlined above in the pharmaceutical industry and in the new biotechnology–pharmaceutical overlap affect the SSI. These recent changes can be analysed in terms of effects on actors, relationships, and systemic outcomes of the pharmaceutical SSI.

In terms of the actors, many types are involved. The large pharmaceutical firms are vital actors for linking the innovation and development to market demand. Moreover, those involved in the innovative activities involve directly or indirectly a large variety of actors, including: (different types of) firms, other research organizations like universities and public and private research centres, financial institutions, regulatory authorities, and consumers, etc. Since the 1980s, various waves of dedicated biotechnology firms have been started, based on new discoveries in knowledge fields and on generic techniques. Financial institutions such as venture capitalists have played an important role in enabling the start-up of small firms—as have experienced people leaving larger incumbent firms. The actors listed above can be seen as different types of specialists—or as component suppliers to the innovative search activities. They provide different types of knowledge and resources for goods and services. In many senses, the large pharmaceutical firms play the role of linking all the elements of the innovative search process to the market for pharmaceutical products. In this sense, they often act as a type of systems integrator.

In terms of relationships, these various actors are linked together through a web of multiple types, numbers and frequencies of relationships. For example, the ability of the pharmaceutical firms to develop and sell new drugs depends on rules and regulations set by government agencies—and they may also choose to outsource certain activities, such as clinical trials. Still these relationships in the web are often asymmetrically distributed, with some strong nodes and varying intensities and frequencies of relationships. Large firms may still dominate some webs. Such asymmetrical attributes are similarly visible in how actors access information and thereby affect demand. This, of course, helps them maintain their role as systems integrator—despite shifting boundaries of the innovation system. However, the large firms are also challenged by other actors that may have access to more valuable information and/or develop networks to organize alternative drug discovery, production, and sales.

In terms of systemic outcomes, the pharmaceutical SSI channels resources both to develop new scientific and technological knowledge as well as selling new products and/or service delivery. Firms spend a lot of resources to find new drugs—and in that sense, the large ones have to explore much 'search space' to find new molecules. However, in more recent years, the search space available to find new drugs seems to be contracting, compared to the golden years of the post-Second World War period. This, of course, puts pressures on the firms to find even larger blockbuster drugs, in order to offset the costs of R&D and regulation.

Based on this description, clearly the pharmaceutical industry can be characterized as an SSI, with changing system boundaries. Over time, the changes in the actors, relationships, and systemic outcomes affect both the innovation opportunities for individual actors as well as future trajectories. Interestingly enough, this industry demonstrates a mix and partial overlapping of different selection principles, which affect individual actions as well as systemic outcomes. These selection principles affect both the search for innovations and potential future profits. On the one hand, firms can allow employees to behave like basic scientists and publish—although there can be economic benefits from participating in scientific communities (Pavitt 1990; Rosenberg 1990). On the other hand, universities increasingly behave like private economic actors, in questions related to patenting and licensing. Indeed, the emergence of hybrid forms of selection and learning (McKelvey 1997*b*) has been one of the most interesting features of this industry in recent years.

This view of the changing system boundaries can be used to identify four issues, which link the empirical analysis of the pharmaceutical–biotech industry with theoretical arguments about innovation systems. These are a means of understanding economic competition—and thereby also economic transformation of the modern, knowledge economy. The four issues are:

- First, the relative importance of the actors and the specific form of relationships and linkages between the actors which may differ over time and across countries.
- Second, the pharmaceutical SSI has been changing over time through the emergence of new agents and new forms of new relations, and through changes in the intensity of these relationships.
- Third, the key capabilities and competitive assets of firms and of organizations involved in innovation have changed, due to environmental selection pressures as well as to internal firm actions.
- Fourth, this in turn implies that patterns of competition and selection processes have also changed in the international pharmaceutical sectoral system of innovation.

These four issues which define our analytical perspective—combined with empirical evidence of European and American pharmaceutical firms, but which cannot be given in detail here—allow us to identify two groups of firms, and to argue that their choice of trajectories is linked to their innovation system. All four issues affect, in turn, whether a firm can be a systems integrator and/or whether other coordination mechanisms enable systems integration.

McKelvey and Orsenigo (2001*b*) argue and show empirically that the innovation strategies and competitiveness of pharmaceutical firms should be analysed relative to positive and negative pressures in a dynamic selection environment. Thus, in the existing, complex organizational setting of pharmaceuticals, the individual pharmaceutical firm is not only reacting to market signals.[2] Perhaps as importantly as market signals, the firm as an organization must transform signals about current and possible future demand as well as new knowledge and innovation opportunities into existing and potential products.

This firm-specific process of transformation of innovations into products for the market requires both internal firm activities as well as external relationships. In other words, making these transformations requires some degree of action, strategies, routines, as well as knowledge and experience. The firm-specific process of transformation of inputs into outputs is to some extent unique to one firm—but some of the market and technical knowledge is also shared with competitors.

Two groups of firms can be defined, based on the dominant strategy and thereby the type of competition. The first group of firms follows a strategy which is more focused on production and imitation, and they thereby tend to compete based dominantly on price. The second group of firms follows a strategy which is more focused on innovation, particularly blockbuster drugs, and they thereby tend to compete based dominantly on innovation (and sustained by patents), although price competition is also increasingly important here. In terms of the national selection environments, we can define the characteristics of the two types as well (which may change from one to the other over time). The first type focuses decisions about pharmaceuticals mostly around political selection processes, in the sense of putting primacy on political types of decisions, such as healthcare provision to all inhabitants, protecting national firms, etc. The second type allows many decisions to be made by market-based selection, where political decisions and healthcare providers act in such a way as to increase the range of decisions affected by the market.

The first group of firms competes on imitation and on lower price for substitutable products, mainly generic pharmaceuticals and/or off the shelf. They spend much less on R&D and spend fewer resources on accessing external information held by other agents or through other network relationships. This first type of firms seems to have emerged to first serve regional, then later national markets, but even these imitative pharmaceutical products are increasingly a type of global, mass market product. Firms in this group put relatively more emphasis on manufacturing and distribution channels than on funding the latest knowledge relevant for future blockbuster drugs. They may continue to exist over time despite increasing market pressure, however, in the two cases of either efficient production and price competition or when protected by national price controls.

The second group of firms relies on blockbuster drugs, protection through patents and other property rights, significant returns on R&D and significant profits. This second type prefers to move into drugs with large and/or expanding markets. Succeeding with this innovation strategy requires that the firm invests extensively in the extended pharmaceutical R&D process, which includes both in-house capabilities as well as control over external sources of knowledge (Orsenigo, Pammolli, and Riccaboni 2001). They need extensive contacts and transactions with other firms and other types of actors, because any information about search strategies and final characteristics of potential blockbuster drugs may potentially be so valuable. Winner takes all.

Tables 15.1 and 15.2 summarize our empirical evidence presented above in terms of the four categories, which link dominant firm strategy to dominant selection environment. They give a framework both for the relative concentration and frequency of certain combinations across these two dimensions, as well as for understanding the range of choices for firms.

TABLE 15.1 *Pharmaceuticals: linking dominant firm strategy to national selection environment*

	Selection around political decisions	Selection around market-based decisions
Innovation firm strategy	Transition period	Dominate global trend; American move first. Global competition, based on innovation (over time, increasingly as linked to price)
Production and imitative firm strategy	Previous periods, especially Continental European	Global competition based on price

TABLE 15.2 *Pharmaceuticals: relative frequency of different combinations*

	Selection around political decisions	Selection around market-based decisions
Innovation firm strategy	++	++++
Production and imitative firm strategy	++++	++

Table 15.1 shows different periods and geographical areas where various combinations are visible. Table 15.2 then relates this information in terms of relative frequency. Tables 15.1 and 15.2 thus provide a visual overview of the changing boundaries of the system.

Finally, there are implications for systems integration, of studying the changing boundaries of an innovation system. These changing boundaries clearly affect whether some firm(s) can act as systems integrators—or whether looser coordination mechanisms lead to a more distributed innovation system. Characteristics of the innovation system—which change over time—seem to lead to different ways of integrating the system—and coordinating many individuals.

In some cases, changing boundaries do not affect the existing power distribution very much. For example, large pharmaceutical firms still dominate in terms of size and in terms of integrating the R&D, testing, production, and sales of specialized pharmaceuticals. Some aspects are outsourced while others exist in-house. However, the profitability and dominance of the large pharmaceutical firms has been challenged in recent years, due to changes in knowledge and in demand. Thus, the relationship between the firm and their strategy to innovate can change over time. This argument is now made, in relation to pharmaceutical firms which follow the strategy of innovation and blockbuster drugs.

The innovative firms have more incentives both to engage in search activities in-house and to be linked into the network. They have more incentives to engage in, and try to control R&D and appropriate value from medical and other knowledge in order to translate innovation opportunities into profits. Because of the obvious limits of in-house firm knowledge when facing complex and multiple knowledge fields, however, they also have more incentives to monitor, identify, and gain access to specialized assets held by other actors. They need both internal and external activities to integrate goods and services. These specialized assets may be held by other actors, thereby providing incentives for innovative firms to increase overall inter-activity in the system.

However, as the boundaries of the innovation system change, so too does the relative dominance of one/a few firms as compared to a looser system. The firm may attempt to supersede the system, and thereby control it more directly. In other words, at times, the system may collapse down to the firm again, if the firm can gain control of relevant knowledge and appropriate returns. Mechanisms which can cause a collapse from a network down to the firm include, for example, M&A and incorporating new knowledge in-house which was previously acquired externally. At other times, the system expands. This may occur because new entrants sell products in order to explore new innovation opportunities. Or, it may occur because new (types of) actors hold more valuable knowledge and other assets.

Time matters in the case of the changing boundaries of the pharmaceutical–biotechnology innovation system. The pharmaceutical firms which chose the innovation strategy have faced many market challenges in recent decades, and have thereby had strong pressures to adapt, even internationally. In addition to the need to understand and integrate new areas of science, there have been significant pressures on these firms' profitability, due to attempts among healthcare providers to implement cost containment policies, legal changes allowing generic drugs, etc.

More abstractly, at points of extreme pressure, the firm which was innovative in the previous period now faces a choice between two diametrically opposed alternative futures. They may either continue the strategy from the previous period—with affects on firm behaviour and systemic outcomes—or else attempt to move to the other trajectory. In the case of pharmaceutical firms, the firm which previously had an innovation-dominated strategy has to decide. On the one hand, the individual firm could 'choose' to continue competing as it has in the past, through innovation strategies and competitiveness based on blockbusters. In this case, the individual firm faces increased pressure to find money to finance R&D expenditures and to maintain external network contacts—while simultaneously requiring that this increasing investment must be financed by future blockbuster pharmaceutical drugs. In this situation, these firms can either use the international sectoral system of innovation to the maximum to obtain first mover advantages on potential innovation opportunities—thereby driving up interactivity and frequency of relationships—and/or the firm can try to collapse the most valuable part of the innovation system done to the firm—and thereby gain control. In doing so, this is usually accomplished through mergers with international competitors.

The other outcome is to focus on production and imitation and thereby move away from innovation. Thus, the firm could choose to give up the game of innovation strategies around these enormous, blockbuster drugs. Rather than merge and/or fight on the international scene, the firm which was innovative in a previous period may try to retreat to the group of imitative firms.[3] In this case, the firm should focus on costs of production and distribution and also reduce in-house R&D and their engagement in international networks. Rather than compete through innovation, the firms would change to concentrate on manufacturing and selling fairly reproducible, substitutable products not protected by patents. In this case, the firm now needs access to a smaller innovation system—and with somewhat different composition and components.

In summary, viewing the pharmaceutical industry as a sectoral system of innovation helps us to identify how and why a firm's choices about future products based on innovations are related to global changes in actors, networks, and systemic outcomes. The changes in markets, institutions, and knowledge over time affect the choices of individual firms—as well as the relative frequency and intensity of interactions within the system.

As argued in this section, this view implies that the innovation opportunity for a firm to act as the key integrator of the overall pharmaceutical system may, thereby, differ dramatically over time periods and national boundaries. There are changing opportunities for the core product firm to integrate from innovative search processes to final product. As these change, this thereby also affects those firms wishing to develop and sell component services and goods. Taken together, the sectoral system of innovation can help us analyse when and why at one point, one large firm may act as an overall system integrator while at other points, many small firms and large firms are linked through other mechanisms for economic and knowledge coordination in the overall system.

15.3   Linux: Users, Developers, and Systems Integrators in Software

As with pharmaceuticals, software is a complex, knowledge-intensive product (Steinmueller 2003). Software development is interesting, not only because of the ubiquitous importance of the resulting goods and service products in the modern economy but also because software requires a high degree of knowledge-intensity in development—and sometimes in use. As with Section 15.2 on the pharmaceutical sectoral system of innovation, this section focuses mainly upon innovative activities, albeit this time as related to computer software operating systems.

This section focuses on how and why changes in the configuration of the system combines market and non-market aspects, and by this, we mean it is necessary to further explore how and why the links between innovation and demand—with market demand and users—affect the behaviour of firms and other actors. Market/non-market aspects have implications for how and why search activities are carried out, and by whom, as well as for specific characteristics of the resulting software development and for potential bundling of goods and services for sale on through market transactions. An important question here will be whether, and if so, how, these system configurations and ways of organizing search activities affect future momentum of development and characteristics of the software. These questions affect, in turn, whether the firm acts as a systems integrator—or whether looser coordination mechanisms dominate.

This section focuses on developments of Linux, which is an open source software operating system, where users, developers and system integrators have fuzzy boundaries between them. Based on work reported in McKelvey (2001*a,b,c*), this section analyses Linux development relative to the reasons for, and implications of, the changing system boundaries. McKelvey (2001*b*, 2001*c*) defines the concept of 'Internet Entrepreneurship' in order to try to capture characteristics of modern innovation in software. Internet Entrepreneurship is defined as having the following characteristics: (*a*) Multiple persons are distributed organizationally and/or geographically; (*b*) despite distribution, persons can still interact in real time and lagged time to create novelty; (*c*) user and developer may be the same person; (*d*) copying and distributing information may be without cost or may be costly; and (*e*) instantaneous worldwide distribution of software and communication over the internet, or worldwide web. Taken together, these features may enable the process of knowledge creation to go about in a new way, as compared to traditional patterns of developing knowledge through R&D in firms.[4]

Is Internet Entrepreneurship an emerging phenomenon? Does this model have the potential to beat, or at least seriously threaten, high-tech firms which invest many internal resources in R&D and appropriate the profits? The answers are respectively, 'yes' and 'no'. The 'yes' to an emerging phenomenon is due to the momentum of development, through this way of organizing search activities. The 'no' to the potential dominance of the model arises because of the software-innovation systems exhibiting multiple ways of organizing search activities. 'Internet entrepreneurship' does not threaten to become a complete substitute firm-based development. Instead, firms and looser networks increasingly interact—thereby opening up more search space for firms as well. This way of organizing search activities is a complement—not substitute—for firm search activities and for firm appropriation of economic returns.

In this case, the integration of the system appears to occur through a loosely coordinated set of economic and social mechanisms. Even within open source software, differences exist in building up institutional structures, based on differing principles and differing degrees of centralized versus loose control of coordination. Many of these innovative search activities may be developed—at least partially—outside the realm either of traditional market formation and/or of the one large firm which attempts to integrate the overall system. This type of loose systems integration seems likely, however, to occur in parallel with existing alternatives.

This section highlights the reasons for, and implications of, the interacting market and non-market aspects of development activities. The development activities within Linux are described in terms of actors, network relationships, and systemic outcomes, as for the previous section. Software development appears to be a very interesting case of evolutionary competition which is highly relevant to theoretical developments in evolutionary economics (McKelvey 1996; Metcalfe 1998).

To make the theoretical and empirical arguments for open source software, it is important to establish that there are often multiple and alternative ways of creating novelty and creating economic value. Freeware, shareware, open source software, etc. compete with commercial, packaged software for users. These different ways sometimes develop in parallel but at other times, they converge or branch-off.

In this case, whether all users = buyers or whether users > buyers affects the potential economic returns to innovation and development. The firm needs to cover its development costs somehow—who pays, if not through future markets? After all, software which is tagged as 'open source software' under the various names and certifications, means that users agree to forgo some property rights in return for open access.

Thus, open source software is interesting in relation to changing boundaries of innovation systems. Here, users may compete with buyers, but users are also often developers. Potential users have to make a choice about whether to access operating systems through purchases in a market or through substitutes obtainable through other channels of distribution. Linux and Microsoft are interesting cases of competing operating systems because they compete over users, even if they do not necessarily compete for buyers. These users may want the software for various purposes, such as to run desktop PCs or else corporate network servers.[5] Users can choose various distribution channels to access the software—from purchasing a license for the operating system, purchasing license and service agreement, purchasing configurations of software even if no license is necessary, compiling own software, etc. Examples correspond to purchasing Windows/Word, purchasing Windows/Word and services from a company, purchasing open source packaging such as RedHat, obtaining programmes from net, CD, colleagues, etc., without purchasing licensing or configuration such as do-it-yourself Linux.

Therefore, this empirical case highlights the issues (a) competing software development leads to alternative characteristics of products, as well as (b) competing over access users affects the incentives to further innovation and development. Moreover, firms innovating in this field may sell both products which are goods or services (or combinations of the two) as well as component products in parallel with widely distributing open information.

Linux is an operating system software available in the public domain, or known as open source software. Linux is an operating system based on UNIX, which was started by one user, but which has been further developed by many others. Around early Autumn 1998 and onwards, Linux increasingly received attention in the professional, management, and popular press. Many articles emphasize the community values and willingness to share in the community of hackers or open source programmers. However, one argument developed later in this section—and which is necessary for understanding changing system boundaries—is that the actual development and the actual use of Linux relies on a much wider range of developers and of users than the popular view expresses.

The most amazing part of the Linux story is, perhaps, that it is at all considered an alternative, or challenge, to Microsoft (Hall 1999). Microsoft, after all, has dominated PC software in terms of current sales and installed base in hardware in recent decades. Moreover, the company has been enormously profitable. In an analysis of the Standard & Poor 500 American companies, *Business Week* (1999) ranked Microsoft as the number one performer for 1998. Microsoft's sales were US$376 billion for that year, making US$6 billion in profits. This meant that the net margin for 1998 was 38.2 per cent, which was a 63 per cent profit increase from 1997. Linux, in contrast, had an estimated total of 7–10 million users in early 1999, and the companies selling packaged versions of it were mainly small start-ups. In the first decade of the twenty-first century, use of the Linux operating system is continuing to increase, whether the measures taken are of number of users, types of applications, or geographical spread.

Differences in product characteristics are useful to understand competition—and competition matters as to whether or not the firm is willing to take the costs and risks of engaging in innovative search activities. Could a firm invest enough money to make a commercially produced alternative to Microsoft? Since its first popular upswing around 1997, Linux continued to spread and gain users, albeit from an initially very low base. Microsoft sells a standardized mass market product available pre-installed on much computer hardware. There are clear network externalities, in that almost everybody seemed to migrate to using Microsoft in the 1990s.[6] Microsoft sells licensing rights. Linux is a non-profit operating system which can provide more or less direct substitutable products to Microsoft—both for the operating system and for related software. Distribution of open source may be through the market—such as purchasing specific packaging—and/or through non-market distribution forms—such as the user configuring his own system, with the help of the internet and CDs. The Linux kernel is neither for sale nor licensing—but goods and services around it may be available through market transactions.

Before moving on to analyse the shifting Linux system boundaries in terms of actors, relationships, and systemic outcomes, a few words are necessary about the dominant media view of 'hacker culture' developing open source software—as opposed to the view promoted here that the Linux phenomenon must be understood as a much wider phenomenon of use. Use is tightly linked to development in open source software in a very different way than in, say, pharmaceuticals, where development and use are separate except for clinical trials. In open source, users can give direct input into software development. In pharmaceuticals, users are necessary to validate scientific tests—but they do not contribute to the underlying medical or pharmacological knowledge *per se*.

The dominant media view is that Linux was developed by a small community of hackers who try out, make improvements, and give feedback (Raymond 1999; Sawhney and Prandelli 2000; Tuomi 2001, 2002). Selection of alternatives is seen to rely on the best bits of code being chosen through consensus, even though the network is distributed worldwide over the physical infrastructure of computers, lines, servers, etc. This has been seen in stark contrast with the Microsoft case, where the firm tries to keep as much control as possible over software development in-house as well as over profits. An influential and well-known article 'The Cathedral and the Bazaar' within the internet hacker's community argues that the public domain software model is superior to the model organized within a firm.[7] If we look at the wider phenomenon of Linux use, however, it quickly becomes clear that relative to the total number of Linux users, very few actually develop the kernel; some engage in development of complementary software bits, while the majority of users use Linux without engaging in direct software development. Even without writing code, this last category of users may still be engaged in the overall software diffusion, through discussion groups or other forms of disseminating information about trials and errors. Thus, the popularity and momentum of Linux development is the user side. Linux relies on a range of users. They will likely affect future momentum for software development and future product characteristics.

Certain characteristics of the Linux software can be identified, which are likely to attract additional numbers of users as well as to attract new types of users that differ from the initial users. These arguments are of three types— (a) the role of skills and experience with similar software, (b) wide potential fields of application, and (c) complementary software and hardware solutions so the overall software is useful.

First, since Linux was based on UNIX, which has been a common operating system in the university world, this in turn implies that many users are familiar with it as well as having access to software applications. Second, the operating system has a modularity structure which makes it potentially useful for a wide range of possible applications. The operating system has the potential to appeal to a variety of users interested in different applications, because Linux can run on many different types of hardware and is argued to be flexible and easy to customize. Third, the use of operating system relies on a series of complementary assets, both hardware and software related. As long as either the core community or other actors are willing to develop these complementary software and hardware solutions, the total attraction of the overall software increases. Indeed, for Linux, commercial companies can come in and sell packaged software around the basic kernel and sell services related to configuring software, installation, help functions, etc.

The three components of an SSI—actors, relationships, and systemic outcomes—help structure the concluding part here, about the implication of changing boundaries for systems integration.

In terms of actors, the previous discussion argued that there is a range of actors actually using Linux, and that these actors can be categorized based on their involvement in the development process. The argument above is that relative to the total number of Linux users, few actually develop the kernel; some engage in development of complementary software bits; while the majority use Linux without engaging in direct software development. Actors may thus be conceptualized in terms of their activities in the system—for example, as related to Linux as a phenomenon.

These two main categories of users may be further subdivided into four types. Table 15.3 relates an analysis of users in terms of their involvement in developing software to an analysis based on the knowledge and skills of users, following arguments made previously. In terms of involvement in developing, users may either be developers or users. In terms of knowledge and skills, users may either be advanced or basic.[8]

Thus, Table 15.3 demonstrates the range of possible users in four types, from the community of Linux developers to users wanting simple solutions for use. Understanding the range of potential actors in these terms allows us also to predict the relative frequency of these types of actors in the Linux system, based on the empirical evidence mentioned previously. Table 15.4 shows expected frequency.

These identified-user groups, expected frequency, and understanding of the overall systemic dynamics of development in open source software, have implications for our next point, namely network relationships.

In terms of network relationships, developing Linux requires various types of relationships. The 'Internet Entrepreneurship' argument defined at the beginning of this section has presented a specific view of the types of relationships involved, which may be widely dispersed in time, place, background, etc.

TABLE 15.3 *Linux: relating user involvement in software development to skills*

	Developer	User
Advanced user	Community of Linux developers	Professional programmers; some hobby programmers
Basic user	Hobby programmers trial and error; can make local solutions	Users who want simple and obvious solutions

TABLE 15.4 *Linux: expected frequency of the different types of users*

	Developer	User
Advanced user	++	++++
Basic user	+++	++++++

Indeed, the arguments made above about the need to increase the total software-package attractiveness to a larger number and wider range of potential users, has implications for conceptualizing Linux network relationships relative to innovation and development. These implications are valid both for identifying specific actors and relationships. The traditional way of analysing a system or network is to look at the specific unit (firm, individual, organization, etc.) and then examine the relationships of that unit to other actors—as relevant to some theoretical/analytical arguments.

In contrast, the argument here is that understanding developers, users = developers, and users are a key to understanding the momentum of overall development within the system. Thus, the network does not have to rely on a fixed set of specific individuals—but also on whether others join.[9]

In terms of systemic outcomes, this overall system analysed here is focused around developing one core operating system, with complementary software. This differs from the above discussion of pharmaceuticals, which focused on overall new drug development in the industry. For Linux, this part of the analysis focuses on the expected relative rates and types of future development, if different assumptions are made about the factors giving momentum to the innovation and development process.

The rate of open source software development has been argued above to be a function of persons joining the network, as related to user characteristics, such as their qualifications to make improvements, their willingness to make changes available to others, etc.

This view has implications for the rate, and thereby we can identify two possible, diametrically opposed, systemic outcomes in terms of rates of software development, namely (1) high rate of development and (2) no development. When software is being developed in the public domain without costs and ownership, then the rate of software development can either go very fast or could peter out completely. (1) *Fast pace*: It could go very fast if more and more users adopt it, particularly if those users have the appropriate expert skills and are willing to share their improvements and the results of their tests with others. This form of distributed invention goes very fast with E-mail and the internet, where changes anywhere in the world can be made immediately available to anyone else. (2) *No development*: However, if nobody uses the software, or actual and potential users stop developing it, then the rate of software development will slow down and even stop. If the user base increases in number and range, then that smaller group where user = developer will play an increasingly important role. Thus, if users use but do not improve or test it in the broader sense of systematic testing for failures, then the rate of change could be very slow. It could be so slow that the software could stop being developed—and even disappear completely.

Thus, if one assumes that individuals are the dominant actors in open source software, then software developments will thereby depend on the future attractiveness—not only to users but especially to user = developer. The likelihood of disappearing completely depends in turn, however, on how far the core and complementary asset software has been diffused. If they have been widely diffused, then there is more likelihood of continuing momentum in innovation and development—because of use phenomena. This assumption depends on the network externalities argument, where existing user base and infrastructure present an investment which can differentiate an incumbent (or developing) system from a competing system (Katz and Shapiro 1985, 1986).

A different systemic outcome is possible for open source software, if we drop the assumption that individuals are the main developers. Assuming that network externalities hold, then use will grow—and with it, market opportunities for core and complementary goods and services. In that case, firms have reasons to engage in open source software development—even if they cannot directly sell the open source software.

Thus, those firms which may benefit from an entrenched network externalities in open source software are those most likely to invest resources to engage in software development. The types of firms that are identifiable through the above analysis of Linux include firms that 'package' open source software distributions, sell other complementary goods and services, sell hardware, etc. McKelvey (2001b) postulates that firms will play an increasingly important role in developing and diffusing Linux—in parallel with the hacker community.[10] To some extent, the innovation and development processes for open source software will converge with commercial software—when market demand and use also do so.

This identifies one possible systemic outcome—whereby firms increasingly take over open source software development in order to sell components or systems integration related to the bundling of goods and service. This systemic outcome may, in turn, feed back and affect momentum among individual developers = users. Individuals may decide to keep contributing to the software development—or to leave it to the firms. Whether or not the actual and potential user = developers will continue making improvement will then partly depend on their interpretation of the firm involved in open source software development—are they allies or foes?

In summary, understanding the momentum leading to different future outcomes of the innovation system is a critical issue for Linux and other open sources software. The actors, relationships, and systemic outcomes together determine the trajectory taken in the past, as well as where the system is headed in the future. These combinations affect (a) the attractiveness of this software, (b) the relative strength of network externalities for the system, and (c) whether or not the momentum will continue to grow or peter out. In short, these changing system boundaries will affect current and future search activities, in terms of rate and direction of search activities, as well as in terms of innovative outcomes.

15.4 Conclusions and Implications

This chapter has analysed the changing boundaries of innovation systems, as linked to demand and use, for pharmaceuticals and open source software. Each section addresses the actors, relationships, and systemic outcomes visible in the case—especially in relation to how the system affects future innovation.

In terms of actors, both cases clearly demonstrate that over time, old actors may continue to exist while new actors may join and contribute to innovation and development. This implies that while existing large firms may dominate at a given point, they are being challenged.

In pharmaceuticals, the existing firms continue to exist but engage in mergers, alliances, etc., while new entrants include actors such as dedicated biotechnology firms focused on the commercialization of discoveries. In open source software, early entrants into the Linux community were individuals who are developers = users, but they were fairly soon joined by other types of actors, such as developers (especially in firms) and users (especially individuals; diffusion of use). The phenomenon of use of open source affects innovation and development processes much more directly than pharmaceuticals.

Even when the overall incentive to join the innovation system is the same for new actors as it is for old actors—such as the desire to appropriate economic returns—the new entrants may engage in new ways of organizing search activities, involving other societal actors. Moreover, they may 'push' search activities into new directions, such that the characteristics of future products (goods or services) may differ from characteristics of previous products.

In pharmaceuticals, the new entrants commercialize new medical, bioengineering, and other scientific knowledge around especially the R&D process (and sometimes the final product, drugs). Over time, the incumbent pharmaceutical firms have to change their internal knowledge capabilities and external knowledge relationships in a network, in order to develop innovation opportunities and sell future products. In doing so, they react to aspects of relationships (see below) and national selection environments. During certain periods, firms are reacting to quite close geographical sets of incentives—where differences in these sets of incentives affect future competitiveness of the actors.

In Linux, the new entrants of both firms who are developers of software and individuals who are mainly users affect future software developments. One way is that complementary software and hardware are developed, such that the alternative facing a potential future user is the overall combination of many bits of software and hardware. Another way is that users = users want different characteristics of products than the initial developers, thereby if their wishes are met, their demand for use affects characteristics of the overall combination of software.

In terms of relationships, the networks are clearly shown to be changing over time, as incumbents change internally, incumbents exit and entrants come in. As the set of relationships change, so too do the boundaries of the system. This affects future possible outcomes for innovation processes.

In pharmaceuticals, the number and type of relationships have expanded over time—due to changes in knowledge, supply of novelty, and demand. Historical relationships between firms and others were shown, however, to have effects on future competitiveness of firms. Competitiveness was argued to be partially dependent upon the choice of firm strategy, which was defined relative to innovation, for example, firm strategy as innovative or imitative. Thus, relationships were shown to impact on firm competitiveness, with longer-term effects on the trajectories chosen by firms and populations of firms in different countries. In Linux, the network is also changing over time, due to the entrance of firms and users. Much of the argument was in terms of the overall attractiveness of the system to new users and about whether the overall system could maintain a certain level and variety of relationships. It was argued that these factors give more momentum to the overall development process—which is quite different from seeing the network as specific relationships *per se*.

In terms of systemic outcomes, it was shown that there are different possible future outcomes for a current innovation system. It was argued that the future trajectory actually taken will depend upon a combination of factors. The analysis proceeded by analysing the different possible systemic outcomes, based on combinations of individual components and system boundaries.[11]

In pharmaceuticals, the strategic choices of pharmaceutical firms were summarized as innovation strategy, for example, blockbuster drugs (and increasingly price competition), or production and imitation strategy, for example, reduce production and distribution costs by producing better known drugs. The combination of firm choice of strategy and of other actors and relationships will affect future overall innovation and development within pharmaceuticals, for example, the extent to which new areas of disease can be treated or existing diseases may be more accurately or more efficiently treated.

In Linux, much of the discussion of systemic outcomes related the phenomenon of use to the effects on momentum in innovation and development. It was argued that whether actors continue innovating as well as which actors invest the resources for additional software development will affect the pace of open source software development as well as characteristics of future software available.

Taken together, the arguments presented here demonstrate

- changing innovation system boundaries over time;
- effects of changing boundaries on incumbent actors and on potential entrant firms or other societal actors contributing to innovation;

- differential possible systemic outcomes, depending on the combinations of actors and networks as related to incentives for innovation and development.

These three statements reiterate the dynamic nature of the analysis of innovation systems presented here, as well as the clear link between the actor's incentives and capabilities, to the overall socioeconomic structure of incentives and of knowledge production.

In making these arguments, this chapter has made it clear that the changing boundaries of innovation systems, as linked to demand and use, can be argued through a combination of empirical and theoretical/analytical arguments. The empirical evidence supports the theoretical explanation, and vice versa. The changing boundaries of the innovation system can partly be explained by how new innovation opportunities emerge as related to changing demand—but also to the relative opportunities and problems of specific actors trying to contribute to innovation and development processes.

This dynamic system perspective presented in the chapter is based on an understanding of changes in the two main aspects of innovations, namely information/technology and market/use. The dynamics of the innovation system is partly driven by changes, on the one hand, in innovations and development and, on the other hand, in market demand and use. These two types of change will, in turn, together affect the boundaries of innovation systems. As those boundaries change, so too will the implications for whom, and how, the overall system is integrated. Shifting boundaries clearly affect the questions of who will integrate the system of demand, and of which actors will be involved.

Notes

1. These cases are based on other work by the author, as referenced at the beginning of the respective sections. The analysis presented here differs from that presented elsewhere, due to the focus here on changing system boundaries. The references to the author's work contain, in turn, references to a much larger body of literature upon which the empirical and theoretical arguments were based.
2. Note that in pharmaceuticals, the 'market' for the product is taken in a loose way to mean the supply and demand of products. This market, as it is expressed, is obviously a social and political process, which is quite different from the idealistic conception of a free market. The market expressed in pharmaceuticals is clearly affected by intermediary organizations and concerns, such as welfare policy, government regulation of safety, doctors' right to prescribe to final consumers, etc.
3. Note that this also implies that the constitution of groups is a dynamic process, constituted by competition and interaction among others, including direct and indirect competitors. Competition has no given or stable outcome.
4. See McKelvey (1996) for analysis of the processes of knowledge production.
5. See the analysis of Microsoft, Netscape, and Linux found in McKelvey (2001a).
6. See Katz and Shapiro (1985, 1986) and Liebowitz and Margolis (1994).

7. This particular piece on why the Linux model works (as well as other writings) has been available since 7 April 1999 at www.tuxedo.org/~esr/writings/cathedral-bazaar. It was originally written for a meeting in Atlanta, which seems to have been an important event in focusing the Linux community and in bringing it to the attention of the broader IT community.

8. Under the assumption that some basic level of skills and experience is useful. The level required of users seems different under different systems if, for example, one compares Linux with Microsoft.

9. See McKelvey (2001a) for discussions about three dominant business models for organizing innovation activities—as well as the likely outcomes over time.

10. Firms will invest in open source software, when they can calculate and/or convince themselves that they will appropriate some returns. The returns are likely to come through demand expressed through another product, whether goods or service. In this case, the firm will have to be convinced that the open source software alternative is growing fast enough to produce enough volume for economies of scale. For example, it may be important that use is spreading to new users, new hardware, and new applications. In the long run, the firms will have to receive some financial returns—directly or indirectly—in order to continue to invest in open source software development.

11. Thus, there is no assumption of functionality, or necessity of system outcomes.

References

BRUSONI, S., PRENCIPE, A., and PAVITT, K. (2001). 'Knowledge Specialization, Organizational Coupling, and the Boundaries of the Firm: Why do Firms Know More Than They Make?', *Administrative Science Quarterly*, 46/4: 587–621.

BUSINESS WEEK (1999). 'The Best Performers'. 29 March: 42–99.

EDQUIST, C. (ed.) (1997). *Systems of Innovation: Technologies, Organizations and Institutions*. London: Pinter Publishers/Cassell Academic.

—— and McKELVEY, M. (eds.) (2000). *Systems of Innovation: Growth, Competitiveness, and Employment* (2 vols.). Cheltenham: Edward Elgar.

——, HOMMEN, L., and McKELVEY, M. (2001). *Innovations and Employment in a Systems of Innovation Perspective*. Cheltenham: Edward Elgar.

GALAMBOS, J. and SEWELL, J. E. (1995). *Networks of Innovation: Vaccine Development at Merck, Sharp & Dohme, and Mulford, 1895–1995*. New York: Cambridge University Press.

GAMBARDELLA, A., ORSENIGO, L., and PAMMOLLI, F. (2000). *Global Competitiveness in Pharmaceuticals: A European Perspective*. Report prepared for the Directorate General Enterprise of the European Commission.

HALL, J. M. (1999). 'The Economics of Linux', *UNIX Review's Performance Computing*, 17/5: 70–3.

KATZ, M. and SHAPIRO, C. (1985). 'Network Externalities, Competition, and Compatability', *American Economic Review*, 75/3: 424–40.

—— —— (1986). 'Technology Adaptation in the Presence of Network Externalities', *Journal of Political Economy*, 94/4: 822–41.

LIEBOWITZ, S. and MARGOLIS, S. (1994). 'Network Externality: An Uncommon Tragedy', *Journal of Economic Perspectives*, 8/2: 113–50.

LUNDVALL, B.-Å. (ed.) (1992). *National Systems of Innovation: Towards a Theory of Innovation and Interactive Learning*. London: Pinter Publishers.

MALERBA, F. (2002). 'Sectoral Systems of Innovation and Production', *Research Policy*, 31: 247–64.

McKELVEY, M. (1996). *Evolutionary Innovation: The Business of Biotechnology*. Oxford: Oxford University Press.

—— (1997*a*). 'Using Evolutionary Theory to Define Systems of Innovation', in C. Edquist (ed.), *Systems of Innovation—Technology, Institutions and Organizations*. London: Pinter/Cassell, 200–22.

—— (1997*b*). 'Coevolution in Commercial Genetic Engineering', *Industrial and Corporate Change*, 6/3: 503–32.

—— (2001*a*). 'The Economic Dynamics of Software: Three Competing Business Models Exemplified through Microsoft, Netscape and Linux', *Economics of Innovation and New Technology*, 11: 127–64.

—— (2001*b*). 'Network-based Dynamics: Does Linux Represent a Real Competitor to Microsoft?', in R. Coombs, K. Green, V. Walsh, and A. Richards (eds.), *Demands, Markets, Users and Innovation*. Cheltenham: Edward Elgar.

—— (2001*c*). 'Internet Entrepreneurship: Linux and Open Source Software', Discussion Paper at CRIC (Center for Research on Innovation and Competition): University of Manchester. www.les1.man.ac.uk/cric.

—— (2001*d*). 'The Search for Innovations: Innovation Management in a Dynamic Selection Environment', paper presented at the 2001 DRUID Conference for Nelson & Winter. www.druid.dk.

—— and ORSENIGO, L. (2001*a*). 'Pharmaceuticals as a Sectoral System of Innovation', EU Report to the Project ESSY, European Sectoral Systems of Innovation.

—— —— (2001*b*). 'European Pharmaceuticals as a Sectoral Innovation System: Performance and National Selection Environments', paper presented at the Second EMAEE—European Meeting of Applied Evolutionary Economics, 13–15 September, 2001.

—— ——, and PAMMOLLI, F. (2003*a*). 'Pharmaceuticals seen through the Lens of a Sectoral Innovation System', in F. Malerba (ed.), *European Sectoral Systems of Innovation*. Cambridge: Cambridge University Press.

METCALFE, S. (1998). *Evolutionary Economics and Creative Destruction*. London: Routledge.

NELSON, R. (ed.) (1993). *National Systems of Innovation: A Comparative Study*. Oxford: Oxford University Press.

ORSENIGO, L., PAMMOLLI, F., and RICCABONI, M. (2001). 'Technological Change and Network Dynamics: The Case of the Bio-pharmaceutical Industry', *Research Policy*, 30/3: 485–508.

PAVITT, K. (1990). 'What Makes Basic Research Economically Useful?', *Research Policy*, 20: 109–19.

—— (1998). 'Technologies, Products and Organisation in the Innovating Firm: What Adam Smith tells us and Joseph Schumpeter doesn't', *Industrial and Corporate Change*, 7: 433–52.

Powell, W. W. and Smith-Doerr, L. (2000). 'Networks and Economic Life', in N. Smelser and R. Swedberg (eds.), *The Handbook of Economic Sociology*. Princeton, NJ: Princeton University Press.

——, Doput, K. W., and Smith-Doerr, L. (1996). 'Interorganizational Collaboration and the Locus of Innovation: Networks of Learning in Biotechnology', *Administrative Science Quarterly*, 41: 116–45.

Prencipe, A. (1997). 'Technological Competencies and Product's Evolutionary Dynamics: A Case Study from the Aero-engine Industry', *Research Policy*, 25: 1261–76.

Raymond, E. (1999). 'The Cathedral and the Bazaar'. www.tuxedo.org/esr/writings/cathedral-bazaar.

Rosenberg, N. (1990). 'Why Do Firms Do Basic Research (With Their Own Money)?', *Research Policy*, 19: 165–74.

Sawhney, M. and Prandelli, E. (2000). 'Communities of Creation: Managing Distributed Innovation in Turbulent Markets', *California Management Review*, 42/2: 24–54.

Steinmueller, W. E. (2003). 'Software as a Sectoral System of Innovation', in F. Malerba (ed.), *European Sectoral Systems of Innovation*. Cambridge: Cambridge University Press.

Tuomi, I. (2001). 'Internet, Innovation, and Open Source: Actors in the Network', *First Monday*. www.firstmonday.dk/issues/issues6_1/tuomi.

—— (2002). *Networks of Innovation: Change and Meaning in the Age of the Internet*. Oxford: Oxford University Press.

16

Integrated Solutions
The Changing Business of Systems Integration

ANDREW DAVIES

SPRU, University of Sussex, UK

16.1 Introduction

Recent literature on business strategy argues that firms should concentrate less on making stand-alone physical products and more on delivering high-value services and solutions to a customer's needs (Quinn 1992; Slywotzky 1996; Slywotzky and Morrison 1998; Hax and Wilde 1999; Sharma and Molloy 1999; Wise and Baumgartner 1999; Cornet et al. 2000; Bennett, Sharma, and Tipping 2001; Foote et al. 2001; Galbraith 2002). All of these authors argue that competitive advantage is not simply about providing services, but how services are combined with products to provide high-value 'integrated solutions' that address a customer's business or operational needs.

Although this recent trend in business strategy has attracted the attention of management consultants, business strategy authors and practitioners, with few exceptions (e.g. Hax and Wilde 1999; Galbraith 2002) there has been surprisingly little academic research on this subject. In an attempt to redress this imbalance, this chapter concentrates on the most cogent and convincingly argued case for the shift to services put forward by Wise and Baumgartner (1999). These authors argue that firms are building on their base in manufacturing and moving downstream into the provision of services and solutions to distribute, operate, maintain, and finance a product through its life cycle.

The chapter aims to test Wise and Baumgartner's claims that firms are integrating forwards into services and solutions by examining recent changes in the strategies of leading international firms. It focuses on suppliers of an important high-cost subset of capital goods called complex products and systems (CoPS), such as flight simulators (Miller et al. 1995), mobile phone networks (Davies 1997) and aero-engines (Prencipe 1997). In contrast to consumer goods industries that produce standardized products in high-volume for large final consumer markets, CoPS are produced as one-off projects or in small tailored batches to meet the particular needs of government, institutional, and business customers (Hobday 1998).

333

Systems integration is a central activity performed in supply of CoPS (Miller et al. 1995; Hobday 1998). It refers to the design and integration of products and systems out of components developed in-house or sourced from external manufacturers. The chapter draws upon original case study research undertaken during a three-year collaborative research project with five suppliers of CoPS—Alstom, Ericsson, Thales, WS Atkins, and Cable and Wireless (C&W) operating in different industries.[1] Studying these firms provides an opportunity to examine the changing business of systems integration as firms face the challenge of moving into high-value services and solutions. Rather than just adding services to existing products, the case studies demonstrate that firms are changing their strategies, occupying new positions in the value chain, and developing the capabilities to offer integrated solutions.

Drawing upon the case study evidence, the chapter argues that firms moving into integrated solutions originate from both manufacturing and services. By proposing that firms are simply moving in one direction—downstream from their manufacturing 'core' into services—Wise and Baumgartner fail to recognize the variety of moves into integrated solutions provision. Several of the case study firms—Alstom, Ericsson, and Thales—did start out as manufacturers of equipment and are going downstream into services. But the other case study firms—C&W and WS Atkins—started as service providers. While these firms are stopping short of moving upstream into making products, they are increasing their capabilities to integrate equipment sourced from external manufacturers. At the same time, they have taken over downstream activities previously handled in-house by their customers. All of these firms—whether they started as manufacturers or service providers—are gravitating towards integrated solutions from upstream and downstream positions.

To offer integrated solutions, the case study firms are developing four different sets of capabilities: systems integration, operational services, business consultancy, and financial services. To deliver different collections of products and services tailored to a customer's operational requirements, firms are developing systems integration as their core problem-solving capability. An in-depth knowledge of their customer's operational systems and the product they have designed, integrated, tested, and delivered, places systems integrators in a strong position to perform the second core capability—services to operate and maintain a product during its life cycle. In addition, firms are developing two 'outer' sets of capabilities—business consulting and financial services—to offer the entire range of services required to provide customers with complete solutions to their needs.

The chapter is divided into two sections. Section 16.1 attempts to build on Wise and Baumgartner's (1999) contribution by presenting a framework showing how suppliers of CoPS are changing their positions in the value chain to offer services and integrated solutions. Section 16.2 examines the empirical evidence for a shift to services and solutions in the five case study firms.

16.1   Explaining the Shift to Services and Integrated Solutions

Redrawing the Boundaries of the Firm: Integration Versus Specialization

One of the most important strategic choices facing a firm is deciding what activities in the value chain should be performed internally and what should be obtained from external suppliers. During the twentieth century, the large vertically integrated firm became the dominant form of organization across many technologically advanced sectors of industrialized economies (Chandler 1977, 1990). These firms grew both by organic expansion and by internalizing activities previously performed by many independent small firms operating in the market. In most cases, vertical integration was conceived as a move *backwards* along the value chain towards sources of supply to ensure a steady flow of raw materials and other inputs to production. The advantages of backwards integration were not confined to firms that produced increasingly standardized consumer goods in high volumes and lower unit costs. Suppliers of technologically complex capital goods—or CoPS—required integrated design, manufacturing, and marketing organizations to ensure that product specifications and services could be tailored and adjusted to diverse customers' needs (Chandler 1980: 24–5).

Since the late 1980s many firms have abandoned traditional backward vertical integration strategies in favour of specialization based on the division of labour. Large integrated firms have been concentrating on a few 'core activities' in the value chain where a firm can gain competitive advantage and outsourcing peripheral activities previously handled in-house (Quinn 1992; Hamel and Prahalad 1994; Domberger 1998). Specialized firms focus on performing activities where a firm has established a core capability and outsourcing their requirements for components and other inputs.

Several authors argue that trend towards outsourcing and vertical dis-integration has given rise to a new type of specialist organization whose core activity is systems integration (Rothwell 1992; Granstrand, Patel, and Pavitt 1997; Brusoni and Prencipe 2001; Dosi et al. 2003, Chapter Six, this volume; Pavitt 2003, Chapter Five, this volume; Prencipe 2003, Chapter Seven, this volume). These firms outsource detailed design and manufacture to external suppliers and contract manufacturers while maintaining in-house the systems integration capabilities necessary to coordinate a network of external suppliers. Systems integrators are more than assemblers of products, because they design and integrate internally and externally supplied components in a finished product, and coordinate and internally develop the technological knowledge needed for future generations of product.

However, an important contribution from the business strategy literature emphasizes a new trend working against specialization. Wise and Baumgartner (1999) argue that competitive success of many of the world's largest manufacturers—from General Electric (GE) and Boeing to Ford and Coca-Cola—has been built on new forms of vertical integration, conceived as a movement forwards along the value chain into services. These authors argue that rather than abandoning manufacturing, many of the world's firms are building on these core activities and moving downstream into services to maintain, finance, and operate a product during its life cycle. Wise and Baumgartner provide convincing evidence to show that as manufacturing physical products becomes less profitable, firms are attracted downstream by the opportunity of performing high value-added services.

This section focuses on Wise and Baumgartner's contribution because it offers a useful framework showing how firms are repositioning in the value chain to provide high-value services. It argues that the strategic choice facing firms is not simply whether they should take advantage of either special-ization or forwards integration. On the contrary, firms are pursuing a variety of different moves into services and solutions provision, depending on where they started out in the value chain. Despite this variety, however, firms seeking to add value by creating unique solutions for their customer must all develop their core capabilities as systems integrators.

Rethinking Business Strategy: Moving Downstream into Services

A mixture of stagnating product demand and a growing installed base of products (reflected in the accumulation of past purchases and longer life spans) is forcing economic value to migrate downstream from manu-facturing to services (Slywotzky 1996; Wise and Baumgartner 1999: 134). Regarded as the key measure of firm performance, added value is the dif-ference between the market value of a firm's output and the costs of its inputs (Porter 1985: 38; Kay 1993: 23; DTI 2002).

Revenues from downstream service activities are attractive because in many industries they represent 10–30 times the value of underlying product sales (Wise and Baumgartner 1999: 134). In other words, the purchase cost of the product represents only a fraction of the total cost of operating and maintaining it during its life cycle. For example, Ericsson estimates that equipment costs represent a small proportion—only 6 per cent—of their customer's total costs of designing, building, and operating a mobile phone network. More than 80 per cent of an operator's costs are in operation, maintenance, and network administration and these costs are spread over a 10-year period.

Besides offering new sources of revenue, downstream services tend to have higher margins and require fewer assets than product manufacturing. By expanding the scope of the product offering to include services, firms can capture life-cycle profits associated with the product and secure more continuous streams of revenue. Services represent an increasing proportion of the total revenues of many large manufacturing firms. In 2001, for example, services (43 per cent) overtook hardware and technology (42 per cent) to become IBM's largest source of revenue (Gerstner 2002: 363).

The promise of recurring revenues is attractive to suppliers of CoPS that are dependent on lumpy sources of revenues associated with the sale of high-cost products—such as rolling stock and mobile phone networks—purchased at irregular intervals. These firms are particularly vulnerable when demand for their products stagnates, suffering from shrinking revenues and profit margins. For example, mobile equipment manufacturers—such as Ericsson, Nokia, and Motorola—currently face a slump in demand for third generation (3G) mobile networks, but are developing other sources of revenue by servicing the installed base of 2G products.

Wise and Baumgartner (1999) argue that the attraction of high-value services is encouraging firms to rethink the focus of their manufacturing strategies. The traditional sources of competitive advantage in manufacturing—backwards integration, developing superior products, and scale economies—are no longer sufficient to guarantee competitive success in many industries (Slywotzky and Morrison 1998: 249; Wise and Baumgartner 1999). Increasingly firms are competing by building on their 'core manufacturing capabilities' and integrating forwards into the provision of high-value services that address each customer's needs.

Downstream Business Models

Three downstream business models identified by Wise and Baumgartner (1999: 137–9) are being adopted by suppliers of CoPS.

Embedded Services.   Digital technologies allow downstream services—such as maintenance or fault reporting—to be embedded in the physical product. By automating activities that used to be handled manually in-house, embedded services—or 'service technologies' (Quinn 1992: 6)—can reduce a customer's maintenance and operational costs. For example, Otis Elevator Company has moved downstream by developing its OtisLine service to coordinate its national maintenance activities. A computer control centre operated by highly trained staff receives information about repairs directly from the lift itself through microprocessors and software. By automating activities previously done manually, OtisLine reduces maintenance costs, lowers error detection rates, and provides valuable information on usage patterns to guide improvements in future designs (Quinn 1992: 181).

Comprehensive Services.   Downstream services that cannot be embedded in the product are provided as comprehensive services to finance, operate, and maintain a product through its life cycle. For example, as well as designing and manufacturing jet engines, GE's jet service division performs maintenance, supplies spare parts, and also offers to service other manufacturers' equipment (Slywotzky and Morrison 1998: 86). Instead of viewing the provision of services—such as spare parts or maintenance—as a way of securing orders for future products, firms are now viewing the product sale as a way of opening the door to the provision of future services. By developing strong relationships with profitable customers, suppliers can become the preferred partner of choice for services provided through the product life cycle. But customer allegiance has to be maintained on an ongoing basis by providing services that minimize the costs of owning and using the product.

Integrated Solutions.   One of the most innovative downstream moves identified by Wise and Baumgartner (1999) and a number of authors (Slywotzky 1996; Slywotzky and Morrison 1998; Hax and Wilde 1999; Sharma and Molloy 1999; Cornet et al. 2000; Bennett, Sharma, and Tipping 2001; Foote et al. 2001; Galbraith 2002) is to provide products and services together as integrated solutions that address a customer's needs. Several of the world's leading manufacturers—IBM, GE, and ASEA Brown Boveri (ABB)—pioneered the move into services in the early 1990s and were among the first firms to create the integrated solutions business models that other suppliers of CoPS are now emulating. For example, GE expanded its financial services division, GE Capital, to offer financial services as a part of an integrated solution package—combining products, maintenance, service, and financing—that its customers required (Slywotzky and Morrison 1998: 82). In 2002, GE Capital accounted for 49 per cent of the firm's total revenues.

Integrated solutions add value by providing different collections of products and services that create unique benefits for each customer. To meet a customer's needs for products and services from a single source—or as a 'one-stop-shop'—solutions providers must take over the risks and responsibilities for performing activities previously handled in-house by their customers and create innovative ways for components to work together as a whole to increase the overall value of the solution for the customer. Integrated solutions providers earn high profits when the value of the integrated package exceeds the value of individual components.

As several authors argue, providing solutions that address a customer's needs means that firms have to view the value chain through the eyes of the customer (Slywotzky and Morrison 1998: 18; Wise and Baumgartner 1999: 135; Galbraith 2002). Under the traditional product-centric approach to value creation, manufacturers have focused their efforts on making a physical product, selling, and delivering it. Beyond basic technical support and short-term warranties, after the product was 'handed over the wall' to the customer, the manufacturer largely forgot about it and the customer took over responsibility for operating, maintaining, and financing it.

Adopting customer-centric thinking means that firms have to rethink how value is created from the perspective of their customers. This involves gaining a detailed understanding of the activities a customer performs in using and operating a product through its life cycle, from sale to decommissioning (Slywotzky and Morrison 1998: 18; Wise and Baumgartner 1999: 135; Cornet et al. 2000; Prahalad and Ramaswamy 2000; Foote et al. 2001; Galbraith 2002). Engaging in a close dialogue with their customers, suppliers have to identify their customer's needs and priorities and then develop the capabilities to offer products, services, and solutions that link uniquely well to a customer's requirements. ABB was among the first firms to adopt a customer-centric approach. During the 1980s, ABB's local customer-facing profit centres became responsible for listening to their customers, identifying their needs for industrial, transportation, and power systems, and providing solutions to match with products and services from ABB's global network of specialized suppliers (Slywotzky and Morrison 1998: 243).

The Specificity of CoPS

Wise and Baumgartner (1999) help to explain the generic moves into services pursued by manufacturing firms across industries. But they fail to consider how the nature and types of services—provided either separately or as complements to a product—are shaped by the specific characteristics of the physical product. In other words, services and solutions differ across industries. Building on previous cross-sectoral research (Hobday 1998), a comparison with consumer goods serves to highlight the distinctiveness of services provided in CoPS.

Services in CoPS

As CoPS are high-cost, customized goods configured to meet the needs of large business, institutional, and government customers, the services provided as complements to the product differ from low-cost, mass-produced commodity goods comprised of standardized components. Compared with the set menu of low-cost, standardized services offered with consumer goods, services in CoPS:

- are customized to meet each buyer's unique needs;
- allow greater scope (range of services) and intensity of services per unit (product) of output;
- provide higher margins and recurring revenue streams during—often exceptionally—long product life cycles;
- occur before, during, and after a product is delivered to the customer.

These characteristics of service provision reflect the particular nature of product design, production, and use in CoPS. Market structures in CoPS tend to be bilateral duopolies or oligopolies: a small number of suppliers provide high-value goods and services to a few large customers. As opposed to arm's-length transactions associated with the sale of consumer goods, suppliers of CoPS are engaged in long-term business-to-business transactions with their customers. This provides opportunities to offer a range of customized services that address a buyer's needs throughout the product life cycle, from product conception through production to decommissioning.

In consumer goods, services are provided after the product has been sold to the final consumer, such as consumer credit facilities, maintenance contracts, short-term warranties, and other forms of after-sales services. Depending on their needs, each customer selects one or more services from a standardized portfolio of pre-existing services offerings. In CoPS, services provided after the product has been handed over to the customer are developed specifically to address each customer's unique requirements. For example, Alstom Transport established a specialized organization dedicated to maintaining the fleet of trains operating on the London Underground's Northern Line for the duration of a 20-year contract. Suppliers have to understand all the activities a customer performs in operating a product so that services can be tailored to support different stages of a long product life cycle.

Since Wise and Baumgartner assume that services are provided only after the product has been handed over to the customer, they fail to recognize that many services offered by suppliers of CoPS are provided much earlier before and during the making of the product.[2] These design-and-build activities are undertaken by temporary project-based organizations undertaken in-house or by multi-firm alliances comprised of subcontractors, suppliers, and customers (Hobday 2000: 873). Systems integrators and prime contractors are responsible for managing projects and engaging with the customer, but rely on internal and external contractors for specialized services—such as project management, engineering, design, and technical consultancy—often provided during different phases in the project life cycle (Gann and Salter 2000). These phases include the pre-bid negotiations with a customer; the bid to contract phase; and the project implementation phase involving conceptual design and detailed design, integration and testing, and handover to the customer.

In addition to these services, the recent demand for integrated solutions has encouraged suppliers of CoPS to develop the capabilities to offer business consultancy and financial services, which are particularly important in the front-end pre-bid phase. Business consultancy services are now being offered by CoPS suppliers to provide customers with advice on how to plan, design, build, and finance the purchase of a product as well as maintain and operate it. Customers differ in the intensity of their needs for consultancy services during the project life cycle. The lower the level of a customer's capabilities, the earlier they will require services from their suppliers.

Customers with limited technical experience may require partnerships as early as the pre-bid phase to discuss business plans, user requirements, and conceptual solutions, prior to specifying and integrating systems. More experienced customers may only request support at later stages.

Financial services play a vital role in the negotiation phase when customers require assistance with financing the purchase of high-cost products. For example, ABB's financial services division—formed in 1983—offers value-sharing contracts which lower the purchase price of a product in return for a proportion of the future value generated during its operation. ABB is paid in part by sharing in the efficiency that it creates for the customer. Value-sharing contracts provide an opportunity for ABB to engage in strategic discussions with its customers during the negotiation stage and can 'open doors to a host of projects that might otherwise have been unavailable to ABB' (Slywotzky and Morrison 1998: 245).

Integrated Solutions in CoPS

The provision of integrated solutions also differs across consumer and CoPS industries. In consumer goods, an integrated solution is typically provided as a 'bundle' of products and services. This means that customers are provided with the same standardized package, or bundle, of products and services at a single price, irrespective of their differences in needs or capabilities (Porter 1985: 425). For example, in the early 1980s, IBM sold low-cost, standardized bundles of personal computer hardware, software, and service support.

In CoPS, bundling is valued by less sophisticated buyers or customers who want the convenience of having a supplier take responsibility for everything. Porter (1985) cites the example of Cessna, the business aircraft manufacturer, which offered corporate customers a bundle at a single price including a plane, maintenance, pilots, a hangar, office space, and landing fees (Porter 1985: 431). More sophisticated buyers of CoPS, on the other hand, are less receptive to bundling because they want to integrate the bundle themselves, they require different collections of products and services, or because they differ in their intensity and needs for various products and services.

To address the different needs and capabilities of their customers, providers of integrated solutions in CoPS typically follow a strategy of 'mixed bundling', offering a customer the option of purchasing either the whole bundle or parts of it from a single source. For example, IT vendors such as IBM and Sun Microsystems offer solutions that allow each corporate customer to select the level of service that addresses its needs, ranging from individual packages to full solutions, encompassing all aspects of a customer's IT requirements, from designing and integrating systems to managing and running computers.

Value-adding Activities in CoPS

To understand how services fit into the supply of CoPS, it is necessary to identify the value-adding activities involved in making, delivering, and using a product to provide services to the final consumer. The analysis of the value chain in Wise and Baumgartner's framework is concerned with how an 'individual firm' can manage upstream and downstream activities to that firm's advantage. To understand how value is added within an 'industry', this chapter adopts the more accurate metaphor of the 'value stream' to refer to the entire set of value-adding activities in the life cycle of a specific product or service, running from raw materials to the final consumer (Womack and Jones 1996: 314).[3]

Moving downstream to gain control of profitable distribution activities—Wise and Baumgartner's fourth downstream business model—is particularly important in consumer goods such as cars, domestic appliances, and soft drinks.[4] Whereas manufacturers in these industries traditionally earned profits by offering consumer credit and maintenance contracts, these high-margin activities are increasingly performed by distributors. Large distributors or retailers are able to use their control over the final channel to the customer to exert purchasing power over their upstream suppliers and to gain customer loyalty. To prevent this erosion of their profitability, some consumer goods suppliers are attempting to move downstream to control channels to the final consumer. For example, Ford has recently transformed its traditional car distribution model by gaining control of dealerships, acquiring a leading car parts and service chain, and developing stronger links with the car buyer of the vehicle life span.

Distribution control is less important in CoPS where suppliers sell directly to large customers in oligopolistic markets. Manufacturers of railway and mobile networks equipment, for example, do not face 'channel' conflicts as they move downstream because they already have direct relationships with their customers—railway and mobile phone operators. They may, however, face conflicts with their customers if they move too aggressively into the buyer's territory, or move without prior agreement.

In some CoPS industries, however, suppliers are prevented from moving downstream because they sell their products through independent firms that control the channels to market. In the business IT and telecom markets, for example, business consultancy organizations—such as Accenture—use their scale and global reputation to exploit and control channels to the business user. To overcome channel conflicts as they move downstream, firms can either develop partnerships with channel controllers or buy the channel. For example, to consolidate its control over channels to global business customers, IBM recently expanded its Global Services division—responsible for business consulting and outsourcing—by acquiring Price WaterhouseCoopers.

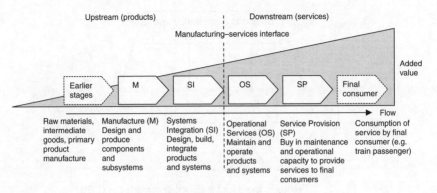

Fig. 16.1 The value stream in CoPS

To account for the distinctive activities performed in CoPS, previous research has identified four main stages in the value stream of a typical CoPS industry, as depicted in Figure 16.1 (Davies et al. 2001). Each CoPS industry may have fewer or more stages in the life cycle of a product. The outputs of one value-adding stage are the inputs of the next. Value accumulates at each stage to make up the overall value stream. Each of these stages in the value stream is progressively closer to the final consumer, such as the railway passenger. The stages include:

1. *Manufacture.* The first stage is responsible for taking raw materials and subassemblies and transforming them into physical components and subsystems that are manufactured to meet an overall system design.
2. *Systems integration.* The second stage adds value through the design and integration of physical components—product hardware, software, and embedded services—that have to work together as a whole in a finished product.[5] Systems integrators are responsible for managing numerous in-house or external contractors responsible for the design and manufacture of components that comprise a system.
3. *Operational services.* In the next stage, an operator or business user runs and maintains a system to provide services, such as a corporate telecom network, baggage handling, flight simulation training, and train services.
4. *Service provision.* In some industries services are provided to the final consumer through intermediary organizations—called service providers. These firms buy in the system capacity they require from external operators and concentrate on brand, marketing, distribution, and customer care activities.

The four stages can be illustrated by the example of mobile communications in the mid-1990s. Suppliers like Ericsson and Nokia were primarily manufacturers of equipment, supplying mobile phone operators with the

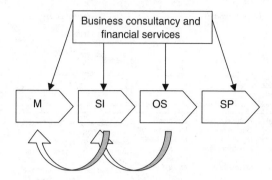

Fig. 16.2 Feedback loops and supporting activities in CoPS

equipment (e.g. base stations, transmission equipment, and switches) required to build a mobile network. At the time, mobile operators had sufficient expertise to perform systems integration in-house. By the late 1990s, a new type of service provider had entered the market. As a so-called 'mobile virtual network provider', Virgin Mobile focuses on developing its subscriber base through brand image, advertising and customer care activities while buying in network capacity from another operator to carry its radio communications traffic.

Rather than a simple linear step-by-step process, adding value involves a series of dynamic feedback loops and iterations between later and earlier stages of product development (Hobday 1998: 694), as shown in Figure 16.2. Systems integrators ensure that manufacturers in an earlier stage of production are able to produce components as integrated packages that conform to an overall design. Through 'learning by using' (Rosenberg 1982), operators and service providers can identify opportunities to improve system performance and feedback lessons learnt into the design of future products. Besides these main value-adding stages, financial services, business consulting, and other services support and underpin the creation of value by providing inputs at different stages up and down the stream.

The line dividing the two segments into upstream and downstream stages corresponds to the traditional manufacturing–services distinction. These segments face different business problems, operate in different market environments and require different organizations and capabilities. Upstream stages add value to the physical product through technology development and manufacture, understanding their customers' requirements, managing projects, and performing systems integration. Downstream stages add value by performing intangible, service-based activities such as managing and maintaining system operations, customer care, advertising, billing, branding, marketing, and other service activities.

Changing Boundaries in the Value Stream

Since the mid-1990s, the traditional boundary between upstream suppliers and downstream customers continues to be redrawn. Buyers of CoPS are focusing on the provision of services to the final consumer and outsourcing non-core activities. Intangible services such as reputation, brand, billing, and marketing are now regarded as more central to the competitive success of these customers than designing, building, or maintaining the systems on which their services depend. To meet this demand, suppliers are undertaking systems integration and operational activities previously performed as part of their customer's business. In full outsourcing solutions, this includes the transfer of assets and staff to supplier firms. Buyers of CoPS are entering into long-term partnerships with their suppliers to ensure that providers of solutions share the risks of performing outsourced activities.

The process of customer outsourcing in CoPS has been accelerated by the liberalization and privatization of former state-controlled sectors, such as telecoms and railways. A variety of customers with different needs and capabilities now operate in competitive markets. Experienced customers (e.g. incumbent operators like Vodafone) often want to perform a broader range of activities in-house. Less sophisticated customers with limited in-house capabilities (e.g. virtual network providers like Virgin Mobile) tend to rely on suppliers for complete solutions to their needs.

Suppliers in the United Kingdom are being encouraged to move downstream by increasing use of private finance in public sector projects. Under the Private Finance Initiative (PFI), introduced in 1992, private sector companies 'design, build, finance, and operate' public sector projects, ranging from schools to complex weapons systems. Under the policy of public–private partnership (PPP), adopted in 1997, public projects are financed partly by private firms, while the state shares some of the risk. PFI and PPP suppliers perform all the activities along the value from systems integration to services provision, as well as financing and business consultancy services.

Although Wise and Baumgartner—as well as other business strategy authors like Slywotzky and Morrison (1998)—identify the downstream trend towards customer outsourcing and forwards integration, they fail to recognize important changes taking place upstream in core manufacturing activities. Since the early 1990s, many large vertically integrated manufacturers across consumer and CoPS industries have been outsourcing a large part of their manufacturing activities, coordinating a network of external component suppliers, and concentrating on performing systems integration (Brusoni, Prencipe, and Pavitt 2001; Prencipe 2003, Chapter Seven, this volume; Pavitt 2003, Chapter Five, this volume).[6] Flight simulation is an early example of the growing importance of systems integration in CoPS. Whereas flight simulator manufacturers traditionally manufactured 70 per cent of the components in the final product, by the mid-1990s these firms were concentrating on performing systems integration and obtaining up to 70 per cent of their components from external manufacturers (Miller et al. 1995).

A new breed of contract manufacturers like Flextronics and specialized component suppliers are growing by making components and products for systems integrators. Often these firms work as partners with systems integrators, supplying critical hardware, software, and services in an overall solution. By effective outsourcing and managing of upstream manufacturers, firms benefit from specializing in systems integration because these activities require fewer assets and generate higher margins than product manufacturing.

Wise and Baumgartner and much of the business strategy literature fails to recognize that a capability in systems integration—rather than broad-based manufacturing—is essential to the provision of solutions. Systems integrators ensure that the value of the solution for the customer is greater than the sum of its parts. They remove the need for the customer to assemble or integrate the products and services that comprise a solution and take responsibility for negotiating with multiple suppliers of a solution's component parts—hardware, software, and services. Because systems integrators have an in-depth knowledge of their customers' operational needs as well as the products they have designed, they are best placed to provide services to monitor, operate, maintain, finance, and support a product.

As a result of the trend for buyers of CoPS to outsource systems integration, this activity is increasingly being undertaken by two contrasting types of firms, or 'hybrid' organizations combining attributes of each:

- *Vertically-integrated* manufacturers that design and integrate components sourced from in-house product divisions, and provide services tied to internally developed technologies and products;
- *Specialized* systems integrators that provide services to design, integrate, and service components and products manufactured by external suppliers.

Since the mid-1990s, however, many vertically integrated manufacturers now provide systems integration as a service by offering to install components and products supplied by their competitors. For example, traditionally IBM's services were offered to maintain and operate IBM equipment. To provide the best solution for its customer, IBM now offers systems integration services to design, integrate, and run systems supplied by major IBM competitors, such as Hewlett-Packard and Sun Microsystems (Gerstner 2002: 130).

The changing boundaries of activities performed by suppliers and customers in the CoPS value stream raise questions about the focus of a firm's activities and its core capabilities. Several authors argue that firms develop distinctive, or core, capabilities to perform activities where they started out in the industry and create organizations that fit their particular industries and value-adding stage (Penrose 1959; Richardson 1972). More recent research has shown how firms tend to grow and diversify along paths set by their original core capabilities (Teece and Pisano 1994).

In other words, there is a 'centre of gravity' in the value stream arising from a firm's initial success in the industry in which it grew up (Galbraith 1983: 316). Firms can be in the same industry but have different centres of gravity—or core capabilities—because of their different starting positions, experiences, and initial successes. Slywotzky and Morrison (1998: 19) argue that as a firm succeeds by learning to provide solutions that address customer needs, its centre of gravity moves closer to the customer. As we will see in the next section, a firm's centre of gravity 'establishes a base from which subsequent strategic changes take place' (Galbraith 1983: 319). But a centre-of-gravity shift of this kind is difficult to accomplish without challenging the current power structure, rejecting traditional ways of thinking and parts of the old culture, creating new organizations, and establishing new capabilities.

16.2   The Shift to Services and Solutions in CoPS: Case Study Evidence

This section uses the value stream framework to examine the empirical evidence for a shift to the provision of high-value services and integrated solutions in CoPS. It draws upon the findings of the first year of a large 3-year collaborative research project involving the case studies of five international suppliers of CoPS:

- Alstom Transport—rolling stock and signalling systems
- Ericsson Mobile Systems—mobile phone networks
- Thales Training and Simulation—flight simulation
- WS Atkins—infrastructure and the built environment
- C&W Global Markets—corporate telecom networks.

Research Method

A case study method was chosen to examine strategic decisions to move into the provision of services and solutions, to occupy new positions in the value stream, and to develop the capabilities required to perform the new activities. The case studies provide a fruitful source of comparison because the firms operate in different industries and perform a range of different activities in the manufacturing and services segments of the value stream. In-depth interviews with up to ten senior managers and engineering directors in each of the five firms were conducted in 2000. This provided an opportunity to study the key motivations and drivers encouraging the firms to adopt services-led strategies. The managers were asked to describe and explain strategic changes in the focus of each firm's activities between 1995 and 2000. This was followed, during the period 2001–2 by in-depth analyses of the overall business organization as well as two major projects in each of the firms to verify the extent and nature of any moves towards services and solutions.

The cross-sectoral sample of firms was designed to examine the differences and similarities in firm strategies across industries. Here we summarize the overall 'headline' findings (for further detail, see Davies et al. 2001). Because of the limited number of firms analysed, the research findings can only be expected to raise hypotheses for further testing by empirical research about the nature of these activities and patterns of behaviour exhibited by firms moving into services and integrated solutions.

Each firm has made successive changes in strategy and altered its position in the value stream to move into the provision of high-value services. While several of the firms started out by adding services to an existing product range, the empirical evidence summarized in Table 16.1 shows that by 2000 all five firms were creating new business models for integrated solutions provision. Rather than simply moving downstream, our research shows that firms occupying the high-value space of integrated solutions provision originate from both manufacturing and services.

Moving From a Base in Manufacturing

Several of the case study firms moving into services and integrated solutions provision have moved downstream from a traditional base in manufacturing. As their traditional centre-of-gravity stage in the value stream—making physical products—has become less profitable, Alstom, Ericsson, and Thales have outsourced a growing proportion of their manufacturing activities and integrated forwards in the value stream (see Figure 16.3). These firms are focusing on becoming systems integrators and providers of services to operate, maintain, and finance products.

(a) Alstom Transport.   Within the diversified Alstom group—one of the world's largest energy and transportation infrastructure manufacturers—the Alstom Transport division undertakes train and signalling system design, manufacture, build and after-care services. Since the mid-1990s, Alstom has been evolving from a 'seller of goods to a system and service provider' (Owen 1997). It outsources up to 90 per cent of components in rolling stock products, but continues to design and produce critical subsystems such as traction systems. Systems integration and after-sales services are becoming an increasingly important source of value added for the firm.

Changes in the UK railway market provided the catalyst behind Alstom's move into services. The break up of British Rail in 1993 led to a growing demand for maintenance outsourcing contracts. In 1998, a Service Business

TABLE 16.1 *The shift to integrated solutions*

Company	Traditional product or service focus (1995)	Integrated solutions (2000)
Alstom Transport—railways	Products • subsystems (e.g. propulsion, traction, drive, electronic information systems) • rolling stock • signalling and train control systems	Transport solutions (e.g. 'train availability'): • systems integrator—turnkey solutions for project management, fixed infrastructure, and finance • services for maintenance, renovation, parts replacement, and service products—'Total Train-Life Management'
Ericsson—mobile communications systems	Products • mobile handsets • mobile system • Subsystem products: radio base stations, base station controllers, mobile switches, operating systems, and customer databases	Turnkey solutions to design, build, and operate mobile phone networks: • mobile systems—complete supplier, systems integrator, and partner • global services—services and business consulting to support a customer's network operations
Thales Training & Simulation—flight simulation	Products—stand-alone flight simulators for commercial and military aircraft	Training solutions (e.g. 'pay as you train'): Training services: networked training; independent training centres; and synthetic training environments.

TABLE 16.1 *Continued*

Company	Traditional product or service focus (1995)	Integrated solutions (2000)
WS Atkins—infrastructure and the built environment	Engineering consultancy, project management, and technical services for infrastructure projects	Integrated solutions for the built environment: • The design, build, finance, and operation of infrastructure across industrial sectors • Total solutions for industry (TS4i) provides one-stop-shop for design, construction, maintenance, and finance
Cable & Wireless Global Markets—Corporate networks	Provides 'managed network services' for multinational corporations: • network design • supply telecom infrastructure and applications • network management	Global outsourcing solutions for a multinational corporation's entire telecom and IT needs on a global basis: • network design • supplies telecom infrastructure and applications • network management • ownership of the network • network operation • business process applications • service level agreements

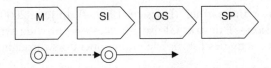

Fig. 16.3 Forward integration: Alstom, Ericsson, and Thales

was created as a result of a strategic review of Alstom's global activities, which recognized the huge growth in the market for rolling stock maintenance services, particularly in the United Kingdom. Alstom offers comprehensive services to maintain rolling stock—functions previously conducted by national railway monopolies.

Besides these contracts for specific services, Alstom provides its customers—UK training operating companies—with complete transport solutions for 'train availability' during the life cycle of the product. In 1995, for example, Alstom won the PFI contract to renew the train fleet on London Underground's Northern Line. Rather than specify the size of the total fleet, the contract only required that ninety-nine trains be available for service each day, for the duration of a 20-year contract. To achieve the customer's targets for train availability, Alstom has built 106 trains and set up a maintenance organization to service them.

(b) Ericsson. Since the late 1980s, Ericsson has moved from being a broad-based manufacturer of public telecoms equipment to focus on one high-growth product segment: the mobile communications market. By 1999, 40 per cent of the world's subscribers were connected to Ericsson's system (Ericsson 1999: 46).

In 1996, Ericsson's Corporate Executive Committee completed the largest planning study in the firm's history. The report, '2005—Ericsson entering the twenty-first century', lays the foundations for Ericsson's current strategy to create an organization which provides mobile operators with 'solutions and services' (Ericsson 1996: 7). The report recognized that deregulation and more competition in telecom markets is forcing operators to move closer to the final consumer in the value stream. Operators are concentrating on supplying competitive services to end-users and asking their suppliers to assume greater responsibility for network design, build, and operations.

As a result of this strategic decision, Ericsson is moving away from its manufacturing heartland into higher value-added services. A growing proportion of Ericsson's products—including exchange equipment, 3G radio base stations and mobile handsets—are now outsourced and manufactured under contract by Flextronics. In 1999, Ericsson combined its resources in service offerings and business consulting activities to create Ericsson Services, 'thus strengthening Ericsson's position as complete supplier, system integrator and partner' (Ericsson 1999: 7). In June 2000, Ericsson set up a new division—Ericsson Global Services—to provide systems integration and service activities for mobile phone operators throughout the world.

(c) Thales Training and Simulation.   As a leading international supplier of simulation systems and training services, Thales Training and Simulation is part of the aerospace business of Thales—one of Europe's largest defence and electronics manufacturers.

In the defence sector, Thales recently changed its strategy in flight simulation markets to focus on being a systems integrator and provider of flight training services. Until the 1990s, Thales supplied its defence customers—mainly military air forces and departments of defence—with stand-alone full flight simulators, as well as computer-based training devices. Thales designed, manufactured, and integrated key components in the final product and its customers used simulators to train pilots. By 2000, however, Thales had outsourced much of its manufacturing activities in order to focus on systems integration. It is working closely with a network of component suppliers to ensure that products are tailored exactly to a customer's requirements.

Thales Defence is taking over responsibility for pilot training and other services previously performed by its military customers. In the words of the vice chairman of Thales, 'Whereas a few years ago you could sell a unit and walk away, generating a profit now depends more on selling services, selling hours on simulator services' (Mulholland 2000). Thales provides military customers with simulators and training services as 'training solutions'. In a shift away from one-off product sales, the firm is tapping into a more continuous source of revenues by providing services to operate simulators and train pilots during the 20–25-year life cycle of a simulator.

However, in civil markets for flight simulators, attempts to move downstream into services have been prevented by the specialized independent training schools which purchase simulators and control channels to market. Performing a role similar to distributors in consumer goods, these training schools have resisted attempts by Thales and other producers to enter the training market. As major airlines have outsourced training, it has been the training schools—rather than simulator producers—which have taken on the training tasks, despite the efforts of Thales and other producers to move into training services.

Moving From a Base in Services

The other two case study firms moving into integrated solutions started from a base in services—C&W as a telecom operator and WS Atkins as a specialized provider of design engineering consultancy services. While both firms are offering an increasing range of downstream services, they are also strengthening their upstream capabilities as integrators of systems using components sourced from external manufacturers.

(a) C&W Global Markets   In the mid-1990s, C&W was a leading international telecom operator providing services to consumer and business markets. In 1998, C&W Global Businesses were created to focus on meeting the highly profitable business demand for internet protocol (IP) and data services. At the heart of this organization is Global Markets, a systems integrator organization which designs and integrates corporate networks, using equipment developed in close cooperation with external manufacturers (e.g. Nortel and Cisco Systems) and network facilities provided in-house. By 2000, C&W's strategy was reformulated in terms of a plan to move from its base as an operator of global telecom networks into the provision of 'total integrated solutions' to its multinational corporate customers needs for voice, data, and IP services.

Demand for integrated solutions first arose in 1997 when some of C&W's largest multinational customers—such as Standard Charter Bank, Andersen Consulting, Chase Manhattan, and Compaq—began to ask for more complex, high-value, outsourcing solutions for their entire telecom and IT needs. Rather than face the difficulties of negotiating with numerous operators in different countries themselves, these customers wanted an external supplier to provide a single point of contact for their end-to-end global IT and telecoms requirements. In global outsourcing contracts, C&W takes over responsibility for network ownership and service performance for a fixed contract period and a fixed price.

To meet its customers' demands, David Sexton, Chief Executive of Global Markets, recognized that 'suppliers must redefine their role as value-generating integrators, rather than low-cost component suppliers' (C&W 1999: 5). To achieve this, C&W has increased the range of activities it performs along the value stream (see Figure 16.4). This has involved moving backwards by developing its systems integration capabilities to design and install different systems—voice, data, and IP—supplied by competing manufacturers, as these are often requested by its customers. At the same time, C&W is integrating forwards by taking over outsourced customer activities, such as e-commerce, security, application software provision, and other business processes. To provide overall solutions to a customer's needs C&W has been seeking to enter into partnerships with large business

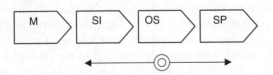

Fig. 16.4 Backward and forward integration. C&W

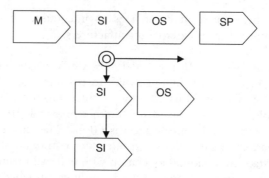

Fig. 16.5 Specialized solutions provider: WS Atkins

consultancy organizations—such as Accenture and PriceWaterhouse Coopers—which undertake the most profitable activities by controlling channels to the business user.

(b) WS Atkins. WS Atkins is a provider of project management, technical consultancy, and support services across sectors as diverse as transport, property management, defence, and public health. During the 1990s, WS Atkins diversified from its original base as a highly specialized design engineering and technical consultancy into the provision of a broader range of systems integration services and outsourcing solutions. WS Atkins is adding value for its customers by specializing in the provision of integrated solutions and selling its services to customers operating in diverse industries (see Figure 16.5).

Growing rapidly by horizontal integration, WS Atkins has filled gaps in its portfolio of systems integration capabilities by recruiting people and acquiring complementary businesses in related industries. In the late 1990s, for example, WS Atkins Rail acquired expertise and complementary technologies by purchasing British Rail's Powertrack Unit, NTES (rolling stock design), Opal (signalling), and Adtranz's signalling business. From this base, the firm has moved into operational services by acquiring firms offering specialized services such as facilities management and property services.

Through its involvement in the Channel Tunnel project in the 1980s, WS Atkins learnt about a new type of privately financed build-own-operate-transfer (BOOT) project which would become widespread in the 1990s. Under BOOT, a private contractor takes the lead in financing, building, owning and operating, and transferring back the completed facility. During the 1990s, WS Atkins capitalized on its Channel Tunnel experience by winning a large number of privately financed contracts under the UK government's PFI and PPP schemes. The firm's growth was also fuelled by business customer demand for outsourcing and support services. By 1999,

55 per cent of the firm's staff were involved in meeting demand for out-sourcing solutions and this activity accounted for 59 per cent of the firm's operating profit (WS Atkins 1999: 9).

Under a strategic review in 1998, WS Atkins was reorganized to meet customer demands for long-term contracts that entail the provision of 'an increasing range of services' (WS Atkins 1999: 6). The firm's strategic vision is to be a customer-focused, service-based organization which is 'the world's first choice supplier for technical services and integrated solutions for the built environment' (WS Atkins 1999: 4). In April 1999, the group was reorganized again to focus on the provision of integrated solutions across three consolidated UK national business streams—Property, Transport and Management & Industry.

Building Capabilities to Deliver Integrated Solutions

The case studies show that firms are pursuing a variety of paths—whether starting out from a base in manufacturing or services—into the provision of integrated solutions. This section outlines the different sets of integrated solutions capabilities being developed by the case study firms, as summarized in Table 16.2.

Systems Integration

To provide customers with physical products that can easily be deployed with services as part of a solution to a customer's needs, the five case study firms are developing their systems integration capabilities. All three manufacturing firms—Alstom, Ericsson, and Thales—are outsourcing a large proportion of component manufacture to focus on being systems integrators. Traditionally, these firms designed and integrated systems using in-house developed components. By the late 1990s, Alstom and Ericsson had developed the capability to offer systems integration as an external service using equipment supplied by their competitors. Alstom is able to design and build rolling stock supplied by its competitors, Bombardier and Systems. Similarly, Ericsson can design and integrate so-called 'multi-vendor systems'—networks composed of several manufacturers' equipment—supplied by other leading competitors, such as Nokia, Siemens, and Lucent Technologies.

As service providers with no in-house manufacturing facilities, C&W and WS Atkins are pure systems integrators. Performing little or no technology development in-house, these firms specialize in providing systems integration services using components sourced from external manufacturers. C&W is developing partnerships with new 'best-of-breed' IP suppliers such as Nortel and Cisco Systems to provide corporate customers with systems that C&W designs, installs, maintains, and supports. WS Atkins designs and

TABLE 16.2 *Capabilities of integrated solutions providers*

Company	Systems integration	Operational services	Business consulting	Financing
Alstom Transport	Designs and builds trains and signalling systems, using equipment developed in-house or externally. Acts as prime contractor in large turnkey projects	Maintains, upgrades, and operates trains	Consultancy-based approach to meet customer needs	Vendor financing and asset management
Ericsson	Designs, manufactures, and integrates mobile phone systems, using equipment developed in-house or externally (e.g. 'multi-vendor' systems)	Maintains, supports, upgrades, and operates mobile networks	Two business consultancy organizations to meet needs of Ericsson and external customers	Considering, but not yet offering vendor financing
Thales Training & Simulation	Design and integration of flight simulators. Coordination of external contractors for component supply	Provides services to train pilots and manages simulator building facilities. Joint venture with GE Capital Training	Consultancy organization to meet customer needs	Revenue sharing agreement for simulators, for example split between TT&S and United Airlines

WS Atkins	Designs and integrates external manufacturers equipment across diverse sectors, such as railway and baggage handling systems	Maintains, operates, and provides services to end-users, for example, setting up independent service provider to design, build, finance, and operate baggage handling services	Consultancy-based approach to meet customer needs	Created joint-venture company, TS4i, with Royal Bank of Scotland to provide integrated solutions for design, construction, maintenance, and finance
C&W Global Markets	Co-ordination of external contractors for component supply. Designs and integrates networks using externally supplied equipment. Developing capability to integrate internet and IT systems. Co-ordination of external contractors for component supply	Designs, builds, operates, and manages a global customer's IT and telecom needs	Consultancy-based approach to meet customer needs	Sometimes takes on responsibility for ownership of networks for duration of contract

project manages the integration of systems supplied by external manu-facturers across diverse sectors. For example, its railway division—WS Atkins Rail—buys and integrates equipment from Alstom, Bombardier, and Siemens as well as more specialized suppliers.

The range of activities performed by systems integrators is increasing as a result of customer demands for turnkey solutions. Under contracts for turnkey solutions, the supplier is responsible for the entire set of activities involved in the design, integration, construction, testing, and delivery of a fully functioning system. All the customer has to do is turn a key. If other products, services, or capabilities are required to provide complete solutions to a customer's needs, systems integrators cooperate with partners in joint ventures or consortiums to carry out those portions of the work. For example, Alstom Transport has established its Systems business unit to integrate components, subsystems and services developed internally or externally by partners in a consortium. By combining skills in project management, systems integration, financial engineering, fixed infra-structure, and civil engineering, the Systems business is able to provide track infrastructure, rolling stock, and signalling systems as a single turnkey package.

Operational Services—Embedded and Comprehensive

The provision of operational services is the second set of core capabilities for integrated solutions. Suppliers are building on their base in systems integration and crossing the boundary into the provision of—embedded and comprehensive—services to maintain, renovate, and operate products. Alstom and Ericsson both offer high-value embedded services. Alstom has developed a train management system to monitor faults on the fleet of Pendolino trains operated by Virgin Trains. Supported by this remotely controlled system, the driver and operator can solve problems in real time while the train is in operation. Ericsson provides a 24-h software-controlled network management service to provide real-time improvements in performance and reliability of a customer's mobile phone network.

All five firms offer comprehensive services to manage, maintain, and operate a product through its life cycle from sale to de-commissioning. Some firms—Alstom and Ericsson—have set up new divisions to provide these services. For example, Alstom's Service Business unit offers services—which it calls 'Total Train-Life Management'—to capture value created during all stages in the operating life cycle of a train, such as maintenance, renovation, spare parts, and asset management. The typical life cycle extends over 30 years—2 years to design, build, and manufacture rolling stock and 28 years to provide services. So, for example, whereas the cost of building a fleet of seventy diesel trains is around £65 m, the service life generates revenues worth £200 m.

As they take over operational activities, suppliers have an incentive to design systems from the start that are reliable and easily maintainable. Being involved in services allows firms to grasp in-service problems and opportunities to improve system performance. Lessons learnt can be fed back into the design and build of current and future generations of systems. Because manufacturers like Alstom, Ericsson, and Thales develop technology as well as integrate systems and perform operational services, they are able to create new feedback loops within different parts of the same firm. System designers and service providers operate in a closed loop, in which responsibility for operational performance and costs remain in the hands of a single organization. By contrast, pure systems integrator firms like WS Atkins and C&W that rely on external manufacturers for equipment and technology development are unable to take advantage of these dynamic feedback loops.

As depicted in Figure 16.6, this can initiate a virtuous cycle of innovative improvements between systems integration and service activities, leading to the design of more reliable and efficient systems being built in the future (Geyer and Davies 2000). For example, instead of building the rolling stock and selling it to the train operator, who then arranges maintenance, overhaul, and train operations, Alstom now maintains, upgrades, converts, and re-deploys rolling stock as usage patterns change, often recycling trains through the plants where they were originally built and designed. In this closed loop, the rolling stock never leaves the oversight of the designer and builder. In the case of Alstom's contract for the Northern Line extension of the London Underground, the managers responsible for maintenance and operational services were deeply involved in the front-end design of the rolling stock. As a result of their recommendations, the train designers made more than 250 modifications to create easy-to-maintain and easy-to-use trains.

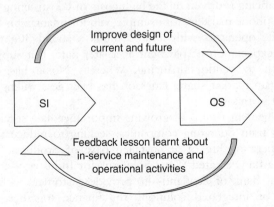

Fig. 16.6 The system-service innovation cycle

Business Consultancy

As part of an integrated solutions package, firms are developing their business consultancy capabilities to advise customers on how to plan, design, build, finance, maintain, and operate systems. Firms are expanding their business consultancy capabilities by creating joint ventures with other firms that have such capabilities; acquiring firms already operating in this field; or by developing business consultancy skills in-house.

Some of the case study firms, such as Ericsson and WS Atkins, have developed these skills internally by establishing specialist business consultancy organizations. Ericsson, for example, established two organizations to offer these services: Ericsson Business Consulting provides advice such as business planning to help other parts of Ericsson implement turnkey solutions; and Edgecom, an Ericsson subsidiary, provides customers with advice on their strategies for mobile communications, such as how to write business plans, produce network designs, finance, and manage their assets, and develop applications for 3G services. Alstom and Thales have developed a consultancy-based approach within their existing business units. C&W, by contrast, has been seeking a strategic partnership or joint venture with one of the major business consultancy organizations because in global corporate network markets these firms dominate the value stream and control access to the customer.

Financing

The ability to provide finance is the fourth capability being developed by some integrated solutions providers. While the growing importance of private finance is generally associated with large public sector PFI and PPP projects, it has also grown in importance in recent years as an industry-led initiative to provide vendor financing and asset management services in capital-intensive telecom, railway, and other large infrastructure systems.

Vendor financing is driven by the high costs of constructing new systems. In 3G mobile phone markets, for example, vendor financing is being offered to help mobile operators with limited funds to build 3G mobile phone networks on expectation of payment at a later date. But suppliers vary in their approach to vendor financing. Whereas Nokia has used vendor financing to gain market share, Ericsson has been less willing to be financially exposed in this way.

Asset management is also of growing importance as a service for customers, such as train operating companies, seeking to reduce the costs and extend the operating life of an installed base of products. In 2000, for example, WS Atkins created 'Total Solutions for Industry'—a joint venture with the Royal Bank of Scotland—to provide customers with a one-stop-shop source of integrated solutions for finance together with design, construction, and maintenance. Serving contracts with an asset value of between £5 and £20m, the joint venture offers to manage assets for customers such as mobile telephone base stations, baggage handling systems, and power stations. The bank supplies the finance (and specific financial services such as equity savings) and WS Atkins undertakes design, construction management, and asset management.

The Variety of Integrated Solutions Strategies

Taken together, these capabilities describe the entire range of activities performed in the provision of integrated solutions. From their different starting positions, all of the firms moving into integrated solutions are developing their core capabilities as high value-adding systems integrators: either of products developed internally or sourced from external manufacturers. From this base in systems integration, the firms are providing operational services to help customers use, maintain, and finance products. Building on these two core sets of capabilities, the firms are less uniform in their approaches to the provision of 'less core' business consulting and financial services. Some firms such as WS Atkins regard these as core components of their integrated solutions. Ericsson, by contrast, has moved strongly into business consulting, but is reluctant about becoming deeply involved in vendor financing.

The case studies also provide an opportunity to begin to distinguish between types of integrated solutions providers which can be represented as a matrix—shown in Figure 16.7—along two different dimensions: the scope of systems integration and vertical or horizontal spread of industrial activities. First, firms providing solutions are developing the capabilities to

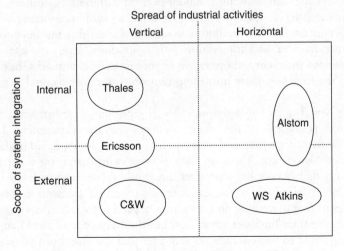

Fig. 16.7 Positioning integrated solutions providers

design, integrate, and deliver: 'internally' developed systems (Thales); systems assembled out of 'externally' developed components (WS Atkins and C&W), or both (Alstom and Ericsson).

Second, vertically-integrated firms offer solutions to customers within a specific industry, such as C&W's development of global outsourcing solutions and horizontally-integrated providers offer solutions to similar customers operating in different industries, such as the solutions that WS Atkins offers. Whereas Ericsson provides internal and external systems integration services within a single industry, Alstom is a diversified firm which provides solutions to customers across energy and transportation systems. The matrix can be used to analyse the position of a division within a diversified firm, such as Thales Training and Simulation which provides solutions—based on internally devleoped systems—within a vertical industry.

Challenges Facing Integrated Solutions Providers

In addition to the development of new capabilities, firms adapting to new positions in the value stream face several wider organizational challenges.

Managing Fluid Boundaries in the Stream

An integrated solutions provider has to understand how far it can migrate along the value stream before stepping over the boundary into what a customer regards as its core activities. Since the mid-1990s, the boundary between supplier and customer has been in a state of flux. Managing these fluid boundaries has become a major issue, particularly where one supplier may be dealing with varying boundaries with different customers, such as operators and service providers. For example, to avoid competing with their customers, Ericsson has traditionally refrained from moving beyond equipment manufacture and integration into operations. Ericsson has recently migrated into the technical operation of mobile phone networks, but has not crossed the final boundary into the provision of services to final consumers.

Creating New Business Organizations.   A major challenge for firms moving into integrated solutions is the need to reconcile the differences between upstream manufacturing and downstream service activities. Manufacturing firms like Alstom and Ericsson face difficulties in managing compartmentalized yet tightly coupled manufacturing and service businesses within the same organization. They can experience a clash of interests between the priorities of manufacturing and resources needed for service provision. Many are changing their business structures, but the frequency of the changes that are being made to these structures indicates that they have not yet settled on a solid strategy and structure.

Some firms are now attempting to resolve these tensions by implementing new business organizations that put the provision of integrated solutions in a category of its own. Ericsson's Global Services division, for example, was set up to support a customer's entire needs for solutions from a single division. In an effort to standardize service offered as components in a solution, Ericsson has developed a portfolio of modular services—called Service Solutions—which address a customer's business and operational goals, from initial business idea and planning, through network integration and service start-up, to technical operation. Depending upon their specific needs and capabilities, operators can select individual modular services or the entire set as a bundled offer.

Accepting the Risk.   In service-based contracts, the risks of late delivery, quality problems, and cost overruns are transferred from the buyer to the integrated solutions provider for the duration of the contract. If the specification is inadequately defined, the risk for the supplier can be extremely high. However, evidence from the five case studies suggests that suppliers of CoPS are prepared to accept such risks. As customers outsource key activities, both suppliers and customers require new ways of monitoring the performance of the system. Many relationships rely on Service Level Agreements (SLAs). Drawn up at the contractual stage, SLAs ensure that the risks and responsibilities for delivering and managing a system during its operating life are transferred from customer to supplier, but equally that clear reward structures are attached to system performance.

Moving from Unique to Repeatable Solutions.   Performance in integrated solutions provision depends on how quickly and successfully firms can move from unique to repeatable solutions (Davies and Brady 2000; Galbraith 2002). The challenge to the supplier is to create organizations that can package and deliver effective and efficient solutions to meet growing customer demand. Suppliers typically invest in the development of a solution with a lead customer so that it can be sold to many other similar customers. Solutions have to be repeatable so that a supplier can get a return on the up-front fixed investment. In other words 'If every solution is unique, the company cannot make much money on them' (Galbraith 2002: 203).

Each of the case study firms have tried to capture the knowledge gained from initial projects for integrated solutions and transfer the lessons learnt to other projects and their wider organizations. In 1998, for example, C&W won its first global outsourcing contract to design, integrate, manage, and operate a network for Andersen Consulting (now called Accenture). Anticipating large demand for global outsourcing solutions, C&W developed a process to learn from this initial project and eventually changed its entire organization in an effort to deliver repeatable solutions (Davies and Brady 2000).

16.3   Conclusions

This chapter began by discussing the recent trend for firms to concentrate on the provision of high-value services and solutions rather than just supplying stand-alone physical products. A review of the business strategy literature identified various business models for moving into services that apply to CoPS: embedded services, comprehensive services, and integrated solutions. The case study firms first ventured into these new markets by adding services to an existing product range, but by the late 1990s they were all focusing on developing strategies for integrated solutions provision.

An attempt was made to reformulate Wise and Baumgartner's argument that firms are simply 'going downstream' into integrated solutions by developing a conceptual framework that is able to account the variety of moves that firms are following into this new activity. The empirical evidence in Section 16.2 showed that rather than simply moving downstream, suppliers of CoPS are moving into integrated solutions provision from different positions up and down the value stream. On the one hand, manufacturers— Alstom, Ericsson, and Thales—are pulling out of their traditional centre-of-gravity stage in manufacturing and focusing on being systems integrators and providers of services to operate and maintain their products. Alstom and Ericsson also offer services to integrate and support their competitor's products. On the other hand, service-based firms—WS Atkins and C&W— are focusing on strengthening their upstream capabilities as systems integrators and moving even further downstream into services previously carried out internally by their customers.

Attracted by the gravitational pull of integrated solutions, the case study firms are developing new sets of capabilities that set them apart from the traditional categories of manufacturing or services. These capabilities are: systems integration, operational services, business consultancy, and financing. Irrespective of whether a firm started from a base in manufacturing or services, providing integrated solutions means a shift in the firm's centre of gravity towards systems integration. An intimate knowledge of their products and customer's needs enables systems integrators to provide operational services. By effective outsourcing and managing of upstream component manufacturers, these firms can concentrate on their core systems integration and operational service activities, while building up their capabilities in business consultancy and financial services to offer entire solutions to a customer's needs.

Future attempts to develop a typology of integrated solutions business models will have to account for the variety and frequency of changes in strategies adopted by the case study firms and the possibility of failure in these endeavours. On the one hand, Alstom, Ericsson, and Thales are focusing on being systems integrators and providers of services tied to products developed in-house. In contrast to Thales, Ericsson and Alstom have also developed the capability to integrate a competitor's equipment if this is requested by their customers. An involvement in technology development enables these firms to benefit from dynamic feedback loops so that knowledge of operational performance can be used to make technical improvements in current and future product generations.

On the other hand, starting from a base in services, WS Atkins and C&W have recently strengthened their systems integration capabilities to provide their customers with optimal solutions using equipment supplied by external manufacturers. Unlike Alstom and Ericsson, however, these service providers rely on external manufacturers to initiate improvements to products and technologies. Whereas C&W offers solutions to one customer segment—business users—within a single industry, WS Atkins is developing solutions for similar types of customers operating in many industries.

As the chapter is based on a limited sample of case study firms, it is not feasible to speculate on whether the trend towards integrated solutions is reflected in a wider change in CoPS industries. The misfortunes of firms moving into services and integrated solutions provision over the past couple of years raises some doubts about whether firms will continue to venture down this road. For example, recent accounts in the business press describe the problems integrated-solutions pioneers like IBM are currently experiencing with their service divisions and the difficulties service support firms like WS Atkins, Serco, and others are having in making money from PFI and PPP contracts. In response to this less favourable environment, firms that have recently moved into solutions provision may revise their strategies or even consider retreating back to their original centre-of-gravity positions in manufacturing or services.

Acknowledgements

Thanks to Mike Hobday, Andrea Prencipe, Ammon Salter, David Gann, Paul Nightingale, and Willem Hulsink for useful comments.

Notes

1. 'Mastering service capabilities in complex product systems: a key systems integration challenge'—funded by the UK's Engineering and Physical Sciences Research Council (EPSRC) Systems Integration Initiative (Grant No. GR/59403).
2. A central problem with Wise and Baumgartner's account is the assumption that all of these services reside downstream in the value chain. This way of thinking about the value chain relies on the traditional distinction between manufacturing and services: whereas manufacturing involves managing physical activities to make a tangible physical product, services related to those products involve any downstream activity required for the product to add value in forms that are intangible to the customer. This definition of services ignores Quinn's observation that many 'functions' performed at the manufacturing end of the

value chain—such as R&D, product design, and engineering—are 'services' when sold externally (Quinn 1992: 175).

3. In his later work, Porter recognizes that a firm's value chain for competing in an industry is embedded in a 'larger stream of activities' which he calls the value system (Porter 1990: 42).

4. In a typical consumer goods industry, value is added through successive stages from raw materials extraction, primary manufacture, and fabrication through product design and high-volume production to marketing and distribution to the final consumer.

5. By using systems engineering techniques, systems integrators are able to prepare conceptual designs for the performance of each component, ensure that components and interfaces are compatible, and modify the design of individual components if a customer's specifications change during the project (Johnson 2003: Chapter Three, this volume).

6. Despite emphasizing the benefits of specialization, the definition of systems integration proposed by these authors implies some form of backwards integration. For these authors, systems integration is an activity performed by firms traditionally based in manufacturing that both: (*a*) develop multiple technologies and combine different bodies of knowledge; and (*b*) design and integrate physical components into a system. This chapter offers a narrower but more inclusive definition of systems integration (category *b*) to account for firms in CoPS that design and integrate systems supplied by external manufacturers, but are not involved in technology development.

References

BENNETT, J., SHARMA, D., and TIPPING, A. (2001). 'Customer Solutions: Building a Strategically Aligned Business Model', in *Insights: Organisation & Strategic Leadership Practice*. Boston, MA: Booz Allen & Hamilton, 1–5.

BRUSONI, S. and PRENCIPE, A. (2001). 'Unpacking the Black Box of Modularity: Technology, Products and Organisation', *Industrial and Corporate Change*, 10/1: 179–205.

—— PRENCIPE, A., and PAVITT, K. (2001). 'Knowledge Specialization, Organizational Coupling, and the Boundaries of the Firm: Why do Firms Know More Than They Make?', *Administrative Science Quarterly*, 46: 597–621.

CABLE & WIRELESS (1999). *Global Outsourcing and the Networked Economy: Telecom's Opportunity to Deliver Real Competitive Advantage*. London: Cable and Wireless.

CHANDLER, A. D. (1977). *The Visible Hand: The Managerial Revolution in American Business*. Cambridge, MA: Harvard University Press.

—— (1980). 'The United States: The Seedbed of Managerial Capitalism', in A. D. Chandler and H. Daems (eds.), *Managerial Hierarchies: Comparative Perspectives on the Rise of the Modern Industrial Enterprise*. Cambridge, MA: Harvard University Press, 9–40.

—— (1990). *Scale and Scope: The Dynamics of Industrial Capitalism*. Cambridge, MA: Harvard University Press.

CORNET, E., KATZ, R., MOLLOY, R., SCHÄDLER, J., SHARMA, D., and TIPPING, A. (2000). 'Customer Solutions: From Pilots to Profits', in *Viewpoint*. Boston, MA: Booz Allen & Hamilton, 1–15.

DAVIES, A. (1997). 'The Life Cycle of a Complex Product System', *International Journal of Innovation Management*, 1/3: 229–56.

—— and BRADY, T. (2000). 'Organisational Capabilities and Learning in Complex Product Systems: Towards Repeatable Solutions', *Research Policy*, 29: 931–53.

—— TANG, P., HOBDAY, M., BRADY, T., RUSH, H., and GANN, D. (2001). 'Integrated Solutions: The New Economy between Manufacturing and Services'. Brighton: SPRU-CENTRIM, 1–43.

DEPARTMENT OF TRADE AND INDUSTRY (DTI) (2002). *The Value Added Scoreboard*. London: DTI Business, Finance and Investment Unit.

DOMBERGER, S. (1998) *The Contracting Organisation: A Strategic Guide to Outsourcing*. Oxford: Oxford University Press.

ERICSSON (1996). *Annual Report*.

—— (1999). *Annual Report*.

FOOTE, N. W., GALBRAITH, J. R., HOPE, Q., and MILLER, D. (2001). 'Making Solutions the Answer', *The McKinsey Quarterly*, 3: 84–93.

GALBRAITH, J. R. (1983). 'Strategy and Organisation Planning'. *Human Resource Management*, Spring–Summer (reprinted in H. Mintzberg and J. B. Quinn (eds.), *The Strategy Process* (2nd edn). Upper Saddle River, NJ: Prentice Hall, 1991: 315–24).

—— (2002). 'Organising to Deliver Solutions', *Organisational Dynamics*, 31/2: 194–207.

GANN, D. M. and SALTER, A. J. (2000). 'Innovation in Project-based, Service-enhanced Firms: The Construction of Complex Products and Systems', *Research Policy*, 29: 955–72.

GERSTNER, L. V. (2002). *Who Said Elephants Can't Dance? Inside IBM's Historic Turnaround*. London: Harper Collins Publishers.

GEYER, A. and DAVIES, A. (2000). 'Managing Project–System Interfaces: Case Studies of Railway Projects in Restructured UK and German Markets', *Research Policy*, 29: 991–1013.

GRANSTRAND, O., PATEL, P., and PAVITT, K. (1997). 'Multi-technology Corporations: Why they have "Distributed" rather than "Distinctive Core" Competencies', *California Management Review*, 39/4: 8–25.

HAMEL, G. and PRAHALAD, C. K. (1994). *Competing for the Future*. Boston, MA: Harvard Business School Press.

HAX, A. C. and WILDE, D. L. (1999). 'The Delta Model: Adaptive Management for a Changing World', *Sloan Management Review*, Winter: 11–28.

HOBDAY, M. (1998). 'Product Complexity, Innovation and Industrial Organisation', *Research Policy*, 26: 689–710.

—— (2000). 'The Project-Based Organisation: An Ideal Form for Managing Complex Products and Systems?', *Research Policy*, 29: 871–93.

KAY, J. (1993). *Foundations of Corporate Success*. Oxford: Oxford University Press.

MILLER, R., HOBDAY, M., LEROUX-DEMERS, T., and OLLEROS, X. (1995). 'Innovation in Complex System Industries: The Case of Flight Simulators', *Industrial and Corporate Change*, 4/2: 363–400.

MULHOLLAND, D. (2000). 'Technology Threatens Sector's Profits, Companies Need to Shift Business to Service, Upgrade Sales', *Defence News*, 7 February.

OWEN, D. (1997). 'GEC Alstom in Career Discussions', *Financial Times*, 19 November.

PENROSE, E. (1959). *The Theory of the Growth of the Firm* (3rd edn., 1995). Oxford: Oxford University Press.

PORTER, M. E. (1985). *Competitive Advantage: Creating and Sustaining Superior Performance*. London: The Free Press.

—— (1990). *The Competitive Advantage of Nations*. London: Macmillan Press.

PRAHALAD, C. K. and RAMASWAMY, V. (2000). 'Co-opting Customer Competence', *Harvard Business Review*, January–February: 79–87.

PRENCIPE, A. (1997). 'Technological Competencies and Product's Evolutionary Dynamics: A Case Study from the Aero-engine Industry', *Research Policy*, 25: 1261–76.

QUINN, J. B. (1992). *Intelligent Enterprise: A Knowledge and Service Based Paradigm for Industry*. New York: The Free Press.

RICHARDSON, G. B. (1972). 'The Organisation of Industry', *Economic Journal*, 83: 883–96.

ROSENBERG, N. (1982). 'Learning by Using', in N. Rosenberg (ed.), *Inside the Black Box: Technology and Economics*. Cambridge: Cambridge University Press, 120–40.

ROTHWELL, R. (1992). 'Successful Industrial Innovation: Critical Success Factors', *R&D Management*, 22/3: 221–39.

SHARMA, D. and MOLLOY, R. (1999). 'The Truth About Customer Solutions', in *Viewpoint*. Boston, MA: Booz Allen & Hamilton, 1–13.

SLYWOTZKY, A. J. (1996). *Value Migration: How to Think Several Moves Ahead of the Competition*. Boston, MA: Harvard Business School Press.

—— and MORRISON, D. J. (1998). *The Profit Zone: How Strategic Business Design Will Lead You to Tomorrow's Profits*. Chichester: John Wiley & Sons.

TEECE, D. and PISANO, G. (1994). 'The Dynamic Capabilities of Firms: An Introduction', *Industrial and Corporate Change*, 3/3: 537–56.

WISE, R. and BAUMGARTNER, P. (1999). 'Go Downstream: The New Profit Imperative in Manufacturing', *Harvard Business Review*, September–October: 133–41.

WOMACK, J. P. and JONES, D. T. (1996). *Lean Thinking: Banish Waste and Create Wealth in Your Corporation*. New York: Simon & Schuster.

WS ATKINS (1999). *Annual Review*.

INDEX